D0857847

Unveiled Voices
Unvarnished Memories

Unveiled Voices
Unvarnished Memories

The Cromwell Family in Slavery and Segregation, 1692-1972

ADELAIDE M. CROMWELL

INTRODUCTION BY ANTHONY CROMWELL HILL

UNIVERSITY OF MISSOURI PRESS
COLUMBIA AND LONDON

Copyright © 2007 by
The Curators of the University of Missouri
University of Missouri Press, Columbia, Missouri 65201
Printed and bound in the United States of America
All rights reserved
5 4 3 2 1   11 10 09 08 07

Library of Congress Cataloging-in-Publication Data

Cromwell, Adelaide M.
    Unveiled voices, unvarnished memories : the Cromwell family in slavery and
segregation, 1692–1972 / Adelaide M. Cromwell ; introduction by Anthony
Cromwell Hill.
           p. cm.
    Includes index.
    ISBN-13: 978-0-8262-1676-2 (hard cover : alk. paper)
    ISBN-10: 0-8262-1676-5 (hard cover : alk. paper)
    1. Cromwell family.   2. Cromwell family—Correspondence.   3. African American
families.   4. Social networks—United States—Case studies.   5. Cromwell,
John W. (John Wesley), b. 1846—Correspondence.   6. Cromwell, John Wesley,
1883–1971—Correspondence.   7. African Americans—Biography.
8. Philadelphia (Pa.)—Biography.   9. Washington (D.C.)—Biography.
10. American letters.   I. Title.
    E185.96.C757 2006
    929'.20973—dc22   2006027685

⊗ This paper meets the requirements of the
American National Standard for Permanence of Paper
for Printed Library Materials, Z39.48, 1984.

Designer: Kristie Lee
Typesetter: Bookcomp, Inc.
Printer and binder: Thomson-Shore, Inc.
Typeface: Adobe Garamond

WILLIS HODGES CROMWELL
AND ELIZABETH CARNEY CROMWELL

my great-grandparents
who broke the bonds of slavery

Contents

꩜

Preface

❧ ❧

This is the story of how one African American family and a key figure in that family, John Wesley Cromwell, my grandfather, established and maintained a network of family, friends, and associates through the years. It is also a testimony to the importance of the writing and keeping of letters.

Throughout his life, my grandfather kept most, if not all, of his correspondence, as well as a diary, a journal, newspaper clippings, and books. The ties with his family—his brothers, his father, and his children—were sustained through letters. These letters are written to him and, with supporting documentation, are exclusively concerned with family matters.

Included here also are other letters written to Grandfather that reveal his activities and concerns beyond the family. Chapters 8 and 9 contain selections of his extensive correspondence with John E. Bruce, a fellow journalist and amateur historian, and Theophilus Gould Steward, a clergyman, chaplain, and author.

In preserving these letters and in writing this book, I have tried to keep the faith of my great-grandfather, Willis Hodges Cromwell, my grandfather, John Wesley Cromwell Sr., and my aunt Otelia Cromwell. This has been a long journey, and for that reason, I am indebted to many, many people: my son, Anthony Cromwell Hill, for his informative and sensitive introduction to this work; William O. Banner, who has been my friend since we were students at Harvard, for critically reading the first part of the manuscript; and Michael R. Winston, the coauthor of the *Dictionary of American Negro Biography,* for reading the entire manuscript and offering many important suggestions for its improvement, which I have gratefully followed.

My indebtedness extends to numerous personal friends and professionals who responded to my requests for help: Edward Howell, Thelma Truitt Howell, my cousin Darrell R. Gordon, and Charles L. Blockson helped me in my descriptions of nineteenth-century Philadelphia; Melvin Ramey, my cousin by marriage, brought me up to date on the family genealogy; Yvonne Simkins, Dores McCree, and Frances Wright added more facts on the family; and Willard Johnson helped me to interpret government documentation.

Most helpful over the years were Donald Altschiller, the history biographer of the Mugar Memorial Library at Boston University, and Willard B. Gatewood, professor of history at University of Arkansas and author of *Aristocrats of Color: The Black Elite, 1880–1920*. The research for this book was also greatly expedited by Judy Capruso and Anatol Steck, curators of the school archives, Sumner School, Washington, D.C.; Randall R. Burkett, bibliographer, Robert W. Woodruff Library, African American Collections, Emory University; JoAnn Elasher and Leila Williams, directors of manuscripts, Moorland-Spingarn Research Library, Howard University; Paul Phillips Cooke, president emeritus, District of Columbia Teachers College; Phillip W. Rhodes, acting director/research services coordinator, Jones Memorial Library, Lynchburg, Va.; Jane W. Rehl, Historical Society of Saratoga Springs, N.Y.; Sherri Ellerbe, historian, Metropolitan A.M.E. Church, Washington, D.C.; Katherine Steko, Cambridge Historical Society; Dennis M. Scott, assistant archivist, Boston College; Gregory Stoner, Virginia Historical Society; David S. Azzolina, Van Pelt Library, University of Pennsylvania; Brian Sullivan, Harvard University Archives; Tommy Bogger, director of archives, Norfolk State University; Peter Drummey, Massachusetts Historical Society; Clifford Muse, alumni records, Howard University; Jim Hughes, Genealogical Society of New England; Barbara A. Burg, research librarian, Widener Library of Harvard University; and Donald W. Gunter, associate editor, *Dictionary of Virginia Biography*.

Other sources include the Buffalo and Erie Historical Society; the Schomburg Research Library, New York Public Library; New Haven Historical Society; Historical Society of Pennsylvania; Philadelphia City Archives; Virginia State Library; Maryland Historical Society; Maryland State Archives; Public Record Office, Kew, Richmond, Surrey, United Kingdom; Maryland Department of General Services, Hall of Records; Colonial Williamsburg Foundation; and the Church of Jesus Christ of Latter Day Saints.

The following people were also of assistance: Barbara M. Solomon, James Dent Walker, Basil Phillips, Frederick Barnett, Ruth Hamilton Shorter, Nancy Burkett, Bettye Collier-Thomas, Felicia Blue, Marva Carter, Preston Williams, Anthony Campbell, Elmer Gaden, John Hope Franklin, James Sicmon, Barbara Maginley, and Pearl T. Robinson.

I have been working on these letters to my family for many years. I am now as old as the many persons quoted in the book and have received so much assistance and support from numerous persons, but I have a special indebtedness to Beverly Jarrett, the director and editor-in-chief of the University of Missouri Press; to Susan King, my patient and knowledgeable editor; and to Kristie Lee, for the very creative and informative design she created for the cover of the book.

The letters of John E. Bruce are in the family archives, the Alain Locke Papers at the Moorland-Spingarn Research Library, Howard University, and the Schomburg Center for Research in Black Culture, New York Public Library. The letters of Theophilus Gould Steward are in the family archives.

The letters included in this volume were transcribed by three Boston University graduate students: E. Frances White, David Johnson, and Cynthia Johnson. Margaret McKinney and Norma Fleming typed the first draft of the manuscript, and Jeannette Sanders assumed the responsibility for the final typing, made valuable clerical suggestions, and with good humor undertook the necessary revisions.

Two books proved to be invaluable sources: Rayford W. Logan and Michael R. Winston, eds., *Dictionary of American Negro Biography* (New York: W. W. Norton, 1982); and August Meier, *Negro Thought in America, 1880–1915* (Ann Arbor: University of Michigan Press, 1963).

Photograph reproductions were done by Sandy Middlebrooks Associates and the Photographers and Prints Division, Schomburg Center for Research in Black Culture, New York Public Library.

The Appendix identifies persons or events not covered in the footnotes.

EIGHT GENERATIONS of the BLACK CROMWELL LINE

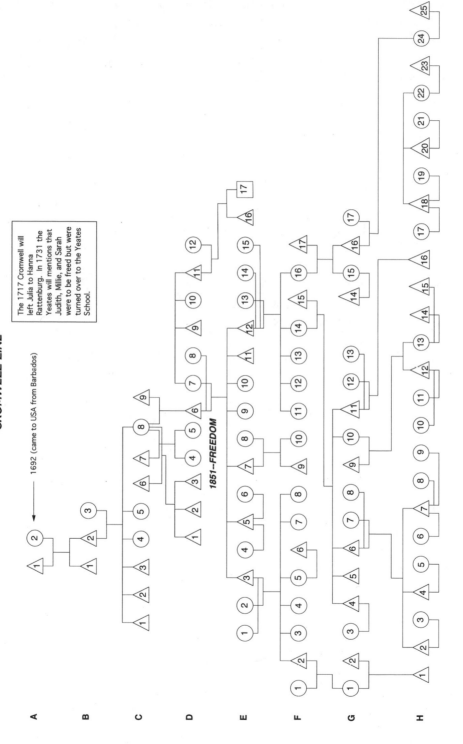

The 1717 Cromwell will left Julia to Hanna Rattenburg. In 1731 the Yeates will mentions that Judith, Millie, and Sarah were to be freed but were turned over to the Yeates School.

1692 (came to USA from Barbados)

1851–FREEDOM

Created by: Adelaide M. Cromwell, Ph.D.
Drawn by: Melvin R. Ramey, Ph.D.
Revised: November, 2005

A.
1. Jack
2. Julia (Judy)

B.
1. Milly
2. Sarah
3. Isaac Hodges

C.
1. Dempsy
2. Isaac
3. David
4. Milly
5. Sarah
6. Harry Thomas (Thominas)
7. Dan Jordon
8. Esther
9. Max (Maxter) Hodges

D.
1. Henry
2. Lydia
3. Eley
4. Sarah
5. Elizabeth
6. Willis Hodges Crommel (Cromwell)
7. Elizabeth Carney
8. Tempie Nancy (2nd wife)
9. Anthony Carney
10. Theresa Carney
11. William H. Carney
12. Nancy Carney

E.
1. Anne E. Conn
2. Lucy McGuinn
3. John Wesley
4. Hester Anne Myers
5. Levi
6. Nancy Myers
7. James
8. Martha Harris
9. Martha
10. Esther
11. William
12. Willis Hodges Cromwell Jr.
13. Felicienne Fouché (1st wife)
14. Celestine (2nd wife)
15. Sarah Charlotte Dangerfield (3rd wife)
16. William H. Carney
17. Also: Simon H., Teresa, Martha, Sarah E., Mary A., Emily E., Martha L., Cornelius

F.
1. Yetta Mavritte
2. John
3. Frances (Fanny)
4. Lucy
5. Martha (Lercie)
6. Alfred Brent
7. Mary
8. Otelia
9. Levi
10. Lavina
11. Helen
12. Minerva
13. Willistine
14. Felicienne
15. George Harry Houston
16. Elizabeth
17. Theodore West

G.
1. Adelaide
2. Henry Hill
3. Mamie Pittman
4. Stanley
5. Harry
6. Willis Cromwell
7. Ethel Marie Fuller
8. Sarah C. Dangerfield
9. Darrell Roth Gordon Sr.
10. Ella Marie
11. George Adolph
12. Helen Dutton (1st wife)
13. Bertha Hart (2nd wife)
14. Hayward Donald Threlkeld
15. Theodora Cromwell
16. Cromwell Payne
17. Roberta Hawkins

H.
1. Anthony
2. Robert Fuller
3. Roberta Periman
4. Bruce Fuller
5. Ester Ford
6. Alice Waters
7. Willis Fuller
8. Pearl Jones
9. Melvina Cutter
10. Florence Helene Bishop (1st wife)
11. Joan Logan (2nd wife)
12. Darrell Roth
13. Francis Elaine
14. Rodrick Hilsinger (2nd husband)
15. Clarence Blake (1st husband)
16. George Adolph
17. Vera Johnson (1st wife)
18. Wendell Houston
19. Christine (2nd wife)
20. Carol Stanley Houston
21. Kathleen Dingle
22. Felicienne Houston
23. Melvin Ramey
24. Ada Fouche
25. Otto Williams

Unveiled Voices
Unvarnished Memories

THE WORLDS WITHIN AND WITHOUT
THE VEIL OF COLOR ARE CHANGING RAPIDLY,
BUT NOT AT THE SAME RATE,
NOT IN THE SAME WAY.

—W. E. B. Du Bois, *The Souls of Black Folk*

author's son

Introduction

ANTHONY CROMWELL HILL

Few African American families have been able to keep an extensive record of their experiences, in slavery or in freedom. Thus, the field of African American genealogy has largely been restricted to the search for the most basic facts of life: births, marriages, employments, residences, and deaths. The Cromwell family is an exception, due largely to the intellectual habits of John Wesley Cromwell Sr., a newspaper proprietor, historian, lawyer, civil servant, and educator in Washington, D.C., who created the archive from which this book is drawn and who instilled in his descendants the appreciation for the historic record that this book, compiled by his granddaughter, my mother, Adelaide McGuinn Cromwell, embodies.

As a result, *Unveiled Voices, Unvarnished Memories,* through its utilization of letters, journals, and documents from several generations, provides an unprecedented view of how one black family thought and survived in American society from slavery in the eighteenth century to freedom and professional accomplishment in the nineteenth and twentieth centuries.

The youngest of the seven children born to Willis and Elizabeth Carney Cromwell, John Wesley—or J. W., as he came to be known—was the last member of the family to be born into slavery, and he would outlive all of his siblings. Partly as a result of that and partly because his life was so rich and eventful, much of this book hinges on his journey from slavery in antebellum Virginia to his boyhood and education in Philadelphia, his return to Virginia as a teacher of the freedmen during the Civil War, his settling in Washington during the latter years of Reconstruction, and the five decades he would spend in the nation's capital as a twice-married husband, father of seven children—three of whom would have remarkable careers of their own—and as a multifaceted and intellectual pillar of the black community.

My mother, Adelaide, born and reared in Washington, D.C., was seven when J. W. died, old enough to have indelible memories of him and of his place in the family and in the closely knit circle of the capital's black elite in those years at the height of segregation, old enough, in fact, to have absorbed some of her first impressions of the family's oral history at J. W.'s knee. But she was too young when he died to have developed a mature relationship with him, even though J. W. lived with his second wife, the former Annie E. Conn, just a few blocks away from the townhouse in which Adelaide was born and where she would grow up and live until she went north for college. For her, J. W. was more a face and a name than he was a man.

Consequently, throughout much of her life, Adelaide would learn about J. W. and his forebearers in much the same way as many Americans, Black and White, have traditionally learned about their ancestors: through memories shared with them by their parents, aunts, uncles, and family friends.

The circumstances of my mother's youth were especially conducive to promoting an interest in family history. The large townhouse in which she grew up, on 13th Street in Washington's Northwest quadrant, was home not only to her parents, John Wesley Cromwell Jr. and the former Yetta Mavritte, but also to three of her paternal aunts, Otelia, Mary, and Lucy Cromwell. A fourth aunt, Martha, the only of J. W.'s daughters to marry, who had lived at 13th Street during Adelaide's early childhood, continued to live nearby after her marriage. A fifth aunt, Fanny, lived with J. W. and his second wife on Swann Street, a few blocks away.

The neighborhood was rich with people who had known J. W. and other members of the family for many years and was marked by educational, cultural, and social institutions in which the family had been long involved.

Equally important, relations between the Washington branch of the family and relatives in Virginia and Philadelphia, the other two significant places in J. W.'s life, were quite close, refreshed by not-so-infrequent visits and correspondence. Even relatives who had moved farther afield to Massachusetts and Ohio remained in the family's orbit not only because Washington was nation's capital but also because it was home to an especially influential black community. Many members of J. W.'s extensive circle of contacts continued to interact with the family during my mother's youth.

From this wide and deep web of associations, Adelaide was inevitably steeped in the oral tradition of the Cromwell clan. But her connection to J. W. and, by extension, to his progenitors was greatly enriched by her bond with her aunt Otelia. As the first child born to J. W. and his first wife, the former Lucy McGuinn,

Otelia might well have been expected to be the one member of her generation to be closest to her father.

This expected closeness, based on the accident of birth order, would be cemented by a confluence of tragedy and character. Shortly after his arrival in Washington in 1871, J. W. had scored first among two hundred applicants for a clerkship in the auditor's office of the Treasury for the Post Office Department. The job had provided him with the wherewithal to pursue his education in the law at Howard University, from which he would be graduated in 1874, the year of Otelia's birth. That same year, J. W. had also been appointed registrar of money order accounts at the Treasury for the Post Office Department and his salary had been raised from fourteen hundred to sixteen hundred dollars a year—very good money at the time, especially for a black man who, a few years earlier, had been pulling down thirty-five dollars a month as a schoolteacher in Virginia.

J. W.'s reliable income from his government post enabled him to enter into one of his two professional passions: journalism. By 1876, he had established the *People's Advocate,* a weekly that would last longer and wield more influence than any previous black newspaper in Washington.

In the 1880s, however, J. W. encountered a series of increasingly daunting reverses. His firstborn son, Willis, named for J. W.'s father, who had engineered the family's extrication from slavery in the 1850s, was injured as an infant and died before his third birthday. Then, in 1885, after Grover Cleveland, the first Democrat to be elected president since 1856, had taken office, J. W. was fired from his job at the Post Office Department because of the *People's Advocate's* "offensive partisanship" in support of the defeated Republican ticket.

Closing his paper after more than ten years of unbroken, vigorous life was a crushing blow to J. W. But that pain was just a foretaste of what he would suffer the next year. After giving birth for the seventh time, Lucy McGuinn Cromwell died from postpartum complications following the delivery of her fifth daughter, Fanny. Thus, in rapid succession, J. W. had lost his firstborn son, his lucrative job, the newspaper he loved, and the lovely wife he cherished. He found himself, at the age of forty-one, a single father of six, plunged into a dark night of the soul that challenged him to the core.

Otelia was just ten years old when this set of reverses began and only thirteen when it culminated in the death of her mother. At a tender age, she found herself immersed in a realm of adult responsibilities and realities. On her deathbed, Lucy McGuinn Cromwell had enjoined Otelia to serve as surrogate mother to her siblings, with special attention to her sister Lucy, who had been born with curvature of the spine, and to keep house for her father. Already a tall and serious girl, Teely, as her siblings called her, was faithful to her charge, as a friend of the family noted in a letter to her father three years later: "I believe that Otelia has the making of a Noble Woman. I believe that now that she has no mother that she as head of her father's home knowing that he appreciates her efforts will surprise him and others in the manner she will keep that home. Indeed it will be very difficult to get a housekeeper-wife to excel her."

Over the next seven years, Teely turned this prediction to prophecy. Not only did she perform her homemaking responsibilities well and without complaint, aided, as her father's salary could afford, by hired housekeepers, she did so without completely losing herself in this domestic role. Always an outstanding student, she excelled at M Street High School (then, arguably, the leading black secondary school in the nation), while holding a part-time job working for Frederick Douglass, who was the District of Columbia's registrar of deeds. Following her graduation from high school in 1891, she matriculated at Miner Normal School, a school for the training of black teachers, where she continued her record of academic success and completed her course of study the following year.

In 1897, Otelia Cromwell applied both to Vassar and to Smith, neither of which had knowingly graduated a black student. Vassar rejected Teely's application; Smith did not, and she enrolled at Northampton that fall. As Smith's first black student, Teely encountered minimal racial discrimination. She was not permitted to live on campus, though, and did not, apparently, participate in many extracurricular activities. Her social life was also probably quite limited, but her contacts with faculty and classmates were decidedly positive.

Teely's success as an undergraduate at a prestigious college set an example for her siblings to follow. In 1905, J. W.'s second daughter, Mary, graduated from the University of Michigan. In 1906, John Jr., the sole surviving son, took his bachelor's, Phi Beta Kappa, from Dartmouth. Like Otelia, Mary and John paid almost the entire cost of their college education themselves, with some help from their father and other siblings. All three of them subsequently attained graduate degrees from Ivy League institutions; Otelia, in 1926, becoming the first black woman to receive a doctorate in English from Yale. Indeed, only two of J. W.'s five children, Lucy and Fanny, did not receive college degrees. Yet, even Fanny, the youngest and frailest, finished high school (still an uncommon achievement in those days), and Lucy, whom Otelia considered the brightest of them all, graduated from Miner Normal School with a teacher's certificate.

J. W. had long been extraordinarily interested in the relationship of black Americans to Africa. As a founder and later president of two important black cultural institutions, the Bethel Literary and Historical Association and the American Negro Academy, J. W. played a significant role in cultivating interest in black history. Along with Alexander Crummell, the distinguished African American minister who would become J. W.'s spiritual guide, Archibald Grimké, Francis Grimké, and William S. Scarborough, among others, J. W. laid the foundation for the politically engaged black intelligentsia that emerged under the leadership of the rising generation of African American scholars, which included Kelly Miller, W. E. B. Du Bois, Carter Woodson, Jesse Moorland, John Hope, Arthur A. Schomburg, Alain Locke, and Otelia.

Already twenty-six years old when she returned to Washington from Smith, Teely resumed her life in Washington knowing that the list of potentially appropriate suitors would be short and that the list was bound to dwindle with each passing year. But because she at once knew and cherished the independence of her spirit and because her maternal instinct had already been amply fed by the roles she had and would continue to play in the family and as an educator, she never felt an overwhelming desire to find her way to the altar. As she explained, the fear of not having the title "Mrs." on her tombstone was never strong enough to force her into marriage.

After teaching for several years at Dunbar High School, John married Yetta Mavritte, a former student. Yetta had been reared in the rural Burrville neighborhood in the Southeast section of Washington, D.C., where her father, William Mavritte, a bricklayer and part-time preacher, had built his two-story house as part of an extended family settlement.

John and Yetta began their marriage by moving into the house on 13th Street, and it was in this house that their daughter, Adelaide, was born the following year. This was not the situation that Yetta, as the youngest, least accomplished, and best-looking member of the household, expected when she married John. From the first, there were tensions that Teely did much to mollify. John remained torn, however, between his sisters and his wife.

Otelia assumed the responsibility for assuring that Adelaide would be groomed to become a woman more like her than like her mother, and she was partially successful in this ambition.

Adelaide readily took after her aunt in many ways, including becoming such a good student that she followed in much the same path of academic excellence that had led Aunt Tee—as Adelaide and, eventually, I would call Otelia—from Washington to Northampton, only she would cover that ground in significantly fewer years. Graduating from Dunbar at sixteen, Adelaide matriculated at Smith in the fall of 1936 and took her bachelor's degree in sociology with honors four years later. Notably, while at Smith, Adelaide continued to demonstrate her interest in the history of her family by writing a paper for a genetics course about the inheritance of a physical trait, piebaldism, in three generations of Lucy McGuinn's branch of the family. Published by the *Journal of Heredity* in Adelaide's senior year, the article was a precocious beginning to her career in scholarship.

Adelaide continued her studies at the University of Pennsylvania and earned a master's degree in sociology in 1941. She went on to earn a certificate in social work from Bryn Mawr two years later. Social work was a field that was much closer to the interests of her aunt Mary than it was to Teely's concerns, but the experience was, in retrospect, perhaps most important because it exposed her to the black community in Philadelphia, the city in which J. W. had first gone to school.

Following her marriage to Henry Hill in 1943 (the same year that he graduated at the top of his doctoral class in chemistry at MIT), Adelaide pursued her academic training along a trajectory that J. W. surely would have appreciated. After teaching briefly at Hunter College and at Smith, in 1950, she joined the faculty of Boston University. In 1953, she received her doctorate in sociology from Radcliffe and cofounded Boston University's graduate program in African studies. At the time, the United States in general and its academic establishment in particular were paying scant attention to Africa, and Boston University was the first to establish a graduate concentration in the field.

For the next fifteen years, Africa and its relations to the United States was the focus of Adelaide's career. She visited the continent several times in a variety of capacities and became well acquainted with a number of the intellectual and political leaders of the post-colonial period, including Kwame Nkrumah, Julius Nyere, and Simeon Kapwepwe. She was also a friend to several members of the emerging generation of African women professionals, such as Frances Wright of Sierra Leone, Mary Antoinette Brown Sherman of Liberia, Winnie McEwen of Nigeria, and Pearl Bruce Jones-Quartey of Ghana.

In collaboration with Martin Kilson, a Harvard political scientist, Adelaide edited a collection of writings by African Americans about Africa entitled *Apropos of Africa: Sentiments of Negro American Leaders on Africa from the 1800s to the 1950s* in 1969. Yet, at the same time, she remained deeply engaged in issues of concern to black Americans and continued to nourish her ties to her family in Washington.

Almost every year during the Christmas season, Adelaide, Henry, and I (their only child) would travel to the capital to spend part of the holidays with the Cromwells at 13th Street and the Mavrittes in Burrville. Almost every fall, my

Adelaide M. Cromwell, Anthony Cromwell Hill, and Felicienne Houston Ramey.

grandfather would visit us over the Harvard-Dartmouth weekend. One year, when I was in my early teens, my mother arranged to have our postgame dinner feature a pig roasted in the fashion that her father had reported the famed sportsman "Diamond Jim" Brady had preferred on his visits to Saratoga when my grandfather had worked summers there as a Dartmouth student. I will never forget the pleasure in his eyes, as he, joined as often on these occasions by his former Dartmouth schoolmate Heine Bullock, sat down at the table as my father carved that pig.

While Aunt Tee's visits to our house were less frequent, they were certainly equally memorable. The most vivid in my memory came when I was perhaps seven. We had moved from the small house in Harvard Square to a much larger, Federalist-era house in Watertown. Toward the end of this visit, Aunt Tee and I took a walk from the house down to Watertown Square, then a fading commercial district where several wide streets intersected.

The intercourse between pedestrian and vehicular traffic was controlled by a series of signals that included not only lights but also sounds in deference to the students at the Perkins School for the Blind that shared the neighborhood. Familiar with this symphony of sight and sound that regulated traffic, I had run so far ahead of Aunt Tee, who did not know these cues, that when we had reached the heart of the square, she had insisted that rather than walking back, we take a taxi home.

Shortly after we had arrived, safe and sound, Aunt Tee, then in her late eighties, told my mother that she found me such a delightful child that, if she was just a few years younger, she would take me back to 13th Street to give me a proper rearing, but she reluctantly acknowledged that she did not have the energy to carry out that role. The point, of course, is not that Aunt Tee lacked the energy to rear yet another generation of the family but that even near the end of her eighth decade, she considered it her prerogative to do so.

A decade later, following Aunt Tee's death at ninety-nine, Adelaide inherited the family archive that J. W. had initiated and that Teely had dutifully preserved. At that time, Adelaide was in the process of turning the focus of her scholarly interest from Africa back to the United States, as the founding head of Boston University's African American Studies Program.

In 1986, Adelaide's biography of Adelaide Smith Casely Hayford, a distinguished educator from Sierra Leone, was published. In retrospect, that book, *An African Victorian Feminist: The Life and Times of Adelaide Smith Casely Hayford, 1868–1960,* which included both the letters of Mrs. Casely Hayford's family and interviews with many who had known her, was the last of three significant precursors to this volume. The first was Adelaide's doctoral thesis on Boston's black upper class from 1750 to 1950. In a preface to the version of the dissertation published in 1994 entitled *The Other Brahmins,* Adelaide wrote,

> When I chose the Negro upper class as the topic for my dissertation in the late 1940s, few students believed such a class existed within the black community. Interest and research had been focused on the black poor, deserving and otherwise. For me, however, if one presumed academically the existence of a lower class and a middle class, such a class had to exist. Furthermore, having lived in three cities—Washington, DC, Philadelphia and Boston— with an old elite stratum within each of their black communities, I was convinced of not only the existence but also the importance of this group.

The other significant precursor of *Unveiled Voices, Unvarnished Memories* was the afterword Adelaide wrote to the 1982 republication of *The Living is Easy,* the first novel by Dorothy West. Originally published in 1948, when Adelaide was engaged in the research for her dissertation, *The Living is Easy* was a fictionalized account of Miss West's upbringing as a member of the fragile black upper class of early twentieth-century Boston.

While initially well received, the novel and its author, part of the younger generation of the Harlem Renaissance, had fallen out of favor during the McCarthy
era, when Miss West's ties to the Soviet Union, a country she had visited with
Langston Hughes and other black intellectuals, brought unwelcome suspicions.
Miss West had then retreated to Oak Bluffs, a community on Martha's Vineyard,
which had long been host to a summer colony of African Americans.

Indeed, it was not until the early 1970s, when Adelaide invited Miss West, by
then her friend of nearly thirty summers on the Vineyard, to lecture at Boston
University that Dorothy began her long ascent out of obscurity. Among the favorite photographs I have taken is one of Adelaide and Dorothy, laughing at the
kitchen table in Watertown, late in the evening in the winter of 1972. Adelaide's
afterword to the reissue of Dorothy's first novel a decade later was quite a modest
essay, written without any anticipation of how extensive the public's rediscovery
and embrace of this work and its author would be. For, even in 1982, it seemed
that there was hardly more public interest or even awareness of the black upper
class than there had been four decades earlier.

Almost two decades ago, following the republication of *The Living is Easy* and
the publication of *An African Victorian Feminist,* Adelaide began to work on the
Cromwell family archive. As she sorted through the family papers, she inevitably
confronted a range of questions and issues that prompted her to reexamine the
oral history of the family, as it had come down to her through J. W., Otelia, and
other relatives.

Until my mother began the research for this book, the history of the Cromwell
family, as remembered by my great-grandfather, was that of slaves belonging to
James Yates who died in 1731 and left them as a group to provide the labor to
support a free school that he had started for poor Whites in Virginia.

After securing their freedom, Willis and Elizabeth Cromwell chose to move to
Philadelphia. With the largest population of Blacks in any northern city, Philadelphia had recommended itself for three reasons. First, it had an established class
of black businessmen who shared Willis's entrepreneurial bent. Concentrated in
the catering industry, this business class, though small in number, confirmed
Willis's belief that African Americans could be economically successful in this
country.

Second, Philadelphia was prominent in both the antislavery movement and
in the development of black institutional life. As early as 1786, Philadelphia was
among the first places in the North where blacks had organized separate Christian prayer meetings, under the leadership of Richard Allen and Absalom Jones,
and had established a mutual aid group, the Free African Society, which would
become the model for similar organizations in Boston, Newport, and New York.

Philadelphia had also been the birthplace, in 1794, of Bethel Church, the founding congregation of the African Methodist Episcopal denomination.

Moreover, since 1830, Philadelphia had played host to a series of national Negro conventions, where free people of color had met to share information, shape strategy, and build bonds that would be so essential to the operation of the Underground Railroad and other endeavors.

The third and perhaps the most important reason that Philadelphia was attractive to Willis and Elizabeth Cromwell was the city's highly evolved system of black private and segregated public schools that afforded, of all the places they considered, the best educational opportunities for the family's youngest child, J. W. Just five years old when the family arrived in Philadelphia, J. W. entered the Bird School, a public institution in South Philadelphia, and did so well that he was admitted to the preparatory department of the Institute for Colored Youth in 1856.

Here, indeed, was antebellum segregated education at its best. With its handsome facilities, challenging curriculum, and skilled and committed faculty, the institute offered, both to its male and female students, an education that was at least equivalent and, in some sense, superior to that which they might have obtained in the best white secondary schools of Philadelphia. The students responded to this stimulating program by mastering skills and developing attitudes that would enable a remarkable proportion of them to attain noteworthy achievements later in life.

Following his graduation from the Institute for Colored Youth in the summer of 1864, J. W. took his first teaching job in Columbia, Pennsylvania. A principal station of the Underground Railroad, Columbia had a large population of recently arrived ex-slaves eager for an education. But, after teaching in Columbia for a school year, J. W. decided that he wanted to return to Virginia to teach in the same state where it had been illegal for him to learn. Thus, at the age of eighteen, he arrived in Portsmouth to open a school for the freedmen.

But for J. W., perhaps the most dramatic and personally relevant change in this occupied city was the number of excellent freedmen schools that had already been established in and around Portsmouth by the American Missionary Association. Taught by graduates of the best colleges and normal schools in New England, New York, and Pennsylvania, who had been inspired to come south to uplift the freedmen, the AMA schools had the additional advantage of being tuition free.

Faced with such competition, Cromwell's private school flourished briefly before it was taken over by the AMA, and he returned to Philadelphia in the fall of 1865. However, his efforts were praised in a letter published in the *Freedmen's*

Record: "Mr. John Wesley Cromwell is a private school teacher from Philadelphia who was born here. He is a young man, very smart, and the only 'live' one in the place. He will soon leave, as the Free Schools will take his pupils."

After a spell with the family in Philadelphia, J. W. enrolled in a teacher training program in Maryland at the Baltimore Association for the Moral and Intellectual Improvement of Colored People, which was established in 1864 under the leadership of Maryland Quakers.

After leaving Maryland, J. W. returned to Portsmouth. That summer, he opened a grocery business that displayed the family's entrepreneurial bent as well as his own commitment to social justice. Because so many illiterate freedmen were being exploited by unscrupulous white merchants, J. W. set himself up as an honest broker, offering a fair price to black farmers for their goods that he sold at a fair markup. He also taught both privately and at the Sabbath school of the Emmanuel A.M.E. Church.

His work attracted the attention of H. C. Percy, the superintendent of the AMA's schools in Norfolk, who urged him to apply for a teaching post. On September 12, 1866, J. W. wrote the Reverend Samuel Hunt, the AMA's superintendent of education, for a commission, noting that "for nearly 17 months I have endeavored to teach the freedmen in different parts of Maryland and Portsmouth and regard it as a privilege." In a letter of recommendation, Percy wrote of J. W.,

> He is of dark complexion, of ordinary intelligence, a graduate of Philadelphia High School, and a teacher of some experience . . . He identifies himself with the people,—has their confidence, and is very well-liked by all who know him. I *think* he will prove a better teacher than most col'd persons yet offered to our Association and as he proposes to *spend his life in* elevating his race, it may be he will do the AMA valuable service. I have known him but one year, but my acquaintance gives me considerable confidence in his abilities.

Percy's notation that "though professing a change of heart, he is not a member of any church," however, raised a red flag concerning J. W.'s application. For the AMA, devoted to spreading literacy among the former slaves as a means of bringing them to Christ, the notion of employing an unchurched teacher, regardless of his other credentials, was unsavory on its face. Hunt asked J. W. to elaborate on his qualifications to be a missionary teacher among the freedmen. Rather than responding with a reference to his religious upbringing in Philadelphia or the generations of Christian practice among the family in Virginia, J. W. did not skirt the issue: he let it be known that because he had grown up in a country whose major Christian denominations had been all too comfortable with the perpetuation of slavery and racial discrimination, he had found it increasingly difficult to espouse a faith in their God.

Instead, with self-assurance remarkable for a man just barely twenty, J. W. responded by emphasizing the secular motives that had inspired him to teach former slaves. He also included what may have been a none-too-subtle dig against some of the white teachers who had come south to work at the Freedmen's Bureau and AMA schools only to depart, disenchanted, shortly thereafter or to turn their attention from teaching to business opportunities.

> It is not my purpose to be South for mere selfish motives to satisfy a ro-
> mantic, roaming poetic sentiment, but to assist in the elevation of my own
> down-trodden, unfortunate, illiterate yet not God-forsaken people. Actu-
> ated by such principles, there is nothing to prevent my missionary spirit,
> energy, and nerve being taxed to the utmost. None can know better than
> myself the requirements of such work, one in which I have been engaged,
> the workings of which I have daily seen, the influence of which upon the
> elevation of my race every one has felt. This hard fare I have experienced.
> I was shot at in Maryland March last and the church in which school was
> held was burned to the ground.

Meanwhile, J. W. was becoming involved in the politics of Reconstruction Virginia. In 1866, he served as a delegate and clerk of the Republican State Convention in Richmond. The following year, he held the same positions at the state constitutional convention. In 1868, he was impaneled on the jury to try Jefferson Davis for treason, but the trial was called off.

Subsequently, J. W. left Portsmouth to organize freedmen's schools in southwestern Virginia. In the summer of 1871, he opened a school in Southampton County, where forty years earlier Nat Turner had raised his doomed revolt. The experience would lead J. W. to an enduring fascination with Turner, while at the same time convincing him that the prospects for a black teacher anywhere in Virginia were insufficiently inviting to maintain his attention. So, that fall, at the age of twenty-five, he moved to Washington to enroll at the law department of Howard University.

Nevertheless, J. W. remained deeply interested in the education of Blacks, especially in his native state. He was the founder and the first president of the Virginia Educational and Historical Association, established in 1875 as an advocate for the education of African Americans in the commonwealth.

In his inaugural address, J. W. stressed that the education of the former slaves and their descendants was a demanding calling:

> The peculiar work of the teacher of colored schools demands as a preparation, more than the elements of knowledge and skill in the best methods of imparting that knowledge,—the teacher must inspire confidence in those under his care, and make them know that they are capable of the highest intellectual endeavors and achievements.

This spirit, incubated among the Yeates School Negroes, nourished within the family by Willis and Elizabeth and burnished by the faculty of the Institute of Colored Youth, would become J. W.'s guiding light. It would be the beacon that shone in every issue of his newspaper, in all of his work as an educator and an advocate for African American education, and, perhaps, in his role as a father. And it would be the torch that he would pass down to his children—Otelia, above all—and that all of them, particularly those who would spend the majority of their lives residing at 1815 13th Street, would pass on to Adelaide.

J. W. offered a view in which his pride and faith in the inherent abilities of the black race coexisted with a confident patriotism and a devotion to the widest high aspirations of the American dream. In this vision, J. W. stressed that

> The future civilization of America is to embrace all of the excellences, and possibly, some of the defects, of all the different civilizations of the world, and that here the ennobling characteristics of different human natures will be found to grace and adorn the coming man. Let us then, by cultivating, as teachers, the excellence of our race characteristic, gradually evolve those qualities, which will give additional color, tone, strength, and beauty to the future civilization of our country.

The story of this family is based largely on family letters, but the correspondence is one-sided, for while John Cromwell preserved many of the letters he received, he usually did not make copies of his replies. He did late in life, however, begin a journal and many of the entries include extended reminiscences about his correspondents and the people and events about whom they wrote.

In the creation of any collection, be it of books, paintings, letters, records, or baseball cards, the unseen hand of the collector is made manifest by his or her choices. In the letters that John Cromwell preserved and passed down to Adelaide undisturbed by Otelia, Adelaide had another opportunity to discover her grandfather's mind at work. Thus, the letters that she has selected for this book reflect her effort to distill her grandfather's own archive to a collection that captures the essence of her grandfather's view of his world.

This is not a book easily categorized. To remain true to her material, to the stories, and to herself, my mother dons several hats reflecting the various attributes and perspectives she brings to this work. Her overarching ambition is to ensure that the family archive is recorded in a manner such that this unique primary source will both enlighten the general reader and serve the community of scholars.

In doing so, she has also brought to bear the benefit of her training and experience as a sociologist specializing in African American and African studies where the knowledge and skills she has acquired over six decades in those fields offer insight on this material. As she is neither a historian nor a literary expert, however, she has not attempted a comprehensive analysis of all the primary material included. She hopes that the publication of this material may inspire others to make more extensive exegeses, especially of the correspondence in the closing chapters of the book.

Chapter 1

SLAVERY

IN THE GRIP OF THE MASTER, 1692–1851

❧

The story of the Cromwell family is one of slavery, emancipation, and freedom. It has been passed on by word of mouth but has been altered and expanded by the less romantic, irrefutable facts of accurate documentation.

John Wesley Cromwell (1849–1927), my grandfather, is the key figure in this story because he was the keeper of the flame. The first published account was based on a lecture Grandfather delivered in Portsmouth, Virginia, on January 1, 1901:[1]

> James Yates,[2] a Scotchman, died in the early part of the eighteenth century. He had no children. To a slave, Julia Cromwell, and her two daughters he left, by his will, their freedom and two of his seven planations. They were cheated of their freedom and the entire estate was devoted to the use of the free schools for poor whites. The posterity of the three were known as the "Free School Negroes." My father, Willis H. Cromwell, was the great grandson of July or Judy Cromwell, being born in 1792, the son of Hodges and Esther Cromwell.

An addendum amplifying this account was provided in *The Free Negro Family:* "Deprived of his lawful heritage of freedom, Willis Cromwell, with the assistance

---

1. "Notes," *Journal of Negro History* 12, no. 3 (July 1927): 563–66.
2. In the oral history passed down to Grandfather, Yates was erroneously called *James,* rather than *John,* which I corrected through further research. Furthermore, the frequent change in surnames often makes it difficult to identify people, so I have chosen to use *Yeates* in this account.

of his wife, ran a freight-ferry boat after hours between Norfolk and Portsmouth, and by this means accumulated enough money to purchase from the 'Free School Estate' himself, his wife, his six children and his son-in-law. Thus freed, the entire family moved to Philadelphia in 1851."[3]

This history, supported by several documents of slave sales, seemed sufficient to Grandfather to establish the experience of the family in slavery and its march to freedom.

For me, however, looking at the material many decades later, several important questions were unanswered: Who, in fact, was John Yeates?[4] What evidence is there that Julia was cheated of her inheritance? What was the Yeates Free School? Where was it located? And, perhaps most significantly, why were these slaves owned by John Yeates given the surname of Cromwell? Then there is the ever-present, intriguing question in black family history: is it possible to trace the family line to Africa or at least to when the first ancestor arrived in colonial America? To answer any of these questions would broaden our knowledge not only of the black family but also the understanding of slavery as an institution.

The first question is how did these slaves get the surname Cromwell? One hypothesis was offered by John Gabriel Cromwell, who researched the Cromwell family line in the United States. Cromwell relied on an account by a P. S. P. Conner, Esq., of 126 South 18th Street in Philadelphia, who was careful to deny that the black Cromwells living in Philadelphia in 1897 were in any way related to the white Cromwells of Philadelphia. Having the same name, Cromwell hypothesized, was the result of "innocent ambition of men who *after* emancipation from the condition in which they were only known as Tom or Nick, and finding themselves at liberty to adopt their own patronymics, sought to identify themselves with such houses as Raleigh, Trevelyan, Sydney, Russell, Talbot or Cromwell; besides that in many cases they did but call themselves after their own masters."[5] Cromwell, writing in 1897, thought any possibility of a blood relationship between black and white Cromwells was not worthy of serious consideration. This might have been the case but not the story. While John Gabriel Cromwell was, no doubt, distressed in noting the presence of black Cromwells in Philadelphia, he did not research completely the early history of Cromwells in this country.

The Cromwell line in America was started by Richard Cromwell, a barrister in Huntingdonshire, England, who had three sons, John, William, and Richard, and one daughter, Edith. John married Elizabeth Todd and had three sons,

3. E. F. Frazier, *The Free Negro Family* (Nashville: Fisk University Press, 1932), 59.

4. John Waylen, *The House of Cromwell, A Genealogical History of the Family and Descendants of the Protector,* rev. ed., by John Gabriel Cromwell (London: Elliott Stock, 1897), 257–62.

5. Ibid., 260–61.

Richard, Thomas, and John; William married Elizabeth Trahearn; Richard married Elizabeth Phillips; and Edith married Christopher Gist. The elder Richard never came to the colonies himself, but he acquired large amounts of land in Baltimore and a large estate in Frederick County, Maryland.

William and John came to the colonies on the *Benoni Eaton* on March 11, 1671. Three months earlier, on December 19, 1670, John and William had been assigned three hundred acres of a six hundred acre grant originally made to George Yates. In 1735, that land was resurveyed and named "Cromwell's Adventure" for William and John, William's grandsons.[6]

I do not know why Richard Cromwell did not accompany his brothers in 1671 or when he arrived, but in any case, after establishing himself in the colonies, he became more affluent than they. Neither John nor William owned slaves. William's will, which was probated in 1680, and cosigned with his wife, Elizabeth Trahearn, mentions his two brothers, John and Richard, and his two sons, William and Thomas, but makes no mention of slave bequests. In his property inventory of May 3, 1684, William noted only indentured servants: four adults and one boy.[7]

Richard, however, did own slaves, whom he bequeathed to his relatives, and these slaves called themselves and were identified before the Civil War as Cromwells. Richard's will was probated on September 27, 1717. His bequests of slaves were to his cousin Joshua, one Negro girl named Phyllis and her increase forever; and to Margaret Rattenbury, one Negro girl named Judith and her increase forever. According to the will, should Margaret Rattenbury die, Judith was to go to her daughter Hannah.[8] Richard had two sons, John and Richard, but apparently Richard was "in need of care." In addition, to his niece Edith Gist, Richard bequeathed two Negro girls, Abigail and Priscilla, and their increases forever. Richard's wife, Elizabeth, and his son John were left the balance of the estate, which included many other slaves who were not identified by name.

In 1728, Margaret Rattenbury wrote her will—she does not die, however, until 1741—but made no mention of Judith, though Cromwell had expected her to remain a slave in the family. By this time, Judith was the property of John Yeates; yet there is no bill of sale for Judith by Margaret, Hannah, or John in the land

---

6. Liber 16, folio 151, box 1, folder 29.

7. The wills of the Cromwell family are located in the archives at the Maryland Hall of Records: Richard Cromwell (September 27, 1717), bk. 14, folio 396, S530; William Cromwell (1680), bk. 4, folio 26, S530; Richard Cromwell (1717), bk. 14, folio 396, S530; William Cromwell (1683–1684), bk. 1, folio 9, Baltimore Co., MDC 4372–33-8–6; Margaret Rattenbury (1741) liber 22, folio 517, S538.

8. Margaret Rattenbury may be the mother-in-law of Richard's son John, who was married to Hannah Rattenbury.

Historical marker for Yeates Free School in Suffolk County, Virginia.

Upper Academy (left) and Lower Academy (below) of the Yeates Free School. (Courtesy of the City Attorney's Office, City of Suffolk.)

records. Those documents would have been in the Nansemond County, Virginia, records, which were destroyed by fire during the Civil War.

Who then was this John Yeates who bought Judith before 1741 and from whom did he purchase her? Assuming Judith was at least twelve years of age in 1692, then upon Cromwell's death in 1717, she was probably about thirty-seven years old. When Margaret Rattenbury died in 1741, Judith, if still alive, would have been about sixty-one years of age. The sale to Yeates occurred when she was between forty and fifty years old and the mother of two girls.

The references to Yeates are scattered. One was provided by William Turner Jordan, who described Yeates as a man of means and as "an educated Englishman of great philanthropic view who settled and lived in this parish during Colonial days." According to Jordan, after "becoming wealthy in lands and some Negroes," Yeates "wished to do what he could possibly for coming generations, gave land and Negroes in trust for the establishment of two public free schools; one in this neighborhood and one in the lower. When the Civil War came on, this institution was worth in money value nearly or quit one hundred thousand dollars, but Lincoln in the sweep of the hand killed the income by emancipation of the Negroes. The lands were sold by act of the Legislature of Virginia, and there remains but two lots and houses on them to tell of the greatness of John Yeates, English gentleman. He more than likely lived on the Pig Point farm at the mouth of the Nansemond River. The old schoolhouse on the above lot was built in 1841."[9] In the official listing of the officers of Nansemond County, a John Yeates is listed in the patent book as having acquired five hundred acres of land on April 27, 1701, in the Upper Parish of Nansemond County near Bennett's Creek.[10] The 1704 Virginia Quit Rolls list a Mr. Yeates as owning four hundred acres of land.

In the *William and Mary College Quarterly Historical Magazine,* the following account is given: "After Norfolk County, next in order is Nansemond County, but as the records of this county are totally destroyed, only an unsatisfactory account can be given of it. We have noticed the gift of Hugh Campbell and we are also told that one Yates left a considerable portion of land for the establishment of two schools in that county."[11]

9. William Turner Jordan, *A Record of Farms and Their Owners in Lower Parish of Nansemond County, Virginia* (Suffolk, Va.: Suffolk-Nansemond Historical Society, 1968).
10. Nell Marion Nugent, *Cavaliers and Pioneers: Abstracts of Virginia Land Patents and Grants,* vol. 3, 1695–1732 (Richmond: Virginia State Library, 1979), 41.
11. "Education in Colonial Virginia," pt. 3, *William and Mary College Quarterly Historical Magazine* 6, no. 2 (October 1897): 82.

Both of these accounts noting the establishment of two schools by Yeates seem to identify Yeates as the owner of the Cromwell family, who would later be known as the Free School Negroes.

Slavery in Maryland and Virginia in the mid-eighteenth century affected the history of the Cromwell family. The slave trade in Maryland and the Upper Chesapeake has not been fully chartered as it has been in Virginia. Marylanders up until the mid-seventeenth century purchased slaves in ones and twos from traders in Virginia or the West Indies and relied almost exclusively on indentured servants to meet their labor requirements for the cultivation of tobacco.

> Four years after the arrival of the first settlers, Lord Baltimore requested his agent to purchase cattle, sows, hens and "Ten Negroes" for use on his lands. His younger brother, Leonard Calvert, who was appointed first governor of Maryland, sought to acquire in 1642 "fourteene negro men- slaves, and three women slaves, of between 16 and 26 yeare old able and sound in body and limbs." Another member of the Calvert family expressed regret in 1664 that he was unable to find a sufficient number of responsible men who "would engage to take a 100 or 200 neigroes every yeare from the Royall Company."[12]

By the last years of the seventeenth century slave labor was seen as more suitable for the needs of the emerging agrarian society; therefore, there was a marked increase in the slave trade. Most slaves reached Maryland by the same means and routes that brought them to Virginia, through Dutch traders and through direct exchange with the island colonies of Barbados and Jamaica. Barbados was the island on which the British developed their first expansive slave system in the New World, and it became renowned not only for the flaunted wealth of its planters but also for the general mistreatment of the slaves and the indentured population.[13]

While slaves continued to be imported from the West Indies, by the 1690s most were brought directly from Africa. In the midst of the growth and control of slavery in the colony of Maryland, it is not surprising that conflict or controversy arose over the ground rules for its introduction.

12. Darold D. Wax, "Black Immigrants: The Slave Trade in Colonial Maryland," *Maryland Historical Magazine* 73, no. 1 (March 1978): 31, 33–34.

13. See Hilary Beckles, *Black Rebellion in Barbados: The Struggle against Slavery, 1627–1838* (Carib Research and Publications, 1987); and *White Servitude and Black Slavery in Barbados, 1627–1715* (Knoxville: University of Tennessee Press, 1989).

One such controversy concerns the case of the *Margaret*, which sailed into St. Mary's River in St. Mary's County on December 25, 1692. The master of the *Margaret*, William Burnett, was not English nor were most of her crew. The *Margaret* had sailed from London to Barbados, where it illegally took on board several Negroes: three men, Sambo, Jack, and Dick; three girls, Judith, Moll, and Maria; two boys, Rough and Dick; and one "mollata" woman. The Negroes were slaves, and the "mollata" woman was an indentured servant.[14]

According to Donnan, Burnett said, "The charge of breach of the laws made against him by the information was illegal and insufficient, for Negroes are not goods nor commodities intended by the said statues, and by no law whatsoever pay any duty or custom either for Importation or Exportation."[15]

The slaves as originally identified were assessed at 103 pounds: twenty-six pounds for the two men, Sambo and Jack; and thirty pounds for the three girls, Judith, Moll, and Maria. During the process of the case, as was made clear, a man named George Luke, obviously a friend or associate of Burnett, had to return to Virginia.[16] The records do not say whether Luke went with or without slaves. In a January 12 record, however, the appraised report of cargo and slaves on the *Margaret* mentions only two unnamed Negroes. My assumption is that Luke, in a private sale with Burnett, took all or some of the others—the women surely to Virginia—and that the two men, Jack and Sambo, were left in Maryland to be dealt with later.

The significance of this story for the history of the Cromwell family is, as recorded by Grandfather, that his great-great-grandparents were Judith and Jack. The circumstantial evidence is powerful that Judith and Jack on the *Margaret* were indeed the ancestors identified by my grandfather: 1) few slaves were imported into Maryland at that time, 2) it was rare that slaves were recorded by first names, and 3) that a slave named Judith was owned by Richard Cromwell and was passed on by will to Margaret Rattenbury.

In his account, Grandfather speaks no more of Jack—who probably was sold

---

14. For a brief reference to this case with names of slaves and their value, see Elizabeth Donnan, *Documents Illustrative of the History of the Slave Trade to America*, vol. 4 (Washington, D.C.: Carnegie Institution of Washington, 1930–1935), 12–13. More expansive accounts of the controversy appear in *Proceedings of the Council of Maryland, 1693–1694*, 490. See also the original correspondence for the Board of Trades, 1689–1695, at the British Records Office, Kew, Richmond, Surrey, UK.

15. Donnan, *Documents Illustrative of the History of the Slave Trade to America*, 4:17–18.

16. According to the Virginia State Library and Archives, early Stafford County records have not survived. Consequently, it is impossible to verify more on George Luke. When Yeates purchased Judith, or from which Rattenbury, is not known.

separately from Judith and probably never came to Virginia—but he does state that Judith had two daughters, Milly and Sarah. If the Judith mentioned in Richard Cromwell's will of 1717 arrived on the *Margaret* in 1692, then she must have been his slave for twenty-five years. Although willed by Cromwell to Margaret Rattenbury, and then to Hannah Rattenbury, his daughter-in-law, Judith does not appear in the wills of either of these women. Consequently, one must assume that either before Cromwell's death, with no change having been made in the will, or after his death, Judith and her daughters became the slaves of John Yeates. Even though they were owned by Yeates until his death in 1731, they kept the surname of their first master, Richard Cromwell.

There are only fragments of family history to explain how these slaves fared after Yeates's death. Unanswered also is the question of whether they were actually cheated of their freedom (which was certainly not improbable) or whether, in fact, Yeates was influenced to change his mind and devote his legacy to the education of poor Whites. Yeates, apparently before his death, had already started a school for his own children in which he taught, and there was certainly a growing appreciation of the need to provide education for the children of white families who could not find or afford private tutors and who did not wish or could not afford to send them to England for their early education.

Beginning in 1635, there was an interest in supporting free schools. Several individuals, including Benjamin Syms, Thomas Eaton, and Henry Peasely, provided generous financial gifts for schools in various counties of the colony.[17] This trend and obvious need could certainly have influenced Yeates. In addition, Judith, by this time a woman of advanced years, was perhaps less able to encourage Yeates to keep his promise to her and to her daughters. It is clear from his will made September 18, 1731, declared to be his last, that Yeates left neither freedom nor farms to Judith or her daughters.

He did, however, make some other dispositions that reflect the social structure of his estate. Two individuals, presumably indentured servants, Wm. Heffler and Edwin Shea, were given some livestock "besides what the law gives at freedom." Tenants then living on his land, Temar Maning and her sister Ruth, were also given livestock. His Negro, Bess, was willed his linen spinning wheel and the hackle, and to his Negroes, Dick and Caesar, he left his old clothes and coarse shirts.

Finally, without mentioning any by name, Yeates made the following disposition of his slaves:

17. "Education in Colonial Virginia," 80.

that my negroes be hired out in the said Lower Parish for convenience of paying the same; there being no occasion to sell any, my estate not being in debt; and there being females among them, may, with God's blessings, be a standing stock of them; and the hire of them and the remainder part of my personal estate undisposed of, together with some rents of my land aforesaid, may be employed in keeping the church on this side of the river in repair, as well as the yearly wages of a school master and school masters in the limits aforesaid forever.[18]

Unlike the indentured servants and tenants, the slaves mentioned in this will do not have surnames. But apparently the slaves, who were owned by the Yeates Free School, saw themselves as Cromwells until Judith's great-grandson, Willis Hodges Cromwell, purchased his family and himself between 1849 and 1851.[19]

According to the family oral history, Sarah, Judith's daughter, married Isaac Hodges and by him had six children—Dempsy, Isaac, David, Milly, Sarah, and Esther—all of whom would belong to the Yeates Free School.

The family Bible provides the only documentation on the direct heirs of Judith and on the slaves of the Yeates Free School.

Sarah Jordan, daughter of Daniel Jordan and Esther, his wife was born March 28, 1787.

Elizabeth Jordan, daughter of Daniel Jordan and Esther, his wife, was born January 5, 1789.

Willis Crummel [sic] was born May 25, 1792, the son of Maxter Hodges by Esther Crummel.

Lydia Thomas, daughter of Harry Thomas and Esther his wife was born the 21st of September, 1800.

Eley Thominas, the son of Harry Thominas and Esther his wife was born the 12th of June 1803.

Henry son of Harry Thominas and Esther his wife was born the 24th of March 1808.

These entries reflect the now rather well-known fact that slaves did indeed think of themselves as husband and wife. There are, nevertheless, some mysteries. There is no mention of Judith or her daughters, Milly and Sarah. Esther

18. Commonwealth of Virginia Will Book, Nansemond County, Va., bk. 7, p. 271.

19. From a catalog of the school published in 1861, we can ascertain the value of these Yeates Free School slaves: Mr. Knob Collector for this year by the scale amount of 30/2/8 3/4; by rent of land hire of negroes 83/47 1/2; by rent of land 36/11/-; by hire of negroes 56/4/2; by rent of land and hire of negroes 41/10/-; by rent of land and hire of negroes 90/-/-.

Crummel is the only member bearing the family name, which she carried probably from her mother, Sarah, one of Judith's daughters, and Esther may have named one of her daughters, Sarah, after her mother. She passed on her surname to her son Willis, whom she had by Maxter Hodges. Willis's father—listed in the Bible as Maxter Hodges—was recorded by Willis's son, my grandfather, as Max Hodges. Willis himself was known as Willis Hodges Cromwell.

There is also the difficulty of determining whether there was more than one Esther—Esther Crummel and Esther with no surname—or whether there was just one, who married Daniel Jordan and had Sarah and Elizabeth, then married Harry Thomas and had Lydia, Eley, and Henry, and who between marriages had Willis by Maxter Hodges. I suspect the latter is true: there is one Esther—Esther Crummel—who had two husbands and an outside child by Maxter.[20]

It is "Willis Crummel" who makes the bridge between slavery and freedom and in a sense becomes the true family founder. On July 28, 1934, in an article in the *Afro-American*, reprinted from the *Portsmouth (Va.) Star*, an interesting account is given of Willis as a slave

> who carried freight back and forth between Portsmouth and Norfolk in a square rigged sail boat, "Daisy," and lived in an old brick house on the wharf where freight from his boat was landed. Cromwell was hired out at $125.00 and his wife at $50.00 for a year's term. These school slaves were permitted to keep all over that amount that they could earn. Willis was trusted by the entire community and held himself among the aristocrats of slavery.[21]

Another account, which originally appeared in the *People's Advocate* on July 14, 1883, described Willis Cromwell as "a ship carpenter and wharf builder" who "eventually ran a freight ferry between the two cities of Norfolk and Portsmouth—a business then monopolized by two colored men—the other being the late Charles Cooper of Monrovia, West Africa, but since run by the captain of the noted Merrimac. From the profits of this business,"

> [Cromwell] accumulated quite a sum, and at the age of fifty-six, he paid . . . more than three thousand dollars for his wife and seven children. One of his

---

20. During the eighteenth and nineteenth centuries, Whites by the name of Hodges were numerous and prominent in Norfolk County, Virginia (see Willard B. Gatewood, Jr., ed., *Free Man of Color: The Autobiography of Willis Augustus Hodges* [Knoxville: University of Tennessee Press, 1982], 5). I don't know how Willis got his name.

21. In *Tobacco and Slaves: The Development of Southern Cultures in the Chesapeake, 1680–1800* (Chapel Hill: University of North Carolina Press, 1986), Alan Kulikoff notes the increasing number of slaves as boatmen but not as owners of boats.

Willis Hodges Cromwell, 1792–1883.

children a daughter, had but recently been married. The "owner" of her husband, L. Bilisoly, the proprietor of a large grocery to whom Mr. Cromwell voluntarily gave his services on Saturday evening, put the husband in jail and threatened to send him to New Orleans, on the pretext that as his wife had become under the law a free woman, her husband would at the first opportunity escape from slavery. He did this knowing that before he would be allowed to send him to New Orleans his father-in-law would secure his freedom, which the sequel proved to be true.[22]

The complete story is considerably more complicated. Willis was indeed married to Elizabeth Carney. But Elizabeth, though a slave, was not one of the Free School Negroes. She and their children belonged to Thomas and Sarah Twine, Sarah having inherited them from a previous marriage. Willis first had to have his wife set free so that she could exercise the prerogatives of a free person; that is, so she could buy slaves. Elizabeth Carney Cromwell's parents were William and Theresa Carney. William Carney was one of the Negro preachers who was not effectively silenced during the time of the Nat Turner insurrection; he continued to preach at the Eastern Branch Baptist Church until his death on February 29, 1844. Elizabeth, the Carneys' oldest daughter, was born in the Eastern Branch, Norfolk County about 1799. Their other children were Anthony, Theresa, Latitia, and William. In 1812, Elizabeth was living in Norfolk County with her stepmother, assisting her in preparing food for soldiers. When her stepmother died, she went to Portsmouth and there met and married Willis Cromwell. They were both slaves. I do not know how she became a slave in the Twine family.

According to the slave purchase document, on January 10, 1849, Willis Cromwell gave to B. W. Dobson, of the town of Portsmouth, fifty dollars to purchase "Betsey" (Elizabeth) Cromwell, then forty-nine years of age, from Thomas Twine.

On January 11, 1849, Sarah Twine agreed that her husband, Thomas, could for the promised sum of three thousand dollars "sell, or dispose of in any manner or form their jointly owned slave, Betsey and her children—James, Levi, Martha Ann, William, Willis, John Wesley and Esther"—their objective being to go to Africa. That same month, Thomas Twine accepted from Elizabeth Cromwell the bill of purchase for her children:

22. Philip S. Foner and Ronald L. Lewis, eds., *The Black Worker: A Documentary History from Colonial Times to the Present*, vol. 1, *The Black Worker to 1869* (Philadelphia: Temple University Press, 1978), 43–44.

James, twenty-five years of age
Levi, nineteen years old
Martha Ann, twenty-two years of age
Esther, fourteen years of age
William, twelve years of age
Willis, ten years of age, and
Wesley, two years and four months

Elizabeth manumitted her oldest son, Jim (James) Cromwell, on July 10, 1849.

On July 6, 1850, the Board of Trustees of the Yeates Free School in the county of Nansemond ordered and directed James Ames, the treasurer of the Yeates Free School, to sell the Negro slave, Willis Cromwell, provided the sum of three hundred dollars could be obtained. Following the directive, on July 17, 1850, Ames reported that "for and in consideration of the sum of Three hundred dollars to me in hand paid by Elizabeth Cromwell (the wife of the said Willis Cromwell) hath bargained and sold and by these presents doth grant bargain, sell and convey unto the said Elizabeth Cromwell, the said Negro slave named Willis Cromwell belonging to the said Yates Free School."

On July 17, 1850, Elizabeth had her bill of purchase for three hundred dollars for her husband, Willis Cromwell, then sixty years of age, from the Yeates Free School.

Elizabeth manumitted her children—Levi, Willis Jr., Esther, and John (Wesley)—on June 14, 1851, and then on June 16, 1851, she manumitted her Negro man "named Willis Cromwell (also my husband)."

Although the documents are not extant, one presumes that Elizabeth's and Willis's other children, Martha Ann and William, were similarly manumitted by Elizabeth. In addition, the document that gave Elizabeth her freedom from Dobson, her arranged purchaser, thus enabling her to negotiate these sales, is also missing.

The Yeates Free School was located in Nansemond County, of which Suffolk in 1742 was established as the county seat. Suffolk was located on the Nansemond River on the line of the Portsmouth and Roanoke Railroad, eighteen miles southwest of Norfolk and eighty-five miles from Richmond. During the antebellum period, agriculture was not as important in this area as trade in tar, turpentine, and slaves. In 1840, there were 4,858 whites, 4,530 slaves, and 1,407 free people of color in Suffolk, making a total of 10,795 persons.[23]

23. Henry Howe, *Historical Collections of Virginia* (Charleston, S.C.: Babcock, 1845), 386.

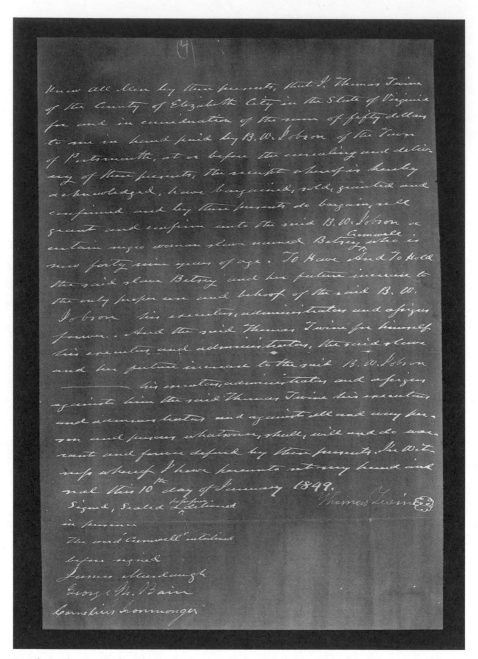

Purchase document for Elizabeth (Betsey) Cromwell. In January 1849 Elizabeth's husband, Willis, paid B. W. Dobson fifty dollars to purchase his wife from Thomas and Sarah Twine.

In January 1849 Elizabeth paid Thomas and Sarah Twine three thousand dollars for her children's freedom.

Purchase document for Willis Cromwell. In July 1850, a year and a half after being freed by her husband, Elizabeth was able to purchase Willis for three hundred dollars from the Yeates Free School.

This was clearly an environment that permitted Willis Cromwell, as enterprising as he was, to acquire the funds to purchase his family. Transportation was important. Apparently although there was a free colored population in the community, Willis Cromwell, now free, was urged by friendly merchants and preachers to go to Liberia where "he could be a free man indeed, and see his children grow up to usefulness if not to distinction." Cromwell "rebuked them for the solicitude for his welfare," saying that "they stood between him and the

In June 1851, Elizabeth manumitted four of her seven children, Levi, Willis, Esther, and John Wesley. She had manumitted her oldest child, James, two years earlier in July 1849.

sun and then blamed him for not seeing." Therefore, with his wife, he toured several northern cities, including New Haven, Brooklyn, New York, and Philadelphia. After this tour, he returned to Virginia and finally decided to settle in Philadelphia in 1851.[24]

24. The *People's Advocate*, July 14, 1983, reprinted in Foner and Lewis, eds., *Black Worker: A Documentary History*, 1:44.

Chapter 2

PHILADELPHIA

THE CITY OF BROTHERLY LOVE?

❧ ☙

Philadelphia appears to be the metropolis of this odious prejudice and there is probably no city in the known world where dislike amounting to hatred of the coloured population prevails more than in the city of brotherly love.

—Joseph Sturge, *A Visit to the United States in 1841*

There is not perhaps anywhere to be found a city in which prejudice against color is more rampant than in Philadelphia.

—Frederick Douglass, *Douglass' Monthly,* February 1862

A cursory survey of the treatment of Blacks in Philadelphia is necessary to assess the accuracy of these epigraphs and to explain Willis Cromwell's decision to settle in this city.

Several studies have been extraordinarily valuable in exploring these questions: Du Bois' seminal work *The Philadelphia Negro* focuses on the black community in the latter part of the nineteenth century and offers a useful schematic overview of the situation of Blacks in that city from the earliest days. More recently, Julie Winch's study *Philadelphia's Black Elite: Activism, Accommodation, and the Struggle for Autonomy, 1787–1848,* provides a more microscopic view of the personalities, activities, and issues that shaped the environment of Philadelphia before

the arrival of the Cromwell family. Stratification in the black community continued to reflect the distinction between free-born and slaves, either as freedmen
or fugitives, well into the nineteenth century.[1]

Interestingly, Philadelphia's black elite was the subject of the second novel by
black American writer Frank J. Webb, *The Garies and Their Friends*. Originally
published in 1856, after Willis Cromwell and his family had come to the city, Webb's
work describes the lifestyle of successful Blacks, the economic difficulties faced by
the poorer Blacks, and the conflicts between Blacks and Whites of that period.[2]

In *Forging Freedom: The Formation of Philadelphia's Black Community, 1720–
1840,* Gary Nash provides the most recent documentation supporting the observations of Sturge and Douglass. Before the War of 1812, Philadelphia had
apparently been a city of true brotherly love between the races, albeit reflecting a dependency of Blacks on well-intentioned Whites. But "the War of 1812
engendered bad feelings between the races, forcing the Blacks to seek more independence and self-reliance in their actions." Nash describes "how the optimistic
spirit of 18th century Philadelphia came to be transferred into the militant anti-
war black sentiment of the 1830s."[3] After the War of 1812, white Philadelphians
at all levels of society threatened the personal freedom and opportunities of their
black fellow citizens. This change in the relations between the races brought more
overt hostility on the part of the Whites: the storming in 1829 of the Shelter for
Colored Orphans as a reaction to the noise in the nearby black church; the de-
liberate burning in 1838 of the newly opened Pennsylvania Hall, a symbol of the
emergence of radical abolitionism; the hurling of boxes of abolitionist literature
into the Delaware River by an angry white mob; and the increasing frequency of
strikes and labor protests as the result of the growing number of Irish immigrants
in competition with native-born workers—black and white.

Not surprisingly, Blacks became increasingly assertive. "By 1834 they had
formed independent families, carved out their own vocations, built their own
businesses, organized separate churches, founded black schools, and formed beneficial, literary and Masonic societies."[4] But these important community building activities were largely ignored by most white Philadelphians who still saw
Blacks as inferior and unequal.

1. W. E. B. Du Bois, *The Philadelphia Negro: A Social Study* (Philadelphia: University of Pennsylvania, 1899); Julie Winch, *Philadelphia's Black Elite: Activism, Accommodation, and the Struggle
for Autonomy, 1787–1848* (Philadelphia: Temple University Press, 1988).

2. Frank J. Webb, *The Garies and Their Friends* (New York: Arno Press, 1969).

3. Gary B. Nash, *Forging Freedom: The Formation of Philadelphia's Black Community, 1720–1840*
(Cambridge: Harvard University Press, 1988), 211.

4. Ibid., 274.

Roger Lane's *Roots of Violence in Black Philadelphia, 1860–1900,* picks up the story after the arrival of the Cromwell family and examines a city increasingly immersed in the struggles and issues of the Civil War and its aftereffects; yet, as the title suggests, the causes or roots of the racial violence were planted much earlier.[5]

Blacks were first brought to Philadelphia as slaves by the Dutch, and in spite of early protests by Quakers, the institution of slavery continued to grow in the city. But voluntary emancipation also increased, and by 1790, there were about one thousand black freedmen in Philadelphia. This encouraged migration into the city so that "between 1790 and 1800 the Negro population of Philadelphia County increased from 2,489 to 6,880, or 176 per cent against an increase of 43 per cent among the whites,"[6] thus setting the stage for a growing antipathy among some Whites toward Blacks.

Aside from this rather rapid growth in population, the racial perimeters of the black community in Philadelphia did not differ markedly in scope or character from those in New York or Boston, where a larger white community only begrudgingly offered any semblance of equality and the black community struggled to survive with some modicum of dignity. The talented and ambitious freedmen capitalizing on the secure, economic foothold Blacks already had in Philadelphia were able to perform all kinds of domestic service, all common labor, and much of the skilled labor.

Leadership and elite status stemmed from membership in the Free African Society formed on April 12, 1787, the first community institution for free Blacks. Additional leadership status came from the black church, itself an outgrowth of the Free African Society. The independent Methodist Church, erected in 1796 (Mother Bethel), was started in 1790 by Richard Allen, a former slave of the Chew family. It was followed by two white-affiliated churches: the First African Church of St. Thomas Episcopal Church, founded in February 1792 by Absalom Jones who, like Allen, had purchased his own freedom, and the Presbyterian Church, built and dedicated on July 17, 1794, and led by John Gloucester. After educating him for the ministry, Gloucester's master, the Reverend Gideon Blackburn of Tennessee, freed him, and Gloucester was then hired by the Presbyterian Evangelical Society, which established the church for him.

The existence of the Prince Hall Masons, installed in Boston as the African Lodge by Prince Hall himself in 1797, was followed by three others: Union in

5. Roger Lane, *Roots of Violence in Black Philadelphia, 1860–1900* (Cambridge: Harvard University Press, 1986).

6. Du Bois, *The Philadelphia Negro,* 17.

Philly & mistreatment of Blacks

1810, Laurel in 1811, and Phoenix in 1814. On December 25, 1815, these three lodges joined with the African Lodge to form the First African Independent Grand Lodge of Pennsylvania, with Absalom Jones as Grand Master, providing the third institutional basis for leadership.

James Forten, a sailmaker and successful businessman, William Gray, a grocer, and Cyrus Bustill, a Quaker brewer, members of the Free African Society, joined Allen, Jones, and Gloucester as the earliest articulate black leaders. In 1793, Forten, Gray, and Bustill, along with these ministers, performed a great service for the white community when a terrible yellow fever epidemic drove white Philadelphians from the city so quickly that many did not have time to bury their dead. These leaders quietly took the work in hand, spending some of their own funds and doing so well that they were publicly acclaimed by Mayor Clarkson in 1794.[7]

According to Du Bois, "The condition of the Negroes of the city in the last decade of the eighteenth and the first two decades of the nineteen, although without doubt bad, slowly improved." The total black population continued to increase: by 1810, there were 10,522 Blacks and 100,688 Whites in the city of Philadelphia. The free black community established six churches and eleven benevolent societies and had started a school by 1770, which had 414 pupils by 1813.[8]

James Forten, along with Absalom Jones and Richard Allen, called a meeting to recruit black troops to fight the British in the War of 1812. The war ended before they were needed.

By 1830, the black population of the city districts had increased to 15,624—a 27 percent increase for the decade from 1820 to 1830 and a 48 percent increase since 1810. By 1847, 47.7 percent of the black population living in Philadelphia proper had come from somewhere else. These Blacks were being forced out of the hod-carrying and stevedoring jobs, which traditionally had been theirs but were now being performed by foreign-born Irish immigrants. Less than half of one percent of adult black males found jobs in factories.

It should come as no surprise that there would be growing friction between the races. Actually, "beginning in 1829 and continuing through the ensuing two decades Philadelphia Negroes were the victims of a half-a-dozen major anti-black riots and many more minor mob actions. Negro churches, schools, homes and even an orphanage were set on fire. Some Blacks were killed, many beaten and

7. Ibid., 18n24.
8. Ibid., 23–25.

others run out of town."[9] The consequence of one of these riots is the major plot in Frank Webb's novel.

In addition to the overt racial action, in 1838 Blacks were disfranchised, even if they owned property, and remained so until 1870 when the Fifteenth Amendment required that they be given the right to vote. Thus the issue of the franchise became increasingly important, serving to express the concern of the black elite and to divide the black community on the basis of class. This was exemplified when James Forten sought the franchise in 1838, but the verdict was that "No amount of property, no talents, no personal worth, no service rendered to country, nothing will be admitted as a reason for relaxing the exclusion of Blacks from the franchise."[10]

In 1848, about one-third of the black population of Philadelphia County lived in Moyamensing with the densest concentration in an area bounded by South and Fitzwater streets from Fifth to Eighth, where 302 families lived. According to Elizabeth Geffen, "They lived in Bandbox row houses, three stories high, with only one room, about ten by twelve feet, on each floor—'Father, Son and Holy Ghost houses' they were called—filled many courts and alleys running off secondary streets, or lined dead-end walls in the rear of the larger houses facing on the street, with access by means of narrow passageways between the front houses."[11]

The values and strengths of the Quakers, strong abolitionists that they were, gave the Blacks some feeling of freedom and hope. Lane describes the reality of Philadelphia for Blacks in the first half of the nineteenth century:

> The life of Philadelphia blacks was full of uncertainties, of unclear lines and half-hidden traps. A number of professionals and entrepreneurs were able to transcend these problems and establish moderately successful careers. But with these few exceptions, all blacks experienced insecurities and contradictions that reinforced their realization that the economic rules and roles followed by the great majority were irrelevant to their own conditions.
>
> There were no signs to show which hotels, restaurants and saloons tol-

9. Theodore Hershberg, "Free Blacks in Antebellum Philadelphia," in Allen F. Davis and Mark H. Haller, eds., *The Peoples of Philadelphia: A History of Ethnic Groups and Lower-Class Life 1790–1940* (Philadelphia: Temple University Press, 1973), 113. See also Sam Bass Warner, "Riots and Restoration of Order," in *The Private City: Philadelphia in Three Periods of Its Growth* (Philadelphia: University of Pennsylvania Press, 1968), 125–57.

10. Winch, *Philadelphia's Black Elite*, 140.

11. Elizabeth M. Geffen, "Industrial Development and Social Crisis, 1841–1854," in Russell F. Weigley, ed., *Philadelphia: A Three Hundred Year History* (New York: W. W. Norton, 1982), 315.

erated Afro-American patronage and which did not . . . although the treatment of blacks varied by class, age and institution, there was no identifiable white group or organization—elite or working class, Catholic or Quaker child or adult—which could be counted on to behave consistently.[12]

The antebellum black community of Philadelphia was extremely poor. Hershberg estimates "the total wealth—that is, the combined value of real and personal property holdings—for three out of every five households in both 1838 and 1847 amounted to sixty dollars or less."[13] Nevertheless, "in 1847, there were 1940 Negro children in school; the Negroes held, it was said, about $400,000 in real estate and had 19 churches, and 106 benevolent societies."[14]

Yet, there was an extreme disparity in economic status among Blacks with the "wealthiest one percent accounting for fully 30 percent of the total wealth."[15] There was within the black community of Philadelphians a black elite, a closed society that was hard for outsiders to penetrate. The backbone of this elite was a small business class dominated from 1840 to 1870 by what Du Bois called the "Guild of the Caterers," a group "that arose in prominence and power as remarkable a trade guild as ever ruled a medieval city. It took complete leadership of the bewildered group of Negroes, and led them steadily on to a degree of affluence, culture and respect such as has probably never been surpassed in the history of the Negro in America." Before this period, "between 1790 and 1820 a very large portion, and perhaps most, of the artisans of Philadelphia were Negroes." Pushed out by foreign competition, by 1837 only about 350 black men out of a population of 10,500 pursued trades. Only two avenues were, therefore, open to the more enterprising Blacks who wanted

> to enter into commercial life in some small way, or to develop certain lines of home service into a small independent and lucrative employment. The white catering business . . . transformed the Negro cook and waiter into the public caterer and restaurateur, and raised a crowd of underpaid menials to become a set of self-reliant, original business men, who amassed fortunes for themselves and won general respect for their people.[16]

12. Lane, *Roots of Violence*, 23.
13. Hershberg, "Free Blacks in Antebellum Philadelphia," in Davis and Haller, ed., *Peoples of Philadelphia*, 114.
14. Du Bois, *The Philadelphia Negro*, 36.
15. Hershberg, "Free Blacks in Antebellum Philadelphia," in Davis and Haller, ed., *Peoples of Philadelphia*, 114.
16. Du Bois, *The Philadelphia Negro*, 23–35.

Robert Bogle, the first prominent black caterer, was followed by Peter Augustin, a West Indian immigrant, who started a business in 1818 and made Philadelphia's catering business famous all over the country. Other well-known caterers were Henry Jones, James Prosser and son, Thomas Dorsey, and Henry Minton. From 1845 to 1875, the fashionable world of Philadelphia's white elite were regular customers of the catering businesses run by these men. Minton, the youngest of the group, came to Philadelphia in 1830 from Nansemond County, Virginia, at the age of nineteen. "He was first apprenticed to a shoemaker, then went into a hotel as waiter. Finally, he opened dining rooms at Fourth and Chestnut. He died March 20, 1883."[17]

Willis Cromwell was probably quite impressed by the business success of this small black elite. Perhaps he met, or already knew, Henry Minton, from his own community, and perhaps it was Minton who gave him the encouragement to come to Philadelphia. In any case, Willis Cromwell knew he had to rely on his business acumen to survive as a free man. That he was successful himself but even more so was his son, Levi, and thereby becoming a part of this small black elite was clearly illustrated in 1883 when in the midst of rising conflict over political power, "a black caucus proposed the veteran abolitionist, Levi Cromwell, for one of the seven positions in the Seventh Ward (on the common branch of the City Council). Cromwell was defeated by 'Uncle Sammy' Williams, the Organization's hand-picked Afro-American candidate who himself went down to defeat in the general election."[18]

In the decades before Willis Cromwell's move to Philadelphia, free black communities, especially in the Northeast, were less secure of their position because of the growing hostility toward them, particularly in Ohio. They began to take hope in the rise and strengthening of the abolition sentiments. The repercussions in the North following the 1830 Nat Turner revolt in Virginia, the publication and wide circulation of David Walker's *Appeal* in 1829, and the publication in 1831 by William Lloyd Garrison of the *Liberator,* with its unequivocal cry for emancipation, had all served to galvanize many the free black communities. But at the same time, the continuing activities of the American Colonization Society were troubling. Therefore, many leaders felt it necessary to organize and act jointly to examine their common predicament and to proclaim their position on behalf of the free Blacks in the country as a whole.

 Meeting first in 1830 in Philadelphia at the Bethel Church, the convention

17. Ibid., 35n19.
18. Lane, *Roots of Violence,* 67.

Philly's violence

movement brought duly elected delegates from six communities: twelve from Pennsylvania, three from New York, one from Connecticut, two from Rhode Island, one from Delaware, and four from Virginia. There were also honorary participants: six from Pennsylvania, one from New York, three from Maryland, one from Ohio, one from New Jersey, and two from Delaware. It is interesting that Massachusetts was not represented until the next convention, when they had two delegates.

Beginning with this convention in 1830 and continuing until 1835, this body, while plagued by internecine strife over the leadership between Philadelphia and New York, which Philadelphia ultimately won, was concerned with many relevant issues: emigration, education (the possibility of establishing a manual labor college in Connecticut), and the improvement of the moral and political standing of the black community, with special emphasis on the need to stress temperance.[19] This phase of the convention movement merged into the formation of the American Reform Society in 1836.

Willis Cromwell need not have understood or been familiar with the issues espoused by these conventions, but certainly the excitement generated by them would have filtered down to Virginia. The continuing increase in the black population—freed and fugitive—the growing necessity for Blacks to be more morally responsible and less involved in crime and violence, and the growing understanding among the black elite that their position was viewed no differently by the white community than that of the less affluent and less responsible Blacks could not have been lost on Willis Cromwell or on those Blacks he met in the city. By 1841, the Philadelphia black elite had moved to such a position of conservatism that one activist described the city as "the seat of all that is discordant, visionary and impracticable."

In spite of such negatives, there was a positive side—the growth of the churches, the importance of education, the stress on morality and temperance, and the possibility of success in business—for certainly there was no black community in the country where a free family would be without problems and anxiety. Philadelphia would have seemed to Willis Cromwell, with perhaps some encouragement from Minton, as advantaged, if not more so, than any other possible choice.

From a white perspective, however, between 1841 and 1854 Philadelphia "was marked by unprecedented civic violence, arising from many causes: an explosive

---

19. See Winch, *Philadelphia's Black Elite,* 91–107; and John W. Cromwell, *The Negro in American History* (Washington, D.C.: American Negro Academy, 1914), 27–35.

increase in population; a complex and unreconciled ethnic, racial, and religious mixture; inadequate housing; a growing and ever-more-obvious maldistribution of wealth; and a volatile social class structure—all exasperated by political ineptitude or chicanery or a combination of both."[20]

As the country drifted slowly toward civil war, slavery and the situation of the Blacks in Philadelphia became intense political issues on both the local and national level. For example, the Democratic presidential campaign of 1856

> candidly argued that a vote for Buchanan's party was a vote of unequivocal rejection of the antislavery party and the Negro. This argument evidently appealed to most Philadelphians. They would not agitate against the peculiar institution of the South, and they could hardly imagine the North's agitating the question of the extremity of civil war; they themselves did not like the Negro and wished to confine him to a restricted and menial role. The whole remaining history of the sectional crisis was to confirm that this was the principal attitude of Philadelphia and to leave the attitude little changed.
>
> With such an outlook Philadelphians did not expect civil war, but neither did they find the sectional controversy, so closely linked to questions of race, altogether remote and abstract . . . [for Blacks] constituted about 4 percent of the population . . . congregated . . . in the very heart of the city, in and immediately adjacent to the wards of the old city where they were most visible and closest to the principal institutions of the city's life. . . .
>
> Living at the core of the city, the blacks were perceived by white Philadelphians as a seemingly necessary but disturbing presence.
>
> . . . Almost equally disquieting was the presence of the blacks' friends and advocates, the abolitionists, a small and unpopular minority but a persistent one, whose cries against slavery in the South carried overtones of racial egalitarianism that seemed to threaten Philadelphia itself.[21]

The Pennsylvania Anti-Slavery Society, founded in 1837, joined William Lloyd Garrison in denouncing the United States Constitution as a proslavery document and in proclaiming "No union with slaveholders." This organization, headquartered at 31 North Fifth Street, had Robert Purvis,[22] at various times,

20. Geffen, "Industrial Development and Social Crisis," in Weigley, ed., *Philadelphia: A Three Hundred Year History,* 307–8.

21. Russell F. Weigley, "The Border City in the Civil War, 1854–1865," in *Philadelphia: A Three Hundred Year History* (New York: W. W. Norton, 1982), 385–86.

22. Robert Purvis Sr. (1810–1898) was born in Charleston, S.C. His father was English and a successful businessman, and his mother, a free-born black woman who was brought to Philadelphia

as its president and vice president and William Still[23] as its clerk. It was able through various activities—an annual antislavery fair and a stream of antislavery lecturers—to keep the issue of slavery alive. More important, however, were the activities of William Still himself, working through the vigilance committee as a conductor on the Underground Railroad. During the 1850s, the Philadelphia Vigilance Committee aided about one hundred fugitives a year. Many of the people helped by the committee proceeded to places farther North, but many chose to remain in Philadelphia.

Legally, Philadelphians took a proslavery position. The passage of the Fugitive Slave Act of 1850 provoked no remarkable outcry among them, and the cases that were tried, on balance, were favorable to the slave catchers rather than to the slave.[24] As late as May 1860, a fugitive slave was apprehended by Philadelphians and returned to the South without much excitement.

Alexander Henry, the mayor of Philadelphia, "refused to be a sponsor or to speak at a meeting to deplore the execution of John Brown, but when parties were formed for the 1860 presidential election, he rejected Republicans and Abraham Lincoln for the Constitutional Unionists and John Bell. . . . The Pennsylvania Democratic Party remained so pro-southern that its chairman in 1859 was Robert Tyler, son of Pres. John Tyler, a Virginian in origin and a friend of slavery."[25]

> The city's congressional delegation showed little sympathy for anti-slaveryism. . . . And in late 1850 none of the major newspapers was friendly to anti-slaveryism. . . . Southern sentiment was so strong in Philadelphia, strengthened it seems, ironically by an ever-active cadre of white medical students that fearing a riot, the police prevented John Brown's widow from stopping over in the city to have her husband's body prepared for burial. Nor

---

in 1819. He became an abolitionist at a young age and befriended William Lloyd Garrison. He worked with Garrison in formation of the American Anti-Slavery Society in 1833. He was active in the annual colored conventions that started in Philadelphia in 1830. From 1845 to 1850, he was president of the Pennsylvania Society of the Vigilance Committee of Philadelphia and a conductor on the Underground Railroad. He refused to pay taxes in Byberry until Blacks could attend public schools and denounced the *Dred Scott* decision. He opposed colonization and promoted black enlistment in the Civil War.

23. William Still (1821–1902) was born free in Burlington County, New Jersey. In 1847, he was employed by the Pennsylvania Society for Abolition of Slavery. While serving as a conductor on the Underground Railroad, Still rescued his brother Peter. In 1862, he wrote *The Underground Railroad,* and in 1859, he started the campaign to end discrimination against Blacks on Philadelphia railroad cars. He wrote *A Brief Narrative of the Struggle for the Rights of the Colored People of Philadelphia in the City Railway Cars* (1867) and a pamphlet entitled *An Address on Voting and Laboring* (1874).

24. Weigley, "Border City in the Civil War," in *Philadelphia: A Three Hundred Year History,* 388.

25. Ibid., 391.

was it possible for the Anti-Slavery Society to conduct a memorial service at the hour of Brown's execution. Rather, a group of 'responsible citizens' organized a larger meeting, attended by over 6,000 persons, to deplore John Brown and to express solicitude for the constitutional rights of the South.[26]

Slowly the issues of slavery and race began to determine the feelings of Philadelphians toward the impending conflict. For conservatives, the preservation of the Union took precedence over other issues, and they began an increasing opposition to Lincoln, the Republicans, and to all they believed. "In July 1862 the Democratic state convention resolved that 'Abolitionism is the parent of secessionism' and 'That this is a government of white men, and was established exclusively for the white race, that the Negro race are not entitled to and ought not to be admitted to political or social equality with the white race.' "[27]

There was, of course, another position, as articulated in the *Inquirer:* "In this war there can be but two parties, patriots and traitors . . . the man who is not thoroughly with us . . . is a traitor of as deep and black a dye as ever was Cataline or Arnold."[28]

During this period, the ramifications of the political struggle in Philadelphia are not of the highest priority to the story of the Cromwell family, but it is clear that "the greatest significance of the Civil War era [for the city] was surely its raising the spectre of the race question. The slavery question was at bottom the race question, and the race question belonged to Philadelphia as well as to the South."[29] For with a large black population already within its gates, Philadelphia refused before and during the war to grant political power to the Republican Party. It wavered even in its dedication to the Union once emancipation and unionism were cojoined until Confederate invasion of the North at last pushed the slavery issue into the background and made the safety of the Union appear clearly paramount.

But for black Philadelphians, at all levels, the franchise, education, and access to public transportation were the main battlefronts. While they had never acquiesced to the overt discrimination they experienced, lacking the vote and still relatively few in numbers, they had not been able to mount any meaningful protest. There had been community indignation over discrimination in public transportation, which was either unavailable to Blacks or provided on a segre-

26. Ibid., 388, 390.
27. Ibid., 404–5.
28. Ibid., 405.
29. Ibid., 414.

gated basis, but this did not become a burning issue until the late 1850s. In August 31, 1859, William Still began a campaign for the desegregation of the streetcars with a letter of protest to the *North American*.[30] Later, in 1861, Still persuaded the Social, Cultural and Statistical Association of the Colored People of Philadelphia, which had been organized in 1860, of which he was corresponding secretary, to combat racial prejudice and to circulate among white leaders a petition for desegregated streetcars. Three hundred sixty-nine prominent white Philadelphians signed the petition, but no changes were made in the system since most white Philadelphians of that class were not the ones who supported or needed public transportation.

Nevertheless, the issue became more heated as the war progressed, "For after the Emancipation Proclamation in 1863 opened the way for the War Department to accept Black soldiers, eleven regiments of the United States Colored Troops were organized in Philadelphia, with many of their recruits coming from the city's own black population."[31]

> It was the outrageous exclusion of black men . . . and of their families, that late in the war, finally began to crack the resistance of the street car companies and the indifference of white Philadelphia. . . . [Even] Robert Smalls, a hero of the Union siege of Charleston and a skilled seaman, but an escaped slave, could not travel by street car to visit his ship *Planter* when it was undergoing repairs at the Navy Yard. The Street Car Committee of the Social, Cultural and Statistical Association joined with the more militant younger Philadelphia Blacks, including the schoolteacher, Octavius V. Catto, to organize a mass meeting of Blacks on March 3, 1864. On December 7, 1864, the Street Car Committee met with the 19 presidents of the street railway companies to plead with them and to point out that New York had already ended street car segregation.[32]

They achieved a modest success: two lines promised to open their cars to all well-behaved persons, and two other lines agreed to run separate cars for colored people. The others refused to change their policies. Even after the passage of the Thirteenth Amendment, these companies refused to capitulate.[33]

It was not until 1867, two years later, when the Pennsylvania legislature required all railroads and street railways to carry all passengers without distinction

30. Ibid., 415.
31. Ibid., 396.
32. Ibid., 415.
33. Ibid.

of color that the policy was changed. This new policy was soon tested, when on March 25, 1867, just twenty-two days after Governor John W. Geary had signed the antidiscrimination bill, "Miss Carrie La Count, a schoolteacher, was refused admission to a car at Ninth and Lombard. She immediately sought the aid of a magistrate, who arrested and fined the conductor. Philadelphia's black community soon held a victory meeting."[34]

The inability to exercise any political power, in spite of the sophistication and competence of its leadership, tended to heighten the internal frictions and dissensions within the black community. Yet, there was no disagreement what-soever about the importance of education to the community. As early as 1770, the Quakers, probably led by Anthony Benezet, at their Philadelphia meeting on January 26 decided that instruction ought to be provided for Negro children. On February 30, it was proposed

> that a committee of seven Friends be nominated by the Monthly Meeting, who shall be authorized to employ a schoolmistress of prudent and exem-plary conduct, to teach not more at one time than thirty children in the first rudiments of school learning, and in sewing and knitting. That the ad-mission of scholars into the said school be entrusted to the said committee, giving to the children of free Negroes and Mulattoes the preference, and the opportunity of being taught clear of expense to their parents.[35]

The school opened on June 28, 1770, with twenty-two black children in at-tendance. "After the war Benezet took charge of the school and held it in his house at Third and Chestnut. At his death in 1784, he left part of his estate to 'hire and employ a religious-minded person or persons to teach a number of Negro, Mulatto or Indian children, to read, write, arithmetic, plain accounts, needlework, etc.' "[36]

But public schools for Blacks were not established until about 1822. When the Bird School, later known as the James Forten School, was opened on Sixth Street above Lombard Street, Willis Cromwell's young son, John Wesley Cromwell, attended this school. By 1838, there were twenty-five black schools: nine free schools, three partly free, three pay with white teachers, ten pay with colored

---

34. Ibid., 421. In *Roots of Violence,* Lane refers to "Miss Carrie Lacount" as Caroline LeCount and describes her as a leading activist of the day (52).

35. Du Bois, *The Philadelphia Negro,* 83.

36. Ibid., 84.

teachers—having all told 1,732 pupils enrolled out of a possible 3,025 children of school age.[37]

By 1856, 2,321 pupils were attending public schools, charity schools, benevolent and reformatory schools, and private schools. Among these early schools was the Institute for Colored Youth from which John W. Cromwell was graduated in 1864.

The racial climate in Philadelphia did not improve as the country slowly moved toward war. It is interesting that Willis Cromwell, now free and a businessman, saw possibilities in antebellum Philadelphia and thus chose to settle there, while John Sweat Rock (1825–1866), a lawyer, dentist, physician, and abolitionist, born free in Salem, New Jersey, chose at approximately the same time to leave Philadelphia for the more stimulating and, to Rock, more enlightening environment of Boston.[38]

37. Ibid., 84–85.

38. Rayford W. Logan and Michael R. Winston, eds., *Dictionary of American Negro Biography* (New York: W. W. Norton, 1982), 529–31.

Chapter 3

THE CROMWELL FAMILY IN THE CITY OF BROTHERLY LOVE 1851–1926

愈灵 灵惫

Arriving in Philadelphia in 1851, the Cromwells lived at 1317 Rye Street between Second and Third streets. As soon as possible, Willis Cromwell started in the retail coal and wood business. His sons chose different paths: James, the eldest, and William went to sea; Levi went to work; and Willis Jr. and John Wesley went to school.[1]

Even while still a slave in Virginia, Willis Cromwell was "looked up to as the general adviser of the large community above referred to, as much because of his independent spirit, industry, and pluck as for any other reason."[2] Consequently, when he settled in Philadelphia, Cromwell, already advanced in age and experience, soon became an active member of the community and gave support to all movements for the amelioration of hardship and persecution against his race. In conducting his retail coal and wood business, he set a personal example to encourage other black men in business, and by his own actions, he supported them by patronizing their businesses even when it inconvenienced him to do so.

1. Willis Jr. also engaged in the retail coal and wood business; James died on June 12, 1863, on the U.S. Sloop of War *St. Louis;* and William was discharged from service on the ironclad *Galena* on February 2, 1865.
2. See Philip S. Foner and Ronald L. Lewis, eds., *The Black Worker: A Documentary History from Colonial Times to the Present,* vol. 1, *The Black Worker to 1869* (Philadelphia: Temple University Press, 1978), 43.

Willis Hodges Cromwell Jr.,
ca. 1839–1926.

John Wesley Cromwell Sr.
(1846–1927), as a young boy.

Willis Cromwell was a fighter. On more than one occasion, he was station agent of the Underground Railroad, and he had no patience with the proslavery arguments frequently expressed in the northern press. My grandfather, John Wesley Cromwell, recalled that once his father had refused to ride in a segregated section of a streetcar in Philadelphia and had challenged the conductor to stop him from sitting in the area reserved for whites. On this occasion, Grandfather added, "a white gentleman on leaving the car handed his Father a card as 'attorney-at-law' and said, 'You are in the right and should you need any assistance, call on me.' "

In February 1858, Willis sought financial support from his church to purchase his sister-in-law "Nancy, a slave woman in Norfolk, Va., held in slavery by Joseph Carter who will sell her for $300.00."[3] In July of the same year, Willis received a letter from George W. Bain—signed "Truly Your Friend"—in response to his correspondence of July 13th. According to Bain, Carter had "agreed to sell Nancy her time for $300.00 and that she had paid $55.00 and expects help from a brother or someone in Baltimore." Bain offered to receive any money Willis might raise and to make sure that it was paid to Carter. After receiving the money from Bain, Carter would execute the proper papers for Nancy. Bain then advised Cromwell to send the money as a bank draft.

Nancy and her husband, William H. Carney, were two of the 110 slaves belonging to Mrs. Sarah Twine, who for many years had promised them at her death their freedom and transportation to Liberia.[4] As Mrs. Twine, then a widow, had no children or near relatives to deprive of their just and promised rights, the slaves put their faith in her promise. William himself had been hired out as an oysterman for most of his life for the sum of $130 a year and thus had managed to maintain his family in a humble way.

Mrs. Twine died in 1856, and shortly thereafter, the slaves learned that their faith had been misplaced: not one was freed, and they were soon to be auctioned off. William and the more intelligent slaves realized that they must make their escape on the Underground Railroad. After finding the appropriate agent to instruct him, William left Nancy and their children—Simon Henry, William, Sarah, Mary Ann, Elizabeth, Louis, and Cornelius—who were still slaves and fled to Philadelphia. As the records indicate, the other slaves were sold: Nancy

3. Nancy was married to William Carney, the brother of Willis's wife, Elizabeth.
4. William Still, "Arrival from Norfolk, VA 1857," in *The Underground Railroad: A Record of Facts, Authentic Narratives, Letters* (Chicago: Johnson Publishing Company, 1970), 453–55.

was purchased by a Mr. Joseph Carter, who was now willing to sell her to Willis Cromwell.

Responding to a query from Grandfather, his cousin William H. Carney, the first black winner of the Congressional Medal of Honor for bravery at Fort Wagner, sent a list of the names of the children of his parents, William H. and Nancy Carney. All nine of William and Nancy's children were born in slavery, and the eldest, Simon Henry Carney, born in 1834, was apparently sold earlier by Mrs. Twine herself, no doubt giving added credence to the feeling that all the slaves would indeed be sold after her death.

Children of William H. and Nancy Carney[5]

1st Simon H.	Born 1834 (sold away)
2nd Teresa (named for our Grandmother)	B. 1836
3rd Martha	B. 1838
4th William H.	February 29, 1840
5th Sarah E.	September 1842
6th Mary A.	May 1844
7th Emily E.	Jan. 1846
8th Maria L.	Jan. 1848
9th Cornelius	February 1852

This comprises all the family that lived to any age.
Please remember us all to your wife and family.

Always yours,

Wm H. Carney.

The Civil War affected the fortunes of the Cromwell family as it did many other free Blacks. Two of Willis Cromwell's sons, James and William, joined the navy; James died and was buried overseas.

The following letters offer some insight into James's family situation and the circumstances of his death.

---

5. This letter was written on stationery of the Office of the Secretary, Commonwealth of Massachusetts.

1863 Jan. 24   U.S. Sloop of War St. Louis
Letter to Willis Cromwell   Lisbon 24th January 1863
from Jas. Cromwell

Dear Father:

I take this favorable opportunity to write a few lines to you and let you know that I am quite well and I hope you are enjoying the same blessing. Your letter I received on the 26th Novbr and I am glad to hear, that my children are doing well and I will continue to leave my half pay to you and I wish, you to use it entirely for the benefit of my children; in regard of my wife, I have nothing to say whatsoever. If she wishes to marry somebody else, please tell her to go ahead as fast as she wishes to.

Now my dear father we have been on a long and disagreeable cruise; we left Lisbon on the 1st of Octbr in search of the Pirate steamer Alabama. We steered directly for Tayal, in which vicinity she had been doing so much mischief. About 10 o'clock p.m. on the 8th Octb, when we were laying in a dead calm, a steamer hove insight; we beat immediately to quarters and prepared for action, but the stranger kept on his course and we came to the conclusion that it must have been a mailboat; but on the next day we found out that it was the steamer Alabama.

The calm continued on the following day and in the afternoon we seen the Alabama hotly pursed by the Kersage; we could not go to her assistance, there wasn't a breadth of wind and we were entirely useless, a silent spectator. The Kersage pursued her for 16 hours and during the night the Alabama gave him the slip in a fog.

We layed around the western Islands for nearly a month, but didn't see that notorius Alabama any more and after we filled our noble little ship with wood and water, we made the best of our way to Cadiz. The commander of the Kersage who was in the harbor at the same time ordered us to Lisbon, where we have been laying ever since. A great many stories are afloat on board our Ship, as to her destination; some say we'll go on the coast of Africa and others say, that we will shortly be ordered home. But nobody knows for certain only man-of-war yarns, not even the commander knows, he is waiting for orders from the department. I would have written sooner but I expected to hear from my wife; but I don't expect, that she will write after you tell her the contents of this letter.

Now my dear father I must close my few lines, give my best respects to all in-quiring friends and acquaintances and while I pray and hope, that the allmighty God may bless you with health and strength for many many years to come, I remain Your affectionate son.

James Cromwell

Please direct:

James Cromwell

On board of the U.S. Sloop St. Louis

Care of American Consul

Lisbon

Portugal

There is an engl. fleet in this harbor. The so much talked about iron ships, the Warrior and the black prince, likewise a line-of-battle ship and two large rams. They are making quite an appearance here.

Dear father please send me the direction of my brother Willis.

J. C.

ENVELOPE

From U.S. Sloop St. Louis

Mr. Willis Cromwell

1319 Rye Street[6]

Philadelphia

Penn.

United States of America

Personal and Unofficial

To Mr. Cromwell

Dear Sir:

Your brother, the late Mr. James Cromwell died on board the U. S. S. St. "Louis," June 12, 1863, at Lisbon, Portugal. On the next day, June 13th 1863, his body was carried ashore,—after the usual naval honors of burial on board ship, in charge of an officer and a burial party and buried in the English burial ground at Lisbon. Your brother was rated at the time of his death as Petty Officer (W.R.C.). If you need officially this information you must apply to the Chief of the Bureau of Navigation of the Navy Department.

Yours truly,

John H. Brooks

Aug. 4, 1863   (Father of Ursuline Brooks)

6. Correct address is 1317 Rye Street.

Passed on to me by my father, John Wesley Cromwell Jr., was a small bundle of artifacts, which he had received from his father, John Wesley Cromwell. These items included a small dagger in a leather case and what my father always thought, for some strange reason, was a rhinoceros's horn—which had been sent home to my great-grandfather, Willis H. Cromwell, either by James before his death or by his officer Mr. Brooks. The "horn" was certified by a staff member at the Peabody Museum of Harvard University to be the lower right jaw tooth of a sperm whale! This tooth had an interesting bit of scrimshaw on it: a flag, a sailor, and the word *Liberty*.[7]

The ties between the family members still in Virginia and the family members in Philadelphia were not broken by the move north. A nephew, Daniel Graham, wrote to Willis Cromwell Sr. just after the Civil War to update him on family affairs. The letter is intelligible, and although his use of grammar and punctuation is quaint, Graham's writing ability is far superior to what most people would expect from a newly emancipated slave.

To Willis from Daniel
  Portsmouth Va. feb. 4th 1866
my Dear uncle I received your kind letter The first an was very glad to hear that you and Family was all well it found me and My family also well I reserved a letter From my Brother the same day But was sorry to here that he had not reserved My letter so I set rit down an rote To him he ask me How you was an when I had heard from you I told him that you Had Been to see me an all the folks here He told me that he was Going into neworends [New Orleans] to be mustered out of the servis. He wanted to here from me I told him the No of your house an Street an if he com by the way of New York and through Philada he must call I went to day to see how your cosen Sarah Norfleet was I fond her very feble an weak she told me to Give here love to you an All the children She is goin to move to

---

7. After some research and good fortune, I was able to identify the symbolism of the scrimshaw design. The composition is apparently copied from a painting on glass that was most frequently found on the walls of the brothels in China "where American and British sailors may have had the opportunity to broaden their esthetic appreciation." The original work, *Liberty in the Form of the Goddess of Youth: Giving Support to the Bald Eagle* (1796), was painted by Edward Savage in Philadelphia. The original picture and the many forms it later took were described by Louis C. Jones, director of the New York State Historical Association ("Liberty and Considerable License," *Antiques,* July 1958, 40–43). My uncle's rendition varies in some details, but in answer to a letter I wrote to him inquiring about the piece, Mr. Jones said this was the first time he had heard of this particular theme appearing on scrimshaw.

Aunt Lydia's to morrow 5th She has Promised to Dou all She can for her I went to Aunt Lydia's she said to me she wood take her And doe all that she was able to due Aunt Lydia an her Husborn Sends there love to you. uncle Henry has Been quite feble but he has Got much better May says she has not Got tim yet But when she du you shall have the cake She an sister Nancy Gives there Best lve To you I saw her son to day an told his that he an his Brother must help to Take care of his mother he said he would Du so I have not heard from the others Very latley I have not seen them sence you was here but tha are not outdoorsy I am going up the river this week And I will tri an see some of them so I will let you know how tha Are Getting along Tel cosen Martha I am very sorry she God a Fall but I am Glad she did not hurt her Self very bad uncle says you was friten Worse so I know you get over it quicker Than if yu was badley hurt so take my Love to you an jack an all the Family Give my love to cosen John Wesley When you here from him a Gain Mirs Wanner had been very sick But she is Getting much better. You did not tell me where you seen Brother Robert Butts soon or not Please to tell Me in your next letter. Margaret and Sister Nancy Both excuses you freely you Says something about being indebted to me not to me Dear uncle I have not Forgot your kindness to me when I was A Boy I shall not Forget you neatley what little I can du For you is no Troble to me so Give my Love to cosen Levi an familey tell Him I hope I shall be able to see him A Gain

Plese to rite soon

I have nothing more to Say at Present but Remain your nephew

Truly in Love untill Death

Daniel Graham

Willis Hodges Cromwell died on July 8, 1883, in the ninety-second year of his life. The funeral services were held on a Wednesday afternoon at the Zion A.M.E. Church of which he was a member and his first wife, Elizabeth, was a founder. The *People's Advocate* ran a piece on his funeral:

> Eulogistic remarks having been made by Revs. B. F. Combash (the pastor), Theo Gould, Dr. B. T. Tanner, F. P. Main and B. Siers, the pastor said a gentleman had requested an opportunity to pay tribute to the deceased, whereupon a venerable white gentleman came forward and said that he could heartily endorse all that had been said, for he had known the deceased for over sixty years in his home in Virginia where he was universally esteemed, both in his business transactions and as a private citizen. He gave a few reminiscences, which illustrated how Mr. Cromwell stood

as a businessman of his race in the community from which he came. This stranger was unknown to the family of the deceased, and he had only heard of the funeral by seeing it announced in the daily papers. The venerable Rev. Thomas Jones paid a most eloquent tribute saying the deceased was the man referred to in the 1st Psalm.[8]

Willis Cromwell was buried in the Lebanon Cemetery. He was survived by his second wife, Tempie N. Cromwell; five children, from his first marriage, Mrs. Martha Ann Armstead, Mrs. Esther Nash, Levi Cromwell, Willis H. Cromwell, and J. W. Cromwell; and sixteen grandchildren. He left his wife, Tempie, in lieu of dower, five hundred dollars, and in equal shares to his children, the residue of his estate, real and personal.

When the family was still in slavery, Willis Cromwell, notwithstanding the rigid law against slaves obtaining an education, secured such instruction for his son Levi that the latter was able to do all the clerical work necessary in the extensive freight business carried on by him and his partner, Charles Cooper. This experience stood Levi in good stead when the family moved to Philadelphia, for by 1861 he was able to secure employment in restaurants. He later established himself in an oyster business and worked in a photographic gallery and on the Ohio and Mississippi rivers. Levi finally established his own restaurant at 227 Dock Street opposite the Merchant's Exchange, which he later moved to 117 South Second Street. He eventually retired because the heart of the business district was moving west and north, and he felt himself too old to move again. In letters to his brother John, he discussed his indecision about retiring.

In addition to his success in business, for the twenty-three years between his father's death in 1883 and his death on December 29, 1905, Levi was the outstanding member of the Cromwell family in Philadelphia's black community. He was a trustee of the Philadelphia Workingmen's Club, a president of the Century Building and Loan Association, a grand director of the S.C. of M. of the Grand United Order of Odd Fellows, and a member of the Ugly Club of New York, Philadelphia, and Newport. At the time of his death, he was treasurer of the Shiloh Baptist Church.

Levi Cromwell had no children, though he was married twice—first to Hester Anne Myers, daughter of Captain Daniel Myers of Baltimore, Maryland, and then to Nancy Myers (no relation). He and Nancy resided at 934 Lombard Street. After his death, Nancy, who survived him by more than forty-five years, purchased a house at 1637 Christian Street, where she lived until her death in 1949.

8. "But his delight is in the law of the Lord, and in his law doth he meditate day and night" (*People's Advocate*, July 14, 1883).

Levi Cromwell, *ca.* 1830–1905.

Levi's Oyster and Dining
Saloon was located at 117
South Second Street in
Philadelphia.

Levi apparently played the role of the wiser, older, and financially most successful brother to his siblings and their children. As John Wesley was his only sibling not living in Philadelphia, it is through Levi's eighteen letters to him, written between 1875 and 1904, that we learn how the family fared in Philadelphia and also gain some understanding of Levi as a businessman.

In his last will, probated March 15, 1904, Levi Cromwell left his estate to his widow, Nancy. After her death, the will specified that the estate was to be divided equally among the children of his brothers, Willis Hodges Cromwell Jr. and John Wesley Cromwell. John Wesley Cromwell Jr. and Nancy Cromwell were named executors of Levi's estate.

                                                    Phila. Dec 27, 75
Dear Brother
    Your favor of the 23d inst is at hand and contents noted. I am glad to hear that you and family are well with exceptions—which I made a note of.

    Father and all of our family are well and I hope was made glad on Christmas by some one that was thoughtful of them.

    I saw them all with the exception of Willis and tried hard to make Esther comfortable.

    I called on Mary Cannon she inquired after you
I hope Otelia was pleased with her lunch and candy. Several of our friends wants to come to Washington to New Year is there any better boarding house then formaly or do colored people go to hotels one whom I have in my mind at this time would like to go to a house that was heated and water closets indoors——

    In regard to Oliver do you think it would pay to notice him would it not injure the whole cause.

    I know that the colored dont have any influence in his philanthropy to anyone but himself, but on noticing further I dont think you intend to publish him but only communicate to him the decision of the Board.

    Wife and Dr. Crummell, and friends [text missing] the sun had made its appearance and air is cooler and improvement on the previous three days I intend to go to all the publishing houses when the days get longer and they get over their holiday bustle.

                                                    Your Brother
                                                    Levi Cromwell
                                                    227 Dock St.

Phil. March 6, 1876

Dear Brother,

Miss Jackson[9] came to see me this evening to say something I hardly know what but the whole upshot of the matter I think they want you at the School but to use her own words "they want a teacher and she wants you, but the salary is so small she hates to offer it to you, but she thinks if you were there you would soon work your way there something that you could get to do to make up your salary and would you communicate to me what is the lowest you would come for."

I don't know that I am capable to advise you on the matter but I do think if you was to give your services at the school from 9 to 3 pm you would want the balance of the time to work up to prepare your self to show them what you could do to get yourself raised in the estimation of other that they might open their hearts to pay a sufficient salary.

Don't be too hasty in refusing to accept be and act as I have in the matter perfectly cool so there will be room and a chance at any time to get a situation if you want it——I suppose it will come out after awhile——I am before the story she told Francine 8 days ago she wanted me to write to you. I didn't pay any attention to it so she called on me. She takes all the responsibility on her self but I don't believe her, if she is truthful so much the better but if not it will tell on her as her last shift has done by working herself down they want some person there that has some face of character and they will have to pay to get them—— You know what politics has come to and we can't expect for it to get much better for a long period, this Committee on the conduct of the Department will skip anything that has occurred in the annuls of the History of our Country it will outskip the honest John Committee that split the democratic Party in twain but it will not be received in the same way it will take the shape of a calamity to our Free Government and will put the shoe string men in the rear of either party.

We want good men that are above bribes men that stand so high above the common herd that they can't be reached men that are willing to serve their coun-

9. Fannie Muriel Jackson Coppin (1837–1913) was born a slave in Washington, D.C. In 1865, she graduated from Oberlin College and was employed by the Institute for Colored Youth in Philadelphia to teach Greek, Latin, and higher mathematics. At the institute, she headed the Girls' Department and was the initiator of many innovations, such as the development of a normal training program and later an industrial training component. In 1881, she married the Reverend Levi Jenkins Coppin, the pastor of the Philadelphia Bethel Church. Reverend Coppin was elected bishop in 1900 and assigned to Cape Town, South Africa, where they remained for four years, thus forcing her to relinquish her teaching post. She apparently wanted to recruit Grandfather to teach at the school.

try for the honor conferred with wealth at their command to make them independent.

Grant is politically dead beyond resurrection after 4th March 1877 he will only be known as a horse Jockey and a Judge of old Rye and Havana all of which I am sorry to have to believe at this late day

If you think worth while you will excuse the letter I wrote last night after eleven so I could tell you news what Miss Jackson said all of which I hope you will understand in short she wants to know will you come to the Institute to teach and the lowest terms and could you get anything to do to make it pay. [letter torn]

If you thought of coming and was in a situation to waite . . .

I think there is material for several volumes that would be saleable if you could collect the facts at hand in a readable manner.

Levi Cromwell

P.S. She wants this to be confidential I say keep it so and after we get the facts from her then if we [letter torn].

Phila July 27–83

Dear Bro

Your favor is at hand.

I am glad to hear that you and family are well. Henry arrived safe and sound and finds his way in the city quite well.

He is very fond of reading Story papers. I told him such trash was not good and I did not like the men around me to read them and to prevent it while with me I destroyed every one that fell in my hands. They scatter them here on the broad east.

There is not time limited to probate wills in this city. I am satisfied to wait for you to come on. I have not seen Lewis to witness the document but I will endeavor to next week and I will let you know.

Mr. Reeves can be obtained at any time. Mr. Throck Morton was buried today—89. The man that George Bain was bookkeeper for here and had father's money when he first came here. Father did not lose anything by him—I called at the house

Yours Afc

It is difficult to determine the relation between Reeves, Throck Morton, and George Bain. Bain was the key and business concerns brought them all together.

Phila Feb. 8, 84
117 South 2nd

Dear brother

It has been some time since I have had a line from you. I hope you are well and your family allso.

Martha remains very weak and is compelled to keep to her room. Levi is with me, for which I am sorry that circumstances had not will'd it otherwise. I informed you of the correction of six dollars of Dickens. I don't know just how we stand financially.

I am sick and tired of the comments on Douglass' marriage[10] and those in the *Recorder* with the outcome are ludicrous; I will never forget Douglass' great speech in Concert Hall in this city about 1872 He said "Let the Negro alone; this continued advising and teaching him, let him alone! let him depend on his own strong arms and head give him the same chance in life as other races if he starves on the corner of the street let [him] starve. There is little room for unfavorable criticism by our people as there are few pure Negroes among those that talk the loudest."

A gentleman has called on me inquire of the abilities of Miss Henrietta Vinton Davis[11] as a reader as I have never heard her I take the privilege to ask you.

Levi

Levi Cromwell
Restaurateur
117 South Second Street

Philadelphia July 3, 1884

Dear Bro-

Your favor came duly to hand—I am glad to hear that you and family are well. We have no cause to complain as to our health. I do not charge you for

10. Two years after Frederick Douglass's first wife, Anna Murray, died, he married Helen Pitts, a forty-five-year-old white woman who had worked as his secretary when he was a recorder of deeds. For a variety of reasons, this particular interracial marriage caused considerable tumult in the country. Many Blacks were against it, but Douglass was already on record for believing that America was a composite nation and that racial cooperation and amalgamation were the solutions to the color problem.

11. Henrietta Vinton Davis (1860–1941), one of the most illustrious black actresses at the turn of the century in the United States, became famous as a leader in the Garvey movement. In 1878, she was the first black woman to be employed in the Office of the Recorder of Deeds, and Frederick Douglass, her employer, became a sponsor of her dramatic career. She later took an active part in the Garvey movement.

Blain Logan election But if you could get a few coppies of the *Advocate* with the article on Theodore Stam (?) Wink I would be glad to pay for them as some of his relatives' desire to have coppies. We will have to wait until Oct. to get grant from Orphans Court to sell 1317 . . .

> Your brother
> Levi

Levi Cromwell
Restaurateur
117 South Second Street,

> Philadelphia, July 7, 1884

Dear Bro.——

I would like to have a few copies of the *Advocate* of June 14. Some of his white friends want them . . . [illegible] to me.

Mr. French requested me to have the Ad discontinued at expiration of the year—please let me know when it expires.

He speaks in the highest terms of the paper and considers it a first class paper as to its quality and good reading matter.

I think it would be wise to sell the house 1317 Rye. The blacksmith left this week. I think I will pay aunt Tempie her $500.

Answer.

> Your Brother
> Levi

Levi Cromwell
Restaurateur
117 South Second Street

> Philadelphia, Nov 13, 1884

Dear Bro:——

I received a letter from D. Graham informing of the death of Uncle Henry.

I am glad that you were there. He was born March 24, 1808. I was not surprised to hear of his death for I saw it plain Tuesday morning—awoke crying and said to my wife is my Uncle Williams dead.

He has paid the debt of all living there is doubt but he is better off. We have lost the election it is too bad that the rebel Hendricks[12] should be President of the Senate; it is hard to anticipate but I hope good will be the outcome of what seems to be too intolerable to bear up under.

Hyman seems to be in a hole; if his brother comes to you for a note or lone you can to him that I will not accept a note for a longer time than 60 days All are well. Willis is eating pie as of yore.

Love to all
Your brother
Levi

Levi Cromwell
Restaurateur
117 South Second Street

Philadelphia, March 30 1885

Dear Brother

Your favor came duly to hand I was glad to hear from you but sorry to hear of the sickness of your children I hope they are better.

I have extended the note to the 15 of April.

I am sorry for Henry. If you had of known there was anything in the manner of Henrys dress you should have endeavored to remidy the same if you could have done so; and then we would have known whether it was prejudice or not; as to my part I am not willing to believe without some proof.—Esthers girl Theresa has been dismissed from school as some said to keep her from passing examination when she was ahead of her class.

---

12. Thomas Andrews Hendricks (1819–1885), who had served as a representative and a senator, governor of Indiana, and vice president under Grover Cleveland, was consistently in favor of slavery. While still in the Indiana legislature, he opposed allowing Blacks to come into Indiana and supported the provision of the new Indiana constitution to that effect. In January 1863, he was elected to the U.S. Senate, and during the single term he served (1863–1869), in addition to his opposition to emancipation, he opposed the passage of the Thirteenth Amendment "on factional and partisan grounds . . . that the times were not propitious, that the Negro was inferior and no good would come from his freedom, that emancipation was a matter for the states and the Southern states were not in a condition to consider it." Hendricks "supported Johnson's plan for Reconstruction . . . He opposed the Freedmen's Bureau and the Civil Rights Bill and any new apportionment of representation. He objected to the Fourteenth Amendment . . . He also opposed the Fifteenth Amendment and the impeachment of Johnson . . . On November 25, 1885, less than nine months after his inauguration as Vice-president, he died suddenly at his home in Indianapolis" (*Who Was Who in America Historical Volume, 1607–1896*, 246).

I saw her father. He said how could you expect her to obey her teachers and would not obey her mother or father; it was her own self will and impudence and if she would go to Mr. Powell he would reinstate her but she refused to beg his pardon. I have done all that I could I wrote her a note prior to her dismissal promising her five dollars if she passed which she could only do by obeying her teachers.

There is nothing to be gained by this keeping up this "color" question it is no use all we have to do is to pass or attend to our duties and we will come out side by side with the fairer and more favored.

I have noticed the young men of your age and class. Some have done well and some have done very bad financially and socially; though some of which [are] schollars and are teachers, but they spend every dollar for drink or invest it in "pollicy".—It is better to court what is called the best society or create society and not spend their leisure moments in taverns.

We have had very interest sociables at the Working Men's Club fortnightly consisting of Lectures Readings Vocal and Instrument. To make it successful we have been giving out tickets that we would have a good audience. Two weeks ago Mrs. Lacount read and she sent for forty tickets (40) and there was not standing room in the hall and stair way two dark fellows both high school boys got furious it was as much I could do to keep them in check; these same fellows don't bring their wives and sisters if they did we would not have to go outside—

I suppose you heard of the death of Dr. Shadd's son.

Yesterday his sister Mrs. Gould died of Typhoid. We have many deaths the winter just past and this present month march.

Give my love to your family. Get Henry's measure. I will send him a suit.

Levi

Phila Apl 8th 1887

Dear Brother

As I am indebted to you I take this opportunity to write you these lines to inform you that we are all tolerably well at present and as I have not heard of your wife lately I suppose she has improved. The weather has been very cold and we have had many deaths in consequence.

I did not see Steward when he was here but I heard of him through Willis. I am glad to know that you have connected yourself to the church and hope that you may continue in the faith and so walk act that many may be attractive thereto by your devotion to the teachings of the Scriptures.

Is Trotter[13] out of danger—I am glad Longuen is Deputy, as it is a good thing it is quite right to keep it in the family.

Your Brother
Levi

Phila. March 3d—90
117 So 2nd

Dear Brother

It has been some time since have heard from you but I know that you wrote to me in January.

I hope these lines may find you and the children well. We are all well at present please give our love to them all.

I am glad that you have caused *The Advocate* to come again. We missed it but did not know from what cause it failed to come to us.

As to the lady Mr. Amos Wilson said from the best of his knowledge she was of good family had owned property in Carlisle but lost it.

I have not been writing lately but I hope to get down to it at least I hope to be able from this forward to keep up my correspondence.

Do you ever hear from Mr. McGuinn does he expect to do anything? My business is very dull and I do not think it will revive to a paying basis in my present location—

The great craze for dazzle and Trust is centralizing everything is gone from 2nd 3d up to 4th and 5th and as I did not go with the first *eb* I am afraid it will be hard to get a place higher that would pay.

13. James Monroe Trotter (1842–1892), born in Grand Gulf, Mississippi, was an army officer, politician, author, and amateur musician. After a distinguished career in the Massachusetts Fifty-fifth Regiment, Trotter moved to Boston and accepted a position in the post office; he resigned in 1882 over an issue of racial discrimination.

At the time of Trotter's resignation, James Garfield was president and thus federal appointments were made to Republicans. Receiving no help from the Republicans, Trotter became a Democrat. In 1883, he worked on the campaign for governor of Benjamin F. Butler in Massachusetts. Newly elected President Cleveland nominated Trotter for the position of recorder of deeds, but his nomination was opposed by Democrats because he was black and by Republicans because he was a Democrat. The debate about his appointment is probably the situation to which Levi is referring. The Senate confirmed his nomination on March 3, 1887, because of the endorsement of two senators. He served as recorder of deeds from 1887 to 1889 but was not reappointed by Benjamin Harrison (Rayford W. Logan and Michael R. Winston, eds., *Dictionary of American Negro Biography* [New York: W. W. Norton, 1982], 602–3). Trotter was the father of William Munroe Trotter (1872–1934), the fiery editor of the *Boston Guardian*.

Of course my investments are good and will be better if I can hold on to them. I think Willis is doing well at his trade barbering. John has a good place. Levi is with me at present—The Nash boys are at Work. Field and wife are at Norristown. Mary and the boys are in Camden—

Mrs. Augustine died last night see Monday Buleton.

Mrs. Hill died Friday and was buried today *Monday.*

As to the charge of the papers more anon—has Dickens paid; how does my account stand. How is Jerome Johnson and family. My regards to all. Speaker Reed by his manly stand against the rebelious Democrats deserves the highest praise of this and the English speaking people of my country. He no doubt will make a formidable candidate for the presidency in ninety two.

We want a man with pluck and foresight. It is a good thing that the majority for at least this session and I hope for all time may be able to do business and be responsible to their constituents therefor.

You need not write as long as I have in answering yours as to write is your business as for myself it seems that I am tired of writing for which I am very sorry.

> Your Brother
> Levi

> Phila July 10 1890

Dear Brother

Your favors came duly to hand.

I am glad to hear that you and family are well we are all tolerably well at present.

Willis' Daughter Lizzie was married Monday the 7th inst to Theodore West—

I think William's wife and children are entitled to pension under the new Law and Esthers children please enter their names.[14] I have Williams discharge—it is dated 2nd day of February 1865—Steamer "Galena" C. H. Wells Capt., Master Boardman Paymaster

My regards to all children and friends—Nash was on the same ship—

> Resfy Your Brother
> Levi

14. Responding to the Democrats' wish to eliminate the government surplus by lowering tariffs, the Republicans sought to increase pensions for Union veterans and their families and to reduce the tariff on sugar—both recommendations were incorporated into a tariff bill introduced in 1890 by Congressman William McKinley of Ohio. As Levi Cromwell was no doubt aware of this legislation, he wrote to his brother John Wesley, telling him to do what he could for eligible family members.

Phila. July 26th 1890

Dear Brother

I wrote you some time recently and requested you to enter Adeline Henderson and the Nash's name on the Pension List—

I hope you received the letter it was a business letter—I wrote to you. I expected an answer immediately and then I would have forwarded you the names and Williams Discharge.

My regard to all we are all well hope you and yours are the same

Resfy Your Brother
Levi

Phila. Aug. 25–92

Dear Brother

Your card received—I received two letters from Mr. McGuinn both of which I intended to mail to you. I misplaced one—I am sorry *that* you *mentioned* it on the card to my house as I had not mentioned it to Mrs. Cromwell or any one of the family. I hope you will live long enough to be more careful. Now as to the letter and cards you send to my house or to any address to me you should at all times mention my wife she takes exception but I have not justified her but she may be right.

I write this before looking at the letter and card.

I would have been glad to have had the girl[15] spend the Summer with us and no doubt would have if you had not omitted her name in the letter. I told her that you sent the letter at the house that she would get it and read it and it was intended for both—She further says that the girl would have been at the house and she would have had the pleasure as well as the care of her and she should not have been forgotten. Otelia will be here Friday 26th Lord willing I will meet her at the Penn Depot at ten I hope she will come by that Road.

Your Brother
Levi

In a letter, written perhaps in 1892—the first and last sections of the letter are missing, and apparently there is no date on the letter—Levi expressed his concern for his extended family.

15. Perhaps this girl is a relative of Grandfather's second wife. The tone suggests she is not a blood relative of either man. Grandfather's children often felt their stepmother "used him" to advance the members of her family.

Now we expect Otelia to come you know she will be fed and well housed—
You know her ability to spare the money and the condition of her health to
undergo the winter travel. Mrs. Cromwell would be glad to have her.

Doughty Miller has been sick for weeks and is still confined in the house. Mrs.
Andrew Stevens is sick she is confined to her bed—I would be glad if you could
look over these books. Greener was here last week and looked over them. Willis
is well and joins me in love to your wife and children and yourself. Xmas is near
at hand and I hope you with your wife and children will have a pleasant time.
Remember me to Jerome and his wife and all inquiring friends.

Three teachers that is a good showing. I hope they will succeed and continue
to improve their minds and take advice from their mother and escape the pitfalls
that people are disposed to lay in the way of the young.

The boy John I hope he will soon be a man—it would be nice if he could
learn to trade and be a business man and not have to hang around and wait for
something to turn up.[16]

Your Brother
Levi

The following eight letters from Levi Cromwell to his brother John Wesley
Cromwell illustrate the understanding post-Civil War black Americans had of
the larger society in which they lived as free men and of how the socioeconomic
forces of the day affected them. As the message in any letter must be understood by both the sender and the recipient, these letters, while written by Levi, a
prosperous and experienced businessman in Philadelphia, discuss matters clearly
appreciated by his young journalist brother, John Wesley, in Washington.

The messages in the first three letters concern two of the most important
political issues of the late 1880s and early 1890s: the pervasive issues of taxation
and tariffs. President Cleveland in both his first and second terms in office was
strongly against protective tariffs and for the elimination of government surplus
funds that only benefited the rich. During this period, the allegiance of Blacks
to the Republican Party of Abraham Lincoln was weakening, as that party increasingly was seen as favoring large business interests and the rich, while the
Democratic Party was emphasizing economic equity and viewing trusts and mo-
nopolies as enemies of the people.

16. The three teachers were Otelia, Mary, and Larcie; John did become a businessman by working as a certified public accountant in his own business.

On March 4, 1893, in his second inaugural address, to which Levi referred in his letters, Cleveland spoke about the problems created by tariff laws, but he made no mention of a particular bill to remedy the situation.[17] He did note that his election was a signal for tariff reform through a more just and equitable system of federal taxation, which would be accomplished wisely and without vindictiveness. Taxation, he said, was necessary only to support the government, not to make the rich richer. He promised to restore self-confidence and business enterprise without dependence on government favor.

Later, in 1894, President Cleveland refused to sign the Wilson-Gorman Tariff Act originally introduced into the House of Representatives by William L. Wilson, a Democrat from West Virginia. This act was designed to reduce the tariff rates and to institute a federal income tax. Arthur Pue Gorman, a Maryland Democrat, refashioned the bill and various senators added 634 amendments, nearly all of which revised tariffs upward. In spite of Cleveland's action or inaction, the Wilson-Gorman Act was passed in 1894.

The entire period from the mid-1880s into the 1890s, called "The Great Upheaval" by Nell Painter, saw the emergence of giant corporations and strong union activity, which precipitated several disastrous strikes.[18] Eighteen eighty-six was seen as a pivotal year with strikes of miners in southern Pennsylvania, reaper workers in Chicago, and streetcar workers in New York.

The 1892 strike at Homestead, Pennsylvania, pitted the nation's largest steel producer, Andrew Carnegie, against the nation's strongest trade union, the Amalgamated Association of Iron, Steel and Tin Workers, which was organized in 1876 and had more than fourteen thousand workers in 1891. Occurring in a factory town a few miles from Pittsburgh, this strike brought the problem of labor unrest, also found in many other parts of the country, close to Levi Cromwell in Philadelphia.

When the Carnegie Steel Company did not accede to the workers' demands for better conditions and higher pay, Carnegie's plant manager, Henry Clay Frick, on June 28th, locked the workers out and built a fence eight feet high and three miles long to enforce his decision. When the workers retaliated on July 6, the company brought in three hundred men from the Pinkerton National Detective Agency to ensure the safety of nonunion men who were employed as

---

17. See Grover Cleveland, "Second Inaugural Address," in *Inaugural Addresses of the Presidents of the United States from George Washington 1789 to George Bush 1989,* Bicentennial ed. (Washington, D.C.: U.S. Government Printing Office, 1989), 187–92.

18. See Nell Irvin Painter, *Standing at Armageddon: The United States, 1877–1919* (New York: W. W. Norton, 1987), 36–71.

strikebreakers. When Pinkerton's men arrived on the scene, a battle broke out between them and the strikers. When the hostilities ceased, 150 of the three hundred Pinkerton men were injured and nine steelworkers and seven Pinkerton men were dead. Governor William Stone of Pennsylvania sent eight thousand militiamen to Homestead to maintain order.[19]

The aftermath of the strike, which included the indictment of many workers and the imprisonment of thirty-five leading union men who ultimately were exonerated, weakened the union and the employment of many Blacks who were among those hired to replace the strikers.

> The last of the soldiers left Homestead in the middle of October, leaving a legacy of intense bitterness and a demoralized work force. The Homestead tragedy, where 16 men lost their lives and thousands lost their jobs, was the first of the tremendous labor upheavals of the 1890s, and it showed that a strong employer could break a union that was strong if the company could hire a mercenary police force and could count on the cooperation of the courts.[20]

The Homestead strike itself would have caused much discussion in Philadelphia, but the fact that the union in question, the Amalgamated Association of Iron, Steel and Tin Workers, was quite hostile to organizing Blacks and, indeed, refused to go on record favoring their organization until 1881 would have caused reaction in the black community. Beyond that, black citizens would have been sensitive to the use of Blacks as strikebreakers during the notorious Homestead strike and before. Strikebreaking was one of the few avenues through which black workers could secure what were, for them, well-paying jobs in industry.

As Levi Cromwell indicates in his letters, the economic situation at the time was very bad. Aside from the strikes in May 1893, the stock market collapsed, and, as a result, banks canceled outstanding loans and several railroads went bankrupt. In six months in 1893, eight thousand businesses and 360 banks (including 141 national banks) failed and farm prices continued to fall. Wages were cut dramatically and unemployment was estimated to be between two million and three million. At least one-fifth of the industrial work force was idle in the winter of 1893–1894.[21]

In the fall of 1893, as the Depression made jobs scarce, groups of unemployed

19. Ibid., 113.
20. Ibid., 114.
21. Ibid., 116.

workers in the far West organized along military lines, calling themselves industrial armies or industrials. Numbering from fifty to three hundred persons, these groups overpowered railroad guards and rode trains for free, looking for employment.

One of the best known of these industrial armies was led by Jacob S. Coxey (1854–1951), a successful businessman from Ohio. Coxey's Army "about 100 strong and led by a young black man carrying an American flag, set out . . . on Easter Sunday [March 25, 1894], . . . Jacob Coxey's sixteen-year-old son [followed] . . . Behind a trumpeter Jacob Coxey, his wife, and baby son . . . rode in their coach."[22] Coxey hoped to rally support for two bills he had introduced into Congress in 1892 and 1894. If passed, these bills would have initiated a vast road building program and given local governments the right to exchange noninterest bearing bonds for treasury notes to finance public works.

When the marchers arrived in Washington at the end of April, they were five hundred strong—having gathered supporters along the way. There, they were repulsed. Coxey was arrested before he could read his prepared speech, and he and his lieutenants were charged with walking on the grass in front of the Capitol. Coxey was sentenced to twenty days in jail and his bills died in committee.

Coxey's endeavors were appreciated by the common folk, Black and White, especially in Washington; but the disorganization they represented hardly enhanced their cause with the people who might have benefited from his success. I can recall my grandmother in Washington reacting to a group of noisy, disheveled grandchildren by describing us as belonging to Coxey's Army!

Phila. Nov. 4th 1893

Dear Brother

Your favor came duly to hand. I was glad to hear from you and your family. That you and they were well, it had been some time since I had written to you but I was not without interest in your welfare in every respect.

We only heard through Phila. papers that there was a stampede in one of the Washington school buildings but later on someone brought me a Washington paper giving the particulars.[23] I was sorry to hear of it but glad that it did result in favorable results—

22. Ibid., 119.

23. According to the *Washington Post*, on October 20, 1893, a panic and near-serious situation had occurred at the Garnet School at 10th and U streets N.W., when Windsor Robinson, a student in the fifth grade, suffered an epileptic seizure while standing beside his desk reciting a lesson. "When he fell, some of the pupils ran about the prostrate boy, and the noise so created thoroughly

I met Tom Boling the day it occurred He stopped me in the street and inquired of your health and family and said he was afraid that there had something happened as he had dreamed of an entertainment at your house—

To-day we expect the Presidents *message*. he will indors the report of the Wilson bill looking to reform the present Tariff law—We in Phila. are very much interested as the present state of affairs make it very dull in all business—My kindest wife all the family seems to be well and seems to be able to get something to eat.

A custom house inspector said that it is a good thing for those that receive a regular Salary these dull times.

Your Brother
Levi

Phila. May 15–94
117 So 2nd

Dear Brother

Yours of May 7 came duly to hand and contents noted. We were all glad to hear from you and your family. I knew that I was indebted to you a letter but I have not been in a writing mood. the times are very dull and I contemplated closing my place when my lease expired and spend some time traveling in the South but after considering the thing over I have decided to continue and I think it is the best thing to do for health and happiness as it is very pleasant to meet my patrons and talk over old times; and perhaps if my life is spared I may make another venture and follow the march of the present tendency of business Westward [to West Philadelphia.]

I am happy and content as my health is excellent my investments are coming up nicely and no doubt will continue; that is if the electric continues to trade.

Please remember me to your children. I am glad to hear that Mamie is home again and I hope that she thinks and can exclaim there is no place like home.

---

frightened the scholars in the room directly underneath and on the same floor. This confusion spread in an instant to the twelve rooms of the school, and then panic reigned." Nine of the children received injuries either by falling or being trampled by those who crowded in the rear. Of the two most serious, one suffered a broken collarbone, and the other, a broken ankle.

Community reaction was swift and concern was expressed for the general safety of the school buildings throughout the city, especially in case of fire. The *Washington Post* reported on October 21, 1893, that the trustees and superintendents (one white and one black) were satisfied that the Garnet School as well as others in the system were fireproof, but they assured the community that the system of fire drills, which had been part of the curriculum and then discontinued, would be resumed.

Mrs. Cromwell send her kindest regards to Mrs. J. W. Cromwell and the children.

This year we have lost many of our friends by death but the Lord has been kind to us; very dear we get along smoothly the Nashs seem to be well Willis is well he was at the house Sunday—Mr. Benjamin Hill departed this life Monday after a month illness

Mathew's death was sudden to me, as I had not heard of his illness. I guess every thing will go on smoothly since Andrew spent a week or ten days at the Capitol.

Mathew was a representative of the Race. He was quite an orator and at all times in public dressed in good style and impressed everyone as a man of wealth and ability. I hope his soul is at rest. I met Mrs. Jones to day on Chestnut Street and she did not spare him for making the second will but I think he should be forgiven for that whereas it often occurs when one make one will they neglect the second and often where millions are at stake

How is Johnny give my love to him and tell him not to join Coxey's Army—

But I hope he will have some original ideas and some day will be able to see them culminate without attempting to march an army of ragamuffins over hill and down dale hungry and footsore, Coxey is no ignoramus the working people are restless something must be done to appease them.

Phila. May 15–94
117 So. 2nd
Sunday night

I hope you will excuse me for not answering your letter ere this, I wrote it and misplaced it.

We are having a stormy day cool and disagreeable. There is nothing new but the steady depression of every thing that grows and are manufactured it seems strange to the unthoughtful mind but it is none the less true.—the market seems to be overcrowded with all kinds of vegetables and are selling at prices that will not pay the picking and freight with the exception of potatoes and apples— We have the same people to eat but they must subsist on less as the fields have produced more than be consumed—though many of the manufacturers are shut down yet there seems to be an abundance of all kinds of dry goods at the lowest prices for the millions for which they have not money to buy or those that have the where with are waiting for lower prices and better goods by the passage of the Tariff bill that will admit free wood and other materials—I will not attempt to discuss the matter as we have not heard much else for the last 4 months and they don't seem to get much nearer a solution of the matter to the satisfaction of the Law Makers. I will venture to say that it would be better to pass the bill as framed by Wilson and let the business community know what to depend upon The people voted for a change and the Democrats promised them a change and we have a bad one; thousands are starving and dying for the want of work and the Congress are wasting months doing nothing towards settling the Country's trouble—Our gold is leaving the country being drawn upon by the wealthy that are taking their wealth to the old country. This has been predicted for years that this massing of wealth by a few could not continue *inequality* of *wealth* it cannot stand it is not honest there is a grinding down of the poor while corporation Directors get immensely rich by speculation and the middle class get poorer— The great Railroads of the country are not making expenses wages must be cut down and the Laborer will be the sufferers—hence strikes railroads will cease to be moved the bountiful crops may rot with wheat at 55 cts *miners strike* if continued we may not have coal for home consumption.

[letter unsigned]

Phila. July 15–95

Dear Brother

Your favor came duly to hand.

I am glad to hear your daughters have passed and were promoted. It shows that they not only inherit aptness from their father more good training at home.

Times are very dull and we can see hundreds well dressed and people that have been well fed and reared in the South walking in the streets in search of employment—

My business is dull but I am in hopes of some change for the better It might be better to close in a financial point of view but then the change from activity to idleness might act disastrously to health.

I hope with the bountiful crops and the cheapness of all kinds of wearing apparel you may be able to pull through, I would not like to see you fall by the way and be unable to assist you such is my condition at this time during the last year my expenses were heavy; draining and paving as well as redeeming and some loaning. I hear of nothing but praise for your wife of which I feel proud and I hope to have the pleasure of her acquaintance in the near future. The *children* remember me kindly to them one and all. The collection is intact the unbound scraps need sorting. It would be good work for your children if you had room for them—with strict orders only to be worked among in the day when light would not be needed

Nothing more at present

Your Brother
Levi

Phila. Aug. 2 1895

Dear Bro.

Your favor came duly to hand and gave considerable thought and some inquiries among merchants and at the Provident.

They are good business people and the house is reliable and I think one seeking investments could trust them with a draft of $2000 without losing any sleep over night. I don't think it is necessary for me to make any further statement.

I don't think you ever have know me to mislead one knowingly

Your Brother Levi

Phila. Dec. 16–96

Dear Bro

Yours came duly to hand and I am sorry that I did not get the papers filed up and sent—

I was somewhat delayed—on account of the children sending me a letter stating that they were going to Boston to reside and I did not want the trouble—

The Short certificate find enclosed I had it in my fire proof—The boy calls at my place two or three times a week to get . . . [illegible] they are trying to keep house with their married sister The boy Theodore is at Boston or Cambridge—As to the hon. Alfred Harmes I know him well and I don't think he has forgotten me. Though I do not see him often. Phillip Garrett is a constituent of his and there are many others in *Germantown* that could be *reached*

My business had dwindled down to nothing since the grand Westward march but I am thankful it is well with me and it is—Mrs. Laws the woman that cooked for me so long died about a month ago and I cannot say that I have been suited since—The sun does not allways shine we must expect to have some cloudy days but when one has health and where with to get food and raiment should be content.

Phila. March 23, 98

Dear Brother

Having nothing of importance to write to you I have delayed to this time. The books are in my possession but the next day the daughter claimed them through a friend she being out of this state and sick; she was by a second or third wife the first is living (divorced) the money is in the hands of a friends with a string attached and I am acting under the advice of my council—and will not say any thing more—[24]

Send me a copy Steel Engraving of Douglass for I would like to know what 500 or a thousand cost.[25] I was thinking it would be a good thing to give away.

Armstead is confined to the house the rest of the family are well I was interrupted by the men soliciting subscription to this land speculation I dont know any thing about them.

I hope you and your family are well, please remember Mrs. Cromwell and I to your Wife and to the children. The winter has been severe and long with much sickness and many deaths

Your Brother
Levi

Phila March 25 1904

Dear Brother[26]

I suppose you thought it strange of not receiving a reply to your sensible letter I have been taking a rest flat in the bed I have been sick for one month ten days had to be helped in and out of bed

The weather is pleasant and I am now venturing out I am thankful to the Lord that it is as well with me as it is

I hope you and family are well

Mrs. Cromwell joins me in love to you all

Your Brother
Levi

24. I do not know the basis of these comments, but I assume they relate to family business with the children of Levi's brother or brothers.

25. John Wesley Cromwell started a business, J. W. Cromwell and Company, to sell steel engravings of eminent colored men. He printed engravings of Frederick Douglass, Blanche Kelso Bruce, and John Roy Lynch "on heavy plate paper, 17 x 22, artistically executed, . . . first class in every way" and sold them for fifty cents for a single copy and $1.25 for a set of three.

26. This is the last surviving letter to John Wesley Cromwell from Levi, who died on December 29, 1905.

[note on back of letter]
You have spent much time and research. Why not get off some one on more of
your lectures.

Willis H. Cromwell Jr. married Felicienne Fouché while on a sailing expedition to Haiti. They were the parents of five children: Elizabeth, Felicienne,
Willistine, Minerva, and Helen.

Although given an early education—he refers to Miss Caroline LeCount as
one of his old school teachers—Willis Jr. apparently spent his adult life as a
barber. His barber shop and residence were at 819 South 17th Street. He died on
March 6, 1926, at the age of eighty-seven; he was the last of Willis Hodges and
Elizabeth Cromwell's children to die in Philadelphia.

From the five surviving letters from Willis to my grandfather, aside from family news and death, we only learn how happy Willis was that John had joined a
church. On February 6, 1887, Willis wrote, "I heard through the papers that you
had embraced religion and joined Metropolitan Church.[27] I am glad of it and
may the Lord bless you and your family and keep you steadfast whereof Christ
has made you free." Willis himself became superintendent of the Bethel A.M.E.
Sunday School in Philadelphia.

It is difficult to know just what prompted Grandfather to take this step. As a
younger man, he apparently had shown little religious zeal; even Levi in his letter
of April 8, 1887, noted his brother's conversion. His wife's illness and death in 1887
may have been a factor, but in any case, once he joined the church, Grandfather
became an important member of the congregation and of the Bethel Literary Society, which was started on November 9, 1881, by Bishop Daniel A. Payne. With
one exception, all members of the executive committee of the society, including
Cromwell, were members of the Metropolitan A.M.E. Church. Later in his life,
Grandfather found less attraction for this denomination and tended toward the
Episcopal Church where Alexander Crummell was pastor.

Most of our knowledge of Willis's life comes from Levi's letters to John. Even
in Willis's last letter of January 31, 1923, written for him by someone else, the
thoughts are simple: illness, family ties, and deaths in the community. There

27. The Metropolitan A.M.E. Church was founded on July 6, 1838, after a merger of Israel Bethel
A.M.E. Church, founded in 1821, and Union Bethel A.M.E. Church, founded in 1838. The name
Metropolitan was first applied to the Union Bethel congregation in 1870 and became official in
1872 when the Baltimore Conference authorized the construction of a new "Metropolitan Church
in Washington, D.C."

is no doubt that love and caring kept families in contact after slavery, but for the Cromwell family, at least, it was the tie between the businessman and the scholar—between Levi, the oldest surviving brother, and John Wesley, the youngest—that bonded the family during these years.

Willis's letters are not very revealing, and there are no extant letters to John Wesley from his other siblings aside from those already discussed.

Of the other son, William, who joined the navy, there is no further mention in the family letters, other than the July 10, 1890, letter from Levi to John Wesley asking him to inquire about William's widow's eligibility for a pension. A daughter of Willis and Elizabeth Cromwell, Martha Ann Cromwell, married John A. Armstead. They had seven children: W. H. F. Armstead, who became the principal of the colored schools in Camden, New Jersey; Rachel, who died in 1880; Martha Ann and Margaret Elizabeth, who died in 1876; Roxcelena and Emily M.; and Levi, who was a minor at the time of his parents' death.

Grandfather, the youngest of Willis and Elizabeth's children—just five years old when the family moved to Philadelphia—was the only child whose childhood and adolescence were not spent in slavery. He is the key person in understanding the intellectual history of the family.

Soon after the Cromwells arrived in Philadelphia, Grandfather was sent to the Bird School, where he remained until 1856, when he was admitted to the Preparatory Department of the distinguished Institute for Colored Youth, located at 716–718 Lombard Street. He graduated from the institution in 1863 at its eleventh commencement.[28]

At the commencement exercises, young Cromwell was one of the fourteen students who participated by giving an oration on "Oratory." Jacob C. White Jr. gave the address and Henry Highland Garnet gave the alumni oration. All the

---

28. The Institute for Colored Youth, probably the most memorable of the early schools for Blacks, was founded by Richard Humphreys, a former slaveholder from the West Indies who had moved to Philadelphia. Following his death in 1832, his bequest of ten thousand dollars to the Friends to found a school was announced. The object of the school was to "instruct the descendents of the African race in school learning in the various branches of the mechanic arts and trades, and in agriculture in order to prepare, fit and qualify them to act as teachers. The Institute was founded in 1837, chartered in 1842, and upon receiving further gifts was temporarily located on Lombard Street [716–718]. In 1866 additional funds were raised and the Institute was located on Bambridge street, above Ninth" (Du Bois, *The Philadelphia Negro*, 87).

There is a discrepancy about the exact date of John Wesley's graduation. The date in the program for the commencement exercises is April 29, 1863; yet, the program for the December 16, 1868, commencement ceremony, for which J. Wesley Cromwell was the alumni speaker, lists him as a member of the class of 1864. Cromwell, however, was awarded his Teachers' Provisional Certificate ("good for 3/4 year only") on October 8, 1864.

graduates had been examined in Latin (Virgil's *Aeneid*, Caesar and Latin composition, and Horatio's *Ode*), algebra, geometry, arithmetic, trigonometry, English grammar, English composition, reading, geography, anatomy, Greek, Grecian history, natural philosophy, sacred history, sacred geography, and history.

At the end of the nineteenth century, there was a growing debate about the appropriate education for African Americans, which has been popularized in the differences between Booker T. Washington and W. E. B. Du Bois. The relevance of the education offered by the Institute for Colored Youth became an issue, and steps were taken to change its classical curriculum to one focused on industrial training. This change was strenuously deplored by John W. Cromwell, who wrote in the *Record* on Tuesday, June 27, 1902, that this shift was "another evidence of the indifference, if not the opposition to the Negro's intellectual advancement on the part of those who once ardently espoused his cause." The editorial then named some of the most outstanding faculty at the institute: Charles L. Reason, Robert Camp, Robert Campbell (the explorer), Ebenezer Bassett, Sarah M. Douglass, Miss Grace Mapps, Miss Mary J. Patterson, and Miss Fanny M. Jackson (the latter two were graduates of Oberlin College). This was followed by a list of some of the distinguished graduates: Jesse Ewing, who went on to the University of Glasgow where he excelled in mathematics; Octavius V. Catto, who at thirty-three was elected superintendent of colored schools and a year later murdered by a mob; John H. Smythe; Theophilus Minton; Joseph E. Lee; Eugene R. Belcher; Charles N. Thomas; and James Fields of Needham.

In this editorial, Cromwell also named a "few outstanding women graduates . . . Sallie Daffin, Mrs. Coredia Atwell, Mrs. Sarah A. Fleetwood, Mrs. Rebecca J. Cole and Miss Laura J. Barney."

But he was particularly disturbed because Fanny Jackson Coppin, who was retiring, was being replaced as head of the school by Hugh M. Browne. Mr. Browne, whose background and experience in education were in the field of industrial training and theology, was coming from four years at Hampton. Additionally, according to Cromwell, Mr. Browne had fired many of the old teachers.

At an early age, Grandfather displayed journalistic and oratorical ability as well as a serious interest in scholarship. An article in the *Press* of Philadelphia, on Thursday, December 3, 1863, reported that Mr. J. W. Cromwell gave the anniversary address at the Frederick Douglass Lyceum. It stated that this society was composed of a number of young men who met weekly for the purpose of improving their minds by speaking and debating on different subjects. Cromwell must have been about seventeen years old at the time.

Chapter 4

THE CROMWELL FAMILY IN WASHINGTON'S "SECRET CITY" 1871–1972

❧ ☙

This story of the descendants of Willis Cromwell and Elizabeth Carney Cromwell focuses on their youngest child, John Wesley Cromwell, and his children by Lucy A. McGuinn Cromwell. The setting for the story is Washington, D.C., which Constance Green refers to as the "Secret City" in her book of the same name.[1]

It is easier to understand why Washington was attractive to John Wesley Cromwell than it is to understand why Philadelphia was attractive to his father, Willis Hodges Cromwell. As the home of the federal government, Washington was the seat of power in the country, but at the same time, it had not been an inconsequential center of the slave trade for the neighboring states of Maryland and Virginia as well as for the more distant points in the Deep South. For these reasons, Washington and Washingtonians, citizens and politicians alike, were more intimately connected to the fate of Blacks nationally than any other city or the people in any other city in the country.

Free Blacks and slaves coexisted in the city. By 1800, there were 3,244 slaves and 783 free Blacks living among 10,266 Whites. Thirty years later, the black population alone was almost equally divided between slaves (6,119) and free Blacks

---

1. Constance McLaughlin Green, *The Secret City: A History of Race Relations in the Nation's Capital* (Princeton: Princeton University Press, 1967).

(6,152). Blacks, slave and free, comprised almost one-half of the population of the city that now had 27,563 Whites. This ratio of White to Black and of slave to free affected the form and control of the policies needed. Nevertheless, as Constance Green noted, "All told opportunities in the city were varied enough to draw ambitious Negroes to the District from the nearby states." She argued that "with the possible exception of New Orleans, no other American city in which the proportion of colored people was high offered them wider opportunities than they had in antebellum Washington and Georgetown." The relation between the races was "far less biased than that of most of the South. . . . Colored people of Washington . . . had developed a cohesiveness rarely equaled among other Negro city dwellers."[2]

But the racial climate in Washington began to change in the 1830s. It was stimulated by the fear and hostility stemming from the Nat Turner insurrection in 1831 in nearby Virginia, by the strengthening of abolitionists' activities elsewhere in the country, reflected in the publication of the *Liberator* in Boston, and by the avalanche of anti-slavery petitions pouring in upon Congress from northerners.[3]

After a slave attempted to murder his mistress and after a botany teacher, new in the city, bought some of his specimens wrapped in abolitionists' papers and was accordingly arrested for being an agent sent to stir up local Blacks, a week's witch hunt was carried on by gangs of white boys and unemployed young men. Their aim was to intimidate free Blacks and to punish those responsible for circulating incendiary pamphlets.

The mayor called in the militia but not soon enough to prevent much property damage, including the smashing of the furnishings of a fashionable restaurant owned by a mulatto, Beverly Snow, who reputedly had made derogatory remarks about the wives of white mechanics. Fortunately, no Blacks were physically harmed and things were brought under control. Nevertheless, the "Snow-Storm" severely damaged the spirit of the community.[4]

Later, the Civil War radically altered the picture. Blacks, slaves and free, were about one-fifth of the city's population at the start of the war, and eighty percent of the Blacks were free. This number was soon augmented by thousands more who flocked to the city seeking freedom. Labeled *contraband of war,* these

2. Ibid., 43, 53, 54.

3. It is quite likely that the paper in question was David Walker's *An Appeal to the Colored Citizens of the World*. Published in Boston, it was considered so inflammatory that a bounty was placed on Walker by Georgia slaveholders, and when Walker died, it was widely believed that he had been murdered.

4. Green, *The Secret City,* 36.

new arrivals were a problem for the city as a whole and especially for the black population with which they were identified and with which any assimilation was painfully slow.

In April 1862, Congress emancipated the remaining thirty-one hundred slaves in the District of Columbia.[5] Between 1860 and 1870, the number of Blacks more than tripled until they comprised almost one-third of the total population. Exposed to this expanding black population comprised largely of individuals ill equipped for urban living, from mid-1862 onward, the white population became fearful and increasingly hostile toward Blacks.

The situation of Blacks was affected, however, not only by the changing values of white Washingtonians but also by the determination and power of members of Congress who had control over the affairs of the city. In 1866, all adult males—Black and White—were given the franchise. Some black Washingtonians were elected and others appointed to local offices, and laws were passed in 1869 and in 1870 prohibiting segregation in public accommodations. A number of Blacks were in Congress, and others taught in the public schools, worked for the federal government, entered the legal and medical professions, or started newspapers.[6] In 1867, Howard University was opened.

The 1870s were, in fact, initially most promising. Frederick Douglass moved to Washington in 1870 and with the Reverend Sella Martin edited a newspaper called the *New Era*, which marked that year as the high point for the black community.

In 1871, Grandfather came to Washington to accept a clerkship in the Office of the Auditor of the Treasury for the Post Office Department, having placed first in a competitive examination for the position over two hundred applicants.

5. This bill, introduced into the Senate by Senator Wilson and signed by President Lincoln on April 16, 1862, had many interesting features. It provided that "all persons held to service or labor within the District of Columbia by reason of African descent are hereby discharged and freed of and from all claim to such service or labor, and from and after the passage of this act neither slavery nor involuntary servitude, except for crime, whereof the party shall be duly convicted shall hereafter exist in said District." "A sum of money not exceeding $1,000,000 was appropriated to compensate owners loyal to the government for their former slaves, it being provided that the average price for each slave should not exceed $300, and the compensation was not to extend to those persons who were disloyal to the government or who should bring slaves into the District after the passage of the act . . . an appropriation of $1,000,000 to aid in the colonization of free persons, including those liberated, as may desire to emigrate to Hayti or Liberia or to such country beyond the limits of the United States as the President may determine" was approved (Edward Ingle, *The Negro in the District of Columbia* [Freeport, N.Y.: Books For Libraries Press, 1971], 14–15).

6. Sandra Fitzpatrick and Maria R. Goodwin, *The Guide to Black Washington: Places and Events of Historical and Cultural Significance in the Nation's Capital* (New York: Hippocrene Books, 1990), 17.

While in this position, he studied law at Howard University and graduated as one of seven in 1874. On the motion of the Honorable A. G. Riddle, he was admitted to the District's bar association the same year.

The other graduates in his class were: James O. Adams from Florida, George W. Boyden from Massachusetts, Augustus Gage from New Jersey, Pliny I. Locke from Pennsylvania (the father of the well-known scholar, Alain Locke), and McGill Pierie and Ambrose Whiting from Virginia. Grandfather gave a talk on usury laws as part of the graduation ceremony.

Rapidly, however, things began to appear less promising in the city. In 1872 the Freedmen's Bureau was ended, in 1874 Freedmen's Bank failed, and in 1878 Congress, which had retained constitutional authority over the District of Columbia, used "local political turmoil, mismanagement, and corruption as excuses to snatch away the limited self-government that it had previously granted the city. . . . Three white, federally appointed commissioners replaced locally elected officials." During the same period, "black Reconstruction members of Congress from the southern states gradually were removed from office and departed from the capital city."[7] By 1878, the colored people ceased to be the major concern of the Grand Old Party and Washington was becoming a less hopeful place for Blacks to live, or so it seemed.

But in 1872 John Cromwell expected to be seen publicly with Lucy McGuinn, and he offered in August 1872 to assist her in the purchase of a sewing machine. Apparently, the relationship had been of some duration.

227 Dock St.
Philadelphia, Pa.,
Aug. 1, 1872.

Dear Lucy:

I am glad to hear that you are going to visit your relatives in Culpepper and in Washington. I hope I will be in Washington when you are there, so as to go around with you.

I saw an account of that grand Republican gathering at the City Springs Park. I hope if you were present you enjoyed the treat to hear Frederick Douglass and Henry Wilson. I guess there was such a gathering as Richmond has never before witnessed. It must have been a grand sight to see Broad and Main Sts at night with five thousand citizens marching and walking keeping time to that music of "John Brown's Soul marching on."

7. Ibid., 18.

You wrote some time ago about a Sewing Machine. I suppose one kind is about as good as another and that all have their advantages and their favorites. They sell here by a party paying in monthly instalments of five dollars. So it takes about nine or ten months savings to buy one. Dressmakers here are so busily kept and so well paid that it is very easy to obtain one.

Do you think that you could pay for one yourself if the first instalments were met?

Does dress making pay in Richmond?

I wish I could be with you now and that there would be a full and free conference between us.

I don't feel like writing any more because I have just had a bitter dispute with a white man about working for Greeley or Grant, and my nerves are not as quiet as I would like them.

With much respect,

Truly yours,

J. W. Cromwell

On November 13, 1872, John Wesley Cromwell, who listed Portsmouth, Virginia, as his residence, married Miss Lucy A. McGuinn of Henrico, Virginia, at the 19th Street Baptist Church of Washington, D.C. It is not known just how the couple met, but Cromwell had listed Warner McGuinn, Lucy's brother, as one of the students in his class in Richmond, so no doubt Warner was responsible for their meeting.[8]

John Wesley Cromwell and Lucy McGuinn became the parents of seven children: Otelia, Mary Elizabeth, Lucy Antoinette, Martha, Willis Robert, John Wesley Jr., and Fanny. All but Willis, who died as an infant in 1881, lived to adulthood.

In 1873 and 1874, as a result of a competitive examination for higher ranks in the Post Office Department, Cromwell was accordingly promoted. On the basis of the 1874 examination, he led the entire office and was one of the two first black clerks to receive such a rank in any department. Cromwell was then appointed chief examiner of the money order department and was subsequently registrar of money order accounts. However, the official dismissal notice that he received on June 23, 1885, from the secretary of the Treasury Department addressed him as being in the Office of the Sixth Auditor classified as "Clerk of Class Three in the

---

8. Warner McGuinn's nephew, also named Warner, a Yale University student, was a recipient of financial aid from Mark Twain.

Office of the Auditor of the Treasury for the Post Office." It is difficult for me to appreciate the significance of these various titles.

In 1875, Grandfather delivered an address in Richmond before the black teachers of that city, which resulted in the organization of the Virginia Educational and Historical Association. On August 24, with only eleven members, this group elected Grandfather president, and he served in this position until 1883. The purpose of the organization was to permit "Gentlemen and Ladies to meet annually to discuss educational and other topics bearing on the infringement on the conditions of colored people in Virginia, especially and of the country generally."

On April 14, 1876, in Alexandria, Virginia, J. W. Cromwell started the *People's Advocate.* The paper's masthead read, "Principles Not Men But Men as Representatives of Principles," and its stated purpose was to "inquire into the existing character of people, and the construction and bearing of their social system . . . to examine the present state of their religion; their morals; their education and their literature; to survey their political status and the position in which they [were] placed." It was to be "independent in politics but give a cheerful support to the principles of the Republican Party."9

T. B. Penn was the publisher of the *People's Advocate,* R. D. Beckley, the business manager, and John W. Cromwell, the editor. A few weeks after its publication, the paper absorbed the *Summer Tribune,* irregularly published at the Culpepper Courthouse, and afterward at the Alexandria Courthouse by the Honorable A. W. Harris. Penn's and Beckley's connections with the *Advocate* were brief and so was Harris's, leaving Grandfather the sole proprietor after only three months in existence. Among its editors, at different times, besides the proprietors were Charles N. Otey, George H. Richardson, and Rev. S. P. Smith who were its regular contributors and correspondents at different periods.

As soon as the *People's Advocate* was launched, Grandfather received the commendation and endorsement of the Republican convention. As editor, he immediately became involved in the politics of the 1876 presidential campaign, vigorously supporting Senator James G. Blaine of Maine, who received an overwhelming endorsement by Virginia's black Republicans at Lynchburg. The convention adopted a resolution offering its allegiance to the National Republican Party. A month later, he advised the Virginia delegation to the Republican convention in Cincinnati to support Blaine, implying that Blaine was the best candidate to restrain the Bourbon conservatives in Virginia. The National Republicans, however, nominated Rutherford B. Hayes, who Grandfather first described

9. The *People's Advocate,* July 10, 1879.

as a man of integrity, but a month later, as crafty, adroit, and unscrupulous. He urged northern Republicans to encourage southern Republicans to align them- selves with the national ticket, and he asserted that the only issue was whether the country will be safer in the hands of the Democrats or Republicans.

Blacks rejoiced over the election of Hayes, not realizing that the election meant a compromise between the North and the South, for although a Republican had won the presidency, conservative Democrats were elected to office in several southern states.

In 1877, the Cromwells moved to 1511 P Street in northwest Washington, and John Cromwell began his long and distinguished career in that city. In June 1877, he bought a secondhand printing outfit and published from Virginia his first "all- at-home" sheet on June 29. Briefly in his employ at this early stage was T. Thomas Fortune (1856–1928), who supervised the mechanical work of running the paper. In 1879, disappointed by the lack of capital and the paper's poor circulation, and responding to the encouragement from his wife, Cromwell moved the *Advocate* from Virginia to Washington, where it was published every Saturday from room 24 of the May Building, located on the northeast corner of 7th and E streets. As a single-sheet weekly, the *Advocate* became "a veritable history of the social life of the colored people of Washington from 1880 to 1890."[10] The paper included liberal comments on political affairs, especially concerning the rights of Negroes protesting discrimination in the restaurants and education. Columns in the paper were also devoted to literature and news items on new books and magazines. Subscribers to the paper were in Maryland, Pennsylvania, New Jersey, New York, Massachusetts, Rhode Island, Ohio, Virginia, West Virginia, Florida, and North Carolina.

In April 1880, Levi Cromwell became the official agent of the *Advocate* in Phil- adelphia. The same year, J. W. Cromwell (as he became more publicly known) was elected chairman of the Conference of Colored Journalists, which met June 3, 1880, in Chicago. J. Henry Cromwell, who became an important advocate for the Blacks of Norfolk, began his journalistic career at the *People's Advocate,* and in 1889, he succeeded John Wesley Cromwell as managing editor.

That John Wesley and Lucy chose to live in Washington dramatically af- fected their lives by providing opportunities for the family to become outstand- ing members of the black intelligentsia. Throughout his long life, John Wesley

---

10. Henry Lewis Suggs describes the *People's Advocate* as "one of the first full sized black weekly newspapers in Virginia for the years 1876–1879" (Suggs, ed., *The Black Press in the South 1865–1879* [Westport, Conn.: Greenwood Press, 1983], 382–83).

Cromwell was known for his intellectual acumen and concern for the political and cultural events provided by the Washington community. His children, each in his or her way, were influenced by their father and were also outstanding members of the black intelligentsia. Washington's black community favored its educators who, in turn, developed an exceptional educational system capped by the existence of Howard University and the Miner Normal School. Black teachers in Washington held more influence than their peers in other black communities did and, contrary to most southern cities, received approximately the same salary as white teachers. Educational and literary activities were taken seriously, and within the scope of these activities, the community revealed its highest potential as well as its least desirable values. The political activities that in other times and places would have been manifest in politics were played out in the arena of education, and it was through educational opportunities that the citizens were rewarded or punished.

Washington, D.C.

Feby 20, 1879

Dear father:[11]

I am compelled to say that it was my duty to have written you before this, but I have been so run with one thing and another that I have put off until now at quarter of eleven tonight to pen you these few lines. I am happy to say that we are enjoying as excellent health as can be expected this time of year. Otelia and Mamie by turns are up and down and then up. Little Lucy keeps as lively as a cricket, constantly chirping as if it were one continual summer. Her mother has as much as she can do to keep the family straight and the house in order. As Otelia goes to school and can now print on her slate, the present which you sent her was very acceptable. If she and you live, she will use some of the paper and the pen to write you her first letter. She "takes" to books, but I do not like it. It is papa what is this for? What is that? and such like questions I do not encourage her and I often regret that I consented to let her begin although her school is held in only two hours and a half a day.

They all send love to papa; they are asleep and I am growing sleeping. My next letter I assure you will not be so long in going as this one.

Your devoted Son,

Wesley.

11. Letter from John Wesley Cromwell Sr. to Willis Hodges Cromwell.

My grandmother, Lucy McGuinn Cromwell, died on April 6, 1887. She and my grandfather had been married for only fifteen years, and she left six children ranging in age from thirteen to two.

Unfortunately, there is no surviving letter to show how John Wesley Cromwell reacted to the death of his wife; he does not even mention it in his journal, though there is an interesting soliloquy on his reaction to the birth of their first child, Otelia, and the pains Lucy suffered during her birth.

After having so many children in rapid succession, Lucy's health began to fail, as Levi and Willis both acknowledged in their letters to their brother John:

> Willis to John 2/4/87

> "I am very sorry that Lucy's health is not too good. Remember me to her and say that I hope she will be well soon."

> And again from Willis to John, 3/13/87

> "Give my love to Lucy and tell her I hope she will get well soon then she might come up here and stay a few weeks and get some rest. Give my love to all the children."

> Or from Levi to John, 4/8/87

> " . . . And as I have not heard of your wife lately I suppose she has improved."

Certainly Levi and Willis also wrote more about Lucy's illness and death, but none of those letters has survived.

After Lucy's death, her sister Winnie McGuinn Lewis came to mother the little brood. Many years later, in April 1931, writing from Oberlin, Aunt Winnie, at age seventy-four, reminiscenced about those days:

> My dear Easter flowers, I did want to send you all a Easter card but I could not so the thought came to me why not write a little letter to all in one and tell them how much I love them on this Easter morn. I guess it was because I was thinking about you when you were children when you wore little gingham aprons. How I wish I had stayed there with you but I am proud of you all just the same and hope you all have a happy Easter and hope I will see you all again some day.

The only account of this period from the children's perspective is from Mary, the second oldest child and the second girl, who wrote in her unpublished autobiography,

> Being one of a family of six children I did not get individual attention. As my mother died when the youngest was one year and the oldest eleven, my father was left with the care and support of them. He entrusted this care to hired people who looked after our physical needs; our spiritual development was left, I might say, to ourselves, for as I remember when my father came home from a hard day's monotonous work, he found surcease in his library. Thus altho we were not allowed to suffer for physical care we were bereft of the love and care of a woman.

Mary does not mention her aunt Winnie's stay, probably because it was relatively brief. Winnie came to meet the need for emergency care following her sister's death, but as her own letter says, she shortly returned to her husband.

These were certainly not easy times for John Wesley Cromwell or for his children. During these years, Otelia, the eldest, assumed a responsibility for and authority over her siblings, which she never relinquished.

Otelia's first letter to her Uncle Charles has survived. In childish scrawl in red ink, she wrote,

> October 30, 1881
> My dear Uncle Charles. I take my pen in hand to let you know that I am well and hope when these few lines reach you they find you the same.
> And dear little Brother is dead and buried and Uncle Charles please send me a doll baby and Mama has another little girl only 2 months old and please send me a baby carriage and Mary. Send her that doll baby and all sends there love and Robert Wigonton sends his love.
> From your dear niece Otelia Cromwell

On August 30, 1886, five years after this letter was written, John Wesley Cromwell wrote Otelia, who was in Culpepper, Virginia, in such a way as to suggest her seniority and responsibility in the family.

> Tell your poor mother I received her message. Send me word when you want to return Saturday or sometime next week. If next week I will try and spend Sunday with you—but no, I guess I will remain here although it is my birthday when we should all be together, for Sunday night there is to

be a special lecture on the Metropolitan Church by the pastor giving the history of its building, expenses, etc . . .

Kiss the children. You have another cousin—it is a girl she lives in Philadelphia and her father is named Willis. I will write to our mother tomorrow.

Your Father

John Wesley's family was important to his brother Levi, who was their only source of financial help. Levi's acceptance of this responsibility is seen in his discussion of his will in letters to John Wesley and the provisions he made for John's children in the will: "And give whatever I die possessed to my dear wife Nancy Cromwell for her use during her life and at her death to revert to the children of my brothers Willis Hodges Cromwell and John Wesley Cromwell share and share alike."

Although Levi died in 1904, his wife, Nancy, lived until 1949. At the time of Nancy's death, John Wesley's children were still alive—only the grandchildren of Willis were alive—but all had made their own way in life; therefore, Nancy left her share of the estate to her family.

John Wesley Cromwell's children's education was always important to their father, and as modest as the family resources were, five of the six Cromwell children finished the famous M Street High School; his son John Wesley Cromwell Jr. was enrolled as a student in the Preparatory Division of Howard University and then at Dartmouth College. One by one, after completing the Normal School, the girls ventured forth to college: Otelia to Smith, Mary to the University of Michigan, and Martha (whom we called Larcie) to Howard. Lucy and Fanny both suffered from a spinal curvature. Lucy finished the Normal School the same year as Mary, in 1896, but had no further schooling. She always lived, however, with her brother and sisters. Fanny remained close to her father and stepmother and did not go beyond high school.

While the educational goals of Cromwell's children were achieved, their adolescence and young adulthood were disturbed by their father's second marriage on October 20, 1892, to Annie E. Conn of Mechanicsburg, Pennsylvania. Although I am not certain how Grandfather met his second wife, the St. Luke's *One Hundred Year History* lists Annie Conn as well as his daughters, Otelia and Larcie, as members between 1873 and 1889, so they may well have met at church.[12]

Therefore, if the church list is any clue, two daughters of John Wesley Cromwell knew their stepmother before he married her. Yet it is difficult to know

12. "Families of St. Luke's 1873–1880," *One Hundred Years: St. Luke's Episcopal Church, 1873–1973,* 134.

exactly how the children reacted to this marriage, as Mary's account of her response is the only documentation we have. Curiously, though older than Larcie, Mary is not listed as a member of the church. Mary wrote,

> It was during my high school life that a change in the domestic life of our family caused me to spend a year in a manufacturing center of Pennsylvania . . .
>
> . . . Returning home I found conditions changed. My father had married. His wife was different from my father. She had none of that austerity and quietness of mind that he had. She was a woman of the world interested in clubs she had whist and enchra [sic] parties of the day of "500" and Bridge not being so popular. In this environment I felt out of place. I began to live more and more to myself.

These were stressful years for John Wesley Cromwell. Years that were not made easier by his second marriage. Sadly, the family never seemed to be one again. Grandfather and his bride, whom he called Effie, moved from 1511 P Street, the family home, to 1439 Pierce Place (now Swann Street). Otelia, who had secured a teaching job, according to Grandfather, moved out of the family home the first week of January 1893.[13] In his journal, Grandfather wrote that it was necessary for Aunt Winnie to come again "three hundred miles from her home to endeavor to bring about such readjustment as will not interfere with the proper training of the younger children."

In her letter, Mary stated that during high school, she spent a year living in Pennsylvania. Perhaps, during this year, Aunt Mary was living with Aunt Winnie, who was then living in Pittsburgh.[14]

In his journal, Grandfather's only comment on the stress in the family at this time was

> Must I put to paper what should linger alone in the chambers of the soul?
> There are thoughts so sacred that there never should be any human soul that could possess the key to them. But when his sacredness is disregarded

---

13. Apparently, my stepgrandmother had purchased the house at 1439 Pierce Place on July 14, 1898, from a Mr. Armistead, and on March 8, 1911, she sold the house to Ida V. Smith. It seems, however, that on June 2, 1911, Ida Smith sold the house back to my grandfather and stepgrandmother. Eight years later, on April 24, 1919, Grandfather sold his share of the house to my stepgrandmother, presumably to ensure that at his death none of his children would have any claim on it.

14. See chapter 3, p. 70, for a letter dated May 15, 1894, in which Levi makes reference to Mary's move.

and the whole world is permitted to gaze within the inner circle of the family and its occurrences; self-interest, self-defense justify a different course of action and the question professed becomes pertinent.

John Wesley Cromwell then drew a line or two across the statement, but he did not remove or erase it.

In the journal the following year, we are told Mary and Lucy were admitted to the Normal School. Although pursuing their educational goals, apparently after Aunt Winnie's intercession, the feeling of the children toward their stepmother continued to be hostile. It is difficult to know how the family members interacted. By the end of the century, Otelia had left for college, followed in 1901 by Mary, and in 1902 by John. Larcie and Lucy continued to live in the family home on P Street. As their letters reveal, however, all the children kept in touch with their father and with their relatives in Philadelphia and New Bedford.

Levi's letters reflect his acceptance of John Wesley's new wife but also refer to her as Mrs. John W. Cromwell, no doubt because he had not yet met her.

On October 20, 1906, Grandfather noted that Otelia and Larcie accompanied him and Granny-Step[15] to the wedding anniversary of a friend, which coincidentally was their fourteenth wedding anniversary. On the same day, Grandfather also wrote, "the only remembrance of our marriage came from Otelia—a gift of some table ware. Today she is the most confiding of the girls just as a daughter should be towards a mother."

Later that year when their stepmother's father died, her ability to attend his funeral, Grandfather reported, on October 22, 1906, was "made possible by the self-sacrifice of Otelia and the other children."

In 1910, Grandfather took John with him to the summer school of the Virginia Theological Seminary and College. John was to be an instructor at the school.

On May 21, 1910, Otelia and John jointly bought a large house on 13th Street, hoping their father and his wife would live with them in it, thus bringing the family together again. Although Grandfather, Granny-Step, and Fanny moved into the house for a brief period, by 1913 they had moved back to Pierce Place. John, Otelia, Mary, Larcie and Lucy continued living together on 13th Street.[16]

In 1913, Grandfather noted in his journal that he took Arthur Schomburg to visit Otelia. The following year when his long-awaited book, *The Negro in*

15. Granny-Step was my name for my grandfather's second wife.
16. John, Otelia, Mary, and Lucy remained on 13th Street for the rest of their lives; Larcie left after her marriage to Alfred Brent.

American History, appeared, Grandfather wrote, "John came over the house for the first time in several years to offer his compliments." Something critical must have precipitated the break in the family relationship as evidenced by a letter of May 1912 to Otelia from Granny-Step:

> My dear Otelia:
> Don't throw this in the wastebasket when you recognize the writing. I am writing you from the depths of a heavy heart. I want your help! I want this coldness to cease. I am very sorry from my inmost soul for my part in this long unnatural family estrangement. Won't you lay aside all the past and forgive and forget.
> Forgive—I make an appeal for father or Lislu—I speak to you myself. I want you to come to me and let me hear you in the old voice say once again.
>
> Mother

After the estrangement, which so far as I could discern was never completely ended, Grandfather, Granny-Step, and Aunt Fanny continued to live away from the family for the rest of their lives.

When my father married my mother, Yetta E. Mavritte, Grandfather was not invited to the simple wedding, which Otelia, Larcie, and Lucy attended. Grandfather, who was only informed about the marriage after the fact, reported that Mary was away at the time. Grandfather felt hurt that his son and namesake "and the sole male descendant in the third generation of the family" had ignored him and, of course, Granny-Step.

My father brought my mother to live with his sisters on 13th Street, where I was born. My parents, as a couple, fit no more happily in the framework of this family setting than had Grandfather, Granny-Step, and Aunt Fanny.[17]

But my birth did serve, somewhat, as a bridge between the two households. Carried by my father, I often visited Grandfather and Granny-Step. Grandfather would come to visit us, in the way of a formal call, but I do not remember seeing Granny-Step in our house. Grandfather kept a letter to him written for me by my father:

17. While I was away at college, my mother wrote me about a visit she made to see Granny-Step and about how bonded they became in sharing stories of the difficulties both had with the children of John Wesley Cromwell.

Industrial School
Bordentown, N.J.
August 21, 1925
Dear Grandfather:

  This is Adelaide. I am up in New Jersey at Bordentown. The place is very pretty and I like it so much. Mother was up here but she has gone to New York and I am here with Daddy.

  Of course you know I had my tonsils cut out before I left home but I am alright now. I am going to stay next week for the tennis tournament and then I am going to Brandy to ride horses. Give my love to Aunt Fanny and Grandma Cromwell.

  Aunt Lucy and Aunt Otelia are in Stockbridge. Aunt Larcie and Aunt Mary are in New York. I think.

  Daddy is alright.

  Kiss and hug.

                              Adelaide

  Grandfather died April 14, 1927, and Granny-Step survived him by thirteen years. As I grew older, I would visit her by myself. My impression is that my aunts Mary and Larcie were largely responsible for the conflict with Granny-Step and, later on, with my mother. Aunt Otelia, Lucy, and Daddy coped.

  Ironically, I believe there was also an estrangement between Larcie and Mary, which was later healed. In 1924, Larcie married Alfred P. Brent and moved into her own home. Uncle Alfred had been widowed and had a child so Aunt Larcie became a stepmother herself.

  My mother and father were divorced in 1940. None of the other sisters married, and my father did not remarry.

  In spite of the strain in the relation between John Wesley Cromwell and his children, the proximity of their residences in Washington and their membership in St. Luke's Church facilitated some form of communication between father and children. Furthermore, neither John Wesley Cromwell nor his children moved away from Washington, and the city continued to shape the direction of their lives. For Washington, more than Philadelphia, and certainly Portsmouth, gave them all an opportunity to be active members of the black "intelligentsia," as they had done elsewhere—Willis Cromwell as a slave in Virginia, Levi Cromwell as a businessman in Philadelphia, and now John Wesley Cromwell as a journalist, lawyer, and educator in Washington. A third generation made its mark in

Washington also: Otelia Cromwell as a scholar and professor, and John Wesley Cromwell Jr. as the first black certified public accountant.

While Washington, D.C., offered opportunities to the children of John Wesley Cromwell and Lucy McGuinn Cromwell, all of whom were born in the District and received their early education there, as a community, the city changed considerably after John Wesley and Lucy Cromwell moved there. The relatively positive relationship between the races that had existed after the Civil War into the early 1870s slowly eroded after the late 1870s into a growing separatism and segregation that limited the opportunities for African Americans in every area. Constance Greene described these changes:

> White Washington in the 1880s enjoyed a material prosperity and amenities richer than any city had ever known before. For Negroes the satisfactions of life diminished steadily after 1878. Between white and colored people such tolerant friendliness as survived the seventies slowly disappeared. The change was gradual enough to permit colored people for a time to persuade themselves that a year or two would suffice to reestablish them on the footing they had attained earlier. Not until the autumn of 1883 did they clearly sense how much the atmosphere had chilled in a decade, and not until the 1890s did they realize that no effort of theirs was likely to restore warmth to the city's race relations.
>
> . . . By the 1890s most Negroes in the District were adhering to the social pattern common in the deep South: conflict within the caste and compliance with or carefully concealed hostility toward the white group outside.[18]

The Cromwell family managed to survive and to some extent prosper in Washington. For them, as indeed was true of most African Americans, education was the only way of overcoming the limitations the Washington environment imposed upon them.

Educational institutions in Washington, though segregated, were designed to challenge the most promising students and to offer employment to the growing cadre of black educators who came to the city, where black teachers could receive approximately the same pay as white teachers. Salaries in the 1890s were nearly "10 percent lower, and the teaching load heavier in the colored than in the white schools. At an annual salary of $750.00, a colored high school teacher earned $74.54 less than his or her white counterpart. In 1890, white classes averaged 41

18. Green, *The Secret City,* 119, 121.

children to the teacher, the colored—47. Otherwise, the two systems ran generally parallel . . . in four examinations given all high school students in 1899, the colored high school scored higher than either the Eastern or the Western High School."[19]

The Washington public school system was a pioneer in educating African Americans. In 1870, nine years before the city had a high school for white children, the Preparatory High School for Negro Youth was started. This school located in a church basement was the first public high school for black students in the United States, and because of its later location on the intersection of First and M streets, it became known as M Street High School. M Street High School was the predecessor of Dunbar High School, which started in 1916 in a new building on First Street and became one of the premier black high schools in the country. Dunbar's reputation was built on the quality of its teachers and the success of its students. Several graduates of Harvard and other distinguished northern colleges, not finding positions in the North, were happy to teach at Dunbar High School.

Howard University, including its faculties of medicine, law, and religion, prepared students for the professions, and the Miner Normal School prepared students for teaching in the public schools and for civil service positions.

As in most black communities, the church in Washington was an important institution. In 1860, there were eleven black churches: six Methodist, four Baptist, and one Presbyterian. The Preparatory High School for Negro Youth was first located in the basement of the Presbyterian Church.

In 1867, twenty-eight black men and women separated from the white Epiphany Church and formed the St. Mary's Chapel for Colored People. In 1873, the congregation had Alexander Crummell as its own black pastor. After a dispute over the property deed, Crummell left St. Mary's and led a majority of his congregation to St. Luke's Episcopal Church when that building was completed in 1879, thus making St. Luke's the first completely independent Episcopal Church for Blacks. The building was designed by Calvin T. S. Brent, Washington's first black architect and the brother of Alfred Brent, who married my aunt Larcie.

Grandfather became a member of the Metropolitan African Methodist Episcopal Church in 1887. His children, however, grew up in St. Luke's, which he himself never officially joined, in spite of his close friendship with Alexander Crummell.

Many outstanding preachers, too numerous to mention, were ministers of these churches, but for the Cromwell family, Alexander Crummell, rector of St.

19. Ibid., 137.

Luke's, was the most important. Crummell was the godfather of John Wesley Cromwell's son John. Cromwell also counted among his close friends Francis Grimké, the pastor of the 15th Street Presbyterian Church, and Walter Brooks, the pastor of the 19th Street Baptist Church. Many of the ministers of the Metropolitan A.M.E. Church, especially Theophilus Gould Steward and John Albert Johnson, were also his close friends.

The Cromwell family, because of John Wesley Cromwell's prominence as a journalist and educator, was an important part of the black socially stratified community of Washington. There was a small educated elite, an aristocracy if you will, comprised of professionals and those fortunate enough to have the more prestigious government positions, secured by patronage or competition. Next was a broader group of those holding lesser government positions and a range of occupations requiring education at least through the secondary school and beyond, which permitted a comfortable lifestyle. This middle group included elementary schoolteachers, less educated ministers, and small business owners. Below these two main groups was the large and growing mass of less educated and often unemployed, who were thought by others, Blacks and Whites, to be irresponsible and potentially criminal.

Housing was segregated but not rigidly so, for Whites still lived in many black neighborhoods. The black community lived in neighborhoods easily defined according to race, always, with one or two exceptions, in Georgetown and in the northwest section of the city. Home ownership was important, and apartment buildings as we know them did not exist. Poorer families lived in crowded single family houses, which they rented; the very poor lived in the alleys, a remnant from the Civil War days. The last of these alleys was not removed until the presidency of Franklin Roosevelt.

The Washington of this period had more cultural and intellectual organizations and less important businesses—successful barbers served white customers only—other than morticians and a printing company, than say Philadelphia or New York. The black community fed upon itself in a peculiar way: lacking political power, it was dependent upon the largesse of Whites and thus directed both its frustrations and discontent, as well as its accolades and recognition, to the churches and the educational system.

Otelia Cromwell's death on April 25, 1972, ended the period of the Cromwell family living in Washington.

Chapter 5

JOHN WESLEY CROMWELL SR.
THE LIGHT THAT GLOWED

As my grandfather, John Wesley Cromwell, was the pivotal figure in the history of this family, it is important to understand him as a person. Beginning with the diary, which he called "Reminiscences," that he kept for only a year in 1863 when he was only sixteen and ending with a retrospective journal, Grandfather believed in chronicling events of importance within the family as well as within his large circle of friends and acquaintances. For him, history was an obsession. He was an editor and a scholar, and as such, his pen was never idle. Yet, it is difficult to know his personal feelings because his responses to the many letters he received were not kept by his children or by his friends, with the exception of a few by John Bruce. But to understand his role in the family, it is necessary that we know the man, especially in his mature years in Washington.

In his diary, we meet a youngster who is an avid reader (he read Sir William Smith's *The History of Greece* for most of the year) and a frequent church attendee (Cherry Street Baptist, Bethel A.M.E., and Gloucester churches). Community activities are important to him. He hears Frederick Douglass speak several times on his recruiting mission to Philadelphia. He is also in the audience when William Lloyd Garrison takes the stage for a speech. With some of his young friends, he organizes the Frederick Douglass Lyceum before whom Frederick Douglass himself speaks. Family illnesses, visits, and marriages are reported: there are entries for William Carney's trip from Virginia to New Bedford with his wife and four children and Willis's marriage in Haiti. There is also a letter dated

Saturday, March 7th from Aunt Nancy saying that William has enlisted in the Massachusetts Fifty-fourth Regiment: "May his blows tell good things for the welfare of his people and may he be remembered with the immortal defenders for Right, Liberty and Equality!"

John Wesley Cromwell reports regularly on the activities at the Institute for Colored Youth where he was enrolled: "Mr. Bassett is sick"; on Friday, March 13, "Mr. Bassett is mad as a bug" and "At school ridiculed"; on Thursday, March 31, "Mr. Bassett gives our class Greek grammar" and "Mr. Catto gives me a slap on my face with a book for giving impudence as he calls it." Mr. Catto said that "I was walking about with my Virginia pedestals." On June 8th, the youngster notes, "I miss my lessons and am kept in school until 7 o'clock"; on Thursday, June 25, "Mr. Bassett orders us to write a composition"; and on Friday, June 26, "composition brought forth!" There are also regular reports on the war, especially on Union troops.

Grandfather's writing is almost always impersonal and even remote. In only a couple of his letters does he write about his own feelings: Saturday, May 30, "I take my usual Saturday evening stroll. Dr. Tumblety, the great Indian Doctor. He advises me to bathe every morning in order to strengthen my chest"; July 10, "Greedily eat some food"; July 11, "Sick from foregoing circumstances"; and July 12, "Heat, heat, heat. Heat overcomes me."

As an older man, Grandfather included in his journal some circumstances that he had recorded earlier in his diary. While the journal is largely a chronicle of broader issues and conflicts within the segregated educational system of the Washington public schools and an equally detailed reporting of activities within the black church, especially the Methodist Church and particularly the Metropolitan African Methodist Episcopal Church, of which he was a member, there were also reminiscences of his early life and his own involvement within the educational system and the church.

A reading of the journal—the first entry is dated March 17, 1891—reveals a man who was proud of his integrity but ever sensitive to the actions of others against and occasionally for him. He remembers his childhood in Philadelphia, especially the Watch Meetings at the Zion Mission Church (of which his mother was a founder) at 7th and Dickinson streets. He also remembers the violence by the white youth of the city during these times: "No church had felt safe to open its doors."

In 1856, as a boy of ten, Grandfather attended Bird's Grammar School. But he included nothing in the journal for the years from 1860 to 1864, though he kept the diary in 1863, which remained in his possession throughout his life. He does recall in his journal an attack of typhoid fever in 1868 and being a patient in his brother Levi's house.

Grandfather also recollected in his journal about not being chosen in 1869 as legislative delegate from Charlotte County, Virginia, by William E. Reed, with whom he had boarded and roomed when he was teaching at Scott's Farm, and about being overlooked as cashier of the Freedmen's Bank in Norfolk because of the preferences of Bishop M. Brown. He recalled, however, that in December 1879 he was elected to the board of Storer College in Harpers Ferry. Thus he ended his thoughts of his early life.

After graduating from the Institute for Colored Youth and teaching for a brief period in Columbia, Pennsylvania, Grandfather at eighteen years of age returned to Virginia where the family had lived as slaves to open a school for freedmen.

Faced with unexpected competition from the American Missionary Association schools that had already been established in and around Portsmouth, which were tuition-free and staffed with well-educated northern teachers, Grandfather's school briefly flourished before it failed and was taken over by the association.

In the fall of 1865 Grandfather returned to Philadelphia, but he soon left for Baltimore where he enrolled in a teachers' training program under the auspices of the Baltimore Association for the Moral and Intellectual Improvement of Colored People. On December 1865, E. W. Sampson, the principal of the association, recommended him as "punctual in attendance, exemplary in deportment and exact and thorough as a scholar" and as someone "who would be a competent and efficient teacher to all who may desire his services."

Grandfather, on the basis of such a strong reference, was employed to teach in the American Missionary Association's schools.[1] He taught for several months in different parts of Maryland and in Portsmouth, Virginia, but in 1866 he was shot at and the church in which he had been teaching was burned to the ground. At the close of the school year, he left the association school and opened a private school connected with the Sunday school of the Emanuel African Methodist Episcopal Church. On September 12, 1866, at the suggestion of H. C. Percy, Esq., he wrote to the Reverend Samuel Hunt, the superintendent of education for the Freedmen's Schools of the American Missionary Association, seeking a commission for the position he had received at the Providence School in Norfolk County. But his qualification to teach was still questioned by Reverend Hunt because he was not a member of an evangelical church.[2] Not denying this but stressing

---

1. In the American Missionary Association archives at the Amistad Research Center in New Orleans, there six letters and four monthly reports submitted by John Wesley Cromwell from September 11, 1866, to July 1, 1867.

2. As earlier, family letters note Grandfather did not join a church until several years later.

his other qualities—his motivation and his teaching methods—and supplying the names of several impressive references, Grandfather was unable to influence Reverend Hunt.

On December 1, 1866, however, with surprising candor for a man only twenty-two years of age, Grandfather made his case to Reverend Hunt:

> I have embraced Christianity, although several times I have struggled for it—even when 12 years old. I have tried again and again. At times I feel as though I could resign all my hopes upon Christ, but then something—I know not what—makes this but momentary. I know I am weak and sinful. I have stated the truth as it is mighty and must prevail. If you as a clergyman can give me any advice upon this, I will be thankful for it.

The matter was settled when on July 1, 1867, Grandfather wrote Edward P. Smith, who had replaced Reverend Hunt, "that on the advice of Superintendent H. C. Percy, he had closed the Providence School on June 1, because the demand for labor was such that there was not sufficient attendance to warrant the continuation of the school for another year." He also added the following suggestion: "Should you resolve to reopen the schools at this point it would be better to have them opened earlier—say in September or as soon as the crops are over and then you will have full schools until March."

While still living in Virginia, following the family tradition in business, Grandfather briefly ran a grocery store and became politically involved. The grocery business was not successful, but John Cromwell became recognized in the political arena. On May 17, 1866, he attended the John Minor Botts[3] convention held in Alexandria, and on April 17, 1867, he was named a delegate to the first Republican convention held in Richmond. Cromwell was elected clerk in the Constitutional Reconstruction Convention (1867–1868), and he was an impaneled United States juror for the term at which Jefferson Davis was to be tried.[4] In

---

3. John Minor Botts, a former Congressman and Unionist Whig, of no mean ability, disliked slavery and tried to steer an intermediate course between Radical Republicans and Conservative Democrats. He was concerned about the increasing strength of the Radical Republicans in Congress and was chair of the so-called Unconventional Convention, which met in May 17, 1866, the first statewide political convention held in Virginia after the war. The day before the meeting of the Republican convention on August 1, 1867, a conservative faction of delegates met and approved a platform presented by Botts that condemned secession as a crime, advocated the enfranchisement of all Confederates except for their leaders, and called for punishment of the latter.

4. After being captured in May 1863, Jefferson Davis was imprisoned for two years for treason and then liberated on bond. He was probably accused of complicity in the assassination of President Lincoln. Davis was never tried and was finally released on bond. He spent his last years working on his memoirs.

addition, he was one of the four colored men on the jury that convicted several government officials of conspiracy to defraud the United States government.

Following these experiences, Cromwell devoted much time to organizing Republican clubs and councils of the Union League Association. In 1869, he resumed his teaching career and organized several schools under the auspices of the Philadelphia Friends. In the fall of 1869 and into 1870, he taught at Wytheville, then the highest grade school in southwest Virginia. In 1870, he was principal of a school held in Dill's Bakery in Richmond, and in the summer of 1871, he taught at a school in Northampton County near the scene of the Nat Turner insurrection. The 1869 census of Virginia lists John W. Cromwell, age twenty-four, as a teacher living in the household of Lewis H. Blair, a white dry-goods merchant in Henrico County.

As the following letter reflects, John Wesley Cromwell was evidently enthusiastic about his educational activities in the South. Also revealing are the ties maintained between freemen in the North and their relatives and friends now living as free persons in the South.

Charlotte C. W. Va
Jan'y 14. 1869

Willis H. Cromwell, Esq.
Dear Father

I will not be able to say much in this letter about my work and its progress, although I have made arrangements to open my first school Monday. It is to be on a large plantation of 1,000 acres where many of the old customs of the old era still cling to the people and where no previous arrangement has been consummated in the establishment of a school. It is five miles from this place and five miles further from the nearest Railroad depot.

I staid in Portsmouth until Sunday night, in Norfolk that night and left the next morning but did not arrive until Tuesday morning owing to an accident that occurred to a previous train.

While in Ports. I found all our folks well. Daniel, Unc. Henry, Godfrey, Aunt Lydia, Max, Aunt Sally and their families in general are well. Uncle Henry's wife is sick and Aunt Lydia would like you to send her some assistance however little it may be.

I found Mrs. Fanny Watton from California here, well, and glad to hear from you through me, and anxious to hear directly in future from both you and Levi.

She will remain in Virginia until the spring when she will pay you and other friends North a visit on her return homeward. Some new houses are being erected in Portsmouth which would slightly improve some portions and adorn the whole were not they checkmated by the ravages of fire in other parts of the city. Among the improvements is a three story warehouse being erected by Bain on the site of our last residence in Portsmouth.

Give my respects to Levi, Esther, Martha, Willis and their families, tell Levi to send me a paper that has an account of the proceedings of the Convention and believe me as ever.

Yours truly
J. W. Cromwell

William J. Simmons wrote the most complete biography of Grandfather to date. A contemporary of my grandfather, he knowingly and a bit effusively described him as the best English scholar in the United States, as both unassuming and retiring, and as having a character for business and honest dealing that marked him as a man of much talent, tact, and industry.[5]

In 1872, after receiving his position as clerk of the Post Office Department, Grandfather turned his attention to the black community of Washington, D.C., where by the late 1880s many intellectual African Americans were seeking a platform or forum from which to address the social changes taking place in that city. Some gravitated to the Bethel Literary and Historical Association started in 1881 by the Reverend Daniel Payne and a select few to the American Negro Academy started by Rev. Alexander Crummell in 1897. Grandfather was a key figure in both organizations: He was a member of the association's first advisory committee and served as president of the "Literary" for two terms. For twenty-two years, he was the corresponding secretary for the academy and served for one year as its president.

The Literary flourished for a decade and a half during which time Grandfather gave several speeches on its programs: "The Ethiopians—Who Were They?" "The Negro in Journalism," "The Colored Church, An Historical Sketch," and "A History of the Bethel Literary and Historical Association." H. L. Pendleton published the latter in 1896. The men of the Literary, and with few exceptions— such as Mary Church Terrell's election to the presidency in 1892—they were all men, debated the pros and cons of segregated institutions, including schools, churches, and businesses. Race pride and racial solidarity, as well as political power, were always on their minds.

---

5. William J. Simmons, *Men of Mark: Eminent, Progressive, and Rising* (Cleveland: O. G. M. Rewell, 1887), 637–43.

Grandfather represented the District of Columbia at the World's Industrial and Cotton Centennial Exposition, which opened in New Orleans in December 1884.

In 1885, before any of his children had reached college age, John Wesley Cromwell was removed from his government position by Grover Cleveland, the first Democratic president since the Civil War, for being too partisan in the articles he published in the *People's Advocate*.[6] Cleveland had run as a candidate of reform in general and of the civil service in particular. The *Washington Bee* reported on November 25, 1893, that four hundred Negroes had been dismissed from government service by Cleveland and that only three black persons had been appointed or nominated, two of whom were rejected by the Senate. The black community believed that President Cleveland removed black Republicans and appointed white Democrats in their place but did not, in fact, remove white Republicans with the same dispatch. A review of the editorials in the *Advocate* substantiates the veracity of Cleveland's charges: Cromwell *was* offensively partisan. He believed that the black man's position in this country could be better served by the Republican Party than by the Democratic Party. He viewed with alarm its intrusion into the South and the Republican Party's gradual acceptance of some southern attitudes toward the Negroes in the 1870s and 1880s and consequently the candidacy and election of Grover Cleveland, a Democrat to the presidency in 1884.

After leaving the Post Office Department, Grandfather practiced law briefly, appearing before the Interstate Commerce Commission for the plaintiff in *William H. Heard v. the George Railroad Company*—probably as the first African American attorney to argue a case before that new body.

John Wesley Cromwell then returned to his first love: education. Having passed the examination for teachers with the highest score, he began his long career of teaching in the public schools of Washington, D.C.[7] In 1897, probably

6. Like many of his generation, Cromwell was a loyal Republican and was influenced, as was Frederick Douglass, by the changing political climate of the day. He often found it difficult to cling to the Grand Old Party and expected little from the Democratic Party. As an editor, Cromwell had a reputation for honesty and fairness, a fact amusingly reported in an article in the *Cleveland Gazette* on April 24, 1886, concerning a libel suit that had been filed against the *People's Advocate,* Cromwell, Lemar, and a Captain W. P. Gray, the author of the alleged defamatory article. As the *Gazette* article noted, the plaintiff, who had brought his case to criminal court and lost, had been badly advised, for "It is a cold deagh sonny, when you catch long headed John Cromwell for libel; he mitely particular how he talk and write."

7. In September 1889, Cromwell was appointed as a teacher of "eighth grade school"—no description given. From 1889 to January 1891, he served as principal of Briggs Schools; from February

at the urging of John E. Bruce, Cromwell applied for the position of assistant librarian at the Library of Congress. In addition to Bruce, Theophilus Gould Steward, the chaplain to the Twenty-fifth U.S. Infantry, T. Thomas Fortune, and Professor Clark of Wilberforce recommended him for the position. He was not appointed, apparently lacking the necessary political clout. But, unless the Library of Congress had more than one assistant librarian at this time, there is a mystery about this possible vacancy, for Daniel A. Murray, after having been a personal assistant to the librarian, Ainswork R. Spofford, since 1871, was advanced to the position of assistant librarian. What prompted Bruce to think there was a vacancy is a mystery.

It is clear from his journal that Grandfather not only loved teaching but also prided himself on the excellence of his students. The undated letter, probably to Otelia Cromwell (Miss Cromwell in the salutation), from the Reverend H. T. Gaskins, whom Cromwell taught in the eighth grade, is a testimony of this fact:

THE LIBERTY BAPTIST CHURCH
. . . Rev. H. T. Gaskins . . .
Pastor
Residence: 155 Randolph St., N.W. Phone Potomac 4635
Church: Phone West 623
Washington, D.C. C. [no date]

My dear Miss Cromwell,

Please be advised that it gives me pleasure to thus favor Mrs. Lee, but it gives me more pleasure to have the opportunity of in a very significant way aiding you the daughter of my Eighth Grd. Teacher who while I was with him (by his character) inspired me to climb, not only inspired me but after I had completed my Theological training at H.U. visited me at my home in Kenilworth and urged me on. The first write up concerning me in a daily paper was by him in the Washington Star.

When I was called as pastor of St. Paul's Church in Maryland it was Prof. J. W. Cromwell who on a very hot day though physically weak made his way there and after hearing me preach thrilled the congregation with his inspiring remarks. Returning home he searched among his papers, found and sent to me

1891 to 1893, as principal of Garnet School; in 1893 or 1894, as principal of Banneker School; from 1907 to 1911, as principal of Ivy City School; and from 1911 to 1916, as principal of Crummell School (Anatol Steck, historian, Museum and Archives, Charles Sumner School, letter dated August 29, 1994).

one of the first copies of a paper he once edited and printed before my birth which contained an account of my father's civic and spiritual activities and also a photo of my father which I now hold and prize as the only picture of my late father in existence.

Please pardon my delay and permit one to assure you that in any way, at any time, anywhere I desire to be regarded as

Your friend and humble servant,
Hampton T. Gaskins

One of the most important occurrences for intellectual life in Washington, D.C., and for Grandfather, was the arrival of Alexander Crummell, a distinguished clergyman and scholar, educated both in this country and abroad. Crummell came to Washington in 1873 after having spent twenty years in Liberia. Du Bois, on first meeting Crummell, "instinctively bowed as one bows before the prophets of the world." He saw Crummell's return to America after having suffered defeat and sorrow in Liberia as coming

> out of the temptation of Hate, and burned by the fire of Despair, triumphant over Doubt, and steeled by Sacrifice against Humiliation . . . turned at last home across the waters, humble and strong, gentle and determined. . . . He fought amongst his own, the low, the grasping and the wicked, with that unbending righteousness which is the sword of the just . . . and brought within his wide influence all that was best of those who walk within the Veil.[8]

Even as the glow of the Reconstruction flame was fading and the national political importance of Blacks diminishing, the black intellectuals in Washington were far from inactive. On December 8, 1877, at the residence of Frederick G. Barbadoes, twelve men met to form an organization "to promote the culture, material progress and educational interests of the colored people of this country." Although this group did not yet have a name, the organizers elected Alexander Crummell as their president and John Wesley Cromwell as their secretary. The following week at a meeting at Cromwell's home on P St., N.W., the group was officially named the Negro American Society.

In addition to Dr. Crummell and John Wesley Cromwell, other important

8. W. E. B. Du Bois, *The Souls of Black Folk: Essays and Sketches* (Chicago: A. C. McClurg, 1903), 216, 225–26.

figures attended the society's first meeting: John H. Smythe, T. Thomas Fortune, Richard T. Greener, William Calvin Chase, Charles N. Thomas, Dr. Alexander T. Augusta, W. H. Jackson, J. D. Baltimore, G. W. Price, and John H. Cook. New members were added at the next meeting. Unfortunately, the organization did not survive the year. Conflicts over membership, goals, and perhaps personality differences caused it to dissolve. Nevertheless, twenty years later, after his retirement from the ministry of St. Luke's Church and a year before his death, Crummell, again with the support of John Wesley Cromwell, reassembled the core of the group. This group, strengthened by the recruitment of some new members, formed the American Negro Academy. The purpose of the academy was to encourage intellectual excellence among the race and to counter the mounting volume of racial propaganda against Negroes. Many distinguished Blacks of the day were elected to membership: Dr. Crummell was the first president, and W. E. B. Du Bois, the second president. During most of its existence, John Wesley Cromwell was the academy's secretary, though near the end of its existence he served as president. Perhaps the academy's most lasting contribution was its publication of twenty-two occasional papers. Three of these papers were authored by John Wesley Cromwell: "The Early Negro Convention Movement," "American Negro Bibliography of the Year," and "The Challenge of the Disenfranchised."

Evidence of Dr. Crummell's early friendship with Grandfather is a letter from Levi, dated December 27, 1875, asking to be remembered to Dr. Crummell. Although Crummell was busy organizing St. Luke's in 1879, he was also having an effect on men such as John Wesley Cromwell throughout the community.

Coincidentally, for me, in trying to understand my Grandfather, one thorny question remained: as an adult, where had his religious affiliation rested? Apparently after some hesitation, he had joined the Methodist Church, and his journal is replete with entries concerning the politics of that denomination. I also found stationery that lists J. W. Cromwell as secretary of the Board of Trustees of Metropolitan A.M.E. Church. His home address, 1439 Pierce Place, is given as the location of the office of the secretary. Finally, there is no evidence that he formally withdrew from the Metropolitan A.M.E. Church. Yet almost from the beginning of Alexander Crummell's arrival in Washington as Episcopal minister, Grandfather was his admirer and friend.

Shortly after St. Luke's Church was opened on Tuesday evening, November 8, 1879 (the official opening was on Thanksgiving Day 1879), John Wesley Cromwell listed himself in the January 17, 1880, issue of the *Advocate* as one of the two members of the church's recently organized choir. According to this piece, he sang bass with a J. William Cole. Furthermore, Cromwell's children and their stepmother all belonged to St. Luke's as did I, his only grandchild. He also was buried from the church.

Beyond his teaching, Cromwell's interests and concerns again went far beyond the classroom to the larger political and civil issues of the day, and once more he returned to the field of journalism with some startling consequences.

After he ceased publishing the *Advocate,* Cromwell was briefly affiliated with *Pioneer Press,* edited by John R. Clifford. When my father was a student at Dartmouth, he frequently mentioned the *Record* and its lively news to my grandfather, but today there is only scant documentation on this paper. There are, to my knowledge, no extant copies of the *Record;* all that is available comes from a few clippings in Grandfather's scrapbook.

The *Record* started as a daily black newspaper on October 24, 1901, with Rev. E. W. Lampton, as the publisher, J. E. Mosely, as the circulation manager, and John W. Cromwell, as editor.[9] If the letters from John Wesley Cromwell Jr. to his father are any indication of the nature of the paper, it seems the *Record* was a spirited paper that was not afraid to cover controversial issues. By June 27, 1902, the *Record* was a weekly paper, appearing on Friday with J. W. Cromwell as the editor.

Apparently, Grandfather's tenure as editor was not without stress, which caused him to resign in 1903. On December 4, 1903, Richard Thompson[10] wrote Emmett Jay Scott saying he never felt much about Cromwell and that Cromwell could be trusted to follow the Booker T. Washington line: "*The Washington Record* under Cromwell's influence is a copperhead sheet. Can't Manley control the policy of the paper? It has no good blood for Tuskegee. Hershaw writes me of Cromwell and his anti-Washington sly digs. He thinks the literaries will discuss Booker T. Washington on the same old lines."[11] On October 15, 1905, Thompson again wrote to Scott describing Cromwell in less than favorable terms: "It is a blessed thing that Cromwell is off *The Record.* Walters may be very little improvement, but his heart is in the right place—and that will help some."

9. There is some confusion about the origin and ownership of this paper. A paper called the *Record,* which was owned by three brothers, Alex, Frank, and Llewelyn Manley, was published from 1897 to 1899 in Wilmington, North Carolina. In 1899, with money borrowed from Congressman George White, another paper called the *Record* was started in Washington, D.C., with Alex Manley as the paper's editor. It was last published in 1904.

10. Richard W. Thompson implied that Manley of the "other" *Record* was involved in the *Record* of which John Cromwell was editor. If this was so, it explains the stress under which Cromwell was working and the basis for his ultimate resignation. It may also be another example of how Booker T. Washington influenced or attempted to influence the policies of the black-owned press. The question is did Cromwell know Washington's role?

11. Louis R. Harlan, ed., *Booker T. Washington Papers* (Urbana: University of Illinois Press, 1972–1989), 7:358, 8:413.

During this period, there was a growing feeling on the part of many black intellectuals that there was a need to challenge Booker T. Washington's leadership and his influence on both Blacks and Whites. Washington himself was not unmindful of this stirring. For "as early as 1900, he had vaguely considered calling a gathering of twelve to fifteen prominent black men to discuss concerted action for racial advancement."[12] A combination of circumstances emerged to encourage these feelings. Three persons, besides Washington, became actors in this drama.

First and foremost was William Monroe Trotter (1872–1934), the editor of the *Boston Guardian,* the fiery newspaper that was unrelenting in its opposition to Washington and his ideas on race relations. When the Boston branch of the National Negro Business League invited Washington to speak at the Columbus Avenue A.M.E. Zion Church on July 30, 1903, Trotter saw this as an opportunity to confront Washington and to end his position as major spokesman for the race. What has been described as the "Boston Riot" began when the meeting opened with a prayer by the pastor of the church, Rev. James H. McMullen. After the preliminary speeches, "William H. Lewis, in introducing T. Thomas Fortune, favorably referred to Washington" and the crowd hissed. Fortune then took over and harangued the crowd. "He was interrupted by Granville Martin, a Trotterite, who was still dressed in his butler's uniform." Martin was ejected from the hall but soon returned, and Fortune completed his speech. "When Lewis tried to introduce Washington . . . pandemonium broke loose again. . . . Scuffling and fist fights broke out all over the hall. Bernard Charles, one of the fighters, was stabbed and then arrested." Trotter tried unsuccessfully to read nine questions he wished Washington to answer. Trotter, his sister Maude, and Martin were then arrested. "When order returned . . . Washington gave a bland account of his leadership and social philosophy with only one interruption." Maude was released almost immediately, but the others were charged. The charges against Charles were dismissed by a jury at the appeals court, but Trotter and Martin were convicted and given the maximum sentence of thirty days in jail.

The ramifications of this episode were extensive. Most notably, it radicalized Du Bois and formed an intellectual bond that saw its fruition when these two brilliant men, Trotter and Du Bois, started the Niagara Movement in 1905. Neither that movement nor the ideological compatibility between the two men endured, but for the time it was critical in the emergence of strong anti-Booker Washington sentiment among Afro-American intellectuals.[13]

12. Louis Harlan, *Booker T. Washington: The Wizard of Tuskegee, 1901–1915* (New York, Oxford University Press, 1983), 63.

13. Ibid., 44–49, 195.

Washington's choice to participate in the conference, T. Thomas Fortune, was the second actor in this drama. Fortune was probably the most militant and most articulate race spokesman in the North, and he was best known for the critical writing in his paper the *Age* on all forms of racial discrimination and on Booker T. Washington. Fortune, interestingly, had begun his career in journalism working for Grandfather on the *People's Advocate*. He was unstable, unpredictable, and later became an ally of Booker T. Washington, serving as his confidant, advisor, publicist, and speechwriter. On November 5, 1903, Washington wrote Fortune suggesting that the *Age* be used to fulfill the need for a strong black national paper. Of course, Washington assured Fortune that he (Fortune) would still be in control, strengthened only by a few additional persons. Always plagued by ill health, financial woes, and alcoholism, Fortune was not fooled but felt, as he wrote to Emmett Scott on February 15, 1904, that he had no alternative. In 1907, the *Age* was sold to Frederick R. Moore through a complicated maneuver engineered by Booker T. Washington.

W. E. B. Du Bois was the third and most important actor in the 1904 drama. His publication in 1903 of *The Souls of Black Folk,* which included his essay "Of Mr. Booker Washington and Others," thrust him on center stage, as it were. Others wrote articles and made pro and con speeches about Booker T. Washington, but this essay "launched the most effective attack on the darling of capitalists who had grasped Washington to their bosom for his accommodationist apostasy at Atlanta."[14] Washington, now anxious to appear to be in communication with all important black leaders, invited Du Bois to Tuskegee and offered him the position of director of research, which Du Bois did not accept. But Du Bois did agree on the desirability of a jointly sponsored conference of leading African Americans.

Washington then made plans to call a secret conference in Carnegie Hall between the 6th and 8th of January 1904. Ostensibly, this meeting of twenty-eight prominent men and women, as described by Washington to Du Bois, was to be conciliatory, "not confined to those who may agree with my own views regarding education and the position which race shall assume in public affairs—shall in every respect represent all interests of the Negro race."

In his detailed and intriguing essay "Conference at Carnegie Hall," Louis Harlan described the considerable jockeying and politicking between Du Bois, representing the "other" faction, and Booker T. Washington over whom to invite

14. Rayford W. Logan and Michael R. Winston, eds., *Dictionary of American Negro Biography* (New York: W. W. Norton, 1982), 237.

and topics to be discussed at the conference.[15] In the fall of 1903, after Andrew Carnegie had assured him of a subsidy to pay the expenses of the conference, Washington finalized January 6–8, 1904, as the date. He then decided to invite some of his white philanthropist friends to meet with the black participants, hoping to impress the black members with the power and prestige of his white allies.

As the conference was designed to be secret—though from its inception apparently certain individuals such as William Monroe Trotter knew and publicized much of the happenings before and during the meetings—few details have survived. Although the black participants remained at odds, Du Bois remembered that the attitude of the white invitees—Andrew Carnegie, three members of the Southern Education Board, William H. Baldwin Jr., Robert C. Ogden, and George Foster Peabody, and three journalists favorable to Booker T. Washington, Oswald Garrison Villard of the *Nation* and the *New York Evening Post,* Lyman Abbott of the *Outlook,* and William Hayes Ward of the *Independent*—"gave a chilling presence near the end of the conference just when it could have been expected to begin resolving the factional conflicts among the Blacks." Whites, apparently, were all most fulsome in praise of Mr. Washington and his work and in support of his ideas, but, according to Du Bois, it was not appropriate to the circumstances.

Kelly Miller, a professor of sociology and mathematics at Howard University, wrote the "Summary of the Proceedings" that did little to capture the ongoing and deep-seated disagreements among the black participants. Nevertheless, the conference did not break up in disarray, and some general propositions were agreed upon, for example, "that an effort should be made to disseminate a knowledge of the truth in regard to all matters affecting our race." Also, by unanimous vote, it was agreed to establish a "Committee with 12 members to be a Bureau of Information and to seek to unify and bring into cooperation the actions of various organizations and sections of the country." Booker T. Washington, Dr. Du Bois, and Hugh M. Browne, the head of an elite industrialist school for Blacks in Pennsylvania, were made members of the committee and authorized to select the other nine members: Archibald Grimké, Kelly Miller, Charles Anderson, T. Thomas Fortune, Dr. Edward H. Morris, J. W. Bowen, Charles Chesnutt, Bishop J. W. Clinton, and H. T. Kealing. Charles E. Bentley of Chicago was named as a substitute for Dr. Morris, who had angered Washington when he

15. Harlan, *Washington: The Wizard of Tuskegee, 1901–1915,* 63–83.

referred to Washington's leadership as a sham in a speech he gave before the Bethel Literary.

While each faction saw some victory coming from the meeting, its real importance was in challenging the leadership and authority of Booker T. Washington, thus making it impossible for him ever again to appear as the omnipotent spokesman for the race, and in propelling Dr. Du Bois into a counterleadership position. Dr. Du Bois immediately saw the need to capture this public split by forming a counterforce in the Niagara Movement.

The February 4, 1904, issue of the *Boston Guardian* had the following headline:

> Editor of The Record Has Resigned
> Mr. J. Wesley Cromwell, the Learned
> and Brilliant Writer, Refuses to be
> Responsible to Editorial Booming
> Booker Washington Written by the
> Latter's Head Printer.

In covering the conference, Cromwell, as editor of the *Record,* had reported the negative opinions toward Blacks by one of the most important sponsors of the meeting, Andrew Carnegie, and by Booker T. Washington himself. Cromwell's account was the only report that included those remarks.

The matter might not have caused such a furor had not Du Bois in the January 1905 issue of *Voice of the Negro,* edited by Jesse Max Barber, made the startling allegation that the Tuskegee machine had spent three thousand dollars during the previous year in bribes to the black press. Washington's many white friends attacked Du Bois, and so persistent was Oswald Garrison Villard in getting the truth that Du Bois was forced to provide the documentation on his charges. He immediately sent urgent letters to those who could and would verify his charges. Grandfather was one of the editors whose support he sought.

> Atlantic University
> Confidential
> Atlanta, Ga. March 15, 1905

Dear Mr. Cromwell:

I want your help in a very important matter. I have been asked by an influential person for some illustrative facts as to Washington's dealing with Negro newspapers. I know that you have some first hand information and I want that information. Your name of course will be suppressed but I want some specimens of the circular matter sent out from Tuskegee, the methods of payment to certain papers, and especially the circumstances of your leaving *The Record.* Anything you say, or any documents sent me will be in perfect confidence and no publication of the facts will be made without previously gaining your full consent. Will you kindly refer to other sources of exact information? They are putting up a pretty conspiracy against Negro manhood in New York but we can beat it if we will. Let me hear from you if possible within 24 hours.

Sincerely yours,
W. E. B. Du Bois

On March 24, 1905, Du Bois, in response to the note he had received on March 13th, wrote Villard an extensive letter giving him in detail the basis for his charges and stating that he had been reluctant to use names because of the probable repercussions—mentioning Cromwell, in particular, who could lose his job as teacher in the colored schools.[16] Although, he added, the "*Record* under Cromwell was always moderate and saw things both to praise and condemn."

As "Exhibit B" of twelve exhibits, he included Cromwell's letter of March 18, 1905, in response to his letter of the 15th:

While I was with *The Record* I got definite information that there was a literary bureau at Tuskegee. In the month of September 1903, Mr. Frank Manly, one of the owners of that paper, almost immediately after the adjournment of the Business Men's Convention held at Richmond, left this city to take a place at Tuskegee. Shortly after this items respecting Tuskegee and Mr. Washington appeared quite regularly. It was rare that this copy passed through my hands.

When your famous N.Y. conference was held, I picked up the salient points of the gathering and gave it out. So accurate was the account that The Wizard was evidently baffled. But Frank Manly suddenly came here from Tuskegee and had published an account diametrically opposite in spirit to the story of Morris' celebrated talk on "Shams" that I had published, as the contribution of a "Staff Correspondent." I was consulted about its publication and the understanding was that it should appear only as that of an "occasional" correspondent and not on the editorial page. When this understanding between me and Mr. G. was violated, my self-respect forced me to resign. It was the general belief that F. M. came here all the way from Tuskegee to bring things to a head and provide a

16. Harlan, ed., *Booker T. Washington Papers,* 8:224–29.

disagreement. I learned from a brother of his that a certain sum—say $40 a month—was received regularly here by the business manager to help float the paper, it will naturally suggest itself to you that Mr. F. M. could not afford to send that amount of his own pocket regularly to help the paper.

> Very truly yours,
> J. W. Cromwell

Du Bois gratuitously added in his letter to Villard, "I was not the first to make this charge. It was common property among colored people, spoken and laughed about and repeatedly charged in the newspapers."[17]

The *Guardian* (there is no date on the clipping) noted Grandfather's resignation: "John Wesley Cromwell, a man of honesty, courage and ability, to say nothing of intelligence, education, learning and literary talent resigned because one Manly, the printer at Tuskegee and part owner of *The Record,* felt it necessary to countermand Cromwell. We congratulate Mr. Cromwell that he refused to be under even the appearance of treason to his race."

Yet, though undocumented, things must have improved at the *Record* and the publicity may not have hurt Cromwell's status, for on May 3, 1905, the *Guardian* again reported on events around Cromwell and the *Record.* The headlines to this article were,

> Cromwell Again Editor of *The Record.* Washington, D.C.
> Colored Paper Passes From Control of Booker Washington.
> J. W. Cromwell Had Resigned Rather Than Conceal part of
> Carnegie Interview. Head Printer of Tuskegee Then Owned
> Wanted Carnegie's Attack on Federal Election Law Omitted.
> New Owner Gives Editor Free Scope.

Unfortunately, there is no documentation, aside from a few newspaper clippings, that provides any information on Grandfather's second affiliation with the *Record,* and he makes no mention of it in his journal. It must have ceased publication in 1905, for unknown reasons.

No longer having a paper to edit, Cromwell wrote articles and began research on his seminal work *The Negro in American History,* which was published by the American Negro Academy in 1914.

---

17. Ibid., 8:225.

In 1904, Grandfather published a twelve-page pamphlet entitled *The Jim Crow Negro*. This character is the happy-go-lucky-creature, ready to dance the jig, act the clown, or sink his manhood in whatever form most likely to elicit the smile and approval of the white man; he was the lineal descendant of slavery days, the good old darkey. This type of Negro, Cromwell wrote, is very influential and deserves careful consideration; he believes himself to be of an inferior race, with no interest in education or in educated Negroes, such as doctors, teachers, or ministers. Cromwell attributed the creeping strength of segregation in American life to the behavior of this Jim Crow Negro whom, he argued, we must "chain, cast out into utter darkness."

Between 1910 and 1911, Cromwell edited and published with R. L. Pendleton four American Negro monographs: *The Confession: Trial and Execution of Nat Turner, Contemporary Evolution of the Negro Race* by Rev. Thomas G. Harper; *Benjamin Banneker* by John H. B. Latrobe; and *Social Evolution of the Black South* by W. E. B. Du Bois.

Cromwell's *The Negro in American History*, described by James F. Hanley as a credible work for its time, was published twenty-nine years after *History of the Negro Race in America from 1619 to 1880* by George Washington Williams and eight years before the first edition of *The Negro in Our History* by Carter G. Woodson, which was widely regarded as the pioneer work in the field of Afro-American history.

The Negro in American History covers the slave trade and slavery, slave insurrections, the convention movement, Reconstruction, wars, the Negro church, education, and other subjects. But its main contents are biographical sketches of prominent African Americans: Phillis Wheatley, Benjamin Banneker, Paul Cuffe, Sojourner Truth, John Mercer Langston, Frederick Douglass, Booker Tallifero Washington, Henry Ossawa Tanner, Edward Blyden, Paul Lawrence Dunbar, Henry Highland Garnet, Alexander Crummell, John F. Cook and his sons, John Jr. and George F. T., Daniel Alexander Payne, Joseph Charles Price, Robert Brown Elliott, Blanche Kelso Bruce, and Fanny M. Jackson Coppin.

John Wesley Cromwell published two articles in the *Journal of Negro History*, edited by Woodson: "The Aftermath of Nat Turner's Insurrection" and "The First Negro Churches in the District of Columbia."[18]

With his lifelong passion for writing and publishing, it is not surprising that

---

18. "The Aftermath of Nat Turner's Insurrection," *Journal of Negro History* 5, no. 2 (April 1920): 208–34; "The First Negro Churches in the District of Columbia," *Journal of Negro History* 7, no. 1 (January 1922).

Grandfather would be a part of that growing group of African American bibliophiles in Philadelphia, New York, and Boston who saw the importance of collecting books in their field of interest. In 1915, Cromwell, with these individuals, organized the Negro Book Collectors Exchange in an effort to centralize all literature written by colored persons. They were "to contact all Negro book collectors throughout the United States, Africa, the West Indies and South America and Europe and request copies of books written by Negro authors and compile a bibliography of all black authors and their works."[19] John Cromwell was vice president of this group and the other officers—all serious collectors—were Henry Proctor Slaughter, president; Arthur A. Schomburg, secretary-treasurer; Rev. Charles Douglass Martin, librarian; John Edward Bruce, publicity agent; and Daniel A. Murray, registrar. I do not know what happened to this organization, but as most of the members were old and as professional librarians began to show an interest in collecting in this field, it probably just disappeared.

During the ascendancy of Booker T. Washington from his speech in 1895 at the Cotton States and International Exposition in Atlanta until his death in 1915, many black leaders and intellectuals felt the weight of his power and the pain of his scorn. Reference has already been made to Booker T. Washington's reaction to Grandfather's reporting in the *Record* of Washington's "secret meeting." Until that time, the differences in educational philosophy between the two men had not been great, for as August Meier noted, "Cromwell had been a defender of industrial education and separate schools since the 1870s and in 1896 defended Washington's philosophy of education before The Bethel Literary Society."[20]

In December 1900, Booker T. Washington also quoted extensively from facts attributed to Cromwell in his *International Monthly* article "The American Negro and His Economic Value." By 1903, however, Cromwell was anti-Washington and a believer in political means of racial advancement.

Meier argued that the break between the two men came in 1902 when Washington wrote a bland recommendation in support of Cromwell's candidacy for the presidency of Langston University in Oklahoma, but there is little evidence that Cromwell really wanted this position.

19. Elinor Des Verney Sinnette, W. Paul Coates, and Thomas C. Battle, eds., *Black Bibliophiles and Collectors: Preservers of Black History* (Washington, D.C.: Howard University Press, 1990), 10.

20. August Meier, *Negro Thought in America, 1880–1915: Radical Ideologies in the Age of Booker T. Washington* (Ann Arbor: University of Michigan Press, 1963), 48, 94, 213.

South Weymouth, Mass. June 30, 1902

Mr. J. W. Cromwell

17000 Vermont Avenue, N.W., Washington, D.C.

My dear Cromwell:

I have been absent from my mail for several days and this accounts for the delay in answering your letter. Enclosed I send you a recommendation which I hope will answer your purpose.

Please let me know when I can serve you in any manner.

Yours truly,

Booker T. Washington

June 30, 1902

To Whom It May Concern:

This letter is to state that I have known Mr. J. W. Cromwell, of Washington, D.C. for a number of years, and that in my opinion he is a man of ripe scholarship and of the highest moral integrity, and he has always sustained the confidence of the best class of people of both races in the District of Columbia and in other places where he is known.

Booker T. Washington

Indeed, Grandfather stated that he had not sought the position, but he did solicit letters of support from Archibald Grimké and Walter Brooks. Whitefield McKinlay asked Grandfather to seek Washington's support. After this time, Meier contends that "Cromwell became an ardent radical . . . declaring that both education and material development wait on and are subordinate to political life." I have no evidence that Grandfather ever intended to leave Washington, D.C., for Oklahoma, however bad things seemed for him at the time in the job market. I think he began to see other dimensions of Washington's persona, but it is quite likely that Washington never forgave Grandfather for the *Record*'s disclosure and for his willingness to support Du Bois. Washington was able to show his hostility in a covert and long-lasting manner through the behavior of Roscoe Conkling Bruce.

Roscoe Conkling Bruce (1879–1950) was the only child of Blanche Kelso Bruce, the second African American senator from Mississippi, and his wife, the former Josephine B. Wilson. After attending M Street High School in Washington, Roscoe enrolled at the Phillips Exeter Academy and later at Harvard College, from which he graduated Phi Beta Kappa and magna cum laude in 1902.

In 1898, the same year 1898 that Roscoe entered Harvard, his father died. Roscoe had not been particularly close to his father because the senator had a rigorous schedule and because Roscoe was away at school. But the senator and Booker T. Washington were friends. After Washington's famous 1895 Atlanta speech, Frederick Douglass's death that same year, and now the senator's death, Washington was indisputably the most prominent African American leader. Before Roscoe entered college, Washington invited the widowed Mrs. Bruce, who was extremely prominent and attractive, to come to Tuskegee as lady principal (dean of women). She accepted his offer and worked for Washington from 1899 to 1902.

By 1900 Roscoe was a junior in college and Washington was being roundly attacked by several well-known African American leaders in Boston—most notably, William Monroe Trotter, the editor of the *Guardian,* George W. Forbes, a librarian, and Clement G. Morgan, a lawyer and politician. As a student Roscoe was receiving public acclaim for his literary and debating skills so Washington felt Roscoe could be of assistance to him by keeping an eye on these dissident leaders, so he enlisted Roscoe to conduct whatever espionage he could. Roscoe rose to the occasion, clipping newspaper articles from the local press and trying to identify all the local Blacks who were the greatest threat to Washington. He monitored lectures given by these detractors and even suggested ways of eliminating their influence, such as closing down the *Guardian* and having Forbes sanctioned by his employers at the Boston Public Library. The result of this activity was information for Washington and for Roscoe the development of a mentor—a protégé relationship with the most powerful black man in America.

Several months before Roscoe's graduation, Washington offered him a position at Tuskegee as head of the Academic Department, which he accepted because he believed Washington was serious about establishing an academic department to broaden the courses at Tuskegee, and also because in spite of his honors, it was the most favorable option he had.

His early family experiences and his time at Harvard had given Roscoe an attitude of arrogance and elitism, of a man only willing to know and respect comparable intellectuals. This manner did not endear him to the teachers or the other administrators in Washington's inner circle who were older but less educated than he. Roscoe, disliking Tuskegee from the first, learned little from his experience there, except that Booker T. Washington was a dictatorial, controlling, and vengeful employer.

In 1905, when the opportunity came, Roscoe sought Washington's permission to accept the principalship of the Armstrong Manual Training School in Washington, D.C. Although requiring Roscoe to stay an additional twelve months at

Tuskegee, Washington did not send a letter of recommendation for him until he learned that his nemesis Du Bois was also seeking a position in the Washington schools. His motivation in recommending Bruce seemed to be an effort to block Du Bois more than to praise Bruce. In any case, Roscoe left in apparent good favor with Washington.

Roscoe was returning to the city of his birth where he and his wife, Clara, had many friends and had moved within a small elitist circle. The schools for Blacks had been imaginatively and rigorously designed. Black teachers of superior education had been recruited. But after 1900 the Board of Education, following the pattern of many other cities, gradually removed African Americans from administrative positions within the schools to ensure that schools for Blacks and the related black faculty and administrators never gained too much power or control. Washington as a city was becoming more discriminatory toward Blacks.

Whether due to Bruce's hard work, discipline, or demeanor, or Washington's endorsement, the white board members were sufficiently impressed to appoint Bruce to the post of assistant superintendent of colored schools, effective September 1907. Bruce was answerable to the white superintendent and the Board of Education, on which ironically his father had served many years before.

Bruce's youth, lack of an advanced degree, and experience in a less-than-rigorous academic institution made him from the first unpopular in this African American community. In addition, apparently his manner of administration was considered high-handed, and it was thought that he favored for promotion only those from his class or circle. Bruce was not considered qualified to hold a position that was certainly the most prestigious position available for an African American in the District of Columbia's public school system, and it is important to remember that there were few, if any, channels of mobility for Blacks at the time in the city. As Willard Gatewood reported, "Controversy marked Roscoe Bruce's tenure as Assistant Superintendent of Washington Colored Schools almost from the beginning." Any protection offered Bruce by his affiliation with Booker T. Washington was ended with Washington's death in 1915. That year although he had enjoyed early support of Calvin Chase, the powerful publisher of the black weekly the *Washington Bee* had characterized Bruce as "the most despised man in the city." Yet, according to Gatewood, "despite the growing opposition among Blacks . . . he remained in good standing with the white majority of the Board of Education."[21]

In 1911, John Cromwell was principal of the Ivy City School, which was to be

21. Willard B. Gatewood, *Aristocrats of Color: The Black Elite, 1880–1920* (Bloomington: Indiana University Press, 1990), 325.

rebuilt and named for Alexander Crummell. No doubt there was much discussion about who would have the honor of being the principal of this new school. John Cromwell was clearly the most logical choice by virtue of his long, close friendship with Alexander Crummell and his long tenure as teacher and principal in the local schools. Furthermore, Cromwell was a known public figure. It should have been a foregone conclusion, but John Cromwell knew he was not a favorite of Roscoe Bruce and knew about the problems in Roscoe Bruce's administration, all of which he must have conveyed to his friend, John Bruce.

On June 30, 1911, John Bruce wrote, "I note what you say about the Alexander Crummell School to be opened in October, and I am mighty pleased that our grand old man of blessed memory is to be thus remembered. And how appropriate this monument to his moral and public worth. What a triumph for the race." Sensing there may be problems ahead, Bruce added in a postscript on August 26, 1911, "I trust nothing unexpected will happen to prevent your appointment as principal of AC."

The records of the Board of Education prove that Bruce's fears were warranted. While Grandfather was kept on as principal when the Ivy City School became the Crummell School in 1911, he was not satisfied with his treatment. On February 18, 1913, he wrote to Dr. William M. Davidson, the superintendent of the schools and Roscoe Bruce's superior, applying for longevity pay of $495 "to which the recent ruling of the Controller of Treasury makes him legally eligible." On February 24, 1913, Superintendent Davidson denied Grandfather's request, citing a January 15, 1913, policy statement made by R. J. Tracewell, the comptroller of the Office of the Treasury. As evidence, Davidson enclosed a copy of the detailed policy statement in the letter. Grandfather, as a lawyer, and being familiar with the governmental bureaucratic subterfuge, was not dissuaded. On January 17, 1914, he wrote Mr. McKinlay (probably Whitefield McKinlay), now making claim for a larger amount—$605—because of the elapsed time. Seeking support from outside the system was of no avail.

In spite of this dispute, Cromwell was still at the Crummell School in 1917, but the following year he was transferred from the Crummell School to the Garnet-Patterson-Phelps School. At Crummell, he had been the principal and had taught sixth grade, but at Garnet-Patterson-Phelps, he was just a sixth-grade teacher. In February 1919, he was transferred again; this time he was moved to the Bell School, where instead of being a sixth-grade teacher, he became a fourth-grade teacher. Roscoe Bruce's letter to Grandfather the same month and year does not mention the last transfer to the Bell School but does indicate a demotion in status or ranking for Grandfather and the anticipation that he might seek some explanation for this demotion.

13 February 1919

Mr. John W. Cromwell, Sr.
1439 Swann Street, N.W.
Washington, D.C.
My dear Mr. Cromwell:

At the request of this office the Supervising Principal of the Eleventh Division has rerated you as a teacher of the 6th grade at the Garnet-Patterson-Phelps School. A copy of this rating is enclosed for your information.

It is my duty to call your attention with some emphasis to the fact that the total rating is only 60. Under the circumstances, I would earnestly advise you to confer at once with the Supervising Principal in reference to your service, and to confer also, if you so desire, with the Superintendent of schools and me.

Sincerely yours
Roscoe C. Bruce
Assistant Superintendent of Schools

Grandfather had apparently shared some of his frustrations and concerns over his treatment with his friend John Bruce, who in a June 26, 1915, letter to Grandfather, wrote that he was not surprised by Roscoe Conkling Bruce's behavior:

Young Bruce is a chip off the old block. His dad was a high roller as I knew personally and his weakness was for rope meat [white women] and Bourbon likker. Naturally he would transmit these native and acquired gifts to his son and heir. I don't think his mother will be able to turn the trick she used to turn—public officials are getting wise to tricks of this class of ladies and more careful in granting of favors to them. I may be mistaken in this but I believe young Roscoe Bruce will have to do without a public office for a long time and that the blandishments and sweet words of his Ma will not avail in restoring his name to the payroll.

In 1919, Grandfather was seventy-three years of age and eligible for retirement, but instead of retiring, displaying a sense of dignity, he applied for and received a leave of absence for educational purposes on September 1, 1919.

By January 15, 1920, the board had received and approved Cromwell's request for retirement. They deemed, since he had reached (even passed) the mandatory age, that his request should be automatically granted "unless in the judgment of two-thirds of the Board of Education such a teacher should be longer retained for the good of the Service."

While Grandfather was suffering in his rejection and lack of appreciation for his stature in the community and years of service in the public schools, his was but a small part of the larger picture. The black community was ready for Roscoe Conkling Bruce himself to leave or to be fired. What had been simmering for several years finally reached the boiling point in 1919.[22] The Board of Education could no longer protect Roscoe Bruce. The Parents' League threatened to go to the Congress if the board did not remove Bruce, whom they charged as being "pedagogically unfit and administratively unfit, lacking educational qualifications and experience, having no constructive policy, recommending inexperienced persons for principals, failing to unify educational work and wasting public money." Not specified in these charges was the additional one of lacking moral character.

But the community was well aware of Bruce's specific failures: he had attempted to weaken the academic curriculum of the schools by replacing it with industrial education more comparable to the Tuskegee model; in 1914 he fired the popular and well-connected Dr. William Bruce Evans from the principalship of the Armstrong Manual Training School; and most important, in 1919, he was at the center of a court proceeding and sex scandal in the black schools after it was revealed that he had allowed a phony white anthropologist known as Professor

22. As far back as 1906, there seems to have been considerable turmoil in the public schools relating to the salaries of teachers and the general inefficiency of the administrators, and John Wesley Cromwell was not unaffected by this. His problem appears to have been primarily with Roscoe C. Bruce, whose opinion of Cromwell, having come to Washington from Tuskegee, could have been influenced by Booker T. Washington. F. L. Cardoza himself, later to come into difficulty with the board, and some other teachers spoke against John Wesley Cromwell's competence. But I believe that this charge was less about Cromwell than it was a stroke to help Bruce and to diminish Wilder Montgomery, then superintendent of schools, a position Cardoza wanted for himself. John Wesley Cromwell was moved, however, from school to school. In 1907, after being transferred to the Ivy City School, with a change in teaching assignment from the eighth grade to the seventh grade, his salary was decreased by four hundred dollars.

In July 1919, the Board of Education appointed a committee to investigate the educational and administrative efficiency of Bruce. During this same period, a Parents' League was organized at the Metropolitan A.M.E. Church with Mrs. Tanner, the pastor's wife, as chairperson and with officers from many other denominations. This group called many anti-Bruce meetings and joined in the battle to oust him. The committee, appointed by the Board of Education under the chairmanship of H. Barrett Learned, submitted a sixteen-page report finding "Roscoe C. Bruce fitted by education, training and experience to serve as Assistant Superintendent of Schools." A member of the committee, Fountain Peyton, a practicing attorney, dissented and submitted a thirty-one page minority report in October 1919, which found that Bruce "does not measure up in his education qualification to the demands requisite for his office . . . has been proven grossly inefficient . . . has wastefully expended public money . . . is guilty of administrative inefficiency through indisputable proof of lack of character . . . shown to be undependable, lacking in directness, candor, frankness and truthfulness . . . and manly insistence." Peyton's report recommended that Bruce be separated from official service in the public schools.

H. M. S. Moens to take photographs of black female students as part of his study to show the physical similarities between Blacks and Whites. The photographs showed the young girls at various stages of undress, and many of them with no clothing at all.

But Bruce, it should be noted, had Afro-American history incorporated at all levels of the schools he supervised as a means of giving the children and youth a sense of pride in their race and self-confidence in knowing the accomplishments of Blacks.[23]

Lawrence Otis Graham, in his study of the Bruce family, *The Senator and the Socialite,* provides a full and fascinating picture of Bruce's next years. In my story, the Bruce family is absent—his mother, Josephine, and his wife, Clara, and his three children—but they are all an important part of this period of Bruce's life. Unable to find a suitable position in Washington, in 1921 Bruce accepted the principalship of a small black school in rural Kendal, West Virginia. Although he disliked it from the start, he was unable to find a better position, so he remained there. His mother, on whom he was most dependent, joined him there and died from a heart attack in her sleep in February 1923. In May of that same year, Bruce resigned his position and returned to the family farm in Hyattsville, Maryland, supporting his family by income from his mother's estate and a chicken-and-egg farm he ran. In 1926, he was offered the editorship of a new volume, *Who's Who in Colored America,* from which he resigned two years later because he did not receive his promised salary. After graduating from the Washington, D.C., public schools, his three children continued their educations in the North at Harvard, Radcliffe, and Exeter. Clara entered and was the first black woman to graduate from Boston University School of Law. Bruce himself applied to but was never accepted at the University of Chicago Law School.

These years for Bruce were frustrating and disappointing, but on August 26, 1927, his fortune at last improved when he and his wife were employed by John D. Rockefeller as the resident manager and assistant, respectively, for the new Paul Lawrence Dunbar Apartments in Harlem. This five hundred-unit family complex was designed for middle-income Blacks who wanted to own rather than to rent.[24]

By the time Bruce had received what he considered to be an appropriate position and status in the black community, Grandfather had died. While alive,

23. "Report of the Assistant Superintendent in Charge of Colored Schools, 1914–1915," in *Report of the Board of Education* (Washington, D.C., 1915), 249.

24. For more on the Bruce family, see Lawrence Otis Graham, *The Senator and the Socialite* (New York: Harper Collins, 2006).

however, learning of Bruce's wandering and lack of satisfactory employment must have given Grandfather a quiet sense of victory. John E. Bruce, writing in his inimitable style on June 1, 1921, summed up the matter in no uncertain way, without mentioning the instigator: Booker T. Washington, Roscoe Conkling Bruce's mentor and friend.

Please note change of address   260 W. 136 St. NYC
                                                 June 1/21

Dear Friend Cromwell:

When I read of Roscoe Conkling Bruce's coup to escape the meat axe I laughed and said to myself "that's a *neat* way Roscoe has discovered to save his feelings and his bacon", the word "indefinite is far reaching and elastic—samething—and we can now sing true CM:-Belainn we rejoice

To see the cuss removed. Amen, *Selah*!

Good riddance of bad rubbish. I received your letter yesterday and noticed that you also had heard the news and was feeling somewhat hilarious judging from your language. I congratulate the Parents League on its victory in forcing from the school such as an odoriferous onion as Roscoe Conkling Bruce, and I join with you in thanksgiving over the event which has eventuated to your evident satisfaction. Like a played out pugilist, Roscoe "caint kum back." He has eliminated himself by that sweet word "*indefinite*"—it means world without end to be, and he wont see the end of it. May we never see his like again. He did you a dirty trick and as you well say "he knows how it feels to be run over by the steam roller."

Yours Sincerely
Bruce Grit

Grandfather was a journalist, an educator, and a lawyer. He was also an organization man from his earliest days in Philadelphia when he was active in groups of importance to young African Americans, and as a young man, the Virginia Educational Association was important to him; but in his more mature years, the American Negro Academy and the Bethel Literary and Historical Association were his favorites. Although he was a Mason and an Odd Fellow, neither organization seemed of importance to him. The A.M.E. Church, of which he was a member most of his adult life, was also of less influence.

Cromwell saw his role as editor, first of the *People's Advocate* and then of the *Record,* as the means of enlightening and influencing black Americans. Aside from the editorial positions he took in these papers, his stands on other issues are less well known. August Meier documented Cromwell's position from available *Advocate* editorials and, more important, from the position he took at many meetings of the Bethel Literary.[25] John W. Cromwell Sr. believed, as did his father, Willis Hodges Cromwell, in supporting black business, even when it was more costly than supporting white business, to give the black man a chance to become an equal partner to his white competitor. He believed there was value in industrial education for Blacks but not as a universal policy; he saw the value of separate schools but as the quotation from his son verifies, not to exclude the possibility of attendance at mixed schools; and most important, he thought that education and material development should be subordinate to a political life.

In 1924, just a few years before his death, Grandfather wrote the last paper published by the American Negro Academy, "The Challenge of the Disfranchised: A Plea for the Enforcement of the 15th Amendment."[26] In this article were his fundamental and final beliefs:

> My opinion is the remedy should take the form of direct legislation to enforce the 15th Amendment by action providing the penalties of fines and imprisonment at the discretion of the United States Court for all discriminations by state, country or municipal officers in the matter of the registration of citizen or citizens, or the casting of a vote where this discrimination exists or is implied. The supreme sanction of the general government guaranteeing impartial, equal employment by the Negro in his franchise in all elections for the nation *should be paramount.*

This, the last pronouncement by John W. Cromwell Sr., is reminiscent of the fires of the earlier fighter in the postbellum South, an opponent of Booker T. Washington, and the survivor of Roscoe Bruce's vendetta.

25. Meier, *Negro Thought in America, 1880–1915,* 48, 50, 213.

26. Ernest Kaiser, ed., *The American Negro Academy Occasional Papers 1–22* (New York: Arno Press and the New York Times, 1969), 3–10.

John Wesley Cromwell Sr., as a young man of about twenty-five years of age, and his wife, Lucy McGuinn Cromwell.

Lucy, Otelia, and Mary Cromwell (left) and Larcie (Martha), Fanny, and John (right), children of John Wesley Cromwell Sr. and Lucy McGuinn Cromwell.

Winnie McGuinn Lewis,
Lucy McGuinn Cromwell's
sister.

Alexander Crummell, the
distinguished minister of St.
Luke's Episcopal Church in
Washington, D.C.

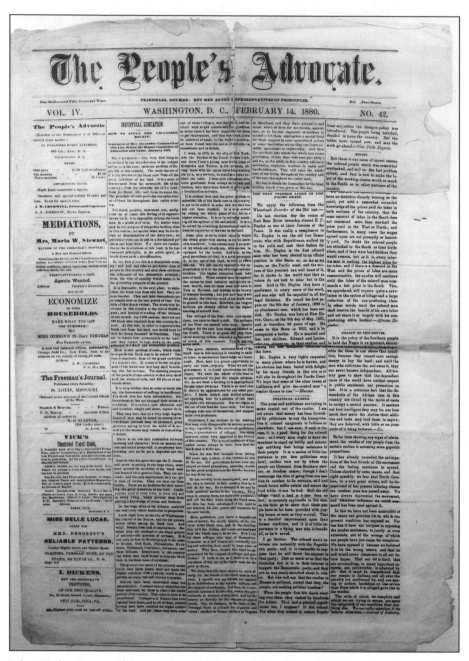

John Wesley Cromwell Sr. was the publisher and the editor of the *People's Advocate* from 1876 to 1890.

The Crummell School, named for Alexander Crummell, in Washington, D.C. John Wesley Cromwell Sr. was principal of the school from 1911 to 1916.

The Bethel Historical Society, meeting for Wilberforce. Pictured here are W. E. B. Du Bois, William S. Scarborough, John W. Cromwell, Kelly Miller, Francis Grimké, William Tunnell, William Calvin Chase, and Jesse Moorland.

Roscoe Conkling Bruce, 1879–1950. (Courtesy of the Moorland-Spingarn Research Center, Howard University.)

Chapter 6

"Ambition for Place or Fame Is Not My Besetting Folly"

Letters from Otelia Cromwell to John Wesley Cromwell Sr.

❧ ❧

Otelia Cromwell was born in Washington, D.C., on April 8, 1874. She was the first child of Lucy McGuinn and John Wesley Cromwell.

Her mother died when Otelia was only twelve years old, leaving her as the oldest of six children and thus with a sense of responsibility for her siblings' welfare, which she manifested throughout their lives. Otelia and three of her siblings—Mary, Lucy, and John—remained in the same household at 1815 13th Street N.W., until their deaths. Fanny, the youngest of the six, lived with her father and stepmother, and Larcie married and moved a few blocks away to 1823 Corcoran Street N.W. Otelia outlived all of her brothers and sisters. She died at the family home on April 25, 1972.

Otelia Cromwell received her early education in the public schools of Washington, including M Street High School, the predecessor of the well-known Dunbar High School. After graduating from the Miner Normal School in Washington, she taught for six years in the public schools of that city before entering Smith College in Northampton, Massachusetts. In 1900, she was the first Black to receive a degree from Smith.

Upon returning to Washington, Otelia Cromwell once again began teaching in the public schools—briefly at the elementary level, later at the high school level at M Street and Armstrong high schools—until 1922.

At this point, the conflict began that she was to have with the Board of Education off and on for the rest of her life. An interpretation of this goes beyond the scope of this profile, but it is important to remember that Otelia Cromwell was attempting to perform in a segregated system as a black woman with more education than any of her black male supervisors and probably more than the Whites on the other side of the line in the same general system. This did not bode well for her popularity, given her reputation for integrity and forthrightness. Her first difficulty was in not quietly accepting a transfer from M Street, the classical high school, to Armstrong, the trade and technical high school. As she wrote in a letter to her father, she felt as if she had been tricked into taking this assignment. She objected but nevertheless was transferred. Records show that while at Armstrong, she was a popular and respected teacher.

After receiving her master's in English from Columbia University in 1910, Otelia spent a summer studying at the Wahrendorf Tochterschule in Rostock, Germany. She later took additional courses at the University of Pennsylvania and the University of Chicago. Then she decided to pursue her graduate studies in English literature at Yale.

During this period, either in late 1921 or early January, 1922, Otelia Cromwell was offered a promotion from teacher of English at Armstrong to head of the Department of English and History in the senior and junior high schools. Apparently, she refused this position because she had already decided to go back to Yale, for on January 22, 1922, the black assistant superintendent wrote her that he "could not subscribe to the policy of allowing the interests of the school system to suffer for the mere gratification of an employee's personal desire . . . it is in the interests of the public school children of Washington that you postpone the date of the completion of the work leading to that degree." "This office," he continued, "is convinced that it is your duty to rely upon the combined judgment of your superior officers with respect to the Head of Department of English and History."[1]

At that time, even without a Ph.D., Otelia Cromwell was undoubtedly the best-qualified candidate available because of her education and experience; hence a compromise between Otelia and the assistant superintendent must have been reached, for she continued to pursue her Ph.D. at Yale but accepted the position as head of the English and history department when it was offered to her again in January 1924.

---

1. The official records show that in 1921 she was granted a four-month leave from teaching at Armstrong, presumably to go to Yale. By September 1922, she had been reinstated as teacher of English at Armstrong. Aunt Otelia's manner was always calm and dignified so she managed to achieve her goals in the system, something her brother John was not able to do.

In 1926, she was awarded the Ph.D. in English from Yale, and her dissertation, *Thomas Heywood, Dramatist: A Study in Elizabethan Drama of Everyday Life*, was published by the Yale University Press in 1928. She dedicated this work to her parents.

In 1927, she appointed a Committee of Outstanding Teachers of English to study the potential of character-building through the study of English. On April 28, 1928, the committee of twenty-four submitted an impressive report of "176 pages which they hoped would measure up to her expectations and meet with her approval."

She returned to Northampton in 1929 to be initiated into Phi Beta Kappa as Smith did not have a chapter when she was a student. The following year, after the Miner Normal School had been upgraded to a four-year college, Otelia Cromwell was appointed professor of the Division of English Language and Literature. She would remain here until her retirement in 1944.

Otelia Cromwell was a consummate scholar as well as an extraordinary teacher. After her first trip to Germany to broaden her knowledge, she made two additional trips to Europe and England. In 1931, Otelia collaborated with Eva B. Dykes and Lorenzo Dow Turner, then the only three Blacks with Ph.D.'s in English, on *Readings from Negro Authors, for Schools and Colleges,* one of the first collections of its kind published in the United States. She also published four articles and two reviews in outstanding journals.[2]

In 1932, Otelia Cromwell was invited to join the Board of Directors of *The Encyclopedia of The Negro* under the chairmanship of Anson Phelps Stokes. This board, which included W. E. B. Du Bois, had only one other woman among its nineteen members and she was white: Florence Read, the president of Spelman College.[3]

---

2. Cromwell, Turner, Dykes, eds., *Readings from Negro Authors, for Schools and Colleges* (New York: Harcourt, Brace, 1931). For more on Cromwell's publications, see "A Question of Motif," *English Journal* 9, no. 9 (November 1928): 508–18; "Preparation for Freshman Composition," *English Journal* 25, no. 7 (September 1936): 551–56; "Essential Values in Education," *Harvard Educational Review* 10, no. 3 (May 1940): 289–99; "Democracy and the Negro," *American Scholar* 13 (Spring 1944): 149–61; "Thomas Heywood et Le Drame Domestique Elizabethan," *Collection des Etudes Anglaises 4,* by Michel Grivelet, 10, no. 1 (Winter 1959): 120; review of *Century of Struggle: The Women's Right Movement in the United States,* by Eleanor Flexnor, *New-York Historical Society Quarterly* 45, no. 1 (January 1960): 125–26.

3. To my knowledge, there has not been a review of the history of the *Negro Encyclopedia*. Based on Aunt Otelia's records, the idea was originally that of Anson Phelps Stokes, the president of the Phelps-Stokes Foundation. Dr. Stokes assembled "representative white and colored scholars and educational leaders at Howard University in the winter of 1931–1932 who discussed and unanimously voted on the need for an encyclopedia, its scope, character of articles, etc." However, as early as 1909, Carter G. Woodson (1875–1950) had made plans to publish an *Encyclopedia Africana*.

Otelia Cromwell was a revered teacher, and upon her retirement, the following statement appeared in the minutes of the Board of Education for the District of Columbia on February 16, 1944:

> The excellence of Professor Cromwell's training was reflected in her teaching . . . She developed among her students a keen appreciation of beauty and truth . . . She daily emphasized the value of thoroughness and open-mindedness in her own classroom preparation . . . The influence she exerted in her position cannot be easily estimated. Encouraging students to pursue graduate work in leading universities, stimulating them to write. She was never too busy to listen to their problems or to entertain them in small groups in her home.

In addition, a former student, then a teacher herself, wrote,

> Dr. Cromwell guided her pupils in the direction of their abilities and awakened them to their potentialities long before guidance, as a term, found its way into educational parlance. Through the years pupils and former pupils have continued to turn to Dr. Cromwell for the spiritual and intellectual guidance begun in this fine pupil-teacher relationship . . . pupils a generation ago paid tribute to the living memory of Dr. Cromwell's outstanding successes as a teacher. Her influence was the only tie that bound this group of persons, but it was enough to call them from all walks of life to do her honor. No words could recapture the élan vital of that meeting.

Well-educated Blacks suffered discrimination by Whites in various forms. Three and a half years after Otelia Cromwell's retirement, the Federation of Teachers Local 27, which included in its membership and leadership some of her former students, wrote the Board of Education requesting that she be awarded the title of professor emeritus. The board complied with that request and accordingly wrote to Otelia Cromwell. After writing to the teachers union to thank them for their intercession on her behalf, however, Otelia wrote to the board itself, refusing their offer and reminding them of the passage of time since her retirement and the obligation of the educational body not the union to bestow such status.

In 1950, at the seventy-fifth anniversary celebration of the founding of Smith College, Otelia Cromwell was one of the ten people to receive an honorary degree. The publicity given this occasion in the *New York Times* and elsewhere caused many friends and classmates to write her congratulatory letters.

Immediately upon her retirement, Otelia Cromwell began what was to be her major scholarly work, *The Life of Lucretia Mott,* which was published by the Harvard University Press in 1958. The years she devoted to researching this book reveal her penchant for thoroughness. No stone was left unturned as she searched for material on every facet of her subject's life: her family, the Quaker movement, and the abolition movement in this country and abroad. A perusal of the dozens of letters she wrote seeking information or thanking those who had assisted her provides a striking example of serious academic research. This book, dedicated to her mother's sister Winnie, seems to be a turning away from racial subjects again, or at least a compromise in that direction, for Lucretia Mott was, as the saying goes, certainly "square on the racial question."

Otelia Cromwell was a member of the Smith College Alumnae Association, the College Club, the Association of University Women, the Writers Club, the NAACP, the Modern Language Association, and St. Luke's Episcopal Church in Washington, D.C.

She was a most distinguished personage, tall and gray-haired for most of her adult life and soft-spoken, but she had a presence and abided by a strict code of ethics and principles. While others were more vocal in their reactions against the discriminatory practices of the day, Otelia Cromwell responded by refusing to patronize the stores in Washington because of their treatment of black customers and by not using public transportation—she walked or took taxis—because no Blacks were employed as conductors and motormen.

Otelia Cromwell was without pretension, and she avoided fanfare and publicity. She preferred to be called Miss Cromwell rather than Dr. Cromwell. When she was invited to send her biography for inclusion in the 1958 edition of *Who's Who among American Women,* the editors "regretfully informed her that her sketch had been inadvertently omitted—through an error that was thoroughly accidental and certainly not intentional" and asked her to please send them another. She refused not because of pride, no doubt, but because of disgust at the lack of efficiency on the part of the editors.

Since 1989, Smith College has celebrated an Otelia Cromwell Day to increase awareness of the many differences that exist within the Smith Community. On April 8, 2004, her 130th birthday, I presented to Smith College an oil painting of Otelia Cromwell, the first black graduate of the college. It was hung in the Neilson Library Browsing Room.

A quiet testimony of her life was the beautiful poinsettia she received each Christmas from a former student until the student herself died.

These letters cover the period of Otelia Cromwell's young adulthood and reflect the responsibility she assumed for her younger siblings, her extended family ties, her higher education outside of Washington at Smith and Yale, and her early career as a teacher in the public schools of Washington, D.C.

My dear Father,[4]

Your letter with the money order was received last week. I thank you ever so much.

We are still having a deliciously lazy time of it. Strange to say the time just flies. One would think that the days would drag in such a monotonously quiet place, but night comes only too soon and when once we tuck ourselves in under Mrs. Hall's heavy blankets sleep instantly takes possession of us. We wake early in the morning but do not get up until nine or there abouts—we feel real wicked at taking so much sleep, for we certainly do not earn it by hard work.

Today Lou has gone to camp meeting held in a grove near Post Deposit. The experience I think will be a novel one for her. These Maryland camp meetings are not at all like the Virginia "big meetings." I wonder if the difference is due to denominational influence. These Methodists up here make the annual camp meeting a source of revenue for the church. There is a gate fee and refreshments of all kinds are sold on the ground. Services are held either in the open air or in large tents struck for the occasion. Often there are smaller tents occupied by families who literally "camp out" for a week or two. In some cases, two or more churches hold camp together—when there is a large crowd gathered from all directions within a radius of twenty or thirty miles. They are occasions for family reunions, but the atmosphere of the church is omnipresent, giving more formality than there might perhaps otherwise would be. Now down in Culpeper there is preaching of course, but the "getting there" and seeing folks, and sitting round under trees eating the dinner which you have brought seem the major considerations. If the Virginians are less religious (and I doubt it), they are more informal and hospitable in their Baptist "Meetings" than are these folks in their camps.

These people anyhow are peculiar. They are really "an institution." They are all of one family and marry and intermarry with no qualms at all. A generation ago they thus kept themselves apart from the other colored people because they con-

4. Aunt Otelia had apparently taken Aunt Lucy as a vacation to stay with a Mrs. Hall in Maryland, who took paying guests. Our family usually went to Brandy, Virginia (near Culpepper), to visit relatives.

sidered no outsider good enough or good looking enough to come in the family. Today they do the same, because there is hardly a person in the neighborhood who is not as Mrs. Hall phrases it "a relative." They are a mixture of Caucasian, Indian and Negro, and are certainly fine looking people. Their houses are small, but well built and neatly kept. It's the Pennsylvania influence that touches here after all, for in our direction we are not four miles from the border land between the two states. The effect of this propinquity is noticed not only in some customs but very plainly in speech also. Farming is the main occupation, more effort being expanded in truck gardening than in raising grain.

Today the weather is almost cold but clear. We have had so much rain that a clear day is a treat.

Love to all.

> Lovingly your daughter,
> Otelia

> New Bedford
> July 28, '92.

My dear Father:

Have just arrived, I did not leave Fall River until 11.50 A.M. because Cousin Emily had to complete her work. I enjoyed the sail up the Sound immensely. Neither Pat nor myself was sea-sick.

From what I have seen of N.B. I think I shall like it very well. Pat says she does not like here, but that is because she wanted to go directly home from N.Y.

I gave Cousin Sarah my ticket to dispose of, which she says she can easily do. The fare direct from N.Y. to New Bedford was $3.55.

Now I tell you what I want you to do. I wish you would get some cheap napkin rings (no two alike) & let the children use them. I don't want them to appear as if they were never used to anything.

The views from the boat were most delightful. Although there was no moon the way was not at all rough. There was quite a number of passengers on board & Cousin Emily made everything pleasant.

Cousin William gave me a most cordial welcome & inquired after you & the children. We left all well in New York. Give my love to the children. Kiss each one for me. Tell Johnny & Larcie to be good children. My regards to Mrs. Wigginton's family. Tell Lucy not to eat too much. All send love.

> Yours—O. C.

My dear Father,[5]

I can't understand why I do not get a line from home. Are you all well? I have written at least twice a week since I've been up here but it has been more than twelve days since I've heard from any of you. You see it is next to impossible for me to answer your letters immediately or write to each one every week for there are five of you. This is my second to you. I've written two to mother one to Larcie and one to Lucy in less time than three weeks. Against that six written by one person I received three, the joint production of five people. I guess it's "out of sight out of mind" with 1439 [their home address].

We are all well. I've something funny to tell you when I get home something which you will appreciate and laugh over.

Uncle Willis and family are well. I thank you for the *Record*.

Love to all—

Otelia

I bet you a penny I write to the family more often than Mame and John do and they have more to tell about than I do.

13—Pine Street
Fall River, Mass.
July 25, 1899.

Dear Papa,

I thank you for the books which I received this morning. On the wrapper I noticed "1463—Pierce Place"—was that written without thought or have you moved? Please tell me.

The Mr. Dickerman whom you met in Hampton is I guess Miss Anna Dickinson's father. She is from New Haven and at college lives in the Hatfield House. She was in one of my classes last year and I always found her an exceedingly pleasant girl.

I find it nice here in Fall River. It is quiet but always cool. Cousin Emily has only herself and husband and I am made to feel perfectly at home. After having boarded so long it is such a relief to have the freedom of the entire house to do what one likes and whenever one likes. I help her with the housework and I enjoy that part too. It was the same way in Philadelphia. Aunt Nancy was so kind

---

5. This letter was sent from Philadelphia when Otelia was visiting her Uncle Willis and his wife, Felicienne, which is odd because she usually visited her uncle Levi and his wife, Nancy. The relationship between Otelia and her stepmother appears to have been warm at this point.

to me, she could not have shown more interest in her own niece. She thinks so much of you too. They have an orderly quiet household. I think there are very few women who have as much as Aunt Nancy has and at the same time are content to spend so little on themselves or do so much work.

I have not seen anything yet of Clara Carney. She wrote to me to come over and stay as long as I wanted with her, but I think I shall not go. Cousin William is going to Philadelphia in September. Clara may go over also.

I received such a kind letter from Professor Moore. I had occasion to write him on business, and he took the opportunity to say several things to me, things that were very encouraging.

Although I enjoyed my stay in Philadelphia I was ever so glad to get back in dear old New England. I could without a regret live in this part of the country for the rest of my days, although I like Phila. better than Washington.

Remember me to all the folks. I am glad you found your visit to Hampton an interesting one. I feel that you will equally enjoy the Philadelphia trip.

I wish you would advise me about my summer reading. There is an excellent library here but when I have all opportunities for reading it seems impossible for me to think of the books I have planned to read "when I have time." I was much interested last winter in M. Paul Bourget and now reading one of Henry James' novels. I am going to read one or two of Balzac also. I can't do much than fiction in the summer time, but I want fiction that is worth my while. Of course everything is Kipling at present but I don't like his style of story nor his setting. Of course he is original both in plot and detail and folks rave over his brevity that is so full and his striking language and so forth but he simply does not appeal to me—that is I never feel particularly desirous of procuring one of his stories, although I must confess that once begun his tales show a force that compels me to finish them. I think I shall read Carlisle's French Revolution during these weeks—Now won't you tell me of some books fiction or non fiction that I need and ought to read.

Write to me soon. You have no idea how much I enjoy reading your letters.

Did you know that there were short articles about my entering Smith in the *New York Herald* and *Phila. Times?* I have not seen them but I was told of them.

Lovingly,
Otelia

Smith College
Northampton, Mass.
November 5, 1899

Dear Papa,

Why have you not written to me—if I had a daughter as nice as I am, away at college I should not give her a chance to think I had forgotten her.

We have had much rain and murky weather. To day the sun shines brightly and it is very warm. We are all wishing for steady cold weather, for then work does not drag so.

My courses are most interesting, but require such close and steady application that I do not have time for anything else except the exercise which Miss Caverno insists upon my taking every day. At Smith the members of the faculty show so much human interest in the students. Class room work, and a high standard at that is required of us, but our health and comfort is so carefully looked after. Here they take a personal interest in us, giving us individual attention where a course presents to any one girl extraordinarily difficulty. When one considers that classes often number one hundred, I think too much praise cannot be given to our faculty.

Now in English 13a, the course is literary criticism open only to seniors, Miss Jordan has given us access to her private study every afternoon from four until six.

It is a small room the walls of which from ceiling to floor are lined with books. In one corner is a large old fashioned desk, a rare mahogany table stands next while curious bits of bric-a-brac are scattered here and there. Miss Jordan is a connoisseur in works of art. The three comfortable chairs and the hassock are filled with girls almost every afternoon—it is such a quiet cosy place to study, and then too it is so convenient to discuss our work there.

I spend most of my time for study on Aristotle—that is relatively speaking. We are reading the *Politics,* and although his subtlety causes us to work on a section an interminable time, when we do get it straight we always feel repaid. The class is small and Professor Gardner is most interesting and always kind. He is an Englishman and did his last work at Heidelberg—his genius, his high standard for scholarship has made our department of Philosophy respected all over the country.

Economics does not give me much trouble. Dr. Moore the head of the department is away ill and the new man is not well seasoned—so lessons are short, and as most of us have about as much other work as we can manage we said nothing the other day when he asked us if we could not do more work.

My most fascinating course is the one in nineteenth century English prose. Miss Hubbard is considered one of the most brilliant of our alumnae. She is an eighty-seven girl, took her Masters Degree at Cornell, taught here a year or two, spent last year abroad studying and is now back this year, full of enthusiasm and most clever and inspiring ideas. We are working on Carlyle now.[6] We have critically read his essay on Burns, Signs of the Times, and Characteristics, made a class comparison of his Cooker's Boswell Johnson and Macauley's criticism of the same book. Next week we have to have papers—mine is "Carlyle's Theory of Biography based on his Life of John Sterling." We are to get no material whatever outside of that book until after we have handed in our papers—then we see what Carlyle's biographers say about him as a biographer. We are now working on the Sarton, but before we take up Newman Shalls' *Heroes and Hero Worship,* Past and Present and Carlyle as an historian. The work is by no means superficial—In each class the entire work is carefully read, an abstract of the thought is required, his method treating the subject as a whole is discussed and all his peculiar mannerisms are pointed out. So often as you know it is so hard to tell just what Carlyle *did* mean that lessons are not prepared in a short time.

Once a week I read German fiction—nothing difficult I attempt, for I do it mainly for recreation. Miss Caverno has a carefully selected German library to which as well as to her other books I have free access.

I am having a very happy time of it this year. Being right down here I can take advantage of so many more opportunities than when I lived up on Round Hill (up Elm Street on northeast side, farther from main campus). I have very few quiet moments and have at times felt much fagged out—but I guess I am no worse for it.

Love to all.
Otelia Cromwell

My dear Father,[7]

I started to write you yesterday, but I am glad I did not for a very blue letter it would have been. You see it rained steadily for several days, and yesterday the

---

6. Thomas Carlyle (1795–1881), Scottish essayist and historian, was born December 4, 1795, at Ecclesfechan in Annandale, Scotland. He trained as a theologian and lawyer, and by the time of his death, on the basis of his voluminous essays and books, Carlyle had become the acknowledged head of English literature. In this letter, Aunt Otelia refers to his essays in the *Edinburgh Review:* "Burns" (December 1828); "Signs of the Times" (June 1829); "Characteristics" (December 1831); *The Life of John Sterling* (1851); and *On Heroes, Hero-Worship, and the Heroic in History* (1841).

7. This letter was probably written while Otelia was at Yale.

weather was at its worst. The sky was a dull leaden all day and the trees seemed so mournful and forsaken in the continued heavy downpour. In the morning I had quite a comfortable and satisfying time, for I studied and then read. By dinner tine I had concluded that after all one's contentment and happiness depend entirely upon oneself. And in great measure I think it does. But in the afternoon I longed to see some people besides those in the house. It's not that I am tired of the country, but being alone in the country during a long rainy time is far from encouraging.

I feel that I am getting rested. I sleep well each night and frequently take a nap in the afternoon. I study an hour or two each morning, I am reviewing the rudiments of German grammar, writing German prose and reading some Lessing. After all is said, I am not sorry I shall have this German to teach, although I was some what vexed when they startled me with the announcement. It will keep me from forgetting what German I know and compel me to master some of the difficulties of the language which other wise I might pass by with just a casual notice. Then too, any study I may wish to make along the line of English will be helped by this German—both literature and philosophy.

I sew in the morning and practise golf in the afernoon.

We have had only one genuinely warm day since I came. It was the next day after my arrival and I firmly believe that the heat I felt was a remnant of Washington weather that clung to me. Last night and the night before I slept under double blankets, and the mornings are almost cold.

My eyes are troubling me—they will have to be examined when I get home. I guess I have not treated them carefully.

Mina Kerr one of my college classmates has written again for me to come up and visit her "some weeks". I wish . . . [letter ends abruptly]

Dear Papa,[8]

Won't you get this order cashed—Please fill in the amount I have in, and close the account. Times are pretty hard these days. My bank book is in my chiffonier drawer—Mamie will get it for you. There is either a dollar and seventy or a dollar and seventy five cents in the bank. Give it to Lou and she will bring it up to me.

I suppose summer school is almost over and I guess you are not sorry.

It's too bad about Cy Shippen.[9] Of course I feel sorry for his father, but my

---

8. This letter was probably written while Otelia was in New York.

9. Cyrus Shippen (a distant cousin, I think) was a graduate of Yale and a teacher at Dunbar High School. I do not know to what Otelia was referring here, for Cyrus never married again and most people did not know he was ever married, but it may be a story related to his sexuality.

sympathy goes out to the girl he married. Cy is certainly nice and I like him ever so much, but I am afraid he has "married in haste."

The world after all is not so large. Mr. Stidum used to teach in this place, boarding at the house of Mr. Hall's aunt. I found it out quite accidentally.

Don't swelter.

Lovingly your daughter,
Otelia

My dear Father,[10]

I have just seen today's *Post* and am wondering at the omission of Mamie's name.[11] Don't try to do anything to have me transferred but use all your energy to have her reinstated if she has been dropped. If she was marked "fair" why was she dropped and Carter & Craig retained. Of course I know you are doing all you can but I am worried sick—do let me know what it all means.

Hastily,
Otelia

Jesse—Wene Farm
North Shore Road
Benton Harbor, Michigan
September 5, 1915

My dear Father,

The relentless strain of summer school is over and Larcie and I are here for a few days before we go to visit Aunt Winnie.[12] We are glad the work is over, and now that it is behind us, it does not seem as hard as we found it while we were actually doing it. There was time for nothing else, literally and absolutely; we did not see Chicago nor Chicago people although the latter were hospitably inclined; perhaps we may be able to come again sometime. But we did find our

---

10. This letter was probably written while Otelia was in New Haven.

11. Mamie is Mary E. Cromwell, Otelia's sister. For some understanding of the machinations within the school department, see Otelia's letter to John Wesley Cromwell Sr., p. 143. Mary, who had degrees from the University of Michigan and the University of Pennsylvania, was not considered to be as strong a person or as good a teacher as Otelia. But according to a former student, "She was a good person."

12. Winnie McGuinn Lewis was the sister of my grandmother Lucy. She lived in Pennsylvania but came to Washington to care for Lucy's children after Lucy died. Later, she and her husband moved to Oberlin, Ohio. When I was about ten years old, she took me to Oberlin to visit Aunt Winnie and Uncle Jim.

work a huge satisfaction and we completed it without being the worse physically although we were fearfully tired after our last examinations.[13]

Although we did not find much time for calling, we did manage to go to see Mr. Barnett for we knew you want us to. Major Lynch[14] also came to see us and Doctor and Mrs. Dan. Williams.[15] All of these friends of yours send their kindest regards to you.

Now we are at Mr. Morris'[16] country home which is beautiful in every detail. We came only Saturday night and already we feel thoroughly rested.

I hope you are well and feel ready for school. I am sorry I have not been able to write oftener, but there was no time for letters and I know you do not care much for cards.

Much love to you

Otelia

130 West 131 St.

New York City

August 1, 1920

My dear Father,

The days are passing by and it will soon be time for summer school to close. We shall be glad for we are tired of the heavy close days which have made the

---

13. Otelia, accompanied by her sister Larcie, took summer courses at the University of Chicago before she enrolled at Yale University.

14. John Roy Lynch (1847–1939) was born in Louisiana to an Irish father and a slave mother. He had a distinguished and multifaceted career: he had served in the military and as a member of Congress and was the recipient of presidential appointments, a strong supporter of the Civil Rights Bill of 1875, and a lawyer. He had moved to Chicago where he practiced law and engaged in real estate. His *Facts of Reconstruction* was published in 1913 and is the best first-hand account of Reconstruction written by an African American. His autobiography, *Reminiscences of an Active Life*, was published posthumously in 1970.

15. Dr. Daniel Hale Williams (1856–1931) was a native of Pennsylvania. He received his MD from Chicago Medical School, and in 1891 he helped to establish Provident Hospital in Chicago. He was the first surgeon to perform a successful heart operation, and he served as chief surgeon at Freedmen's Hospital in Washington and at St. Luke's Hospital in Chicago. He left both hospitals because he was disgusted with internal conflict and bureaucratic controls. He was one of the one hundred charter members of the American College of Surgeons.

16. Dr. Edward H. Morris (1860–1943), a native of Kentucky, was educated in Chicago. He was a criminal lawyer and an assistant attorney in Cook County. He was also active in Republican politics and was elected to the Illinois legislature in 1890 and 1902. He attended Booker T. Washington and Andrew Carnegie's "secret meeting" but spoke disparagingly of Washington in his famous "Sham" speech before the Bethel Literary Society.

work and time drag. Lucy and I expect to go to Bedford Springs on the fourth of the month. Mary will come home and Larcie will stay on up here for a bit.

Mrs. Josephine Turpin Washington[17] is here again this year and has asked for you.

Lucy and I have been to see some good plays: John Drinkwater's *Abraham Lincoln,* St. John Devine's *Jane Clegg* produced by the Theatre Guild, James Forbes; *The Tamms, Mrs. Fair, Footloose* at the Little Theatre and *Lightnice.* They are all fine plays but different in kind. Next week or rather this week we want to start to see some musical comedies.

We are all well, and thankful to be well in the face of illness among one or two of our friends. You know that Majette Gregory is still far from well and Blanche Nugent is recovering only slowly. So we are thankful to be on our feet.

I hope you are having a nice summer after your little trip up this way. All send love.

Your daughter
Otelia

My dear father,[18]

After thinking the matter over carefully I have decided that I do not want to bother about the head of languages. Between you and me I am not teaching the subject I care much for or in which I believe I can do my best work. The money is not everything. The time has come for me to try to do some graduate work and I want to work in English. Can't I be transferred to the M Street High School to teach English? You know (you remember) Bruce Evans got me over to this school on false pretenses, he said I was to have English until the transfer was made. If

17. Josephine Turpin Washington (1861–1949) was born in Richmond, Virginia, and educated at the Richmond Institute and at Howard University. She was a copyist for Frederick Douglass when he was recorder of deeds. Beginning in 1877, Washington was a prominent newspaper contributor to the *Virginia Star,* writing on educational, moral, social, racial, and purely literary subjects. She was published twice in the *People's Advocate:* "Notes to Girls," a series of letters, and "Higher Education for Women," originally an oration before the Young Ladies Literary Society of Howard University in 1885. She held teaching positions at Richmond Institute and at Selma University, leaving the latter to marry Dr. Samuel H. H. Washington.

18. It is difficult to estimate the exact date of this letter. Aunt Otelia was apparently still teaching at Armstrong Manual Training School in 1914, where she obviously did not want to be. This letter provides some insight into the politics involved in Washington's black public schools, revealing how someone working for the schools survived and was rewarded. On the whole, public school teachers in the system were well educated and better paid than were teachers in other segregated systems in the country and accordingly were among the elite of the community. This letter identifies just a few of these individuals.

Parker Bailey gets the English Directorship why can't I be transferred to the M Street to teach Eng. in his place. Now I don't know about trusting Dr. Atwood for I believe he wants to get Lottie over there to teach English but I ought to have the first chance because I am in the system. I should not be surprised if Miss Burrill makes a strong fight for the English head. I believe they will give Miss Cooper[19] the language head. They won't wait to put her out or reduce her, and she can certainly do it better than any one else in the system for she has taught

19. Anna Julia Cooper (1858–1964), born a slave in Raleigh, North Carolina, received her BA from Oberlin College in 1884 and her MA from Oberlin in 1887. She taught at Wilberforce College and St. Augustine College, where she married George A. C. Cooper, who died two years later. In 1887, she was appointed to teach mathematics and Latin at M Street High School. During this period, she emerged as a feminist, public speaker, and author. In 1893, she addressed the Special Meeting of the Women's Congress in Chicago, and in 1900, she attended the first Pan-American Conference in London. When she first arrived in Washington, Mrs. Cooper roomed with the Crummell family and had the opportunity to meet many outstanding black intellectuals. She was invited to be the first woman member of the American Negro Academy. In 1902, she was appointed principal of M Street High School, becoming the second black female principal in the school's history. Under her leadership, the school strengthened its classical curriculum and became a showcase for the best and the brightest students, who for the first time became recipients of scholarships from northern colleges. Mrs. Cooper was frequently in conflict with the system. The 1904–1905 school year was one of turmoil as allegations of insubordination and personal impropriety by Mrs. Cooper and rumors of student misconduct circulated about the city. Oliver M. Atwood made the charge that the students were guilty of drunkenness for which no evidence was found. Mrs. Cooper became the center of controversy. Community opinion for or against her depended largely on so-called revelations in the press, and in October 1906, the board decided not to reappoint her. It was speculated that her stress of classical rather than industrial education had run counter to Booker T. Washington's ideas on education and his long arm of influence. But it is more likely that her opposition to the ideas of "P. H. Hughes, the white director of high schools who had asserted that the pupils of the M Street High School were incapable of taking the same studies in the same time as the other schools of like grade in the city" was the real source of her difficulties. She was retained as principal, but her administrative methods were rebuked and her loyalty to the director of the high schools was questioned. The following year Mrs. Cooper was replaced by W. T. Sherman Jackson. She left Washington to teach at Lincoln University in Missouri but, after four years, returned to Washington to teach Latin at the M Street High School. Meanwhile, she pursued graduate study at the Sorbonne in Paris and was awarded the Ph.D. in 1925. In 1930, Mrs. Cooper became president of Frelinghuysen University in Washington, D.C.. Frelinghuysen's collegiate level courses for employed colored persons were held in her home during the evenings. The classes were taught by volunteers. In 1937, the institution lost its charter and could no longer award degrees. Mrs. Cooper became registrar, and few students enrolled. Her position was largely ceremonial. The school, in some form, lasted until 1951. Mrs. Cooper wrote or edited several books as well as three autobiographies. The controversy around Mrs. Cooper was reflective of the hostility between the Board of Education and the teachers in the system at that time. Teachers other than Mrs. Cooper were dismissed; most were rehired. In his journal, John Wesley Cromwell documented the events with historical accuracy and journalistic skill. He paid particular attention to the firing of Francis L. Cardoza, a supervising principal, who sent an anonymous letter to the members of the

the four languages. Bruce Evans treated Mamie mean. The idea of putting her in the same class with Nina Grimké.[20]

If you can get my transfer to teach *English* in the *M Street* without any trouble, do so. You must let Mrs. Gitterman[21] know the truth about my work—You had better not write again but go to see her and explain. Don't ask her to do any thing for me. I do not want it and was sorry you wrote her at first. Please be sure to see her today. Call her up by phone to see if she is home, then go over to see her. Now don't do anything toward getting me the language head for I do not want it, or any other head.

Love to Lucy—

Hastily

Otelia

[note on back of letter]
After you see Mrs. G. let me know what she says.

---

board noting the incompetence of Wilder Montgomery, assistant superintendent, for retaining in the schools John Wesley Cromwell and several other teachers. The case was thrown out and all the named teachers received commendation for their work from the superintendent.

20. Nina Grimké is Angela Grimké (1854–1956), the daughter of Archibald H. Grimké. Nina graduated from the Girls Latin School in Boston, the Boston Normal School of Gymnastics (1902), and later the Department of Hygiene of Wellesley College. Interestingly, Nina's first appointment was in physical education at Armstrong where she, too, was unhappy. In 1907, she received an appointment to teach English at M Street. Why not Aunt Otelia? The Grimké name meant more than the Cromwell name.

21. Mrs. A. Gitterman gave a course, "Free Lectures to the People," in the school department. According to minutes of the Board of Education, she had some political power, which they did not wish to offend. On February 22, 1905, Representatives J. A. Goulden and I. E. Rider of New York wrote Mr. W. F. Roderick, the secretary of the Board of Education, that "No one in this country is better qualified to inaugurate the lecture course and to assume entire charge of the work. Were she left free and unhampered, as she should be, these lectures would prove eminently successful and profitable. It was with the understanding that such should be the case that *Congress* made the necessary appropriation." Grandfather was clearly seeking some type of influence outside the system that would assist his daughter. Washington was under the control of the Congress and that its local citizens had no vote, so one had to seek help from those who had access to power. How he or Aunt Otelia knew Mrs. Gitterman or why he thought she could be of assistance, I do not know.

The movement in the system of administrative personnel is also interesting. Since Anna Cooper was a "fly in the ointment," she was not going to be rewarded so she removed herself by retiring. With the new building, Dunbar, on the horizon, it seems there was some jockeying for position. Edwin C. Williams was principal of M Street, the same year Dunbar was opened. But then a new person, Garnet C. Wilkerson, appeared. Mr. Wilkerson taught at M Street from 1902 to 1912, and from 1912 to 1916, he was principal of Armstrong. But in 1916, Mr. Wilkerson was made principal of Dunbar, where he remained until 1921 when he was promoted to assistant superintendent.

65 Edgewood Ave.
New Haven, Conn.
July 13, 1922

My dear father,

I was sorry not to see you just before I left or to see you so little when I was home. The hot weather as well as the desire on my part to get a complete rest from the work I am now doing made me inactive and it was second nature to feel that everyone else wanted to be still also. I hadn't the conscience to call you up to come over, and whenever you did come there was always someone calling. I suppose it is the size of our family that brings the visitors; then too, I suppose, folks dropped in more frequently than usual, because I had been away several months. All of which goes to account for my not being able to have a long talk with you during my three weeks' stay.

But, I don't know that there was so much to say, simply more details about Yale and my work than I had put into my letters.

Well, I am back in New Haven where at least the nights are cool even after hot days. I have a large room facing west with three windows. In the mornings I work in the Yale Library which is a quiet roomy place in the summer time; in the afternoons I work in my room, that is at present while I am making a general survey of my subject and it is possible to bring enough reading matter home from the library to occupy me for several hours. Later on when my work becomes more detailed involving a ceaseless verification of opinions from many sources I shall be compelled, I think to do all my reading in the library.

Although I am not absolutely certain—I shall not know for sure until the Department approves—I think I shall work on some phase of Elizabethan drama. From many points of view it would be comfortable to select a subject relating to the Negro but two difficulties stood in the way: the improbability of my being able from what I know of the possibilities of the field to get something that would be big enough for the kind of book I've got to write (Haytian literature excepted which would moreover fall into the French department); and, more important, the fact that any work which I might do in that line would be absolutely independent because, naturally, I'd know more about it than any of the folks here. In one way the independent work would show a certain kind of power, but on the other hand, my main object in being here is to learn scholarly method and to benefit by scholarly criticism. Most of all, I want the work I may do in the years to come—if years are granted me—to be critically sound. This is my only opportunity for training, and training is needed for any output which is more than ephemeral or interesting to an unrestrictive group of general readers.

After this dissertation is done—but it may take two years to write it, some do—I shall be free and better trained to do something that will perhaps appeal more strongly to you—but I'm not sure and am promising nothing. "Sufficient unto the day."

There are some changes in the schools, nothing however which holds any attraction for me. Ambition for place or fame is not my besetting folly, just to be on a public pinnacle a visible target for all the shafts that the crowd will fling. I am glad that I have a sense of values which makes me happy in doing what I am doing—work that I like which still leaves me time for study, time to keep unembittered and perhaps to do this writing some day.

I expect to go to Northampton to visit the Cavernos in a week or so. Miss Caverno goes to Greece next winter. They wrote me early last fall to come up, but I never had time during the winter for anything but my work.

I hope you keep well. Love to you

> Your daughter
> Otelia

Otelia's (left) and Mary's (below) college graduation photos. Otelia graduated from Smith College in 1900 and Mary received her degree in 1905 from the University of Michigan.

Otelia (top right) as young teacher at Armstrong Manual Training School. Garnet C. Wilkerson is also pictured here, top left.

John as a graduate
of Dartmouth.

On his summer breaks from Dartmouth, John worked at the Grand Union Hotel at Saratoga. (Courtesy of the Saratoga Springs History Museum.)

John Cromwell (seated on left) with his bridge-playing friends. Robert Pearson and Victor Daly are standing. Also seated is Caesar Barron.

Yetta Mavritte Cromwell and Adelaide.

Board of Directors for the *Encyclopedia of the Negro,* 1932 (l. to r.) front row: Otelia Cromwell, Monroe N. Work, Charles H. Wesley, Benjamin Brawley, W. E. B. Du Bois, Eugene Jones, Alain Locke, Waldo G. Leland; middle row: James Weldon Johnson, Charles T. Loram; back row: W. D. Weatherford, Arthur A. Schomburg, J. E. Spingarn, Clarence S. Marsh, Anson Phelps Stokes, W. A. Aery, James H. Dillard, Florence Reed, and Mordecai W. Johnson. (Courtesy of Phelps-Stokes Fund.)

At Otelia's fiftieth class reunion, she was awarded an honorary degree from Smith College. Otelia is seated on the far left in the front row.

John's fiftieth class reunion at Dartmouth College.

Chapter 7

"John Had Never Given Me a Moment's Uneasiness"

Letters from John Wesley Cromwell Jr. to John Wesley Cromwell Sr.

꧁ ꧂

According to my aunt Otelia, on his deathbed my grandfather uttered, "John had never given me a moment's uneasiness," as he spoke of his only surviving son. Unquestionably, John Wesley Cromwell Jr. was held in high esteem by his father, his sisters, and even his uncle Levi, who made him the executor of his estate.

John was born in Washington, D.C., on September 2, 1883. His older brother, Willis, had died while still a baby and his parents' next child following his birth was a girl, Fanny, who slowly developed a severe spinal curvature. John's mother, my grandmother, died shortly after Fanny's birth.

I know nothing of my father's early childhood except that he felt then and forever under the strict surveillance of his older sister, Otelia. I assume he spent an average but not-too-happy childhood for the reason already discussed. But as the only boy and next to the youngest child, he, unlike his older sisters, was not alienated from Granny-Step and Aunt Fanny.

Grandfather kept this brief letter my father wrote to Santa Claus that he described as "the first legible letter of John W. Cromwell, Jr., written December 23, 1890":

Dear Santa Claus
    Please bring me forth a drum.
                little friend.

John went to Howard Preparatory School[1] where he prepared to enter Dartmouth College. His choice of Dartmouth was based on two considerations: first, it was less expensive than Harvard, and second, he was familiar with other Blacks in Washington, such as Winfield S. Montgomery, who had graduated from Dartmouth. Montgomery's son Wilder P. Montgomery entered Dartmouth the same year as John.

After receiving a Phi Beta Kappa key and a bachelor's degree from Dartmouth in 1906, John remained an additional year and received a master's degree. After a year's placement at the General Electric Company in Lynn, Massachusetts, as a part of the apprenticeship program the company had with Dartmouth for its most promising students, John returned to Washington, much to his father's joy.

His first position was as a Latin teacher in the elementary schools, and then from 1908 to 1921, he taught mathematics, German, and bookkeeping in the high schools. In 1920, having scored highest on the competitive examination for the Higher Class Teachers, John began to teach mathematics at Dunbar High School, where he remained until 1930.

From October 1930 to June 1931, John was the comptroller at Howard University. In 1931, he began to practice as a certified public accountant, having received his credentials in 1921 in New Hampshire. John was the first Black practicing CPA in the United States.

John had three abiding loves: Dartmouth College, where he was known as "Oliver," mathematics, and bridge. Almost all of the satisfactions of his life were related to these interests. After graduating from Dartmouth, he continued to support the school to the extent of his resources for the rest of his life. When he grew older and could afford it, he never missed a class reunion.[2] He followed a family tradition of recommending the best and the brightest of his students,

---

1. Howard Preparatory School was established in 1867. The three-year curriculum consisted of three years of Latin, two years of Greek, one year of arithmetic, and one year of algebra. James Monroe Gregory, the school's principal and a tutor, was the only African American teacher in the school, which was closed in 1907.

2. After my father's death in 1971, I sent a contribution in his name to the head agent for the class of 1906, Edward B. Redman. Writing from the Hanover Convalescent Home, Mr. Redman, in an unsteady hand, replied, "Thank you very much for your gift to the Alumni Fund in memory of John. The boys will be very glad to see his name on the list for they all thought a lot of him. . . . We are very glad that you are one of us."

whom he prepared well in mathematics, Latin, and German, to Dartmouth and to other equally well-known colleges. Sterling Brown, the distinguished black poet who graduated from Williams College, always told me that my father was "the best teacher he ever had." John was as strict an overseer of the bookkeeping skills of the employees of his clients as he was exacting as a teacher in the classroom. Miss Neely, the longtime manager of the famous Harrison's Restaurant on U Street in Washington, never failed to tell me that when Mr. Cromwell went over the books, he made her "account for every penny."

At Dartmouth, John learned to love sports, particularly Ping-Pong and sculling. After leaving college, he played tennis often and well. Between 1914 and 1917, he was awarded three tennis cups by the Negro Tennis Association; one cup was for a doubles match he played with Talley Holmes, a 1910 Dartmouth graduate and the founder of the American Tennis Association.

John's love of cards started when he was a student at Dartmouth. When he was only a sophomore, he won his first bridge puzzle prize, which was awarded by *Vanity Fair*. Later in 1929, as a result of his publicized success in solving a bridge puzzle, he was invited to join the Knickerbocker Whist Club of New York City. Five days later, when the club learned that he was black, the invitation was rescinded.

In 1932, at Hampton, Virginia, John became one of the founders of the American Bridge Association. He was active in the development of this organization for black bridge players—who were not welcomed into the comparable white organization—which at the time of his death had eight thousand members from all over the country.

It was not easy for an independent thinker to function smoothly within the limitations of the segregated society of Washington, especially if one were not following the traditional and more independent careers of law, medicine, and the ministry. By the time John was an adult, the government jobs available to Blacks were rarely, if ever, commensurate with their abilities. Furthermore, segregation created domains of control and dominance that were not always favorable to the most intelligent and independent.

John was not an agitator or a belligerent person, but his sarcasm, though camouflaged by a warm smile, coupled with his intelligence, did not endear him to his less intelligent or less competent superiors. Although he was popular with his students, especially those of quick mind, John was not favored for promotion within the school system beyond that which could not be denied him. In 1930, after having worked in the school system for ten years, in spite of his experience, training, and popularity with the students, John Cromwell was bypassed in the selection of a chairman for the mathematics department in the schools in favor of a less-qualified but politically more acceptable individual.[3] Taking this as a sign that he did not have favor at the higher levels of the school system, on October 25, 1930, John Cromwell submitted his resignation and accepted a position as comptroller at Howard University. In leaving his position at Dunbar High School for an administrative one at Howard University, for which he was eminently qualified, John Cromwell undoubtedly thought he would be in a freer and less parochial environment where the ultimate authority was a black university president not a white superintendent. This notwithstanding the fact that Dunbar had a better national reputation among its fellow high schools than Howard did among its fellow universities. In retrospect, John Cromwell was being naïve. The Cromwell family had acquired much knowledge of the workings of the public schools in Washington, beginning with John Wesley Cromwell Sr.'s long career as a teacher and principal in the system, but had little knowledge of the inner workings of Howard University. John himself had attended Howard Prep and his father had graduated from Howard's law school but that was all; life had carried them both into quite different directions.

John Cromwell soon found the same types of problems at Howard he thought he had left behind in the public schools. The oppression was the same when the junior person was better qualified and lacking in the appropriate subordinate manner. So on June 14, 1931, he submitted his resignation to Howard University. Although asked to reconsider, he refused but agreed to write his reasons for resigning. In a letter of October 21, 1931, to Mr. Emmett Jay Scott, the secretary-treasurer and business manager of Howard University, John described in some detail the circumstances prompting his decision. These included not being given sufficient authority and status and thus ultimate fiscal accountability (should there be any question about the expenditures of funds by federal authorities, clearly John Cromwell did not intend to be accused of fiscal irresponsibility unless he had been in a position to make the decisions relative to these matters); poor working conditions; too few staff working for wages that were too low; competent clerks receiving pay equal to that of regular laborers; and stenographers and bookkeepers having what he thought were extremely responsible positions being paid less than clerks to individual deans and professors.

3. The preferred candidate, a woman, who had graduated Phi Beta Kappa from Oberlin College, obviously had an excellent educational background. My father's objection, I believe, was to her lack of experience in the school system, certainly as compared to his. Appointments not made on the basis of examination clearly reflected influence and personal preference or, more simply put, politics.

Emmett Jay Scott, John Cromwell's superior, had never graduated from college, though he had attended Wiley College in Texas for three years. He had gained his prominence as the private secretary to Booker T. Washington from 1897 until Washington's death in 1915. He was the person who guarded the entrée to Booker T. Washington and thus wielded considerable influence during Washington's lifetime. Not chosen as Washington's successor, Scott came to Howard University. Before the appointment in 1926 of the university's first black president, Mordecai W. Johnson, Scott was the university's most important black administrator.

One does not have to be steeped in the lore of black university politics to sense the predicament in which John W. Cromwell Jr. found himself. The ultimate control of the management of money became a problem for him. Consequently, in June 1931, less than a year after he had come to Howard, Cromwell submitted his resignation, though he did agree to stay on until a replacement could be found. That same month, Cromwell applied for reinstatement to his old job in the public schools.

There were regulations pertaining to the right of reinstatement.[4] Former employees seeking reinstatement must have resigned under proper conditions and must have had an excellent rating when they worked in the public schools, and they also had to apply within five years of their resignations. Appointments had to be made from the eligible list, and teachers applying for reinstatement had to outrank all on the eligible list, except those teachers on leave of absence. Because he met all the stipulated requirements, John Cromwell assumed his reappointment would be automatic. Here, he was also naïve.

Thirteen months after he had applied for reinstatement, on July 22, 1932, John Cromwell received a letter from Garnet C. Wilkerson, the first assistant superintendent of schools. (Wilkerson was in charge of the segregated schools. His supervisor, Frank W. Ballou, who was white, was in charge of all the schools.) In this letter, Mr. Wilkerson stated that he "expected to place Cromwell's name before the Superintendent of Schools, effective September 1, 1932." Then in three rather long paragraphs, Mr. Wilkerson spelled out the conditions under which this appointment would be made. First, although he hoped his recommendations would "occur at the earliest possible moment," the Board of Education was now subject to restrictions in salary and regulations of employment imposed in the provisions of the economy bill. Second, on the basis of this bill, certain provisions

---

4. Upon inquiry, his sister Otelia was told, "All your brother has to do is send in his application and his reappointment will be made automatically at the time of the first vacancy."

applied specifically to all employees of the federal government and the District of Columbia. Briefly put, "salaries for teachers then in the service and all persons employed during the fiscal year of 1932–33 year were to be cut 8 1/3 percent. Furthermore, no vacancies could be filled until a formal application to fill such vacancy shall be presented through the designated channels to the President of the United States and receive his approval."

"Therefore," continued Mr. First Assistant Superintendent, "the school authorities had to present through the designated channels to the President of the United States a request for permission" for John Cromwell once again to teach in the public schools. Mr. Wilkerson assured him that this was being done and that it was their "confident hope that they would be able to fill these vacancies."[5]

John Cromwell was to be notified immediately when the authorization came down from the president, and this was expected, "although the procedure will cause a slight delay," concluded Mr. First Assistant Superintendent. John was also to reply immediately about his availability "according to the aforementioned terms," meaning the reduction in salary.

Four days later on July 26, 1932, John Cromwell wrote Mr. First Assistant Superintendent accepting the position "in spite of the salary cut," but he requested an early notice of his reappointment "in order that he may make proper provisions for leaving my present position."

On August 1, Mr. Wilkerson informed John that his office "had just received word that the President of the United States is withholding for the time being his approval of our recommendation for the filling of the position at the Cardozo High to which we recently advised you that we hope to recommend you." Therefore, he wrote, "under the circumstances this office cannot recommend you for appointment in September, 1932."

On October 10, 1932, Mr. Wilkerson again wrote to John Cromwell:

> This office is requesting permission of the President of the United States to fill the position of the Mathematics Department of the high schools of Divisions 10–13.
>
> The records of this office show that you are No. 1 on the eligible list to teach mathematics. Should the President of the United States authorize the use of salary for this purpose, an offer of appointment will be made to you.
>
> . . . We are governed by the rules pertaining to the new appointments;

5. The case of Charlotte Corbin to teach Latin in the public schools was also before the board. Her request for reinstatement was denied.

i.e. placements of $100 per year for each year of prior service not to exceed five years in the case of senior high school teachers. This means in your case that your beginning salary will be $2,300 per year.

Wilkerson ended the letter by asking whether John "would accept an offer made under the foregoing terms." When John Cromwell resigned from the public schools, his salary was thirty-two hundred dollars per year. A cut of nine hundred dollars was quite considerable for a salary so small.

On October 24, 1932, John Cromwell replied in some detail, thanking Mr. Wilkerson for the offer, indicating an inconvenience in the timing of the appointment, thus "waiving this appointment or any similar one coming during this semester." Then stating his dissatisfaction with the terms "and in case of reappointment would be sure to test it," and with the inconsistencies as they applied to his case, but being very confident that "Mr. Wilkerson and other officials are anxious that no injustice be done," Cromwell suggested that he "be appointed to Miner Teachers College as Assistant Professor which would secure my former salary and be detailed either as teacher in Dunbar or assigned to your office as statistical assistant for I am sure you could use one."

This letter is interesting because it appears as if John Cromwell was offering the Board of Education and Mr. Wilkerson a way to solve their predicament without involving the president of the United States. One is inclined to speculate about the origin of this suggestion if, indeed, John thought it was going to be taken seriously. I think the idea may have come from Otelia, who was then teaching at the Miner Teachers College and, as has been said, was constantly supportive of her family. However, there was apparently no desire on the part of John's former superiors to make his life easier, to reward him in any way, or, for that matter, to consider a solution that would serve more effectively the students of the Washington schools. As reported earlier, John Wesley Cromwell Jr. was an excellent teacher of difficult subjects, therefore exposing promising students to his teaching could only have strengthened the system.

But that was not to be. Mr. Wilkerson wrote John Cromwell again on February 3, 1933, that his office was requesting permission from the president of the United States to fill a position in the mathematics department at Dunbar High School (not Cardozo any more) within the next week or ten days at a salary of twenty-three hundred dollars. After noting that John was the number one candidate on the eligible list to teach mathematics, he informed him that "this office has the honor to offer you this appointment provided the President of the United States authorizes the use of the salary for this purpose." Cromwell was asked whether he would accept the position and "when we might expect you to report for duty."

Even though he was being asked, or invited, to return to his old school at a greatly reduced salary, to serve under a chairperson whose lack of qualifications was one of the reasons he had resigned in the first place, on February 6, 1933, John Cromwell wrote Mr. Wilkerson that he would accept the position on the terms outlined and that he would report for duty on March 1. But this begs the question, why did he choose to accept this position under these terms? The answer is simple: this was the Depression and other options were probably nonexistent in Washington. There were bills to be paid, even though John and his wife and daughter shared a home with his sisters. These circumstances were well known to the superintendent and the first assistant superintendent.

A week later, on February 13, 1933, John Cromwell, who apparently was still working at Howard University, was invited to Mr. Wilkerson's office for a meeting the following day at three o'clock. It is important to remember that in this somewhat restricted environment of a segregated Washington, and particularly in a segregated school system, there is no doubt that the "Cromwell case" was on everyone's lips. People lived in close proximity to one another and had occasion to meet on the street and at social affairs. Mr. Wilkerson's home was not too far from ours and no more pretentious. Three of John Cromwell's sisters were teaching in the system: Mary at Dunbar, Otelia at Miner Teachers, and Larcie at an elementary school. Otelia Cromwell had also had a confrontation of sorts with Mr. Wilkerson: it was he who had asked her to delay completing the work toward her doctorate. She had not complied with his request.

This meeting was the first of several that John Cromwell had with Mr. Wilkerson. John recorded that at the February 14 meeting, he was questioned about whether he had any plans to press suit on this case. He was also informed that a strict reading of the rules for reinstatement would show that the superintendent did *not* have to reinstate a former teacher, but that he *may* do so. Even though John was on the eligible list, the superintendent was not obligated to reinstate him. But as he was on the list, John did have certain vested rights.

Apparently, John Cromwell did not report to work on March 1 and/or was not given the final papers to do so, for on March 15, a month after the earlier meeting, he was called in for another conference with Mr. Wilkerson. At this time, the possibility of John Cromwell bringing a suit was also discussed as well as the rumor that Cromwell had remarked to Dr. J. Hayden Johnson, a black member of the Board of Education, that he was glad to get out of the system.

Cromwell said that he did not remember making the remark, but that in any case, it obviously had not affected his relationship with Dr. Johnson with whom he frequently played bridge.

At this meeting, the question of Cromwell having to take a physical examination was also introduced; it seems that this was a new requirement for all new teachers. Cromwell rejected this suggestion on the basis that he was not a new teacher and that during the twenty years he was teaching he had taken less than a week's absence because of illness.

During this time, John Cromwell met Dr. Johnson socially and was cautioned by him to "make good" with Dr. Ballou, the superintendent, as "they did not have to reappoint him." Dr. Johnson further urged him to tell Dr. Ballou "that if those were my sentiments at that time, they had changed now."

On March 20, John Cromwell met with the board a third time, this time accompanied by Otelia, who, because of repeated interrogation about why her brother wanted her present, voluntarily withdrew. Once again, John was asked whether he was going to bring suit. He agreed not "to antagonize [the] School Board," and he again requested to be placed at Miner Teachers College at his previous salary rank.

According to John Cromwell's notes on the meeting, Dr. Ballou was clearly annoyed with him and his requests. Dr. Ballou said "it was his duty to act in the public interest in these days of economy and saw no reason to pay a man $3,200 when he could get another perhaps just as good for $2,300."

John Cromwell did not alter his position and accordingly was not reappointed. He subsequently brought suit against the Board of Education (*U.S. in the Relation of John W. Cromwell, Appellant v. Marion Wade Doyle, President, Board of Education, District of Columbia*). The suit was argued on October 27, 1937, by the firm of Cobb, Howard, and Hayes and was denied on November 16, 1937. John Cromwell's lawyers planned an appeal, but it was never made. As a qualified certified public accountant, however, John Wesley Cromwell Jr. was able to develop a successful, if small, accounting firm.[6]

Throughout his life, John Cromwell Jr. remained close to his sisters and even shared a house with them. But perhaps his closest relationship was the one he had with his father while he was a student at Dartmouth. His letters to his father during these five years exemplify the bond between them.

6. See Theresa A. Hammond, *A White-Collar Profession: African American Certified Public Accountants since 1921* (Chapel Hill: University of North Carolina Press, 2002), 16–18.

For John, Dartmouth was more than an academic environment: it separated him briefly from his older sisters and gave him a sense of himself and the larger world of Blacks and Whites in which he would live.

In the spring of 1969, two years before he died, in an attempt to learn more about the campus life of black students at the turn of the century and to contrast it with the growing turmoil I was observing on campuses all around me, I interviewed my father about his college years. In our living room in Washington, against the noises of children and cars in the street, he responded to my questions. I regret not having followed up this interview, but distance and time did not permit.

SPRING, 1969

Interview of John W. Cromwell Jr., Age 85

By Adelaide Cromwell, His Daughter

At His Home in Washington, D.C.

AC: Daddy, I want to ask you about your college days. How did you happen to go to Dartmouth?

JWC: I selected Dartmouth from among four colleges—the colleges known as "Little Ivy League": Amherst, Williams, Wesleyan, and Dartmouth. Dartmouth was about the same size as those others, in those days. And looking through catalogues, all of which were sent me and which I read quite thoroughly—of course, I wrote for them myself and all like that—it seemed to be a little cheaper. In those days, you judged a college by its tuition. And Dartmouth's tuition seemed to be about fifty or sixty dollars cheaper than the others. Harvard and Yale were about $150 a year in those days.

AC: What was Dartmouth's?

JWC: Just about $110. Amherst and Williams were a little bit more.

AC: You told me how you had to go up there in those days, by stagecoach. Who went with you? There must have been some other people from here. The Montgomerys, for example.

JWC: Well, young Montgomery was in my class. His father was there in the 1870s.

AC: When you decided to go did you and Montgomery go together? How did you get there?

JWC: I went up. I was working in the hotel in the summertime, you know.

AC: Already you were?

JWC: Oh yes. Where did I work?

AC: You had begun to work before you went to college?

JWC: Yes.

AC: Where were you working?

JWC: At Saratoga and Atlantic City and places like that.[7]

AC: So what did you do?

JWC: You want to know how I got up there?

AC: Yes.

JWC: Well, I found that I had been given a scholarship, which was sort of beneficiary aid and was available to almost everyone who wanted one—whether they needed it or not. And . . .

AC: By Dartmouth?

JWC: By Dartmouth. And I had decided to take the entrance examination even though my certificate from Howard Prep admitted me, you know, in the hope that I might secure one of the opening scholarships—prize scholarships, you know. Well, somehow, I was doing all the writing, there was nobody else and they forgot to send the questions down here for me to take the examination so I had to resort finally to my certificate. Well, I didn't know enough about the various things you had to do. I had to take up everything, including my linen, I believe. And everything like that.

AC: They took linen up too?

JWC: Yes. Anyway, like a fool, I thought I'd get up there a day before school opened, you know. You see, which was a foolish stunt. Meanwhile Teelie was spending the summer in Fall River with a cousin of ours, on the Cromwell side, cousin William Carney.

AC: Carney, yes, I know who he was.

JWC: He was my father's first cousin.

JWC: Anyway, I had decided I would go up there. I had saved about fifty or sixty dollars, something like that, from my labors in the summertime and decided I was going up there. Teelie had found out there was a new line, a boat line running from New York to Fall River that was much cheaper to travel than by the old Fall River line. So I had to go that way and I checked my trunk. And I lost it on the way. In other words, it was the porter who left it, took my money and left it on the docks, you know, undelivered. I had to take a train from the Fall River line to the railroad station of the Boston and Maine, which came to New York, New Haven, and Hartford. Well, anyhow, I missed it. I was going to stay a couple of

7. Before going to Dartmouth, John worked during the summer at the Hotel Strand in Atlantic City. While in college, he spent his summers working at the Grand Union Hotel in Saratoga.

days in Fall River anyway. She wanted me to stop by and stay there. So I stayed there, losing my trunk temporarily on the way. Anyway, I had to. I decided that I'd go by train from Fall River to Boston and go across the town from the South Station to the North Station to go to Hanover. Anyway, I got up at four o'clock in the morning and went there. Had numerous directions. Teelie wanted to go up with me, but I vetoed that!

AC: Why?

JWC: Oh, she'd get in the way. It was natural for somebody to go with you. Anyway, I vetoed that and I got off. I took the 7:00 a.m. train from Boston, which meant I had to take the 4:00 p.m. train from Fall River to get to Boston. And I got up there and was very much frightened at the big station.

AC: What, in Boston?

JWC: Yes, South Station and on the other hand the Boston and Maine was across town. Anyway, I got over there and arrived in White River Junction about one or two o'clock. Well, I met these stagecoaches for the first time. And I paid my passage and told them about my trunk, and he gave me a ticket—an exchange slip—and I got in one of these stagecoaches and went on up. They still have them there—one or two—they bring them out for ceremonies at certain times of the year. I got there by inquiring about certain things. I had to go to change and register and such as that. I did all of that in about two or three hours. I found my room in Dartmouth Hall—old Dartmouth Hall.

AC: You were still a day early?

JWC: Well, maybe a day early. Yes, I guess I was, from actual opening day. Anyway, I found my way and did registration, got the key to my room. Nothing else, I had no furnishings to put into it or anything like that.

AC: Was a bed already in it?

JWC: I think the bed was there. Anyway, I met President Tucker and talked to him, talked to the dean and everything and all in a short time. Finally, I was walking across the campus and I saw Matt Bullock.[8] He was on the football squad playing that day and he came over and spoke to me. And I . . . I don't know what I said or anything like that, but I told him about losing my trunk. He said, "Well, come down and room with us until it comes," you see. So I went down with them.

AC: Who was "them"?

8. Matthew W. Bullock (1881–1972) graduated from Dartmouth in 1904 and from Harvard Law School in 1907. He was an important civic leader, and he served as special assistant to the Massachusetts attorney-general from 1925 to 1926 and as a chairman of the Massachusetts Parole Board.

JWC: A fellow named Marquess[9] and Dr. Graves[10] and a fellow named Jeffries, too. Anyway, I managed to get a little bit to eat that night. I couldn't get a job. I inquired two or three places—all were loaded up. And everything like that. Then after two or three days I was somewhat adjusted.

AC: Do you remember the first contacts you had with white students?

JWC: What do you mean contacts?

AC: I mean you mentioned Matt Bullock, so?

JWC: Contacts, well, several introduced themselves. You'd meet them on the way. "Jones, my name is Smith," so on, like that. "Where are you from?"

AC: Daddy, do you remember when you first began to meet some of the members of your class?

JWC: Yes, that day.

AC: Did they seem surprised to see you there?

JWC: Some of them wanted to know how did I happen to come up there and so forth.

AC: Most of those guys were from New England? Weren't they? Those white fellows?

JWC: Well, here and there.

AC: You had good contact with the faculty? What were your first recollections of working with the faculty on the campus?

JWC: Me and the faculty?

AC: Yes.

9. John Miller Marquess (Dartmouth 1904) was the son of a physician. He came to Dartmouth as a junior and was a member of Dartmouth's track team as a middle-distance runner. After graduating, he spent most of his first career years in Oklahoma, where he became politically active as a Democrat. Later, he joined the Republican Party. His highest honor came in 1932 when he was chosen to second the nomination of President Hoover at the Chicago convention. In 1915, he became president of the Colored Agricultural and Normal College in Langston, Oklahoma. In 1932, he moved to Philadelphia and engaged in the real estate business. At the time of his death, on May 3, 1936, he was the exalted ruler of the Quaker City Lodge of Elks and the head of the Eastern Federation of Negro Republicans.

10. Allen B. Graves (Dartmouth 1905) was the son of a truck man in Lynchburg, Virginia. He received his early education in Lynchburg and at the Howard University Preparatory School. He completed his first year of medical school at Dartmouth Medical School and then entered Harvard Medical School. He left Harvard after only six months because a promised scholarship did not materialize. He transferred to Howard University Medical School, from which he graduated in 1908. He was licensed to practice in New Jersey and New York, and he chose to live in Harlem, New York. For two years, he worked on the Pennsylvania Railroad as a dining car waiter to acquire some capital before he actually starting to practice medicine in 1910. Graves was active in the YMCA, the Urban League, and numerous medical societies, and he served as president of the Harlem Medical Association. He died at his home in Harlem on February 3, 1957.

JWC: It began in about a day or so—taking of enrollment, assignment of text-books.

AC: Did you get any feeling that they regarded you in a special way because you were a Negro?

JWC: No, no, no, I wasn't sensitive about that.

AC: You weren't?

JWC: No.

AC: How soon did you know you were going to major in the sciences?

JWC: Maybe not for a year or so.

AC: You didn't?

JWC: No.

AC: Can you think of anything that happened to you because you were a Negro? Looking back, of course, I'd be hard put to answer that about Smith, I'm just asking you to see whether you can recollect further than I can about your experiences?

[*long pause*]

AC: Did students show any avoidance or make any comments about you or the other guys?

JWC: Didn't notice so much.

AC: Did the Negroes, those fellows, Mr. Bullock and Dr. Graves, did they talk about the problems of being Negro students up there when they met in their rooms?

JWC: Didn't think so much—was a difference between poor students and not so poor. Most of the Negroes were in the poor class.

AC: You mean you think that the fact they were poor made more of a common bond than that they were Negroes?

JWC: I think so.

AC: What about the poor white students?

JWC: They were the same as the others.

AC: What do you mean by that?

JWC: They were all classified economically, you see, and they had just as hard a time making ends meet as the Colored.

AC: I see. There weren't any Negro students during your time who had any money?

JWC: By having any money, you mean able to pay their way, is that what you mean?

AC: Yes.

JWC: Well, one or two.

AC: Who was that?

JWC: Marquess had a little bit of money.

AC: Where was he from?

JWC: From the South, graduated from Fisk, was up there taking a couple of years. Montgomery would have been a higher class economically than I was, you know.

AC: Did he associate with you all, too?

JWC: No, not to any extent.

AC: Why not?

JWC: Just a naturally a snob, that's all.

AC: Was he Phi Beta Kappa too, Daddy?

JWC: No.

AC: What did he major in?

JWC: Well, I guess he majored in biology.

AC: Oh, that reminds me, how do you fit Dr. Just in this category?

JWC: Dr. Just[11] came the next year, well, he was more of an upperclassman to people like Talley Holmes[12] and people like that. He was pronounced a snob.

AC: Who? Dr. Just?

JWC: That's right.

AC: Where was he from?

JWC: Charleston, South Carolina.

AC: How could he afford to be a snob?

JWC: Just that disposition.

AC: You mean he didn't bother with any black students or white ones either?

JWC: Don't know about that. He went around with a few of the boys from his own school, Kimball Union Academy, you know.

AC: They were White?

JWC: Yes.

AC: And he didn't go around with any colored fellows the whole time he was there?

11. Ernest Everett Just (1883–1941) graduated Phi Beta Kappa from Dartmouth in 1907 and was the first recipient of the Spingarn Medal from the NAACP in 1915. In 1916, he received a Ph.D. in zoology from the University of Chicago. Just taught medicine at Howard University and was an associate at the Marine Biological Laboratory in Woods Hole, Massachusetts. For more on Ernest Just, see Kenneth R. Manning, *Black Apollo of Science: The Life of Ernest Just* (New York: Oxford University Press, 1983).

12. Talley Robert Holmes (1889–1969) graduated from Dartmouth in 1910 and enjoyed a successful career as a realtor in Washington, D.C. He was John Cromwell's lifelong friend and frequent tennis partner.

JWC: Never did. He might have looked up and associated with two or three people who had been there longer and made something of a reputation but he didn't even meet people like Talley Holmes.

AC: He was in Talley Holmes's class?

JWC: No, he was way ahead of Talley. Three years ahead of Talley. Senior when Talley was a freshman.

AC: He was a year behind you, though?

JWC: Yes, a year behind me.

AC: How did he regard you?

JWC: Well, don't know. He condescended to regard me pretty well because he couldn't do otherwise.

AC: Because he was a scientist and you were a scientist?

JWC: No, I was in the same class. Both of us poor, and everything like that, and both of us upperclassmen in a certain sense, and I didn't have to take any fat from him or anybody else, you see?

AC: Wonder how he happened to go to Kimball Union. Do you know?

JWC: I think he told me one time. Some white woman or someone was interested in him. Wanted him to go to Lincoln first but he decided to go to Kimball Union. So he went to Kimball Union instead of going into the senior class at Lincoln.

AC: And then from there on to Dartmouth?

JWC: That's right.

AC: About how many Negro students were in your class?

JWC: Negro students?

AC: Yes.

JWC: Just Montgomery.

AC: Just you and Montgomery?

JWC: Uh-huh.

AC: Oh, I didn't realize that.

JWC: King afterward came up there.

AC: Who did?

JWC: King, a little black man. You saw his picture in the reunion book.

AC: Yes. And then behind you in the class of 1907—Dr. Just and Heine.[13]

JWC: Yes, Dr. Just. No, Heine was two or three classes behind that.

13. "Heine" was W. Henry Bullock, who was in the class of 1909 but did not graduate. He lived in the Boston area and was the younger brother of Matthew Bullock. My father always said Heine was a better student than his brother and a better athlete. I do not know why Heine left Dartmouth, but I believe it was purely for financial reasons. In later years, when my father made his annual trip to visit me and to go to the Dartmouth-Harvard game, he always invited Heine, whose life had been spent in working-class jobs, to the game as his guest.

AC: Mr. Bullock was in what class?

JWC: 1904.

AC: Dr. Graves?

JWC: 1905.

AC: And Marquess?

JWC: 1904. He came up there from Fisk.

AC: What did you all do for recreation?

JWC: Various things, spectator sports, played cards.

AC: Who was the best cardplayer?

JWC: In college?

JWC: Well, couldn't tell, there wasn't any formal contest. Certain groups became known as playing a good game of whist. You know it was before the days of bridge. Good checker players.

AC: Cribbage?

JWC: I learned cribbage after I had been there about a year.

AC: Ping-Pong?

JWC: Yes [*with considerable feeling*]. I learned Ping-Pong.

AC: Tennis?

JWC: No, I didn't play any tennis.

AC: Wouldn't you say you were among the best cardplayers?

JWC: Yes, that's right.

AC: Well, why are you so modest?

JWC: Well, it wasn't anything. There wasn't any formal title or anything like that.

AC: Who was the best cribbage player?

JWC: I didn't play that for a long time. I remember one Sunday afternoon the guy who taught me went insane. Hyde Brown—one Sunday rainy afternoon.

AC: Was he White or Colored?

JWC: White.

AC: Hyde Brown. Where was he from?

JWC: From New York state or someplace like that.

AC: How did he happen to teach you?

JWC: Well, I happened to be in his room that day—to kill time.

AC: He suggested it to you?

JWC: I suppose he did, but I learned how to play, and I taught a lot of people after that time how to play.

AC: You did. Now, what else was I going to ask you? I don't suppose you all dated any girls in those days up there?

JWC: Weren't any up there. Hardly, one or two.

AC: I suppose you fellows came down to Boston.

JWC: Yes, in Boston we'd meet them on holidays and at games and such things as that.

AC: What were some of the girls' names? Do you remember? Was that Knocka Lee?

JWC: There were some around Boston. I didn't meet them until three or four years later. Knocka Lee, Bessie Trotter Craft.

AC: Bessie Trotter Craft, Knocka Lee. Was Emma Newman of that group? Or was she younger?

JWC: She was younger.

AC: I was just trying to think of some of the others who were around. Who was at Harvard then?

JWC: Harvard had about twenty colored students. A fine bunch. And whenever we'd come down there for the holidays or something, some of them made things very pleasant for us, you see. Then of course in any group you had some who were snobs. Locke was a snob.

AC: Was Locke there at the same time?

JWC: Yes, a year later.

AC: Who else was a snob?

JWC: Birnie.

AC: Oh yes, T. C.'s father. Who were some of the nicer ones?

JWC: Well, Ned Chesnutt. French Tyson.

AC: Ned Chesnutt? Where was he from?

JWC: From Ohio.

AC: Oh, was he the brother of the writer?

JWC: He was the son of the writer.

AC: Who else? Was that before Louis Wright?

JWC: Yes, before Louis Wright.

AC: The other man's name down to the beach.[14] I guess that was French Tyson.

JWC: No, he didn't stay down to the beach. His daughter is Mae Baker or something like that.

AC: What was the name of the big football player at Brown? You know?

JWC: Fritz Pollard? Oh, that was ten or fifteen years later.

AC: Oh, was it? Now, I want to ask you one more question for now and that is how did Grandfather feel about you going to Dartmouth?

JWC: Oh, he was very encouraging.

14. Highland Beach was a summer resort for Blacks outside of Annapolis, Maryland.

AC: He was?

JWC: Yes, that is the reason why some of these colored people around here don't like Poppa to this day, because he didn't send all of his children to Jim Crow colleges.

AC: Is that right?

JWC: Yes, that's right.

AC: You mean that there was a kind of dividing line in those days?

JWC: Well, those who had ambition usually wanted to go to white institutions, you see, for part of their education, if not for all.

AC: And Grandfather didn't feel that was right—to go to Jim Crow schools?

JWC: No, he encouraged us. Of course he didn't give us any help because he wasn't in any position to, you see.

AC: But he encouraged you to go?

JWC: Oh yes.

AC: Do you have any recollections, Daddy, of Dr. Crummell at all? A man called me up about him by the way. Do you have any personal recollections of his coming to the house?

JWC: Oh yes, tall and stately, tall black man, you know. English educated.

AC: What kind of accent did he have?

JWC: British, but not pronounced.

AC: Did he stop to talk with the children?

JWC: In the house? Well, not ordinarily. He came in as a matter of time of day, never thought of it as a special visit.

AC: Who else came in the house often in those days? This man, Mr. Slaughter, was he a friend of Grandfather's?[15]

JWC: Not any particular friend. He was a man there from Kentucky working in the printing office, and he associated as much as he could with people of a literary type, you see. And that was how he'd come in, but he was a good bit younger.

15. Henry Proctor Slaughter (1871–1958) was a typographer, journalist, leader of fraternal organizations, and book collector. He was the only Black to take the examination for the position of compositor at the Government Printing Office, and he worked there from 1896 to 1937. Although he had received his bachelor of law degree in 1899 and his master of laws degree in 1900 from Howard University, he never practiced law. He was active in Prince Hall Masons and Odd Fellows and was a member of the American Negro Academy, secretary of the Kentucky Republican Club in Washington, and a committeeman at the inaugurations of Presidents William McKinley, Theodore Roosevelt, William H. Taft, and Woodrow Wilson. His lifelong hobby was collecting books, pamphlets, music, photographs, prints, and manuscripts relating to black people. His ten-room house contained more than ten thousand volumes, many of them rare. He had one of the finest private collections of books on black history and culture in this country.

AC: Who was in Grandfather's circle—his cronies?

JWC: From that bunch?

AC: Yes.

JWC: Kelly Miller, two or three at Howard, round there.

AC: Give me some names? Kelly Miller,[16] Dr. Crummell, Grandfather. How about Murray?[17]

JWC: Yes, he worked at the Library of Congress. Yes, he was the father of Henry Murray. He was one of the litterateurs.

AC: Who else?

JWC: I wasn't.

AC: Oh, I'm not talking about your generation. I'm talking about your father's generation. Who else? How about Fred Douglass? Did he ever come to the house? Do you remember seeing him at the house?

JWC:I don't remember ever seeing him at the house.

AC: Apparently Grandfather did a lot of meeting with people.

JWC: Oh yes.

16. Kelly Miller (1863–1939), educator, essayist and intellectual leader, was a graduate of Howard University. Having passed the civil service exam during the first administration of Grover Cleveland, he was appointed clerk in the U.S. Pension Office. He privately studied advanced mathematics from 1867 to 1887 at the U. S. Naval Observatory, and from 1887 to 1889, he studied mathematics, physics, and astronomy at John Hopkins, which he was forced to discontinued for financial reasons. In 1890, he was appointed professor of mathematics at Howard University where he spent his entire career, later becoming dean of the College of Arts and Sciences. Although a mathematician by training, Miller's interest turned to sociology, and for ten years (1915–1925), he taught sociology and served as head of the department. From 1907 to 1919, as dean, Miller was a tremendous influence at Howard and was an important factor in student recruitment. As a lecturer, Miller felt free to criticize Washington, Du Bois, and William Monroe Trotter, and he wrote extensively about his views. As a college administrator, Miller played an important role in modernizing the curriculum at Howard and also in introducing the systematic study of the Negro to the curriculum. Miller was a member of the American Negro Academy.

17. Daniel Alexander Payne Murray (1852–1925) was a librarian, bibliographer, and biographical researcher. In 1871, he became a personal assistant to the librarian of Congress, during which time he became proficient in several languages and acquired invaluable research skills. In 1881, he became assistant librarian, a position he held until his retirement in 1923.

In 1900, Murray compiled a preliminary list of 270 books by "Negro" authors. By 1904, the list was expanded to five thousand books. He worked for twenty-seven years on a mammoth project—a six-volume "Encyclopedia of the Colored Race" or "Murray's Historical and Biographic Encyclopedia of the Colored Race throughout the World." Among those he sought as assistant editors were John E. Bruce, John W. Cromwell, William S. Scarborough, Arthur A. Schomburg, and Richard R. Wright Jr. This work was never published.

When Murray died, he left a book-length manuscript, "Bibliography of Negro Literature and Historical Sketch of Negro Authors and Authorship," which contained almost five hundred biographical portraits of Negro historical figures and more than 250,000 index cards with book titles and background information on events significant to black people worldwide.

AC: I am trying to find out who these other people were and you aren't much help!!

The thirty-nine letters included here are from John W. Cromwell Jr. to his father. The letters begin in August 1901, when John was working in Atlantic City, before he left for Dartmouth, and end with an undated letter from West Lynn, Massachusetts, probably written in the fall of 1907, when John was an apprentice at the General Electric Company, before he returned to Washington for good.

It is interesting, given the relationship between the children and their father's second wife, that three letters from John to his stepmother have survived. The first was written at the same time he wrote another to his father, but the letter to his stepmother addresses different problems, such as clothing. In the second, written after he was settled in at Dartmouth, John explains to her and through her to the other members of the family something of his circumstances there. The third, penned during his first lonely Christmas, is a thank-you letter for a box of food. In all three letters, he calls her "Mother."

Clearly, John Wesley Cromwell felt closer to his son than to his daughters, for he kept most, if not all, of John's letters and not those, with a few exceptions, from his daughters, Otelia and Mary, who were also away at college during roughly the same period. Regrettably, John Cromwell Jr. kept none of his father's letters to him. John's letters reveal not only the close bond between him and his father but also the closeness among the children of John Wesley Cromwell. Financial assistance was always needed and when possible provided; even the smallest amount was appreciated. Important, too, was the need to work, to have a job, and jobs in Hanover were less easily found than they were in larger cities such as Boston or New Haven. Summer employment was crucial. John Cromwell worked at the Grand Union Hotel in Saratoga Springs, New York. Apparently, this was his mainstay. Poor students, like John, could not afford to go home on holidays, and he spent many holidays in cold isolation on an almost deserted campus.

Understandably, a man of John Wesley Cromwell's talents and interests would have wanted to know all about his son's academic experiences at Dartmouth: what courses he was taking and why, and he, in turn, could offer, at a level unusual for parents of college students, but most certainly unusual for black parents, understanding and advice, which was appreciated by his son.

Although the letters do not reflect it, at this time there was a lively debate over what kind of education—classical or industrial—was most useful for Blacks. My father only makes reference to this debate in his interview with me. It is odd that

Grandfather apparently did not share with his son the problems and conflicts at the *Record*. John seems completely oblivious of them, only wanting more news from the *Record*.

In the letters, the priorities of the Cromwell family are clear. Education was expected to be rigorous. Clothing was discussed only because of the climate, and little attention was paid to recreation or extracurricular activities. One's future goals were important.

Neither the interview conducted sixty-two years after he left Dartmouth nor the letters written while he was a student reveal rancor, bitterness, or even racial prejudice. College was serious business, and John Wesley Cromwell Jr.'s goal was to get an education. His father expected him to excel, for the future of the race required persons of competence with a seriousness of purpose.

Indeed, it is only in letters written to his friend John Bruce that John W. Cromwell Sr. freely expresses his paternal pride in his children's accomplishments, because for all his brilliance, his own formal education, compared to theirs, was limited and inferior.

August 5, 1901

Dear Papa,

I received your letter last week and I was very sorry to hear that you were not able to take that trip to Hampton for I know that it would have been beneficial to you from a standpoint of health. But prospects of a trip to Phila. will repay you.

I have not seen nor heard anything of that man of whom you spoke but I shall diligently look him up. I wrote a letter two weeks ago to uncle Levi, but I assume he did not receive it as I have not been answered as yet. If you go to Phila. I wish you would bring that full-dress suit home for I shall not have any room for it, and some clothes which I intend to buy in Phila; unless I purchase a suit-case.

Hoping to hear from you soon,

Your son,
John

August 19, 1901

Dear Father—

I hope you will not think hard of me for not writing before but I've been so hard pressed that I didn't have time.

I am so sorry to hear that Lou Kelley is dead; it was quite a shock to me.

Hereafter I'll try to write every week.

Uncle Levi was down here last week, but I did not see him as he remained only one day. I think I'll be home on the 15th of September.

Your son,

Johny

Hanover, N.H.

March 29, 1902

Dear Father:

The other day I received five dollars by money order: the handwriting was unfamiliar to me, and inasmuch as the letter contained a bill of a concert to be given in honor of Lieut. Tomey. I thought you had sent it; if you have I thank you ever so much. My expenses are $27.13 and including the money which I have received from Otelia and Uncle Levi, I have $18. in all.

Almost every Saturday evening we have some eminent speaker to give us an informal talk; last evening Mr. Ames,[18] who has traveled extensively in Cuba and the Philippines addressed us; during his talk he spoke of his interview with a southern planter. "Well, Colonel do you employ white or colored help on your plantation" "Neither" says the colonel, "I employs 'niggahs!"

This shows how adverse the southern crackers are to giving us a decent name.

This morning I received a letter from Cousin Lizzie inviting me to spend the Easter recess with her and her family but I shall be obliged to decline. The recess lasts from April 1 to April 15th. I don't suppose this vacation will be as dull as Christmas, before there are generally about 50 to 75 students remaining in Hanover. Besides these the baseball and track team candidates are given only one week.

I thank you for your kindness in defending the students who have been suspended from Howard. Please don't let this be your only effort along this line, but whoop it up until those in authority take cognizance of it. It won't do any harm and will incidentally help to fill up. Papa, why do you have accounts of these kids' parties appear on the very first page? I am glad to hear that you are at last a Mason.

Love to all.

John

18. Oak Ames (1874–1950) was an instructor of botany at Harvard University, an author, and a promoter of economic botany. His interest in orchids took him to the Philippines, the Caribbean, South America, and other regions of the world.

In this and in a subsequent letter, my father refers to student unrest at Howard University, but aside from this, it has been difficult to get any details on the circumstances of the conflict. The archives of Howard University[19] reveal nothing, and there are no extant copies of the *Record*. But the basic reason for the unrest is not a mystery: the students felt that a black institution should be led by a black.

For many decades after the resignation of General Oliver O. Howard, the president of Howard University, there was considerable conflict over the leadership of the university. The trustees refused to elect John Mercer Langston, the eminent dean of the law school and vice president of the university, to replace General Howard. Instead, they elected a series of white presidents who, according to Raymond Wolters, ultimately had their power so severely circumscribed that the black deans—George William Cook and Lewis B. Moore—were actually in control of the institution.[20]

Predictably, the students became involved in this issue.[21] During the tenure of Jeremiah E. Rankin, who was president of the university from 1890 to 1903, students began to express their feelings. A few years after the unrest, Dr. Furmann J. Shadd, a professor of materia medica and therapeutic and secretary and treasurer of the medical school, commented on the students' behavior: "There has been disorder and occasional open rebellion on that hill for over two years." President Rankin resigned after one of these upheavals.

This is the situation about which my father was inquiring and about which I could find no more details.

In any case, acknowledged or not, after Rankin's resignation, the students continued to protest. In 1903, when John Gordon, a white Presbyterian minister who had been named president after Rankin's resignation, attempted to restrict the power of the deans by limiting their terms to one year, it became a matter of public interest and controversy. The students, siding with Cook and Moore, hissed at the president during chapel. One hundred students walked out in open defiance. The deans then refused the president's demands that the students be suspended.

The matter of Gordon's tenure as president involved the larger community, and many sought his resignation. As Archibald Grimké, who was among those

19. Walter Dyson, *Howard University, the Capstone of Negro Education, a History: 1867–1940* (Washington, D.C: Graduate School of Howard University, 1941), 63.

20. Raymond Wolters, *The New Negro on Campus: Black College Rebellions of the 1920s* (Princeton: Princeton University Press, 1975), 78.

21. See data on the controversy in the *Washington Tribune* (December 17, 2005) and in other undated clippings on file at the archives of Howard University, Washington, D.C.

against Gordon, pointed out, the issue at hand was how the white president of a black school should behave vis-à-vis the black community. Apparently, the community felt that "Gordon had chosen to live as a white man though heading a black institution. In order to get himself and his family into the social swim of the capital, he accepted the color line, sent his child to white schools in Washington, held himself aloof from black students and professors and found various ways to avoid inviting black dignitaries to dine in the president's mansion." Grimké insisted that Gordon should decide whether he wanted to be president of Howard or whether he wanted to be a white man enjoying all the privileges to which he would be entitled because of his color.

William Sinclair, the financial agent for the university from 1888 to 1903, called a public meeting, which was presided over by the Honorable George H. White,[22] with Sinclair himself as secretary. As a result, those in attendance at the public meeting submitted a report to the trustees stating that "the student body, the alumni and the friends of the university believe with singular unanimity that [Gordon] is not the right man for the place, either by feeling or education, and he has deeply wounded on more than one occasion the sensibilities of his students and of colored men connected with the teaching force of the institution." The report also delineated the many other deficiencies of President Gordon: "he has not the wherewithal of up-to-date wide awake and resourceful education to meet these needs, to attack successfully the peculiar problems of the University in education, finance and in institutional reform and re-adjustment."

At the same time, another group in Washington supported Dr. Gordon and felt that charges were being made against him because he was persona non grata to some of the deans under him and to a small percentage of the students. They believed that the controversy had been fabricated to get Gordon out to make room for someone else. William Calvin Chase, the editor of the *Washington Bee,* was among those who supported Dr. Gordon.

There was a persistent rumor, however, that the matter had been initiated by a former member of the staff who had collected funds for the university on the understanding that one-third were to be his. The staff member was later discharged, as it was decided that Dr. Gordon could collect the money himself, at less expense to the university. Apparently, one individual was seen as the instigator, as the person who created the petition and stirred up the students' interests, and the suspicion fell on Dr. Sinclair. Further fueling the controversy was the fact

---

22. George White was elected to represent North Carolina in the Fifty-fifth Congress in 1896 and in 1898. He left Congress on March 4, 1901, as the last of the post-Reconstruction congressmen.

that while Dr. Gordon was the son of a respected abolitionist, Alexander Gordon of Pittsburgh, and therefore initially thought to have the proper credentials, he was also the brother-in-law of Tennis S. Hamlin, the president of the Board of Trustees.

Amid the cries that there should be "a colored president for a colored school," Gordon resigned in 1906. Maybe the time was not right, but there was so much disagreement over the choice of a black candidate that another white president, Wilbur P. Thirkield, was selected. Thirkield resigned in 1912 to become a bishop in the Methodist Episcopal Church and was not replaced by a black candidate.

GIMBEL BROTHERS
Philadelphia
Atlantic City Office   August 6, 1902

Dear Father:

I suppose you have been disappointed at not having received a letter from me but I did not have time to write one and send it in time for the papers.

I left my job and went to work at a large hotel as messenger but I am not making any money. I get only $12 per month make on an average of $.20 a day but I expect to go to a better job on Saturday.

It seems as though everything is working to keep me from making any money. I heard that Ada Thomas was here but I have not seen her as yet.[23]

The colored bathers at Wall's are becoming more and more every day. Of course you know that Mrs. Cardozo is running a hair dressing establishment down here.

Since the shooting affair,[24] the white people have been using every way to keep the colored people from lounging under the piers and several have gone so far as to try to make the papers work to that end, but one came out in strong condemnation of those who were endeavoring to accomplish such a purpose. And too another thrust has been made at the colored people. A law has been enacted prohibiting people from going through the streets in bathing costume in as much as the bath-house-keepers refuse to rent to colored people.

23. This could be Adah B. Thomas (1863–1943), a registered nurse and civil rights leader.

24. This is probably a reference to a crime well described in the headlines of the *New York Times* of August 25, 1902: "Fleeing Slayer Wrecked after Shooting His Wife and a Man. [Leander] Smith Put to Sea. Rescued while clinging exhausted to overturned boat. Put ashore and captured by Trick." The shooting occurred in the basement of Hotel Canfield, where the victim, Boyd Clinton, was head waiter.

The Cuban X Giants "The Colored Wonders" have been here for a series of games. This team is easily the equal of any in either league.

Among them is Mr. C. A. Oliver, a former classmate of mine, who for years was a star back and pitcher on Howard's varsity.

I have not as yet written to either Uncle Levi or to Otelia but I intend to on Saturday.

Hoping all are well

I remain

John

GIMBEL BROTHERS
Philadelphia
Atlantic City Office
8-8-1902

Dear Papa:

I hope you will look over the fact that I did not write you sooner but I having heard nothing of your return was waiting to hear from you.

I am sorry that I am unable to come home but you know that $7 is not to be despised, especially by one in my circumstances.

Will you please have the following books sent with my trunk, Homer's Iliad, Xen Anabasis, Greek Grammar and Lexicon, Joynes German Grammar, King and Wentworth Algebra. All of these are at home. Will you also send me that Harkness Latin Grammar (if you have one to spare) and any other books you think I might need. I have all the paper and pens that I need.

I shall make about $65 which with $20 that I have now in the bank will make $85. Out of which I have to pay my expenses. I shall have to buy a suit and an extra pair of pants, two pairs of shoes and an overcoat later on. I shall be compelled to pay $50. expenses right away and inasmuch as I have not received a position as waiter, my board will cost me $3. per week, that is if the position isn't settled.

So if you can give me the money for one pair of good shoes I think I won't need any more just yet from you.

I shall, unless something happens, be in Phila. on Thursday next and I leave on Monday the 15th.

Hoping you are in good health.

I am

John

P.S. Please send some copies of *The Record* for I like to know what is going on.

GIMBELL BROTHERS
Philadelphia
Atlantic City Office
9-8-1902

Dear Mother:

I received your letter this morning and was quite surprised to hear that you were in Washington. I suppose you would like to hear how I am in respect to clothes. Well I have two suits (1.00 a suit) of Fall underwear so I won't need any other until the 1st of Nov. I bought four colored shirts at a sale so I need only white ones size 14. I have enough soap to last me the winter so I am allright there. If you can afford it get me the little things as neckties, handkerchiefs, collars and cuffs and I will be more than thankful. If the trunk is there by Saturday it will be in time for I don't need them till Monday.

When you write a letter again mail it to Phila. and tell me all that is going on. Otelia is going only as far as Boston with me.[25]

It would only be a useless expenditure of money for her to accompany me to school since she knows no more than I do about buying a cot and a washstand and a couple of chairs.

Be sure and send me plenty of bed-clothing and towels.

Respecting an early reply

I am

John

Hanover, N.H.
10/4/1902

Dear Mother:

I hope you will excuse my delay in writing for I thought I would try to have some system and therefore decided to write every Saturday.

I have changed my room and I am now staying in a suite of 4 rooms with three colored students for, you see in that way I don't need to buy so many things since the rooms up here are absolutely bare of furniture. If you can send me a couch cover I'll be ever so much obliged.

When you sent my trunk you forgot to put in some towels which I most need.

---

25. Note the change of plans in the earlier interview. My father was also helped and loved by his older sister Otelia, but he did not always take kindly to her concern. She was a mother figure whom he loved but often resented.

When you send those please put in some cover for the winters up here are 20°
below zero (you know I am only 100 miles from Montreal).

When I came here I thought I would walk right into a place but I was disappointed. This college is just full of poor students who of course get all the chances
and a freshman has no show.

I hope to be able to get something soon since I hate to burden Lucy who is so
kind to lend me board money.

Hoping to hear from you soon.

John

Hotel Strand
Atlantic City

Hanover
November 2nd 1902

Dear Father:

I just received a letter from uncle Levi in which there was a five spot to help
me out in buying an overcoat. I took it and bought shoes and paid my laundry
bill.

The lessons are somewhat hard especially Greek and English.

If you have time please write to Mr. Baugh about a position next summer; I
have already written to Uncle Levi concerning the same but it won't hurt to be
on the safe side.

Gym work has not yet begun but I think it will commence about Thanksgiving.

I have gained a little in weight and am hoping it will continue to increase.

Hoping to hear from you soon.

I remain,
John

Hanover N.H.
December 14, 1902

Dear Father:

While reading *the Boston Guardian,* I saw an account of the J. C. Price Literary
Society,[26] and thinking that you might be able to dispose of a few pictures, I send
you this notice.

---

26. Joseph Charles Price (1854–1893) was a clergyman (A.M.E.), educator, editor, orator, and civil
rights advocate. He received his BA (1879) and his theology degree (1881) from Lincoln University.

The weather has been extremely cold, the temperature running from 150 above to 250 below; it snows every other day, but one soon learns not to mind it is never sloppy.

The gym course which began last Wednesday will prove quite beneficial to me I hope; I have already lost two pounds but I expect to regain it in time.

Last week I saw two deer which had been shot a little out from the town.

I have not an overcoat, and if you are able to give one I don't think I shall burden you any more until March when the term bills are due; Clothiers from Boston are here every week or so, and I can buy a good heavy one that will last me three or four years, for $15. The little one that I bought last fall is so small that I cannot get it on.

I read about Prof. Miller in the *Guardian;* his speech, so I learned, was not so well received because of its dual character. I was very much impressed with that paper for I really think it is the best Negro paper I've seen; I did not see anything striking in the editorials but what caught my eye especially was the large amount of news concerning our people, for there were notes from almost every town of prominence in the east.

I find that the colored people of the north hold Booker T. Washington in very low esteem: They regard him as a "toady" and as a "white man's niggah" I find that my inability to compose coupled with my bad chirography is quite an obstacle in my path.

I see that St. Luke's has enlarged her hall; I think Rev. Waller had long contemplated such, but I didn't think that it would be done as soon.

After the 23rd hardly more than ten students will be left at Hanover, for so great is the exodus at the time, that the rail road has to provide special trains.

Please tell the others to drop a line now and then, for I always rejoice on receiving a letter from home.

John.

He was licensed to preach in 1876. Price assisted in the establishment of Zion Wesley College—later named Livingstone College—in Salisbury, North Carolina, in 1882. He is often ranked with Frederick Douglass as a powerful orator, but he refused to be considered for the bishopric. He served as president of the National Afro-American League and also of the National Equal Rights Convention. Although a Democrat, he did not participate in party politics. Only his premature death, at the age of forty, kept him from being acknowledged as one of the most influential Blacks of the latter part of the nineteenth century.

Hanover, N.H.
12/28/1902

Dear Mother:[27]

I received your nice box last night and am very much pleased with the contents. I think the cake is the best of all inasmuch as the chicken was somewhat spoiled because of the delay in delivering.

Things are rather dull up here all the fellows are away except ten or twelve. I suppose Larcie is beginning to prepare for the "Rosebud party" which is considered to be the leading social among the young folks.

I've been promised a job for next winter, therefore my board is assured. The weather is somewhat mild today, being about zero. I read in the *Record* about "The Negro Academy."

I pay now only $3.25 a week for board thereby making $3.50 pay for board and laundry.

Hoping all are well and are having a fine time during the holidays.

I remain,
John

Hanover, N.H.
January 5th, 1903

Dear Father:

I suppose you had given up hope of receiving a letter from me, because of my great delay in answering your letter: the rooms have been so cold during the holidays that one could hardly sit in them.

I have passed a quite pleasant recess even though the place was almost deserted; I've played cards and checkers, done a little reading and the rest of the time I spent in snow shoeing. College opens Wednesday, and then we will be occupied with our work. The exams begin about the 28th of January.

The weather has been rather sloppy for the past few days; therefore walking has been extremely disagreeable. Tell Otelia and the other girls to write me sometime.

Love to all,
John

P.S. I enjoyed your candy very much.

27. This letter was written on stationery from the Hotel Strand in Atlantic City, where John apparently had worked the previous summer.

Hanover, N.H.

March 8th, 1903

Dear Father:

I rather expected you to roast me because of my failure to pull a 95 mark in English. Of course I should have made more than 60, but still my low mark was not the consequence of previous inattention in Prep., nor in public school, for my good exam in English shows that; but it was due to my inability to write themes, an art which does not fall to the lot of everyman. However, I am improving and expect to acquire a fairly good use of English. This semester, in addition to the regular theme work, we have a course in oratory; in this course each freshman speaks two declamations, and the third one he composes himself. I have already spoken once: mine was Kellogg's "Spartacus to the Gladiators". Taking the criticism of the students as criterion, I did very well.

This course causes many men to fail; consequently our classes are augmented by the presence of many sophomore and juniors.

In regard to W. Mont, my work is considerably better than his. He is few points ahead in English but that's all. I don't know his marks exactly for I am not very intimate, and I don't care so much as to inquire; but in the opinions of the fellows he is not considered to be either an exceptionally good scholar, or a fellow. Concerning my standing in class, I know very little except that English pulled me down. I have a rank of 83 or 84 percent and I don't think there are any more than ten or twelve higher than that.

I don't feel like trying for any high marks as long as I have English on my list, for I know it is impossible to secure them; however, next year I shall be free of it and then, if I feel like it, I may do some work. Up here, no one except the grinds does any hard studying. If a fellow receives 50 he is satisfied, still, although I am making no great attempt to secure high honors, 50 will not satisfy me.

I will now proceed to tell you something about our life in the gymnasium. As yet I can discover no great good it has done me, but as long as it does me no harm I can be satisfied. We go over there, put on light clothing and commence to toss the medicine ball; afterwards, we take a few rounds on the parallel bars, plying rings, suspended ladders, dumb bells etc. then after having taken a cold shower we depart, each to his particular room. Otelia can explain the different apparatus to you. I suppose you would like to hear something about the social side of college life. In the place there [are] fraternities to which no colored men belong, because, you know, all fraternities north and south, are affiliated in a united order of fraternities. College Hall is the social headquarters of the college; in it there's a room containing all the daily newspapers, another smoking and lounging room with all the current magazines, another a trophy room. In another part of the room are ping-pong, and card tables and pool and billiard rooms. This semester I am not doing much in Latin; we have a dry Prof. and we all go to sleep during the recitation.

In solid Geometry, I am in the same section as W. Mont, and I am making him look like the proverbial thirty cents. For the past 3 or 4 days we have been having problems in computation as (what is the ratio of tetrahedron to a cube both having the same edge). Such problems, I have been the only one able to work.

It is gradually becoming warmer up here; the snow is rapidly melting thus causing disagreeable walking. Did you receive the *Aegis* which I sent you a couple of weeks ago. I sent it by mail and if you have not yet received it, please let me know at once. Also send Mr. Baugh's address.

John

Hanover, N.H.
May 30th 1903

Dear Father:-

I suppose you will think that every good letter, which I write is but the forerunner of a bad one; for I am sorry to say that the café which I am working closes to-morrow night; but I guess I can eke out this year all right. The Rathskeller which has recently been established in College Hall has driven the café out of business. It seems as though I certainly play in hard luck for I thought I had a steady job for the next three years.

I have made my electives for next year; they are as follows: Math, History, French, German, and Physics. I shall begin Chemistry the second semester. I've dropped Latin and English for next year, but shall resume them in my junior year. At Dartmouth the group system is in vogue; there are three groups: Math, History, Languages. One must make a major in one group and a minor in each of the other two. Math is my major.

A major subject lasts three years; a minor two years. The object of this system is to prevent students from electing all the cinches, and to make sure they know something about three subjects, I see from the *Star* the university has at last chosen a new President. What do you know about this Rev. Gordon? I don't remember having seen his name among those which appeared in the *Record*. I thank you ever so much for the money which you sent me. School closes on the 25th, but the exams end on the 19th consequently I won't be obliged to remain over.

Love to all
John.

Hanover, NH.
6/7/1903

Dear Father:

I hope you won't think hard of me for not answering your letter before now, thanking you for your kind gift, but to tell the truth I had just written to you when I received your letter and I should have written immediately, had I not known how distasteful 150 word letters are to you. I thank you ever so much for all you have given me, and I hope to be able to do something for you this summer. I am glad to hear that you are going to have a chance to visit New York. I wrote recently to Mr. Baugh concerning my job this summer, but inasmuch as I have not received an answer it's hard for me to say when I shall begin work. The exams commence Wednesday and continue until the 20th.

The other day I inquired my status of the English instructor; he said if I passed a good exam as I did last semester, I had a chance of pulling a good mark.

I think I shall adopt teaching as an avocation. Although this may displease some members of our household still it seems to me to be by far the best policy for a person to make teaching his aim in life, rather than, after having made a bid for a professional plum, to accept teaching as a consolation prize and as a haven of last resort. With this aim in view I shall endeavor to make myself fit in Math and modern languages for work in secondary schools. I don't suppose I shall be able to come to Washington before next Christmas, unless something good falls upon me. When you see me you'll probably find the same 5'4" 117 pound boy which left your home last July. What's the matter with the *Record?* It has not appeared for two weeks, much to my disappointment.

John

Hanover, N.H.
6/14/1903

Dear Father:

I suppose at this time, you are beginning to computate long rows of figures for your reports; while I on the other hand am just now enduring the exams, which are coming in quick succession. I made 95 in the German exam tied for first place: The Professor said he was much disappointed because I didn't get a hundred.

I have not heard from English or Greek, but I feel sure I am up to 85 in each subject. I have yet to take Latin, Solid and Trig. I am due to arrive in Saratoga June 22nd, two or three days after the exams. I received a card this morning from Mr. Baugh. I have been working for my board at the hotel for 4 days, and I think I stand a good show of receiving work for next year.

That was a good strong editorial on Howard in this week's *Record;* I liked it very much.

I'll be in Hanover over Saturday, so I'll be able to receive next week's edition. The next letter I write will be from Saratoga, because the exams, packing up, etc will keep me from having anything much to say. Last night all but the freshmen, enjoyed "wet-down." All students arranged in order of classes, march around all the halls, and then back to the campus, where lemonade is served. The sophomores, as generally do spoiled that which was intended for the freshmen.

Will Larcie have to be appointed before those of the graduating class?

Love to all.

John

Grand Union
Saratoga Springs
6/28/1903

Dear Father:

Well I am in Saratoga at last. This hotel is the largest I have ever seen; it accommodates about 1500 people: some of its halls are 300 yards long. I would make a good bit of money if the bellboys had all the privileges that boys usually have. We have nothing to do with the small baggage, nor do we make anything on the pressing; still I think I shall be able to make a little over a hundred. Mr. Baugh is a very fine head bellman; all the boys like him. John Beckett is also running bells up here. Of the 45 bellmen at this hotel about 30 are students. The Harrisburg contingent is very strong. I left Dartmouth a week ago yesterday and began work Sunday morning. The work up here is rather hard, but I think I shall be able to stand it. Of course we have the usual hotel food; such as brown sugar instead of granulated. This hotel believes in employing colored men. The two mail clerks are colored teachers from Harrisburg, besides the head gas man is colored. Berkley Waller is secretary to the head waiter. The dining room is so long that a person at one end cannot recognize another at the other end. For recreation the fellows play whist, which is the card game of the higher class of the colored gentry. A nephew of Uncle Willis is working on my watch. There are about ten different springs in this town. The bellmen at this hotel can drink free providing they go before 7:00 a.m.

Please send *The Record.*

Love to all
John

Address the letter care of Mr. J. Baugh

10/15/1903

Dear Father:

I thank you ever so much for your kind and generous gift and you may be sure that I shall spend the same judiciously. I hope that you in giving it did not deprive yourself of anything. Today is a holiday, it being athletic Field Day. Tomorrow almost the entire college will journey to Newton Center to see the football game between Dartmouth and Williams. I have not secured a job as yet, but I am still trying. Work is harder to get this year owing to the fewness of boarding houses.

We are still having fine weather, the air is dry and crisp, and everyone is enjoying it.

I see that Messrs. Trotter and Martin have been sentenced to jail for thirty days. I suppose when he is again free, he'll go traveling around the country delivering lectures against Booker. I don't seem to be able to get the hand of my subjects as yet though I suppose they come around in a short time. I think I told you before that I am rooming with a Jeffreys, cousin of Mr. Hunter of Metropolitan Church fame. I saw in the *Star* that Howard's new president was given an enthusiastic reception by the students of the Medical School and I judge from his address that he believes in college education along modern lines. Tell mama I'll write Sunday; also tell Otelia and Larcie that when I've read their lengthy epistles, I shall take a day off to answer them.

Love to all
John

Myles Standish Hotel
South Duxbury, Mass.
Hanover, N.H.
12/6/1903

Dear Papa:

I thought I would not wait for you to answer my letter, for I know you don't have the spare time to write very often though when you do get the chance you certainly write a fine letter. We have been enjoying skating for a couple of weeks, but now the snow is falling fast and we have said goodbye to the bare ground until next April. I have decided to elect chemistry next semester instead of Graphics which I shall drop. Next year I am going to take History as you suggested.

I shall continue math, though I am not going to take civil engineering for it is not much use for a fellow who is a poor drawer to take this course. I could get through it alright, but I don't like it and I should not like to enter upon a profession, for which I don't care.

I should like to go to Boston this Christmas. Some of my Harvard friends said I could stay with them, so my room rent would cost me little or nothing and I could board very cheaply at one of those restaurants, so if you can afford me some money so I can take the trip.

I shall probably pass through Washington about January 30th; I won't stop over for it would only set the gossips on P.P.[28] to asking questions. I hope mama's father is getting better; has she gone to Mechanicsburg yet? Tell Otelia to please send me those books namely, analytical Ge, and Calculus.

Love to all,
John

Hanover, N.H.
January 12th 1904

Dear Father:

I suppose you are just recovering from the effects of a Merry Christmas and are ready to return to the classroom. I remained in Hanover until the Monday after Christmas when I went to Boston. It was about 45° below zero in this town during the last cold snap and no one escaped without having some part of his body frozen. While in Boston I met all the New England College men, who were spending their vacations in Boston. You asked me in your last letter to tell you

28. Pierce Place, the name of their street.

what I intended to do when I finish college. It is my intention to teach higher Math. in some southern college if possible. I shall be unable to go south this winter owning to a change in the schedule of the exams, which do not end until February 10th. Mr. Baugh starts south on January the 19th, so you see I would have to leave school before the end of this semester, something I should not like to do. If you get a chance please send me some colored Washington newspapers as I should like to learn what's going on in the capitol.

Love to all
John

Hanover, N.H.
January 13th 1904

Dear Lucy:[29]

I am unable to go south this winter owing to a change in the schedule of exams, which do not end until February the 10th. I should have to go on the 19th of this month if I should go at all, something which I should not like to do. Will you be able to renew your former offer of lending me $15. per month, as I am certainly broke at the present time. What kind of Christmas did you have? I was down to Boston for the last week of the recess and I enjoyed myself very much. I saw Tyson and Chesnutt on their return from Washington: they spoke of having seen some of the family. Tell Otelia I never received that Analytic which she sent me. How is everyone on Pierce Place? Is Fanny going to school this year?

If you lend me that $15. per month, I guess I shall be able to pay that $50. from another source.

John

Hanover N.H.
January 18th

Dear Father

What has happened at home? I have not heard anything from any of you since the 13th of December. How is Fanny? I hope she is recovered by this time. I remained in Hanover during the holidays; they were rather dull but I did not mind them much. The first semester examinations are almost due. According to my plans I shall remain in Washington only during the month of March.

---

29. As I recall my aunts, Lucy had the sweetest and caring disposition of them all. This letter is included as it portrays the support John received from his sisters, in this case, his sister who was least able to offer help.

I wish you'd see about that job; I want to be sure about it. I see that the Negroes of Washington are going to give three balls during the Inauguration.

I read Prof. K. Miller's address delivered to the Educational Society of Boston, and liked it very much.

I have made my electives for next semester: they are as follows—chemistry, Physics, French, Geology, mathematics and Logic. I am unable to continue German this semester because of conflicts.

Hoping all are well and wishing for a speedy reply.

> I remain,
> John.

> Hanover, N.H.
> January 24th, 1904

Dear Father:

I suppose it is just as easy a job for me to receive a Rhodes scholarship as it would be for a blind person to find a needle in a haystack; nevertheless I should be very glad if such an opportunity should come into my hands.

I'm not taking History this year, because I dropped it for Graphics. You all seem to have the same opinion concerning the latter subject; that it may be acquired by anyone with patience: if such were the case no one would be spending any time on it. It is easily in the class with painting, sculpture, and music. If I were just beginning my college course, I should certainly go to Harvard, because of the facilities which they offer for self help: I suppose that out of the 28 colored students at Harvard, 25 pay less than $175.00 a year for expenses.

Will you please send me the *Souls of Black Folk* which I forgot to bring with me. Is Lucy going to send me any money? The club at which I am boarding collects board every week, as inasmuch as I am already two weeks behind, I am in a very embarrassing position. The examinations begin next Saturday and I hope to do well on them. I see that *The Age* is copying from the *Guardian* in the matter of heading their local news.

At present we are having very warm weather for this locality.

Hoping to hear from you soon.

> I remain,
> John

Hanover N.H.

February 7th 1904

Dear Father,

I've just received an answer from Uncle Levi, which I enclose in this letter. I have taken all but one of my examinations. I did not do very much in them because I was unable to study for them on account of being obliged to work during the exams on my graphics in which I am pretty far behind. I owe $15.00 for board and it's only through the manager of the club that I have been allowed to stay so long, for board bills are due every Wednesday night.

I think I should be able to borrow enough money from the girls to pay my board, and I could let the term bills go over to next fall.

I am somewhat sorry that I did not go to Florida last January and if necessary, repeat the college year.

I understand how Uncle Levi feels about lending me money as long as I have three sisters receiving salaries. I read Prof. Adams' letter to you I don't think I would stand show, so I am not worrying over the matter.

Laboratory fees and books will cost me about $6 this term.

If you can please send me something so it will reach here Wednesday night.

John

I thank you very much for the book.

Hanover, N.H

2/11/1904

Dear Father:

I have passed all of my examinations and am entering upon a new semester. I received your letter Tuesday morning. I should be glad to get money by any means because I certainly need it though I don't like the idea of paying 6% for it, but if you can't get it any other way, I shall have to accept it on this condition. I agree with Uncle Levi in what he says concerning the girls; it is not as if I wanted the gift of their money. I only want to borrow it, and if they can't trust me it speaks very badly for themselves who are of the same blood as I am. Can't you send me something right away, for if I don't pay my board bill within a day or two I won't be allowed to eat at this club, and furthermore I can't begin the laboratory course until I pay the fee. I even had to borrow this stamp.

John

Hanover, N.H.
February 28, 1904

Dear Father:

The reason why I have not written before now is because I was waiting to hear from my marks, which I did not find out until yesterday; they are as follows: Graphics 60, Physics 70 to 80, German, French and Mathematics 80 to 90. I should have been given a much better mark in German but I had a Southerner for a Prof. so I could expect as much. I don't have him this semester for which I am thankful. These marks don't suit me at all. I hope to get better this semester. I thank you very much for the money which you have sent me.

The other day a fellow asked me to work a problem in simultaneity quadratics. I worked it and it was such a unique one that I thought I would send it to you. $y2 + x = 7, x2 + y = 11$.

This semester I am taking Elementary Chemistry, Physics, German, French and Differential and Integral Calculus: the latter I find very interesting. We are still having zero weather and the snow still covers the ground. I have read Dr. DuBois' book. I suppose you are having splendid weather down in Washington just now. This time next year I hope to be coming down to Washington to attend the Inaugural Ball.

Will you send some of the colored newspapers when you get a chance? I noticed in the *Guardian* that you had resigned from *The Record*, I was glad to hear that for I don't think you were receiving the proper returns for the energy which you were putting in it.

John

Hanover, New Hampshire
March 13th, 1904

Dear Father:

I suppose you have expected to receive a letter from me ere this, but I find it so hard to get news enough for a long letter, that I delayed my answering until now. I thank you very much for your kindness in procuring the money for me and I hope I won't be obliged to trouble you so much again. I have read all the articles to which you referred—some I like very much, others not so much.

I meant to send you a solution of that problem in my last letter, but I sealed it up without having enclosed the problem: it is thus:

$y2 + x = 7$, $x2 + 7 = 11$, let $y = a-b$, $x = b (2a - b) = 3$, then $a2 - 2ab - $
$$b2 + 2ab - b2 + 3 = 7$$
$$a2 = 4 \; a = a$$
$$b(2a - b) = 32 + a - b = 11$$
$$b2(4a2 - 4ab + b2) + 6b$$
$$(2a - b) + 9 + a - b = 11$$

$y = a - b \; 2 - 0 = 2$

$x = b (2a–b) + 3 + 0 (4–0) + 3 = 3 \; 4a2b2 - 4ab3 + b4 + 12ab - 6b2 + $

$y = 2$, $x = 3 \; 9 + a - b = 11$

$(3)2 + 2 = 11 (a = 2) \; 16b2 - 8b3 + b4 + 24b - 6b2 + 9 + 2 - b = 11$

$(2)2 + 3 = 7 \; b (b3 - 8b2 + 10b + 23) = 0b$

The ground is still covered with snow, and the thermometer still hovers around the zero mark. I suppose in Washington at this time the fields are green and the air is mild.

I am sorry to hear that Fanny is sick. I suppose she would be better if she should to go into the country for a year or so or else take some outdoor exercise. I weigh about 130 pounds just now and expect to weigh more by the end of the year. I am going to get my term bills deferred until next fall when I hope to be able to pay them. School closes for the Easter recess on April the 1st and commences April the 13th. I was extremely sorry to hear of the action of the Maryland legislature and hope it won't be enacted.[30] I see by a Boston paper that Cardinal Gibbons has spoken against it and I suppose his opinion will affect a few of Irish democrats. We are nearly through the differential calculus and will take up the Integral Calculus after Easter.

Remember me to all.

John.

Hanover, N.H.

April 10th, 1904

Dear Father:

I was glad to hear from you at this dull period even though your letter was not up to the standard. During vacation I have been working at the hotel juggling

---

30. My father was referring to a Maryland disfranchisement contest in 1904. This was in the Poe Amendment to the state constitution, which was designed to disfranchise Blacks. It passed the legislature and was submitted to the people, and the Colored Voters Support League was organized to fight it. After securing the help of Booker T. Washington and the Committee of Twelve, which had been formed after the secret conference, the amendment was defeated by nearly twenty-five thousand votes, helping to stop the creeping spread of disfranchisement that was moving north from the southern states.

with the pots and pans for my board. It is pretty hard work but I don't mind, and besides I have a show of getting work after vacation in which case I shall be able to pay my board money or my tuition. I wrote to Mr. Baugh today for a job; I guess I am all fixed for the summer. I have another Prof. in German this semester and he is all right, I have an average somewhere around 95.

I thank you very much for the papers which you send me: they were all of more of less interest, but did not give me Washington news, which I most desired. Henry's paper I think is as good as any. At present we are having plenty of fine weather. Everything is quiet and lonely. We usually pass the days in playing ball or cribbage.

Only two colored contingents went away for the recess.

School begins next Thursday morning. I suppose you attended Dr. Gordon's inauguration; I hear the students are very well pleased with their new president.

I thank you very much for what you sent me.

John

Grand Union

Saratoga Springs, N.Y.

August 26th 1904

Hello "Pop":

I was glad to hear that you were having a fine time in West Virginia with Mr. Clifford[31] and I suppose you are now at home ready for the winter work. I had only $20. at hand for the season has been very dull. I hope this will suffice. I won't answer your letter just now for I am writing this note in the post office.

Hope all are well

I remain

John

P.S. I attended to that bill.

---

31. John Robert Clifford (1848–1924) graduated from Storer College at Harpers Ferry in 1875 and received his law degree from Shaw University in 1893. He taught for fourteen years in West Virginia's public schools and was principal for one year. He was the editor of the *Pioneer Press* in Martinsburg, which he started in 1882; it was the only printing plant in the city run by a black man. Clifford practiced law, and he was a 33rd degree mason and ex-grand master of the Lodge of Odd Fellows. He was married to E. C. Franklin and was the father of eleven children.

Grand Union Hotel
Saratoga Springs
Sept. 11, 1904

Dear Father:

I received your letter and the *Jim Crow Negro*[32] a little more than a week ago, and I must say that you have expressed my thoughts exactly. I loaned it to Mahoney of Howard Theological Dept. and he spoke most highly.

Last year during the June exams I entered a prize exam in Analytic Geo. and the differential and integral Calculus, for the prizes of $25 and $15.

In the written exam which I enclose, you were allowed to take any book into the examination but you see they would not have helped much. I left on the next day for Saratoga and did not take the trouble to write back concerning the award. The other day I wrote to the Dean about my bills and I received a letter which I enclose. Be sure to return both to me sometime in October when I am in school.

Yesterday I received a letter from the Comptroller of the dining hall to the effect that he would be unable to give me a job this year and you can imagine that I feel pretty blue, but I have not yet given up hope.

Love to all.
John

Hanover, N.H.
November 18th 1904

Dear Father:[33]

I received your letter Wednesday noon and in view of the circumstances have made haste to reply. I received the things you sent me the night before; everything was swell and pleased me greatly. I like the shirts especially. I wish to thank all of you for the sacrifices which you have made for me. I am very grateful to Lucy for her very timely assistance and I promise to pay every cent when I shall have secured work after graduation.

---

32. A little pamphlet Grandfather wrote decrying the demeanor and values of the obsequious Negro.

33. This is a particularly informative letter because Grandfather, who had no understanding of a liberal arts curriculum at that time, was obviously asking his son to be more specific about his choice of subjects. This is not the only letter in which Grandfather expresses his concern about the curriculum, but it is the clearest.

Such a sacrifice as you made to secure tickets for the concert certainly deserved a better reward than to be 87th in line. Please thank Uncle Harry for his kindness in having me booked at the Arlington for March.

You were speaking to me some time ago about the class of subjects which I am pursuing in college: In the modern college one can not take all the subjects that are offered, and I think one should elect such subjects as can be only acquired with the aid of an instructor, and leaves the others to his own diligence. I started at a disadvantage that is trying to pursue a scientific course when I was a classical student; consequently I am taking now the Physics and Chemistry which should have been elected freshman year. I don't see how I can take any of the social subjects without spoiling my course which is about the hardest in college.

After Christmas, I am going to spend some time in the library 2 or 3 times a week in an endeavor to make up my deficiencies in those branches. At present the weather is only about 10° below zero and it feels like summertime.

Enclosed you will find my application for a position of bellman at the Arlington.

Remember me to all,

John.

Hanover, N.H.
December 28th 1904

Dear Father:

I suppose you think I am somewhat slow in answering letters and I guess you are right, for I have been putting it off for so long. How is Fanny? I hope she is better by this time. I am remaining in Hanover during this recess and on account of this; I am looking forward to the end of the holidays. The elective blanks are out for next semester and I think I shall simply continue the subjects which I am taking this semester. How are you enjoying the holidays? I see from the *Star* that this Inaugural promises to surpass all previous ones in brilliancy and in the number of visitors to Washington that week. It is somewhat dull in Hanover just now, there being only about 30 students who have remained but still we are managing to pass away the time in doing various things. According to my present plans I shall reach Washington on the night of the 26th of February.

I wish you would send me Mamie's address when you write.

Hoping you will excuse this note, on account of the dullness of the season.

I remain.

John.

Hanover N.H.

May 24, 1905

Dear Father:

I hope you will excuse my long delay in answering your letter; the fact is that I've been waiting to see whether I could get a job for the remainder of the year and my board bill is settled. I wish however you would send me $5.00 this week and then I shall be able to pay back the money I borrowed to send to Mr. Baugh in order to bind the contract. I thank you very much for the papers which you sent; the *Record* is showing much improvement, especially in the last issue. I think the greatest fault lies in lack of quantity rather than quality, but I have no doubt that this deficit will soon be remedied.

When you get time send me those circulars from the scientific departments. I am going to stay through commencement this year and cinch a job for next year. The exams begin next Friday. I thank you very much for the check. It seems a great pity that the girls are too tight to contribute their shares to Mamie's expenses; they seem afraid to lend a little of their money.

My bills are due June 1st, if you can't send me all of it without putting yourself in a hole, send me what you can. Tell Mama I'll write to her within a day or two.

I judge from the papers that Dr. Gordon is stirring things up a little at Howard. Love to all

John

Hanover N.H.

September 17, 1905

Dear Father:

I arrived in Hanover Thursday night and went right over to the hotel where I am to work during the year. I paid all my bills for the year and bought some clothes. I received that $200. gift despite Baugh's attempts to block me. It was secured for me through the efforts of Mr. Rbitta, a Howard Medic, who went out of his way to benefit me. I won't say anything more about it or everything which old man Baugh said to injure me, and I hope you won't mention it outside the house.

I paid all my expenses and they ate up all of the $200. But inasmuch as I have a job, I shall only have to look after the small bills like washing etc. College does not open until next Thursday and at present it is rather dull.

I remained in New York for six days, the guest of one of my bell-boy friends at the Grand Union. I had a very pleasant time and on that account, I was very sorry to leave.

Hoping all are well,

I remain,
John

Hanover, N.H.
9/29/1905

Dear Father:

I received your letter this morning and I can judge from its contents how much you were deceived by your friend. I asked you particularly not to say anything about this money, because I promised not to say anything about this matter but I see you can't keep a secret and I shall be more reserved in the future. Mr. Baugh told you some things but he did not tell you the whole truth; he did not tell you the reason why he had his son to wait on this lady; he didn't tell you why he was so anxious that the boys should not obtain a gift from this lady. He did not tell anything of the inside matters and I won't say anything about them not until I come home which I hope will be Christmas. Of course I showed contempt for him after this matter; I told him in plain English what I thought of him and his methods. The reason why he took me to Saratoga every year was because I did his work and he had no trouble with me. The reason why he did not fine me was that he had no occasion to and he knew I wouldn't stand to see him take my deposit money for nothing. He is nothing but a hypocrite and a grafter; if I choose to tell the proprietor all I know about him he would not have the Grand Union anymore. Only for my promise not to say anything to him or about him, I would have long ago put a yeast-cake under him before the proprietor.

You don't need to tell me to respect old age; I respect it when it deserves respect. I trust you won't go to the trouble to correspond with him further. I regret it very much that you mentioned the fact of my receiving money for I thought you would be the last to do such a thing. He has done his dirt, but I promised not to rekindle any coals. As to my playing races, I only played them a little as I and every other boy always does. As to staying out half the night, it makes me laugh to hear such a morally perfect man as he is, to say such a thing.

John

Hanover N.H.
November 25, 1905

Dear Father:

I humbly beg your pardon for having judged too rashly your ability to keeping a secret, and I also hope you will overlook my long delay in answering your last letter. At present I am somewhat overworked in the line of studies: I am taking General Astronomy, Conversational German, Analytic Mechanics, Quartermium Organic Chemistry, Quantitative Chemistry, and Education. I am compelled to take Education in order to comply with the Group System, or else I would not be taking it, for I don't intend to teach, if I can find anything else to do. At present I am out of a job, having been laid off during the dull season.

It is the custom for the freshmen of every hall to give their upper classmen a banquet every year. This year I presided at our banquet.

I want to come home Christmas in order to find out all the particulars concerning the position for which I am trying. How is the *Record* progressing? What has Dr. Sampson done concerning the office position? I think he has been somewhat slow.

Hoping all are well.

I remain,
John

Philadelphia, Pa.
1/5/1906

Dear Father:

I received your letter yesterday and I certainly will carry out your instructions when I return to Hanover. The business as far as I am concerned is settled for the present and I am in a hurry to return to school. I wish you would send me by special registered letter the wherewithal for my carfare. I should like to receive the $5 which you promised me and about $10 or $12 more which I think Lucy and Larcie will lend me. Otelia and Mamie have already contributed their quota and I am loath to impose on them.

If a package comes from Hanover N.H. for me, please mail to me at Hanover. All send love.

John

Mamie gave me $4, Otelia $5.

Hanover, N.H.

3/11/1906

Dear Father:

I received your last letter and more than glad to hear from you; I appreciate the kind advice which it contained and will certainly give it my earnest consideration. I am to take the examination for Computer Nautical Almanac this week on Wednesday and Thursday and the examination for assistant examiner Patent Office April 18–19; if I had waited for you to send me the Manual I would have been in the soup as usual. Concerning whether I was thinking of studying a profession I can say no with reference to Law and Medicine which are already overcrowded with Negroes: but I have many times wished I might pursue chemical engineering, inasmuch as tuition is $250 to $350 for a year at the recognized schools I have given up the idea. Really I don't know what I shall do, if successful I possibly and probably shall enter the Civil Service; then too I have a chance to teach mathematics or Physics and Chemistry in Florida. I have received a graduate scholarship equivalent to $325 for next year, and I may return to try for an A.M. in Astronomy and Math a distinction never as yet acquired by a Negro to my knowledge.[34] The truth is however that I am tired of going to school and being compelled to beg for pennies, so to speak, and I am anxious to get out and see if I can't make a few dimes myself.

Don't *publish* this fact that I've received a scholarship, in the *Star* for colored people get an erroneous idea of matters relating to such things, and think that every time a man receives a scholarship he must have won it after an exceeding hard and tedious examination. I have *not* won it, but persons in authority have told me that I may have one if I want to return.

At present I am undecided for the reason stated on the other page. My senior bills are falling due, one of $7. due Wednesday of this week.

Remember me to all.

John

P.S. Please remember what I said, for I don't care for a lot of Jim Crow notoriety.

---

34. John Cromwell accepted the graduate scholarship and did receive the master's degree.

Hanover, N.H.
4/21/06

Dear Father:

I received your letter the other day and was more than pleased with its contents. You have a certainly good reason for advocating Dr. Moore for President and I agree with you that he is qualified for the place nevertheless I don't think he deserves it over Kelly Miller even though the latter is somewhat of a fence-straddler as you describe him.

I took the examination for Computer Nautical Almanac over a month ago but as yet I have received no notice how I came out. It came so early that I was not qualified to take it and on that account I do not feel very confident of having passed it. It made me very sore to solve correctly all the hard problems in higher algebra and calculus and fail on two in Solid Geometry in which I was rather rusty. It is a bare possibility that I attained the passing mark of 70. I don't think I shall like to teach unless I can get a berth in the college Dept. of Howard University, no High School for me, certainly not the Washington High School. There remain only about 7 weeks of school and I am eager for them to pass by. I am trying my best to receive P.B.K. pin something only three or four colored men have attained to do this. I must make an average of 90.7 this semester, a rather hard job with the kind of courses I am carrying. I have not as yet secured a summer job although I stand a chance of getting a position in the Dining room at Saratoga. Many thanks for the School Report.

Love to all
John

Saratoga, New York
7/16/1906

Dear Father:

I suppose you think I have about forgotten you, inasmuch as I have waited so long before answering. I was glad to hear from you, and I thank you very much for the ten which you sent me.

I was very disappointed in not hearing from you while I was at Hanover. If you received my letter I think the least you could have done was to have answered it and not kept me in doubt as to whether you were to come or not.[35] I had a

---

35. Grandfather apparently did not come to Dartmouth for John's graduation. Unfortunately, there is no letter of explanation, but it was probably because of a lack of funds.

program mapped out for you, had engaged tickets for the concert, etc. I began work on July 10th; as yet things are rather slow, no money coming in. Mr. Baugh seems very anxious to make friends with me; he is afraid that I will knock him to the proprietor, but I don't think I'll trouble the old hypocrite. I think I'll come home September 1st and stay until school reopens. I see from the *Record* that a new set of grafters is occupying the trustee bench.

Love to all,
John

Grand Union
8/20/1906

Dear Father:

I received your letter the other day and was more than glad to hear from you and to learn all the news. I was surprised to hear the different changes the Board of Education had made. I think Mattingly although young knows more about the mathematics than the other teachers, but he no doubt received the position because he is an Amherst man and at the same time a P.B.K. man.

I should think Otelia would secure the head of the German department without much trouble, in fact I don't see anyone to run against her.

This is the worst season Saratoga has seen for many years; I don't expect my total earnings to exceed $60 if they reach that. I shall leave Saratoga August 31st and expect to reach Washington on Saturday. I shall probably take a civil service examination during September.

Will close with love

John

Hanover, N.H.[36]

Dear Father:

I hope you will pardon my long delay in answering your letter as well as my ill-timed slang which appeared in my last letter. At present I am in Hanover, remaining during the spring recess. As to what I shall pursue next year if I return, will probably be advanced courses in Celestial mechanics, including Perturbations and work in Practical Astronomy and . . . [illegible]. I wish you would send me within the next week or so, copies of the school bills which have been presented

---

36. This letter was probably written in winter 1907.

to Congress especially the one which I saw Christmas. If you can't procure these for me, let me know and I shall try another source.

I have very little to talk about other than the dullness of the recess and the lateness of spring.

Hoping all are well.

John

Hanover, N.H.
10/25/1906

Hello Lucy:

Well I suppose you are back in Washington by this time enjoying the many comforts of home. Did you have a swell time in Pennsy? Doubtless you availed yourself of the golden opportunity to pay your respects to Aunt Charlotte better known as the dangerous one.

Many thanks for the "fivey" it came in handy.

It seems as though I will have cut off writing home I never get my letters in fact I have already decided to demote Larcie on account of the extreme length of the last letter she wrote me.

They are evidently raising the devil in Washington schools in regards to the colored people, aren't they? At any rate they won't be able to do us much harm.

At present this vacation is fine and dandy, nothing doing otherwise. Got to attend a recitation so I must cut this letter short.

John

Hanover, N.H.
11/28/1906

Dear Father:

I received your letter the other day just after I had written to Lucy.

I was very much surprised to learn that Otelia and Mary had refused to advance me the money for the trip home. My ink is all out so I am compelled to finish this letter in pencil. I did not ask them to give me the money only to lend it.

As to my remaining in Hanover during the next recess I don't want to do it inasmuch as I have had previous knowledge gained from seven out of eight vacations which it has been my lot to pass here. Hanover is a college town in the true sense of the word; when the students leave the college is dead. All of the dormitories with the exception of one or two are closed thus necessitating one's removal. The eating clubs suspend during that period thereby causing one either to board himself or to eat at the hotel at the rate of $6 or $7 dollars per week.

If I stay up here I figure it will cost me somewhere about 16 or 17 dollars. If I go to Boston, I fail to see how I can get out of it much less than $30.

It seems to me that it would be better if I could get out of this town for at least two Xmas out of five years. Hanover is not a town of the size of Northampton or Ann Arbor and even if Otelia and Mary did remain away from home several years at a time I see no particular reason why I should pass 8 out of 9 vacations in this town. I am not so particular about coming home if they don't want to see me but I do desire to go somewhere. What is a vacation for but to furnish recreation? I wish you would keep in touch with Profs. Lightfoot and Miller as to how things are going on the hill.

Well regards to everybody.

John

28 Nelson Street
West Lynn, Mass.

Dear Father:

I've just received your letter and in view of the circumstances I am hastening to reply. I am very grateful to you for your endeavors to land me a position. In regards to the position in Morris Brown College I will say first that I am not over anxious to go down South; second the salary is not at all enticing. You may tell Bishop Turner that I will come to Morris Brown College for the minimum salary of $800. for school and board and room. I am willing however to teach any other work they may me wish to in chemistry, Physics, German and Latin. These terms I think are cheap enough for anybody especially to a southern school with all its petty rules and regulations.

At present I am being nearly worked to death in this factory here in Lynn. I can make about $10.00 per week which enables me to pay my expenses of $8.00 and gives me the large sum of $2.00 for summer recreation. If you hear anything about positions [at] Howard or Union let me know.

Love to all,
John

Chapter 8

THE TWO JOURNALISTS

THE FRIENDSHIP BETWEEN JOHN EDWARD BRUCE AND JOHN WESLEY CROMWELL SR.

֍

Just recently two books have been published about John Edward Bruce, but to date, his influence has not been incorporated into the existing and growing reservoir of works on the black experience in general or on black intellectuals in particular.[1]

One can only speculate on the circumstances that brought John Bruce and John Wesley Cromwell together—a chance meeting in Washington perhaps or a common interest in journalism or mutual friends. In any case, on the basis of their correspondence, it is clear that after a rather formal beginning, Cromwell and Bruce enjoyed a rich and lasting friendship, nourished by their mutual affection and high regard for Dr. Alexander Crummell, the American Negro Academy, and the history and culture of Blacks here and abroad.

Unfortunately, only a dozen of Grandfather's letters to Bruce survive, though from Bruce's letters it is clear that Cromwell wrote as frequently as Bruce did. Grandfather was ten years older, had more formal education, and seemed the more solid person in his thinking and his affiliations. Bruce was given to expansive discourse on a range of subjects, political and literary writing, more as a journalist than as a scholar. Although he wrote many literary criticisms, Grandfather's

1. Ralph L. Crowder, *John Edward Bruce: Politician, Journalist, and Self-Trained Historian of the African Diaspora* (New York: New York University Press, 2004); William Seraile, *Bruce Grit: The Black Nationalist Writings of John Edward Bruce* (Knoxville: University of Tennessee Press, 2003).

John Edward Bruce, 1856–1924. (Courtesy of the Schomburg Center for Research in Black Culture.)

solidity, stability, and caution were strengthened by his responsibility as an editor of a weekly newspaper and as the sole provider for his second wife, Annie, and his daughter Fanny, and by his history of employment—first by the United States government and later by the Board of Education of the District of Columbia. To appreciate the significance of this friendship, Bruce's life, particularly his later attraction to Marcus Garvey, must be examined.

Bruce was born enslaved on February 22, 1856, on a plantation in Piscataway, Maryland.[2] His father had been sold to a Georgia slave owner, and his mother, Martha E. Clark Bruce, was given permission by her master, Major Harvey Griffin, to work for herself on the condition that Major Griffin would receive half of her earnings. Bruce and his mother were freed in 1860 when the first regiment of Union soldiers passed through Maryland on their way to Washington. They, too, went to Washington, where his mother found a relative, Busie Patterson, who had been the body servant to Senator Thomas Hart Benton of Missouri. Martha Bruce worked as a sweeper in a ladies' seminary. In 1864, Bruce and his mother went to New York and later to Stratford, Connecticut, where his mother worked as a housekeeper and he first attended an integrated school. After two years in Connecticut, Bruce, now twelve years of age, and his mother returned to Washington. Martha and the young John Bruce obtained jobs: she, as a cook, and he, as a waiter and assistant doorkeeper in Joseph Haire's Café, an establishment adjoining Ford's Theatre, where John Wilkes Booth frequently came. From 1867 to 1868, Bruce worked as a "general utility man" for Gen. F. T. Dent, the father-in-law of President Ulysses S. Grant. Busie Patterson was a father figure for the young Bruce; and when he was twelve or thirteen, Busie introduced him to Henry Highland Garnet and Martin R. Delany.

Washington, the so-called Capital of Colored Aristocracy, was an exciting environment for Blacks during the postwar period, and Busie Patterson introduced Bruce to this scene. Patterson was not only a trusted valet to a powerful politician but also the proprietor of a boarding house frequented by many important Blacks. After being exposed to this social scene, however, Bruce developed a distaste for the black elite, whom he felt to be excessively concerned with gaining the trappings of social respectability and imitating Whites. These elites, he believed, shared an exaggerated color phobia that stressed straight hair, light skin, and white spouses and avoided contact with ordinary Blacks.

Bruce's hostility toward these types of Washington Blacks characterized his

---

2. This account of Bruce's life was taken from a letter he sent to my grandfather in anticipation of its later publication.

thinking and writing for the rest of his life. He felt hampered by a lack of formal education, family resources, and strong contacts within the black community. As a result, meeting men such as Henry Highland Garnet, Martin R. Delany, John Wesley Cromwell, and especially Alexander Crummell strengthened his resolve to fight the so-called mulatto power of the colored aristocracy. These mentors all stressed independent thought, racial self-reliance, and an energetic respect for black history.

When Bruce was eighteen, he began his long career in journalism as a helper in the office of L. L. Crouse, an associate editor and Washington correspondent for the *New York Times,* who was the brother of the governor of Nebraska and well connected to the political scene in Washington. Bruce also became the special correspondent for the *Progressive American,* published by John Freeman, a prominent black journalist who from 1871 to 1887 led the fight to appoint African American teachers in New York's public schools. From 1877 to 1880, under the pen name of "Rising Son," Bruce wrote letters for the *Richmond (Va.) Star,* and under his own name, he sent letters to the *St. Louis Freeman's Journal,* the *Indianapolis World,* and the *St. Louis Tribune.* He then became a Washington correspondent for the *Chicago Conservator,* the *North Carolina Republican,* the *Fayetteville (N.C.) Enterprise,* the *New York Freeman,* the *Reed City Clarion,* the *Detroit Plain Dealer,* the *Christian Index,* and the *Cherokee Advocate.* He also contributed special articles to several New York City papers, including the *Herald, Times, World, Mail,* and *Express,* and to the *Boston Transcript.*

Aside from these numerous affiliations, Bruce himself established several journals: the *Argus* in 1879, whose editors were S. S. Lacy and Charles N. Otey, a friend of Grandfather's; the *Sunday Item* in 1880, the first Sunday paper published by a black man in America; the *Washington Grit* in 1884, a campaign sheet dedicated to the success of the Republican Party and the advancement of Afro-Americans. With Charles W. Anderson, Bruce started, and served as an editor for, the *Chronicle, Devoted to the Interests of the Negro Race and the Republican Party.* Later, Bruce was an associate editor of *Howard's Magazine.* In 1884, Bruce also began writing regular columns under the pen name of "Bruce Grit" for the *Cleveland Gazette* and the *New York Age.* Bruce became popularly known as "Grit," and his articles and editorials were reprinted in black newspapers across the country and in parts of Africa and Europe.

At the turn of the century, Bruce left Washington for New York. He went first to Albany (Yonkers) and later to New York City. For most of his adult life, he held a minor position with the Federal Port Authority, from which he retired in 1922. He was married twice: first to Lucy Pinkwood, and then in 1895 to

Florence A. Bishop of Cleveland, Ohio, who was twenty years his junior. He and Florence had a daughter, Olive Bruce (Millar), who died in 1943. There were three grandchildren: Onaway (Onnie) K. Millar, Mrs. Agnes B. Conway, and Edwin L. Millar.

Aside from his prodigious work as a newspaperman, Bruce wrote essays, short stories, plays, poems, and song lyrics, and he composed music. His organizational activities were varied. At one time, he was president of a Shakespeare Society, vice president of a Gold Coast mining company, and a member of the Afro-American League, a militant organization started by T. Thomas Fortune and disbanded in the 1890s. Bruce became the financial secretary of the league's successor, the Afro-American Council, in 1898. He was also a member of the American Negro Academy in 1900 and the Literary Bureau of the Republican Party, and he was a founding member of the Niagara Movement (1913) and the Loyal Order of Sons of Africa, which was organized to unite black folks all over the world. In 1911, he and Arthur A. Schomburg founded the Negro Society for Historical Research, and in 1918, Bruce cofounded the Hamitic League of the World with George Wells Parker and Rev. John Albert Williams.

In his introduction to *The Selected Writings of John Edward Bruce,* Peter Gilbert offers some insights to the breadth of the man and the range of topics of interest to him, which

> included politics and the duties of Negro citizens; the legitimacy of force and violence as methods of obtaining black rights; the attitude of Caucasians toward the colored races; the use and misuse of the terms "Afro-American," "Colored," and "Negro;" the urgency of race pride and solidarity; the use of the study of black history to uplift the black race and to heal the psychological damage of racism; the use of black organizations and cooperation to combat white oppression; the common destiny of all colored races; and the desirability of creating a free black nation in Africa.[3]

Bruce was largely outside the mainstream of black issues during his lifetime. He stood apart from the arguments of self-help espoused by Booker T. Washington and the recognition and support of the Talented Tenth of W. E. B. Du Bois. Bruce, in fact, stressed economic independence, self-help, and race pride as well as the need to demand political and civil rights. Blacks, he felt, should be a part of America but not a part of white society.[4]

3. Peter Gilbert, ed. and comp., *The Selected Writings of John Edward Bruce: Militant Black Journalist* (New York: Arno Press, 1971), 2.
4. Ibid., 4.

Bruce's expectations about and subsequent disappointment around World War I were turning points in his life. Initially, he was supportive of the war, and "he had high hopes that the Negro's part in the conflict would bring to Blacks the appreciation of Whites and provide an opportunity for true democracy in the United States."[5] But in spite of the patriotism and heroic acts of black soldiers and civilians alike, racial prejudice did not decrease; on the contrary, "there was mounting racial friction. Some twenty-six race riots erupted across the United States during the 'Red Summer' of 1919, and lynchings in the South increased markedly."[6] Not surprisingly, Blacks displaying a new militancy reacted with force.

Bruce was disappointed rather than surprised by the white man's failure to grant democratic rights to Blacks after the war. And since the black man's security had not been included in any world peace plan, Bruce felt Blacks, as well as Whites, gained little from the war. Cassandra-like, he predicted in 1919 that "We are not through with war . . . let no man deceive himself about this. This present upheaval is the result of a misunderstanding between the white races. There is yet to be a settlement between the white and darker races."[7]

Bruce's disillusionment following World War I and the growing popularity of Marcus Garvey probably accounted for his change of mind about Garvey, who in 1918 he had initially described as "wasting valuable time telling people things which in the last analysis are pure buncombe . . . rhetoric mixed with frenzy . . . oral gymnastics . . . the idea is all right, but the method is wrong . . . all gas."[8] When Bruce actually heard Garvey speak, though, he changed his mind about the man and soon was a Garvey follower and a regular contributor to the *Negro World,* Garvey's newspaper.

While an activist in many ways, Bruce had not been a joiner of politically oriented groups; therefore, his attraction to the Garvey movement was definitely out of character. Apparently Bruce was also reluctant to seek prominence in the United Negro Independent Association (UNIA) and wrote Garvey accordingly:

August 17, 1920

My dear Mr. Garvey:

I have just learned that my name has been proposed by a member of the Convention now in session for the post of President of the American Sector of

5. Ibid., 6.
6. Ibid., 7.
7. Ibid., 7–8.
8. Ibid., 8.

the League or Association, and I hasten to advise you in all courtesy, that I am not a candidate for this office, not that I do not feel it an honor to be considered worthy to occupy and serve as such officer, but that I feel that a younger and more active man that I know myself to be should be selected to fill this post. I am at one with the organization in all that it is attempting, has attempted and will attempt under your leadership to do towards the consolidation of the Negro race and for the ultimate redemption of Africa from the plunderers and buccaneers of an alien race who would barter their God for his image in gold. I do not understand your "back to Africa" movement slogan to mean what the critics have mischievously interpreted it to mean. I think I see with tolerably clear vision that your purpose is to lay the foundation broad and deep, so that the Negroes of the coming day will know better than we, who are now blazing the pathway and preparing the race for African nationalization, how to possess and hold and develop the heritage which the Almighty has given to the black race . . . [9]

In January 1921, however, a Reverend (or Bishop) C. S. Smith in a letter to the *World's Work* referred to John E. Bruce as the only national character among Garvey's followers. Bruce, in the April 2, 1921, issue of the *Negro World*, refuted this assessment: "I have never claimed, and I have never aspired to be a national character. I have always preferred to be a gad-fly and free lance journalistically."

Nevertheless, Bruce slowly began to advance in the hierarchy of the UNIA. At the 1921 convention, he was nominated as Garvey's candidate for the position of secretary general but was defeated by Fred A. Foote. Yet Bruce's role was still visible, for in the parade at the convention he is listed as a high official but without a title.

Before the convention, Bruce described the democratic quality of the UNIA: "There never was an organization of black and colored people in America in which the color line is so conspicuous by its absence and so unpopular as in the U.N.I.A . . . the destiny of all peoples of the Negroid race . . . is identical . . . only the intellectual snobs among us . . . are constantly worrying about class, color or physical appearance."

Garvey characterized Bruce as a "true Negro" and undoubtedly appreciated Bruce's role in the organization. At the first UNIA court reception, held in Lib-

9. This is the only page of this letter now preserved in the Bruce papers in the Schomburg Center for Research and Black Culture, Manuscripts and Archives Collection.

erty Hall in August 1921, Bruce, described as a noted journalist and writer, received the honor of knighthood of the Sublime Order of the Nile for "distinguished services rendered to the Negro race."

Bruce was in a position to broaden Garvey's contact with black America as well as with Blacks abroad. He provided the key linkages for Garvey to such persons as Edward Blyden, Alexander Crummell, Frederick Douglass, Dr. Mojola Agbebi of Nigeria, and J. E. Casely Hayford of the Gold Coast.

When Duse Mohammed Ali,[10] the editor of the *African and Oriental Review,* arrived in New York in October 1921, Bruce interceded in reestablishing the friendship between Garvey and Mohammed, which had been broken in London when Garvey, while working for Mohammed, had acted unprofessionally. Reputedly, Garvey had also stolen some of Mohammed's ideas, such as the slogan "Africa for the African." Bruce paved the way for Garvey to appoint Mohammed head of the African Affairs Department of the UNIA and to become foreign affairs columnist for the *Negro World.*

Bruce, like Garvey, saw the value of using the arts for the purpose of politicizing the UNIA membership. One play written by Bruce, *Preaching vs. Practice,* expressed Garvey's hostilities toward unscrupulous black preachers. Another play, *Which One,* provided an excellent example of the use of this medium for political education. The main characters were Sennebundi Ayai, an African UNIA diplomat and three young ladies—one from Martinique, another from the British West Indies, and another from America—all of whom were in love with the hero, who was leaving for Nigeria on UNIA business. Between the romantic escapades, the audience was treated to monologues extolling the virtues of the UNIA. The set was liberally decorated with the red, black, and green of the UNIA, and the hero and the lady of his choice announced their intention to be married in a liberty hall in Africa. Another Bruce creation, *The Odious Companion,* was serialized in the *Negro World.* By the end of December 1921, Bruce was referred to as "Sir John E. Bruce, K.C.O.N."

In many ways the year 1922 and the third convention of the UNIA were the pinnacle of Garvey's leadership and of Bruce's significance to the organization. After a number of accusations over irregularities in the UNIA, on January 12,

---

10. Duse Mohammed Ali (1866–1945), the son of a Sudanese mother and an Egyptian father, was an editor of the *African Times and Orient Review,* a monthly magazine. He was interested in Africa but especially in a campaign for home rule in Egypt. His mixed ancestry made him sensitive to the presence of an invidious color bar in England, and his writing often reflected his bitterness at the insults directed toward the people of color there. He was the author of *In the Land of the Pharaohs: A Short History of Egypt from the Fall of Ismail to the Assassination of Boutrous Pasha* (London: Stanley, Paul, 1911).

1922, Garvey and three officials were arrested and indicted for using the mails to defraud in the promotion of the Black Star Line and the Universal Negro Improvement Association. They were released on bail of twenty-five hundred dollars each. But it was not until May 1923 that the government's case against Garvey and his associates began. All the while plans were being made to make the third convention, which was to be held in New York, a big success. Yet at the same time, there was brewing conflict within the organization.

During 1922, before the convention, Bruce had been very active and now identified himself in correspondence written in Garvey's behalf as "Special Secretary for the Pres. Gen'l Universal Negro Improvement Association." In this capacity, he was given several assignments and responsibilities. He approached New York senator Caldor to use his influence to have Garvey's case postponed until after the convention, with the promise of a large vote from UNIA members in New York.

Bruce also used his contacts to silence any influence Du Bois would have when he went to Africa. Bruce cabled Casely Hayford to let him know that Du Bois was coming and that he "was bent on mischief due to the failure of the Pan-African Congress scheme. Financed by Joel Spingarn, a Jew and other interest (white) inimical to African independence. Watch him. Letter follows, make no committals."[11]

During the convention itself, there was much activity, some of which involved Bruce. He was, for example, made chairman of the Committee on Social Conditions among Negroes. The other members were Miss Henrietta Vinton Davis, Dr. Leroy Bundy, Robert L. Poston, and Miss Nicholas.[12]

The two cases of impeachment brought before the convention revealed conflicts brewing within UNIA. A Dr. Gibson, after a hearing, was impeached for being a disloyal member of the association and unfit for lack of proper credentials to serve as surgeon general. Bruce testified in Gibson's behalf. Dr. Gibson's professional credibility was challenged, though he had graduated in 1915 from the College of Physicians and Surgeons in Boston.[13]

---

11. Tony Martin, *Race First: The Ideological and Organizational Struggles of Marcus Garvey and the Universal Negro Improvement Association* (Westport, Conn.: Greenwood Press, 1976), 136.

12. The committee was charged with finding a way to establish common bonds among Blacks in the interest of pure morals and discourage this indiscriminate social intermingling of the worst of us and the best of us. The committee made four recommendations to correct this condition: have good home environment; stress parental responsibility; stress respect for parents and elderly; and emulate good examples of social etiquette from other races, as for instance the attitude of the Japanese youth toward those of riper years. The committee concluded that it was necessary to impress upon our youth the importance of courtesy, clean speech, correct manners, and good character as the hallmarks of true ladies and gentlemen.

13. Graduates of this college were not certified as physicians in Boston.

Adrian Johnson, a speaker at the convention, was also impeached, for not being up-to-date in his financial obligations and for conspiring "to disrupt the Convention and damage the interests of the Association." Bruce testified that he had heard Johnson threatening to kill somebody. Both Gibson and Johnson were eventually cleared of some of the charges made against them.

Bruce was one of Garvey's most vehement defenders. In a letter written several months before the convention to J. R. Ralph Casimir,[14] an ardent Garveyite and poet, Bruce gave his view of the government's case against Marcus Garvey:

New York, U.S.A.

February 16, 1922

My dear Mr. Casimir,

It is comforting to receive your sympathetic and gracious letter of February 3, 1922, in which you express your sincere interest in the arrest of the President General of this Organization by the Postal Authorities upon a charge of defrauding the mails, a charge of which Mr. Garvey is an innocent as yourself. He is very much pleased with the interest which members of the Divisions all over the Country and the World are showing in his behalf and feels as they do that the matter will find a solution when the true facts are brought out.

There is more in this charge than appears on the surface, and we strongly suspect that the local politicians are more directly interested in putting the U.N.I.A. out of business because of its large influence with the masses who vote that is the Post Office Department.

At the last election held here in the City of New York, the successful candidate for Mayor, who is a Democrat, addressed a large gathering at Liberty Hall a few days before the election, and by a strange coincidence, when the election came off he was elected by an overwhelming majority. Mr. Garvey was at this meeting and he was called on to make a few remarks but he adroitly evaded this attempt to bring him into American politics and only spoke informally, expressing the hope and wish that the people would use their best judgment and support the candidate they believed would serve their interests. The Republicans subsequently held a meeting in Liberty Hall, at which Mr. Garvey was not present because of illness and this meeting broke up in a row. The local Politicians, who are interested

14. In 1919, J. R. Ralph Casimir was a founding member of the Roseau, Dominica division of the UNIA, and he served as its secretary from its inception until its dissolution in 1923. He was inspired by Paul Lawrence Dunbar and corresponded regularly with many UNIA figures. He remained loyal to Garvey during his trial and imprisonment and retained his devotion to Garveyite ideals throughout his life.

in the various candidates of the more important City offices and especially the Republican Politicians, have attributed the election of the Democratic candidate for Mayor to the personal influence, exerted on the masses of the Colored voters in Harlem through the U.N.I.A., of Mr. Marcus Garvey. They are looking to the future, not only as regards New York, but other States where the U.N.I.A. is strong, and are fearful that in coming State and National elections, the U.N.I.A. may prove to be a dangerous factor to the Republican Organization throughout the Country, consequently, the scheme is to frame Mr. Garvey on the charge of using the mails for fraud.

If you know the game of politics, you can perfectly understand the meaning of this recent attempt to discredit the founder of the Universal Negro Improvement Association and destroy the organization . . . It is safe to assume that neither one nor the other will be accomplished by those who have undertaken the task.

The examination into the merits of the case has been postponed three times thus far by the Government, because of its failure to find any incriminating evidence against Mr. Garvey personally or the Organization generally. Certainly, if it had any facts whatever, upon which to base its action, these postponements would not have occurred.

The President General directs me to thank you most cordially and sincerely for your kind and sympathetic interest in this matter, and to assure you that he appreciates more than you can ever know, the fine spirit that has prompted you to write him so sympathetically.

Yours fraternally,
UNIVERSAL NEGRO IMPROVEMENT ASS'N
MARCUS GARVEY, Pres. Gen'l.
Per John E. Bruce
Special Sec'y to Pres.-Gen'l.

In the case against Garvey and his associates, which began in May 1923, the government contended that they had used the mails to promote the sale of Black Star Line stock after they were aware that the financial condition of the company was hopeless. Garvey was found guilty, fined one thousand dollars, and sentenced to five years imprisonment at the Atlanta penitentiary. Freed under heavy bail, Garvey continued his role as provisional president of Africa and conducted a vigorous campaign in the United States and abroad to prove his innocence. He also attempted to implement his program of colonization in Africa—to Liberia. Because of a variety of circumstances, including the defaulting on the part of the Liberian government, that plan failed. From then on, Garvey's position of eminence and power declined.

Garvey's conviction in 1923 touched off a flood of lawsuits against him and the UNIA. In August 1924, a federal grand jury indicted him on the charge of income tax evasion. Finally on February 25, 1925, Garvey's appeal for the reversal of his 1923 conviction was denied. During the same month, he was committed to the Atlanta penitentiary for the term to which he had been sentenced. In November 1927, after having served half of his five-year sentence, Garvey's sentence was commuted by President Coolidge, and he was deported to Jamaica.

During his last years, John Bruce remained loyal to Garvey, and when Bruce died on August 7, 1924, funeral services were held at Liberty Hall, and Marcus Garvey gave one of the eulogies. As befitting "His Grace, Duke of Uganda," at his death, the UNIA held three memorial services for Bruce. Bruce was appointed duke of the Nile in 1924.[15]

John Edward Bruce was a prodigious letter writer, and he maintained a global network of friendships that supplied him with useful information. There is no evidence that he himself ever traveled abroad. Grandfather was, apparently, one of his favorite contacts. They corresponded frequently, commenting on the issues of the day, activities, and personalities.

Bruce was aware of his tendency to write long, extensive letters. In his letter of September 22, 1904, he wrote, "I have yours of Sept. 19th and I thank you for it. I was ashamed of myself for boring you with that long letter of which you speak and which you say you have read in installments. Reading after me becomes a discipline I fear rather than a pleasure."

John Wesley Cromwell kept sixty-five letters from John Edward Bruce. The first letter was written on December 8, 1896, and the last, on August 15, 1923. Twenty-five letters were written between 1896 and 1899, thirty-four between 1902 and 1911, and eleven between 1920 and 1923. Those written between 1902 and 1911 are the longest and therefore the most difficult to incorporate into a story that is not exclusively about Bruce. For this reason, only excerpts of selected letters from 1902 and 1911 are included. The letters from 1896 to 1899 and those from 1920 to 1923 are quoted in their entirety. They are not too long and give the flavor of Bruce's style of writing and his concerns of the moment. Regrettably, there are no letters from the so-called war years. Perhaps there was little or no correspondence during this period; but it is more likely that Grandfather lost those letters. The letters from 1920 to 1923 reveal the thoughts of one old man

15. Martin, *Race First,* 43.

to another and describe the emergent leadership of Marcus Garvey. The letters included here are reproduced exactly as Bruce wrote them—both as to style and grammar. Bruce was sixty-four in 1922, and he died two years after he wrote the last letter. Grandfather was seventy-four when he received that letter and lived seven more years.

December 1896–December 1899

State of New York
Treasurer's Office
Albany, Dec. 8—1896

Personal
J. W. Cromwell Esq.

My dear Mr. Cromwell, I beg to thank you for your good favor of 6th inst. rec'd this Am which I have carefully read and digested. The sending of the *cast* to Mr. Cooper instead of to a member or committee of your society was done upon the representation to me that it would help Mr. Cooper's[16] circulation in that he was going to print a cut of the cast and have a glowing write up of the Literary etc. It was my extreme desire to lend a hand to a struggling member of the craft that moved me to send it to Cooper and not that I wished to offer any discourtesy to the association or to any member of it. I assumed whether rightly or not, that Mr. Cooper would represent me in this matter and that he would state the reasons why the cast was sent to him. I don't like to feel or to think that Mr. Cooper is capable of resorting to sharp practices in this matter yet when you tell me that there is an incidental bill of $11.00 to be paid on the cast, you arouse my curiosity and excite my suspicions. I have repeatedly assured Mr. Cooper since the arrival of the cast, that I made no charges to the Literary for packing or expressage that I was quite willing to contribute the amount I had paid out of my own pocket to the Literary and therefore hoped he would make no demand for these items $7 for packing $4 on acct of express charges. He wrote me that he paid the $3.00 balance and that he and Hershaw would see

16. Edward E. Cooper, the founder and editor of *Indianapolis World* and *Freeman and Colored Americans,* was heavily supported by Booker T. Washington. Bruce was extremely interested in black history and in the value of cast likenesses of black persons of note. In a letter written as late as 1923, he wrote about a likeness of Frederick Douglass he was sending to the Negro academy through Cromwell. Bruce thought that reproduction of this cast could be sold by the academy for income.

that I got mine. Then it was that I wrote him that I should make no claims upon your exchequer as I was quite willing as an evidence of my good will, and a proof of my race loyalty to relieve the association of this additional expense. I make this statement *subrosa* with no desire to impinge the motives of Mr. Cooper. I authorize you to say to Bethel Literary that I have *no bill against it and have not sold it anything.* You can draw, as you doubtless will, your own conclusions. I've done a little drawing myself since reading your letter and have been led to employ the language of Madame De Stael:—"The more I see of men, the more I like dogs." There are some mighty poor imitators of Machiavelli among the crop of "Afro-Americans" of this generation and I shall quietly dissociate myself from those whom I have been led to believe were at least honorable in some things. The whole situation has been misrepresented to me which accounts for my sharp letter to you. Thanks for the pamphlets. I am sending you a batch of English and West India newspapers by this mail and some valuable school documents.

Very truly yours
Bruce

State of New York
Treasurer's Office
Albany Jany 11 1897

J. W. Cromwell Esq.
Washington, D.C.
My Dear Sir;

I beg to return herewith as per your request my endorsement of the proposed American Negro Academy, and to thank you personally, as well as the gentlemen associated with you in this movement for your courtesy and kindness in extending me an invitation to cooperate with you in this laudable effort. I assure you of my entire willingness to do whatever I can to promote the success of the American Negro Academy and to make it a fixture among the *great* institutions of this caste-cursed country.

Very truly yours
Jno E. Bruce

11 Congress St.

State of New York
Treasurer's Office
Albany Feby 19, 1897

J. W. Cromwell Esq.
Washington, D.C.

Dear Mr. Cromwell I have your good favor of 15th inst with inclosure-draft of your presentation speech before B.L. [Bethel Literary] last Tuesday for which I beg of you to accept my heartfelt grateful thanks. It is refreshing to read a deliverance like this and to note the absence of Tommyrot and gush. You just said enough and said it in your usual forcible and frank manner.

The *Negro Academy*—I know of nothing at present to interfere with my plans of coming to Washington and being a good listener at the preliminary meeting to perfect a permanent organization of the academy, however should anything intervene—I shall notify you in due time and will request you to act as my proxy. I am in favor of J. W. Cromwell for President or for any office he desires because I believe him to be in everyway qualified to give direction to the course and policy of such an organization and because I believe that in all such movements intended to show the capabilities of the Blacks, that the Blacks should lead whenever they are found to possess the elements of intelligent leadership. Certainly no man who knows you, will for one moment question your entire fitness to provide over such a body.

I think the entrance fee should be $5 or $10—and that the annual dues should be $5—the former could be paid in two installments this I think and believe is a fair rate considering the work to be done by the academy, but I am willing to abide by the judgment of the majority and to hold up my end with the rest of the brethren.

Very truly yours
J. E. Bruce

State of New York
Senate Chamber
Albany, Feby 26, 1897

J. W. Cromwell Esq.
Washington, D.C.

My dear sir; I had arranged to leave here for W. on Monday next, having secured leave of absence and a pass from Dr. Depew, but my wife has succumbed to a malignant attack of La Grippe, and I am necessarily obliged to abandon the idea of coming to Washington. I looked forward to an enjoyable trip and a profitable and interesting meeting of the friends of the movement in which you are a leading spirit. In consequence of my inability to materialize will you be good enough to act as my proxy which I authorize you to do?

Faithfully your friend

J. E. Bruce

[marginal note] If for any reason you cannot so act my good friend Dr. Crummell will do so. Kindly advise me.

State of New York
Treasurer's Office
Albany, Mch 16, 1897

J. W. Cromwell

Washington, D.C.

My dear Sir, Your esteemed favor of 8th instant was handed to me this Am at office where it had lain since its arrival. I have been away from work for some days on account of sickness in my family and have not had until today opportunity to go for any mail which might be for me in office. Kindly send all letters for me to my residence, 11 Congress Street.

I gladly enclose the amt for the entrance fee to membership in *Negro Academy* and congratulate you on your election to the office of Treasurer as I note by the dispatches.

I presume you have read Mr. Fortune's article in the *Sunday Sun* March 14th?[17] I haven't time to register and so take risk of sending it this way.

Fraternally Yours.

J. E. Bruce

---

17. The "Color Line" by Fortune originally appeared in the *New York Sun* on May 16, 1897. Fortune's article was written as a response to an earlier piece by Edward Blyden, "Africa's Service to the World." On Thursday, December 3, 1897, in a column, The Color Line, subtitled "Bruce Grit Warmish on the Subject—Taps Editor Fortune, Defends Dr. Blyden," Bruce's response appeared in the *Star of Zion,* the denominational paper of the A.M.E. Church. Fortune had attacked Blyden's reaction to the South, where Blyden had noticed the prominence of mulattoes over Blacks. Bruce stated that the mulattoes had raised the color line and explained that Blyden's statement was the result of his Liberian experience when indeed the mulattoes did lord their position over Blacks. Bruce felt that mulattoes in the United States had raised the color line but that Blacks here would not evade the issue. He further criticized Bishop McNeal Turner for attempting to establish mulatto rule in the African Methodist Episcopal churches under his jurisdiction. This attempt, Bruce felt, had "fortunately been miscarried and which bids fair to destroy the usefulness of the African Methodist Church in the dark continent, because of the ability to supplant *black* preachers who have demonstrated their ability to succeed and to put into their pulpits *American* mulattoes. The Blacks in Africa will not stand for this sort of discrimination even if it does have the sanction and active support of a Bishop who *calls* himself a Negro."

11 Congress St.
Albany
March 23, 1897

J. W. Cromwell, Esq.
Washington, D.C.
My Dear Friend Cromwell

Both card and letter to hand together with receipt for remittance for $5 for which thanks.

The card served its purpose as you intimated it did and that anxious feeling characteristic of a colored man whose mind is between doubt and certainty in such circumstances "have gone." I thank you for the prompt and business-like acknowledgement of my letter and its contents.

I fear the office seekers—many of them at least will reach the conclusion arrived at by the brother of sable hue who sought the mission to Dahomey—as portrayed in Texas Steer "offis seekin is mighty po bizness." It always is for men who do not know their limitations, and I judge that there are quite a few of both races now in Washington seeking office who are thoroughly unfit by education experience and training for some of the offices they aspire to fill. Fortune has just written me that he is a candidate for public printer and has requested me to write the President in his behalf. He has no more chance of landing in the place than a bob-tail bovine or any of the dozen applicants who weigh more politically and mentally than he does. But Timothy wants to have some fun I assume, and at some time in the future will write learnedly if not wisely of the ingratitude of political parties, the while posing as a victim of the indifference and lack of appreciation of the party now in power in refusing to recognize his claim to one of the biggest and most responsible offices within the gift of the President. I have written to the President whom I know personally, a letter asking him to give Mr. Fortune's application the consideration it merits. As the entire male [Negro] population of this state is only 36,925, I do not apprehend that our genial and versatile friend will reach the goal of his towering ambition or write *Hon* before his name as Public Printer. Here is presented a clear case of a brainy young man who does not know "where he is at" and who does not apply the ordinary rule of common sense in the game of politics. There will no doubt be a great number of disappointed men in Washington during and after the Fog Days who now blindly believe themselves fitted for offices that they want to fit. I shall be glad to do anything I can to advance your interests in the direction of securing the appointment as Asst. Librarian of Cong. Lib and will cheerfully send you a letter in a day or so. Congressman Mahoney of this state has secured for me the appointment of a lady friend of my late mother's as attendant. And has just written me that Mr. Spofford will be returned in the position of Librarian. A place in this library is a good thing to have and means that the holder will hold on for life if he or she attends to business. I would greatly like to see you made Asst. Librarian and will do anything in my power to help you succeed. There is no good reason why you shouldn't as you are in every way qualified to fill a place of this character. I know Mr. Melville Dewey only slightly. He is not here much. He is a very able man and he sustains the same relation with our great state Library that Spofford does with the Cong. Lib. He's courtly and a learned genius and a student, an omnivorous reader and a strict disciplinarian. Just as soon as your candidacy becomes known there will be a dozen Negro and tan colored applicants for the same place. I agree with you that this would be just the place for you and you would be in touch with all that is going on in literary circles not that you are not now, but your scope would be wider and your opportunities better for obtaining needed and useful information for your work than they are at present. I'll do what I can for you and will try to influence some "good people" in your behalf.

I took the liberty to send you today some views of the interior of the state capital and other papers which I thought would interest you, together with photographic views of a memorial jug of the late Fred Douglass which I designed and when I am rich enough I shall manufacture and sell. I trust you will receive the latter in good condition.

I give you heartiest thanks for your generous expression of interest in my wife's health, and am glad to be able to say that she is better and able to be about her housework. I indulge the hope that you and your immediate family are in good health and appetites.

Believe Me
Very Sincerely
J. E. Bruce

11 Congress Street
April 27th, 1897

My dear Cromwell

I have only recently returned from a trip thro' the state in the interest of our New York exhibit and find among a multitude of letters and papers your esteemed favor of each instant, which I have read with interest. I can fully appreciate the force and point of your opening paragraph and have no complaint to make because of your failure to connect with this point as often as you could wish. Great men must pay the penalty for being great, distinguished, and useful. It is characteristic of the brethren to become cold and indifferent where a cash consideration is involved. You do not surprise me when you say that they are not taking hold as readily as you had believed they would. I still believe that there is something radically wrong with the Negro and that he must for a long time to come, lack the elements of true race pride and public spirit. *The Negro Academy* is the place for ambitious writers, and the mentally deformed of the race who are willing to be helped and they ought not to hesitate to give it a hearty support morally and substantially. I send you the names of a few of my friends who I am sure will be glad to identify themselves with the academy if asked to do so. Prof. W. H. Perry, 2909 W. Walnut St., Louisville Ky. Prof Perry is a school teacher and a writer of creditable verse; he is also a black man. A. S. White Esq. 515 Court Place, Louisville Ky. is a Lawyer, black as Dinah's shadow and withal a brilliant fellow, a good speaker and an able writer. R. H. Shirley D.D. a native of the Friendly Island a fine scholar a polished gentlemen resident at Coxsackie, NY. I believe that all of these gentlemen will be glad to join the academy. If you write them kindly mention the fact that I suggested their names to you.

I am waiting patiently for Brother DuBois' deliverance.[18] I always read him carefully I like his style and his way of putting things. "The Solvers Solved" discloses the fact that he is a man of breadth and observation. I shall be glad to do anything I can to advance the cause championed by Ex-Congressman Murray and am under obligation to you for courtesies indicated by your letter. I will endeavor to deserve the honor thrust upon me and the confidence of those responsible for it. The mss. of my book is almost ready.[19] I am having it type written to avoid errors. The Principal of the Elizabeth City N.C. Industrial School who was my guest here a few days ago gave me an order for 3 dozen copies to start with—The white brethren are responding handsomely and I ain't kicking. Senator Wetmore sent me an order at Rochester for 5 copies I shall gather it all for the millionaires in this section I can reach. I have hundreds of names of good people. Sent you some Belfast and English papers recently did they reach you?

18. This is an interesting early assessment of Du Bois. I found no reference to Du Bois' lecture, "The Solvers Solved," in the Du Bois papers at the University of Massachusetts at Amherst. Du Bois' earliest printed article, "Strivings of the Negro People," appeared in the *Atlantic* in August 1897, three months after the reference quoted by Bruce.

19. In 1897, Bruce wrote an article entitled "Toussaint L'Ouverture," which traced the history of the slave trade in the New World. The same year he published "A History of Negro Musicians" in the *Boston Transcript*. He had not published any book at this time.

My kindest regards to Dr. Crummell when you see him, tell him he owes me a letter.

Very cordially and sincerely yours
Bruce

State of New York
Treasurer's Office
Albany, May 6, 1897

J. W. Cromwell, Esq.
My Dear Mr. Cromwell.

On my return from New York City, I found on my table a number of pamphlets which you were kind enough to send me, among them Mr. DuBois' *able* and *truthful statement* of the Negroes side of the case.[20] I shall take plans to give it a rereading and to fulminate liberally on its salient points. Mr. DuBois possesses the wonderful faculty of stating things with great clearness and perspicuity. He'll probably be accused by the demagogues and Negroes—of drawing the color line.

Is Dr. Crummell in town? I wrote him recently for his book and photograph of himself for our New York exhibit in Nashville. Leave here Saturday for New York return Tuesday

truly yours
Bruce

11 Congress Street
Albany July 28, 1897

My dear Mr. Cromwell

Your very chatty letter of yesterday is in front of me and all the points it covers are noted. I am pleased to learn that *Transcript* article suited you.[21] There is so

20. In his essay "The Conservation of Races," published in 1897 as *Occasional Paper,* No. 2 by the American Negro Academy, Du Bois discussed the real meaning of race, which in the past had been "the law of race development, and what lesson had the past history of race development to teach the rising Negro people." As one of the eight distinctly differentiated racial groups, as defined by historians and sociologists, Du Bois promoted cultural pluralism. His argument was that Negroes had given America its only native music and folk stories, its deepest pathos and humor; therefore the Negro should not be absorbed into American society but should maintain a separate unity and spirituality and should fashion separate racial, educational, business, and cultural institutions and organizations, such as the American Negro Academy, while at the same time insisting on equality of opportunity.

21. On July 14, 1897, the *Boston Evening Transcript* published a long article by Bruce entitled "Negro Song Writers, Ambitious Work Done By Them As Composers." In the article, Bruce makes

much to be said about Negro Music and melodies that one cannot do full justice to the subject in a column and a brief. To my mind the Negro possesses the only voice in the United States which an inhabitant of the Pleiades would call melodious in conversation and from the first accusation of Twang applied to the whole country by Foreign Nations.

I did not for lack of space credit the Negro with having produced the only nature music or folksong (with a few exceptions) that the country possesses. Songs so beautiful so close to nature so full of pathos that the white brother, beginning with the corked minstrel and ending with the student at the Boston Conservatory of Music or Prof. Paine of Harvard takes off his hat to them as soon as he knows enough, whatever really . . . [illegible] of the American soil in the band tunes that live and you see the brethren in their picturesque outfits and actually hear their melodious voices. This in the symphony which created such a furor in New York Musical circles a few years ago and evoked from the local critics a flood of letters to the newspapers such as only narrow-minded critics can write when they find that foreigners who know music also know where to look for it when they come to the United States. But enough of this.

The reports of the conference[22] at Hampton were not very full and we of the East were disposed to think there wasn't very much accomplished at this gath-

---

reference to some documentation he had received from "Professor John W. Cromwell, a leading educator in the District of Columbia," which indicated that the song "Listen to the Mocking Bird" was written by a street minstrel, George Milburn. Bruce had done considerable research for this article in which he included titles and composers of seventy-one songs, which he considered the best of over 450 numbers composed by African Americans. He anticipated a greater number in the future.

22. Hampton and Tuskegee held well-publicized annual conferences to foster the ideals of self-help and racial solidarity with economic development and moral virtues. Beginning in 1904, emphasis was placed on co-operative insurance features and building and loan associations as forms of collective endeavor calculated to help the masses. An outgrowth of the spirit of the Hampton conferences was the Negro Organization Society of Virginia, which was established under Hampton Institute auspices in 1909. The Tuskegee conferences were similar in spirit to the Hampton conferences, and like the Hampton events, Tuskegee's conferences were attended by eminent persons from across the nation. Booker T. Washington invited some seventy-five farmers, mechanics, teachers, and ministers to a conference at Tuskegee in February 1892. Some four hundred to five hundred men and women, particularly farmers, came and took the pledge: "Self-respect will bring with us many rights now denied us—to buy land, cultivate it thoroughly, build houses with more than one room, tax themselves to build better school houses, extend the school year to six months at least, give more attention to the character of their leaders, especially ministers and teachers, keep out of debt, avoid law suits, treat women better, have conferences similar in aim to this in every community where practicable."

After 1892, these conferences at Tuskegee were held without the election of a chairman. The only requirement was common sense and no discussion of matters black people present had no power to remedy. These conferences grew so large that they were extended to two days: a farmers' conference

ering when too many of our future great get together it generally happens that they don't accomplish much real practical good because one is afraid to move, or to speak his thoughts and of adverse criticism. The tendency to worship the fellow who has in anyway distinguished himself and to regard him as an infallible being is another draw back. Eyeglasses, titles and silk hats are sometimes potent forces in Negro gatherings. Booker Washington's Alabama Conferences are more prolific in results I fancy than these cut and dried affairs such as you had at Hampton recently. It doesn't follow that because a Negro is highly educated that he is necessarily a practical man or a safe counsellor, lots of our highly educated men have yet to be *educated*. But I am prejudging the work of your conference simply because I haven't seen over a dozen lines in print about its work. I shall hope to have some longer information direct from you, and then I will eat the language above recorded. Heretofore all these gatherings have been similar in scope and purpose. The tendency to soar away from those whose conviction calls these gatherings together has been too frequent. Still I hope this Hampton praise meeting was a gratifying success oratorically and along practical common sense lines.

I have had two letters from Mr. Dorsey since the appearance of my article I could not wait on him, because the Boston people telegraphed me for copy. Mr. Dorsey's first letter was a vindication of the accuracy of your memory. It contained practically the same information you gave. His second letter contained a long list of vocal and instrumental music by Negroes sent through him by Mr. Briggs with his compliments.

The accove now at Nashville is a Phila boy, a youngster of perhaps 25 or 8 years of age. He is constitutionally lazy is a great Dude and is passionately fond of female women who spoil him because he is an excellent performer on the Pianoforte.

Brother Fortune broke loose in Washington before he went to Hampton and all the "politicaners" up this way are laughing over his idiotic display of nerve. He threatened to defeat McKinley in 1900 and was presumably as serious about the matter as he ever was about anything in his life. It seems that the President is not moving fast enough in the matter of Negro appointments as he and a few

---

was held on the first day, and on the second, a workers' conference (See Louis R. Harlan, *Booker T. Washington: The Making of A Black Leader, 1856–1901* [London: Oxford University Press, 1975]). Yet, in July 1899, Cromwell was chairman of the committee on statistics. Other chairs that year were Rev. Francis Grimké, Dr. Furmann J. Shadd, Archibald Grimké, William S. Scarborough, Lucy C. Laney, Victoria Earle Matthews, Harris Barrett, Andrew F. Heliyer, George W. Carver, and Alexander Prerves.

other political Hessians would wish and they are sure displeased thereat. Brother *Tim* is not as well balanced in his intellectuals as he might be or could be if he didn't try both with tangle foot and dream dreams no mortal ever dared to dream before. I am doing Negro authors now and have a great list. What are you doing about the library job?

Faithfully yours
Bruce

The Chronicle
Published Every Thursday
Devoted to the interests of the Negro Race and The Republican Party
Office, 150 West 37th Street

Editors and Proprietors
Chas. W. Anderson
John E. Bruce   Albany Nov. 29th 1897
Dear Friend

I have your esteemed favor of 27th inst, advising me of the forthcoming meeting of the Academy Dec. 28–9. In reply to your queries I have to say that I have not heard of any great doings in the literary world by the brethren except one book in course of preparation, the joint product of three men, which is to be published by J. L. Nichols Co. at Naperville, Ill. The authors and compilers of this venture as I learn are a German Doctor somebody, Booker T. Washington and one other.[23] The book is largely statistical and biographical, and I suppose as usual will be as inaccurate as some that have preceded it. The burden of its song of course will be the Negro. My own venture remains in *status quo* pending the arrival of valuable manuscripts from abroad which have been promised. I am in no particular hurry to rush into print. I am positively sure that my matter will keep until I am ready to bring it out in book form. The J. B. Lyon Co. here have offered me $600 in cash for my Mss. My personal friend Col. Cole, R. R. Commissioner, advises me not to sell. I shan't sell.

I notice that Mr. Fortune's *Sun* article on the color line is being republished in the western weeklies. *The Statement of Denver* had it in full last week. I have felt called upon to reply briefly to one or two statements in it. In the *Star of Zion* my article will probably appear this week.

---

23. H. F. Kletzing and H. H. Crogman, with an introduction by Booker T. Washington, *Progress of a Race; or, The Remarkable Advancement of the Afro-American Negro from the Bondage of Slavery, Ignorance and Poverty, to the Freedom of Citizenship, Intelligence, Honor and Trust* (Atlanta, Ga., Naperville, Ill.: J. L. Nichols, 1898).

I have not seen in print other that Mr. Fortune's letter anything in opposition to the work of the Academy but I have come in contact with an element here and in New York who privately oppose it on the grounds that it is a distinctly Negro venture and calculated to arouse bad feeling among those who do not believe in separate Negro organizations of any character. These objectors however are not the most influential or intellectual of their class their social standing overbalances their intellectual standing by a number of ounces.

On the whole I have been very much gratified by the notices given the work of the Academy by such papers as the *Lagos Weekly Record* and the *Jamaica Advocate* which are in the strongest sympathy with its work and see the magnificent possibilities that await it as one of the agencies for the uplift of the American Negro in the realm of learning and letters.

Very truly yours
J. E. Bruce

11 Congress Street
Albany, N.Y. June 20, 1898

My dear Mr. Cromwell

I thank you most sincerely for copies of Dr. C's splendid address.[24] I have sent copies to Ex Gov. Flower at Watertown, N.Y. and W. M. Crane, Lt. Gov. Map (at Dalton). If they read it I am sure that they will do something. Permit me to suggest that you communicate with these gentlemen both of who are millionaires and kindly disposed towards the race. I think Mr. Flower if written the right sort of letter would give half if not all of the amt desired for object stated—He is very vain and fond of flattery and though a democrat is a staunch friend of the Negro race.

Hastily Yours
J. E. Bruce

You might send a copy of the address also to Mr. Zenus Crane, brother of Lt. Gov. who is a wealthy paper manufacturer and a most excellent gentleman. B.

---

24. "The Attitude of the American Mind toward the Negro Intellect" was Crummell's first annual address as president of the American Negro Academy and was published as *Occasional Paper,* No. 3 by the academy. Crummell insisted that educated Whites had done nothing to help the intellectual development of Negroes and that Negroes must do this themselves. He traced the attempt by Whites to keep the Negro ignorant and uneducated before and after the Civil War. Whites only wanted Negroes to learn to work with their hands, but Negroes, he asserted, also needed civilization and culture through higher education.

Albany, N.Y. Feby 28, 1899

J. W. Cromwell, esq.
Washington, D.C.
My dear Mr. Cromwell,

 . . . I note what you say about toning down on the Negro business and will govern myself accordingly. I see your point and thank you much for making it visible to my vision. There is no danger present or remote of my failure to stand up for the race.

 I cannot resist the temptation which occasionally presents itself to sail into these ethnological . . . [illegible] and tell them things.

 As I grow older I see with clearer vision the duty and the work before me as a Negro, and the utter senselessness and folly of the claims put forth by the so called superior Negro or "natural bridge between the Anglo-Saxon and the Blacks to superior mental and moral excellencies." I am beginning to see and to understand that diplomacy of a superior order must be the weapon by which the Blacks must overcome this intellectual minority of misguided and dissatisfied fools among us who see nothing worthy of commendation or imitation in the black race. Occasionally I shall be constrained to break loose. Yet I shall always respect your judgement and try to be good.

 I return herewith with my endorsement the ballots sent for signature. I know Mr. Grimké[25] and the other two gentlemen by reputation and believe that they will be valuable acquisitions to the academy. I cheerfully give my vote to them.

 I am just now not in funds of my own and don't dare *touch* treasurer of the firm Mrs. Bruce as she has only recently paid a note on our house up the country

25. There were two Grimké brothers: Archibald (1849–1930) and Francis (1850–1937). Their father was Henry Grimké, a gentleman farmer and scion of an aristocratic white family, and their mother was Nancy Weston, his slave. Both were born at "Caneacres," a plantation near Charleston, South Carolina. Upon their father's death, the boys were freed, but were later enslaved again by their white stepbrother. After overcoming many difficulties, they lived as de facto free people of color and were freed by the Emancipation Proclamation. At that time, their aunts, Sarah M. Grimké and Angela Grimké Weld, Boston abolitionists, acknowledged their relation to the boys and assisted in their education—first at Lincoln University in Pennsylvania and then at Harvard for Archibald and Princeton for Francis.

Both brothers had distinguished careers: Archibald, the more diversified, was a lawyer, journalist, and diplomat, and Francis, a minister in Washington, D.C. The District of Columbia, in fact, became the permanent home of both brothers, who were also active in the American Negro Academy, of which Francis was a cofounder. Archibald was elected to the academy and served as president from 1903 to 1916. Bruce later seems to express the feeling (how widely I don't know) that the Grimké brothers were dominating the academy. I would assume, however, that this reference is to Francis, for Archibald was still living in Boston at this time.

and isn't feeling amiable today I will send on my dues at the earliest opportunity. You can always count on my support and cooperation.

Melville Dewey is one of the *whitest* white men in this neck of the woods. He has a head as big as a dinner plate and a great big soft spot in it for "weuns." He is a man of about 40 or 43 at most has a sunny disposition is full of jokes and a good humor and the owner of a "*think thing*" that is well stocked with brains and practical ideas. I think he would be glad to know you and to correspond with you in respect of the matter to which you refer. There is quite a collection of Negro literature native and foreign in the State Library much more than I expected to find in it. If you write to Mr. Dewey, I have no objection to your saying that you know me if you think it advisable or necessary. He knows me well and might be inclined to question me about the scope of the work you contemplate doing. Anything I can do or say to help along command me.

Yours very truly

J. E. Bruce

Our yaller cousins will be pleased with this article from the *Sun* of yesterday and Fortune will doubtless reproduce it entire in the current issue of his journal of news and opinion. The problem's expanding shakily.

Albany, N.Y. Apl 4, 1899

My Dear Mr. Cromwell,

Your esteemed favor of yesterday at hand contents noted. Am glad to learn that you have been able to find out something in the Troy matter without the assistance of "able counsel." The Dan Chew I spoke of is the same Dan Chew who used to spill ink in the Recorders Office, and who for a long time after he got out, was a familiar character in about the City Hall. He used to wear high water pants, frayed at the bottom, and a sardonic smile. He doesn't look a year older though he is tolerably bald and still retains his "capacity" for calamity juice or any other liquid pizen. I know the whole family of Chews. These two here have reached out farther and gathered in more than the rest of the family could have ever hoped to do. Dan and Fred who is his cousin are making money "lawing" here among the buckras they look wise six days in the week and git back to their natcherals on Sundays. Drop Dan a line. He says he is a great race man. He will be able to do you some good now that you are Editor in Chief and Publisher of the *Negro American Year Book.*

With regard to my friend Peregrino I have to say that so far as service to the race is concerned he has been fighting its battles in the press in Buffalo and

Pittsburgh Pa. for the past six or seven years and that he is endorsed by the leading business men and politicians of Buffalo in the highest terms who know him as a thinker and writer of great force and ability. I am glad you are sending him some literature on the Academy, it will be promptly acknowledged. I should be glad to see him a member of the Academy and if it is necessary that he should give a clean bill as to respectability, character, etc. I think from what I know of him that he will be able to satisfy the necessary two third in these respects. He is respectably connected in Africa his grandfather being an Arabic scholar at Accra on the Gold Coast. He is a man of family and as polished and cultured a gentleman as I wish to meet. You will see his hand in the *New York Sun* at no distant day and you will be pleased with the song he sings. He's black all over and shows his teeth like the late Dr. R. H. Cain. I assume that if he applies for membership that the judgment of his vouchers should be accepted as a guarantee of his fitness to mix up with the brethren. I shouldn't hesitate to vote for any man whom you endorsed because I have confidence in your judgment and believe you would not propose a name for membership who was not fit. I will have the *Spectator* sent you.

I saw Mr. Dewey on Monday and had quite a chat with him. He is a splendid man and greatly interested in po' we.

Yours truly
J. E. Bruce

My Dear Mr. Cromwell,

I sent you on Saturday last $2 annual dues to the Academy which I trust you received. I have read Mr. Love's excellent paper and will as soon as the local political excitement here abates somewhat, address myself to my consideration of it. It is a very meaty and very pointed argument. Did you see Olin Perry's editorial on the work on the Academy a few weeks ago? Yes, I met Mr. DuBois and think he is very much of a man. I like his gait, and his language. He is a fine looking fellow and like all men of real ability who know how to be so he is modest. If some of our soft head scholars knew a third as much as he, this country would not be big enough for them. There's nothing new here. Jim Matthews has been re-nominated for Recorder by the Democrats the Republicans have fused with the silk stocking Democrats and nominated a Democrat of the . . . [illegible] for Matthews place. All the blacks will vote for . . . [illegible] including myself.

Yours truly
Bruce

Albany N.Y. Oct. 19, 1899

J. W. Cromwell, Esq.
Washington, D.C.
My Dear Mr. Cromwell

Your good favor of yesterday at hand, glad to learn that you received cash O.K. The Crummell Club gives promise of great usefulness here and the members are quite enthusiastic, and very much in earnest in their work. One of the first biographical sketches to be read before it will be one on Dr. Crummell by a bright young lady member Miss A. E. Moore. I will drop a line to Mr. Downing[26] and request the loan of some of his information *in re* to the Dr.

With respect to the engraving of him "I will endeavor to try" to triangulate a scheme to put through the matter, and will bring it up at our next meeting which occurs on Tuesday evening next.

I do not know that I have any of the pictures you refer to, though I have seen them at various times, and places, and think well of the idea. The only one in the bunch that I would care to frame and hang in my parlor, would be that, of that magnificent and eloquent Negro Joseph C. Price whom I know well.

Very truly yours
J. E. Bruce

NATIONAL AFRO-AMERICAN COUNCIL
John E. Bruce—11 Congress Street

Personal

Albany, N.Y. Nov. 10, 1899

My Dear Mr. Cromwell

Yours of yesterday at hand contents duly noted. I return herewith the Australian ballots duly signed and crossed as per your request and hope the gentlemen will get by.

26. George Thomas Downing (1819–1903) attended old Mulberry Street School in New York and Hamilton College in Oneida County, New York. He served as agent on the Underground Railroad and assisted in the rescue of Anthony Burns. From 1857 to 1866, he led the fight that resulted in the abolition of separate publicly supported schools in Rhode Island, and he advocated for the division of political support by Blacks between the two parties. He was also a successful caterer in New York City, Newport, Rhode Island, and Providence. For twelve years after the Civil War, he had charge of the restaurant in the House of Representatives. He worked with Frederick Douglass, urging President Johnson to adopt a more liberal Reconstruction policy, and helped to repeal New York state laws requiring Blacks to own $250 worth of property to vote. He worked against Jim Crow cars on the B&O Railroad, for the opening of the Senate gallery to Blacks, and for the abolition of the nine o'clock curfew and passage of a public accommodation law in Washington in 1873.

Fortunately for Matthews he failed to pass under the wire, as it has been discovered that the democrats (3) in number who did win, outplayed their party false by selling out to republicans boodlers had Matthews won he would have been accused of being one of the conspirators. The fight was against Judge Herrick, Dem of the Supreme Court who has splashed mud on the Ermine judicial by mixing up in politics in this county.

The Negroes stood by Matthews to a man, with but few exceptions—the exceptions being the Negroes in the state employ who were bulldozed into voting for his white democratic opponent. Matthews ran ahead of the ticket and was defeated by only 300 votes. Bishop Walters was here to see me the day before yesterday and we had a long talk about his interview and its probable effect on the Negro. He tells me that all the bigwigs now in office who are opposing his stand advised in secret council that he take that position with a view to driving McKinley to terms with the black contingent. He proposes to uncover these moral cowards and tell what they said where they said it and why they said it. If you will read the *Star of Zion* this week you will there see something on the subject. I am going to stand by the Bishop in this fight because I know he is no more of a democrat than you or I. He is one of the few Negroes in public life who has no axe to grind—who has the courage of his convictions and who is not obliged to "bend the supple hinges of the knee . . . may follow fawning." The contemptible hypocrisy and snivelling cant of the Cheathams[27] and Lyons[28] et

27. Henry Plummer Cheatham (1857–1935) was born a slave on a plantation near Henderson, North Carolina. After emancipation, Cheatham was educated in the Henderson public schools and at Shaw University. He became principal of Plymouth Normal School in Plymouth, North Carolina, and later recorder of deeds in Vance County, North Carolina.

By pursuing some questionable political strategies, Cheatham was elected as the only black member of the Fifty-first Congress in 1889. He was elected to the Fifty-second Congress and was again the only black member. While in Congress, he introduced more than fourteen bills relating to Blacks in general and to his constituency in particular, none of which was passed.

He ran again in 1894 and in 1895 but lost both times. In 1898, he lost to his brother-in-law, George H. White, who represented the Second Congressional District until 1901. White was the last African American in Congress until Oscar Stanton DePriest (1871–1951) was elected in the Third Congressional District in Chicago in November 1928.

McKinley appointed Cheatham as recorder of deeds for the District of Columbia. He was confirmed by the Senate on May 13, 1897. After four years, he returned to North Carolina and in 1907 became superintendent of the Colored Orphanage at Oxford, which had been opened in 1882. He remained in this position until his death in 1935.

28. Judson W. Lyons (1860–1924) was one of the few southern lawyers to openly oppose Booker T. Washington. President McKinley appointed him registrar of the Treasury, and after Roosevelt became president, Lyons unsuccessfully sought Washington's assistance in securing a reappointment. According to August Meier, Lyons had begun to identify with Washington's critics, and he also had become one of the light-skinned elite in Augusta who were associated with the anti-Bookerite movement. Lyons was the last African American to serve on the Republican National Commit-

al is as disgusting as it is nauseating. These ethnological betweenities whether in politics or outside of it are always ready to sell the race for a mess of pottage.

A year ago Lyons as one of the signers of the address to the county issued by the Council subscribed to the sentiment and advice therein given—that the Negro should divide his vote. I sent you a copy of that address read it and see wherein it differs from Bishop Walter's advice which was not that the whole voting population of the race should go with the Democrats but a part of it whenever and wherever it was found beneficial. I am a republican but I am against McKinley and his Philippine policy battling guns and the Holy Gospel are not good civilizing agents. Expansion is going to prove a dangerous experiment for this government. Those who tire of a Republic and sigh for the splendors of an Empire will get more than they bargained for before this "cruel war is over." John Sherman[29] with a clearness of vision almost amounting to prophecy sees dangers ahead for this nation if it carries out its threat to subdue by force of arms the liberty loving and courageous people beyond the sea, who are fighting to preserve their inalienable rights to life, liberty and the pursuit of happiness. Yankee Pride cannot recede it must go on and the fate that awaits it is yet to be recorded. "Pride goeth before a fall" and when it falls it will dash itself to pieces. I am glad the democrats won out in Maryland for more reasons than one. Republican victories elsewhere will only hasten the crisis which is the inevitable result of over confidence and the feeling of general almightiness which overtake Republicans in off years. Walters believed that Blacks should be both Democrats and Republicans.

Very truly yours

J. E. Bruce

The following two letters are particularly informative because they describe Bruce's personal contacts with Booker T. Washington and some additional anecdotes about Washington's way of relating to white people, especially northern

---

tee; in 1908, however, he lost this post to Henry Lincoln Johnson. He accordingly demanded a recordership as a reward from the Taft administration (*Negro Thought in America, 1880–1915: Radical Ideologies in the Age of Booker T. Washington* [Ann Arbor: University of Michigan Press, 1963], 237, 252).

29. John Sherman (1823–1900), senator, secretary of the Treasury, and secretary of state, was born in Ohio. He was a younger brother of Gen. William Tecumseh Sherman, a founding father of the Republican Party in Ohio. John Sherman was elected to the House of Representatives in 1854, and although he first supported President Andrew Johnson, he later voted to impeach him. Sherman took the lead in writing the Reconstruction Act of 1867, which provided for the military operation of ten states until they ratified the Fourteenth Amendment. Sherman was identified with those who opposed the creation of an American empire in the aftermath of the Spanish-American War.

philanthropists. At this time, several years before Washington delivered his famous speech in Atlanta and was dubbed "leader of the Negro race," northerners
and southerners, Black and White, had been debating whether black schools
should have a classical or an industrial educational curriculum; what, in fact,
was a classical curriculum for Blacks; and similarly what did industrial education imply, training to be a skilled worker or to be able to do the least skilled
work deemed appropriate for Blacks. Of course, many black leaders preferred
not to make a choice and saw value in developing institutions that provided or
tried to provide both kinds of education. Even John Cromwell, who fought the
changes in the curriculum for the Institute for Colored Youth, was quoted by
August Meier as being among the early supporters of industrial education from
the 1870s.[30]

But in common parlance, the name of the game was money. Therefore, how
such philanthropic organizations as the John F. Slater Fund decided to allocate
their funds became the critical determinant for what type of curriculum would
be taught in a particular school; in other words, the schools would teach the
curriculum that the organization supported. Schools competed vigorously for
their allotments. Washington was ever watchful of the growth and support of
institutions that could or did compete with Tuskegee for the available funds.
Throughout this book, it has been revealed that Washington used several methods and other people to achieve his ends.

In the letter of November 21, 1899, Howard Burke Frissell (1851–1917), the
second president of Hampton Institute and accordingly due some respect, was
the chosen warrior to block the awarding of funds to the Elizabeth City Training
College of North Carolina in which Bruce had some interest. Known officially
as the Elizabeth City Colored Normal School and Institute, it was founded on
March 3, 1891, when House Bill 383 was enacted by the North Carolina General Assembly, establishing a normal school for the specific purpose of training
black teachers to teach in the common schools of North Carolina. Peter Wed-
dick Moore (1859–1934), the distinguished educator, was the principal from 1891
to 1928.

Bruce accused Washington of spying on this institution to obtain information
that would harm its chances for funding. Frissell was not personally implicated,
but he must have been the spokesman for the negative report. It is not clear why
Bruce favored this school; it may be only that he deplored Washington's methods

30. Meier, *Negro Thought in America, 1880–1915*, 94.

and Frissell's role. In his letter of April 27, 1897, however, he does mention the principal of the Elizabeth City School as a guest in his home.

Using all his journalistic skills, Bruce revealed in these letters Washington's hypocrisy in presenting himself and his true feelings about others. Bruce refused, however, to discount Washington entirely, and angling for some financial support, he described him as a great educator and an overworked statesman, not a political leader. One wonders what Bruce's true feelings were or whether his observations were examples of Washington's power—a man too powerful to be publicly discounted. Washington had too many friends in high places, and Bruce himself existed through political patronage.

National Afro-American Council
John E. Bruce—11 Congress Street,
(Financial Secretary)
Albany, N.Y. Nov. 21, 1899

Personal
J. W. Cromwell Esq.
My Dear Cromwell

Yours of Nov. 19th at hand contents duly noted. I have had no correspondence with Bishop Walters on the subject of Dr. Frissell's proposition to blacklist certain schools. But a gentleman interested in Negro education in the south and who gives liberally to the cause, who was in New York at the time wrote me today, that Dr. Frissell at that meeting arose and said substantially that there were too many of these alleged industrial schools, and that something should be done to check them. He then attacked the Elizabeth City, N.C. School in which . . . [illegible] I am interested alleging that it was represented to be according to a report of some man who had been sent there to investigate it. Who sent him he did not state nor did he state what were the conditions discovered by this spy. This school gets an annual appropriation from the state of $500 per year and has many liberal friends all over the North particularly in Mass. and Albany. Its general agent here G. A. Mebane has in Boston run upon white people who have been giving to Booker Washington and who tell him that they do not approve of the Washington idea of educating the Negro to be servants and they have cut the subscriptions in half giving him the larger half and Washington's man the smaller half because they have pledged themselves to give so much to Washington annually. Washington has heard of these things and he has never lost an opportunity through his agents to dig at the Elizabeth school. The suggestion is Washington's not Frissell's though Frissell advanced it. Neither of the colored men present, Washington included, opened their mouths in favor of the school. Mr. Washington is not popular in Boston and hasn't been since he got up a fake banquet which was managed by his coin hunters and was reported to be given by the leading colored citizens of Boston in his honor. The affair cost $700 and was a bold stroke intended to impress the philanthropic white people with the idea that the Negroes in Boston lionized him. He did not show up at the feast until 9:30 his spokesman alleging that the train was delayed. A few minutes before that time Washington who had been in his room all day resting up he left his hotel and entered the Banquet Hall. In the meantime some of the Banqueters were busying themselves trying to find out things and one man got up after the master of ceremonies had tapped for order and Mr. Washington who by the way had not received a single cheer—had been seated—and wanted to know who was paying for this spread the colored or white people of Boston? That he did not propose to be a party to such a transparent fake as this banquet manifestly was by giving Mr. Washington his endorsement. He left the banquet hall and others followed. The newspapers got hold of it and roasted Washington unmercifully and since that time he has kept a man on salary as he keeps Tim Fortune . . . [illegible] white people out of their money while he tramps over the country dealing out platitudes and hogwash about the future of the Negro. The most dangerous Negro in public life today is the crafty Booker T. Washington. I am told by a gentleman who has lately visited Tuskegee that every time he buys land for the school he has his choice of a plot as his commission. This is allright—if he can fool the buckras let him go on but if there is going to be any attempt by proxy to kill off other schools Washington will hear something drop. Bigger men than he have been laid low by overreaching themselves. Washington loves money and in his mad ambition to get it he will kill off or try to do so to every Negro who stands in his way. He can't last long at the pace he is going. I understand that there was no definite action taken with regard to blacklisting struggling Negro schools, the matter was talked over informally, and the Elizabeth City School was selected as the object of attack by Dr. Frissell, there were no resolutions offered on this subject. Washington was the softest . . . [illegible] of any of the bunch of Negro educators in the South. The houses on his land around Tuskegee are all built by the students. He gets his lumber and bricks free. And his stock, horses, and cows and sheep are fed out of the money appropriated by the Yankees to maintain the school. A white man told me the following story about Washington confidentially and vouched for its truth. Washington was in New York for a few days seeing people of means and before he left delivered before a wealthy club his thumbworn and worked to death essay on democracy and education—and took up a collection of checks and cash for Tuskegee as usual. After the lecture he went down to the Hoffman House Café on 5th Ave. and ordered supper. It was then about 11:30. At the Hoffman they serve whiskey to guests in small decanters holding about two good stiff drinks. My friend says that about 12 he strolled into the Café for a bite and saw and recognized Mr. Washington sawing a beefsteak in half and with a napkin tucked under his chin and his liquor poured out ready to go to its long road home. He said "Good Evening." Mr. Washington bowed and spoke and pushed his counter glass beside his liquor glass. Seeing this movement and desiring to put him at ease he said, "Ah Mr. Washington I see you indulge. Waiter bring me some of the best brandy you have in the house . . ." Mr. Washington acknowledged that he drank a little especially after much speaking as his system needed a tonic as a stimulant. The gentleman then complimented him on his speech—he had not known before where he had seen the gentleman or who he was and when the gentleman gave him his card he tells me that Booker acted real nervous—like and tried to blush. This story was told to me in confidence by the President of the Bd. R.A. Commissioners with the remark that Washington is a "damned fraud."

I have all of his European letters but my wife has clipped and scrapped them and packed them away in the garret. Am going to Boston in the morning early and haven't time to look them up. If you will drop a line to Moses DaRocha, Esq., 25 South Clark St. Edinburgh, Scotland he will get the name and address you want. He is a friend of mine a young medical student at Edinboro and I think a member of the society you refer to. Bishop Walters expects that all that gang of trimmers will get out of the council and is prepared for any break they make. I saw Bishop Grant's interview in the *Albany Journal* about that time and noted its effect. As I noticed the effect of Bishop Walters interview in the appointment of Calloway as Commissioner to Paris. Calloway was here to see me several days before his appointment and was here after he got it. You know Cooper, Brother Cromwell why moralize on his editorial deliverances. Cooper is sui generis. Thompson is the editorial *Janus* of the outfit but Cooper gets the credit and the damning. I see Booker has bought Thompson and has subsidized the *American.*

Yours truly

J. E. Bruce

Personal
Boston, December 8, 1899
My Dear Mr. Cromwell

Mrs. Bruce has forwarded to me your two abbreviated communications, here, and I hasten to reply to them.

I have come here primarily to witness the ovation of the colored citizens in Boston to the Wizard of Tuskegee Dec. 1. They didn't ovate neither did they rise and sing "Hail to the Chief" when half hour after the time announced for the meeting to open the Wizard entered the church on the arm of Chairman Plummer and took his seat on the platform. There was some cranning of necks on the part of the women but no other demonstration—I went to church early and got a seat in Amen corner where I could see and hear and not be seen. I took a few notes of Booker's speech which was a sort of oratorical *potpourri* trimmed with nigger jokes and impossible yarns about every man in several different places at the same time and who did things that the average colored men doesn't usually do. They were oratorical lies uttered with the greatest nonchalance by the orator and with such splendid effect that his audience roared at his keen humor, the few bald headed whites in the audience laughed until they grew red in the face and the humor dripped from Booker 'jes as nacherly as grease on a hot griddle turned sidewise.

His next most irresistible point was the Negro didn't put enough dignity, skill and brains in the humbler avocations such as bootblacking, waiting and other common laboring work and he was apprehensive that unless the Negro bestirred himself he would be driven out of these employment by the whites, who appeared to have a monopoly of these essentials—the applause on this point was led by a white man who sat in the front seat and who was evidently hard of hearing as he kept his hand to his ear and leaned over to catch all the wisdom that dripped from Booker's lips. After this he told jokes by the gross evidently for the benefit of his white hearers at which everybody laughed most heartily. The speech was commonplace enough I assure you, and the Negroes gathered in knots after the meeting and compared notes the consensus of opinion among them being that the wizard had not said a thing.—They came to be amused and got what they came for. After the show I went up to the chancel to speak to Mrs. Jewell daughter of Robert Hamilton of *Anglo-African Magazine*[31] fame

31. The *Anglo-African Magazine* was started in 1859 by Thomas Hamilton of Brooklyn. Written entirely by black men and women, its purpose was to expose the condition of Blacks and "to uphold and encourage the now depressed hopes of thinking black men." After Thomas Hamilton's death, his brother Robert Hamilton took on the magazine. It ceased publication in 1865.

who introduced me to a number of her friends who came to shake hands with the Wizard and I held quite a reception alongside the Wizard. Soon he discovered who was sharing honors with him and he came over and greeted me cordially. I told him he had made a most amusing speech and in a monotone he said "these Boston Negroes are mostly fools, they are all clothes and no brains" then he quickly added, "I didn't mean to say that for there are some very cultured and refined people among them." I said, "Yes that's so." "I want to see you," he said, "wait and walk over to my hotel with me"—I said, "Washington you are a diplomat" and left him to speak to Bob Teamoh and Doctor Courtney whom the former wished to introduce. Both of these men spoke of his speech disparagingly and assured me that the meeting had been gotten up and paid for by Washington who is crazy to get an endorsement from the Negroes of Boston *but* they said the Negroes of Boston are not with him they don't like his methods. On the way to his hotel he talked of the Boston Negroes' ignorance and alluded to them as scoundrels and cut-throats and suggested that I give them a dig for their apathy towards Tuskegee saying he couldn't afford to do it himself. He evidently wanted to say something more to me but the party that went up Beacon St. with us kept him busy answering fool questions. . . . [text missing] mind and I didn't urge him because I have something on my mind. The white newspaper account of the meeting discovered to readers next day that Booker made one speech and printed another. His printed speech was part of his Atlanta speech. Part of democracy in Education and part of Atlanta interview with a few paragraphs from his "One Point of View" as published in *Howard's Magazine* for November. It was declared on the rooftops and street corners that the bluest blood in Beantown from the Lt. Governor down would occupy seats on the platform and that the Mayor would preside. The only white man on the platform was Mr. Edwin W. Read editor of the *New England Magazine* who was literally dragged up there by Chairman Plummer who looks like a retired bootblack. Not one of the prominent white men invited sent letters of regret nor did the chairman even allude to their absence. So much for the meeting. I went around and interviewed a lot of our fellows, Ed Brown, Wolff, Dr. Johnson, Judge Walker and a score of the most prominent of the better element as to [the] cause of their absence from the platform and they told me about that famous Banquet at Young's Hotel which cost Booker $400 and said they could not stomach any more of the self-effacement oratory. And had no sympathy with this work—that he tried to occupy the dual position of man and mendicant and was more mendicant than man which is I think a correct estimate of his industrial action planorama. I have talked with a good many white men here such as Major Higginson of Lee Higginson Banker,

F. C. Foster, Banker, E. Dwight, Cotton Broker and many others who say that it is time Mr. Washington was doing something *practical,* time that he was getting his race in line to help him carry the burden of Tuskegee—that the colored race cannot be said to be making progress along industrial or other lines when white men have to pay the bills, that the rich Negroes Washington tells about in his speeches ought to be told that it is more blessed to give than to receive—that the kind of talk one hears in Boston among the solid men and they are going to quit giving money after while to anybody. I forgot to state that Booker took all the credit for the defeat of the Hardwick Bill,[32] and hugged himself several times during the evening. You say you read my letter with surprise—I am sure there ought to be no occasion for surprise. If in reading my pieces about Booker you fail to discover the snake's hand that's your fault. The article I wrote about him *in re* the Council incident was the subject of many letters. . . . [text missing] I had prepared a syndicate letter raking Booker for his moral cowardice and exposing his lack of moral courage as the logical successor to Frederick Douglass (God save the mark). Fortune telegraphed me and Washington came to see me at Albany to get me to hold up for peace sake. I went to Saratoga to see Fortune at Booker's expense. At our interview I told him I wanted to be fair to Booker. I wouldn't lie on him for him or about him that I knew some things that he knew and the public would like to know concerning his attitude toward the Council. Fortune said it's all over now, what use stirring this thing up. Write a letter giving the fact regarding the meeting in the church where Booker was denounced and send it to these papers giving me a list of papers and send in your bill. I told him that if I wrote such a letter I should say in it Booker is not the leader of the Negro race and has never pretended to be such a leader nor does he aspire to be. He agreed— I then added that I must have guarantee from Booker that the bill would be paid before I wrote a line. He telegraphed Booker at Boston stating the dozen letters manifolded would in judgment of Bruce Grit cost $100. My expenses to Saratoga

32. While the white primary and the poll tax had earlier been employed to disfranchise the Blacks, many politicians felt that they were not sufficient barriers. Responding to Georgia's newly elected governor, Allen D. Chandler, who said that the black vote was a "constant menace" that "tainted society," Senator Hardwick of Washington County introduced a bill in 1899 requiring that all those registering to vote pass a literacy test, with an escape provision in the form of a "grandfather clause" that would permit the 12 percent of the Whites who were illiterate to vote. A coalition of white ministers, labor leaders, and machine politicians joined Blacks to oppose the bill, and twenty-four Blacks, including John Hope, petitioned the legislature against the measure. Booker T. Washington came to Georgia to help covertly to organize resistance to the Hardwick Bill. He wrote T. Thomas Fortune complaining of the lack of initiative on the part of the Blacks in Georgia. In any case, the Hardwick Bill was overwhelmingly defeated in 1899 by a 137–3 vote and again defeated in 1901 by a 114–17 vote.

three days $20—what answer? In an hour answer came back ok go ahead BTW. And then I wrote the famous defense of Booker which you *saw* which as I say was intended to take him out of the political leadership business and dump him in Tuskegee as the great apostle of industrialism. If he looms up in the political arena that letter will tell him to get back. In my article in *Howard's*. I tried to emphasize the fact that he is not a politician but the founder of a great industrial school, that his tastes run to industrialism. I have left myself room enough to turn around three times and I have some very bad damaging documents from Booker and his fictus Actiates Tim which will only be used when it becomes necessary. If Booker stays in his place he can go on. But if he gets going something will surely drop. He is a diplomatic darky and I thinks he sees things in the air. I believe in the work as he is doing with the black belt of Alabama because I think it is necessary and helpful to the blacks of that section. But I draw the line when he attempts to make his kind of industrialism contagious and to make it apply to Negroes in other parts of the country.[33]

Negroes in Massachusetts and New York find openings as expert accountants, Bookkeepers, and clerks in white business houses. It depends on the Negro himself whether he is given recognition in these callings. The smarterer who has been dipped in a weak solution of accomplishments cannot get a foothold anywhere north or south. But the really competent Negro who has character, ability and respectability can catch on and hold on in these parts. I notice here that a number of the District messenger boys are colored that the superintendent of one of the biggest constructing firms in the East the firm that built the New Boston Depot is a black man and all the men who are under him are Irish and Dagoes (this man superintended the building of this depot). Now I must quit writing I am doing a little work for the *Transcript* here. The editor affeared does me the compliment of using one of my articles as editorial and has written me to that effect.[34]

33. Bruce underestimated Washington's control over the black media and overemphasized his own power. See Louis R. Harlan, "Damming Niagara," in *Booker T. Washington: The Wizard of Tuskegee, 1901–1915* (New York, Oxford University Press, 1983), 84–106, to see how extensive and insidious Washington's influence and control were.

34. It is likely that Bruce is referring to an editorial, "Color and Labor," that appeared in the July 7, 1897, issue of the *Boston Evening Transcript*. The piece is several paragraphs in length and reflects rather specific knowledge of the issues and personalities relating to the African American experience. It is based on an article by T. Thomas Fortune that called attention to the labor problem in the South, which was exacerbated by the lack of white laborers and the refusal of white employers to employ Blacks on an integrated basis or at an equal salary with Whites. Fortune wrote, "The solution is not found in attitude of mill owners or white operatives but in a satisfactory understanding between those of black and white people who are compelled to work in order to live."

Certainly attach my name as a voucher on Bishop Walters' application or on that of any other good man. I shall try to come to Washington though I have breathed so much free air up this way I am afeared your atmosphere will affect my lungs.

With every sincere wish

Cordially yours,
Bruce

HOWARD'S AMERICAN MAGAZINE
DEVOTED TO THE COLORED RACE

Personal
Jas. H. Howard, Publisher
Thos. Wallace Swann, Editor
John E. Bruce, Associate Director

Albany, NY, Dec. 25, 1899

J. W. Cromwell Esq.

My dear Mr. Cromwell, I give you hearty thanks for your good letter of 22nd inst. which reached me yesterday and which I have read with much pleasure and profit. I had a very enjoyable trip to Boston and met some splendid people there of the other race which I do not regret. At Cambridge I had the pleasure of an introduction to Mrs. Ole Bull and Miss Helen Longfellow in their houses. In nearly all the houses of the blue bloods I visited I saw either an oil painting or crayon of Douglass. Dr. Bartol in Boston has a large oil painting of Douglass in his "parlor" and a crayon portrait of him at head of first landing of stairway. In his study there are portraits—steel engravings of other anti-slavery Negroes. I assure you that I was greatly pleased to see these things in the houses of the best people of Massachusetts. Over at the state house in the main office of the secretary of state I saw on the wall just as I entered the room a good picture of my old friend Lewis Hayden big as life. There are still some good hearts in the nation and I am glad of it.

I am pleased to know you received *The Transcript* and that the little squib about the Academy has brought some inquiries. I wish some time you would send me in their order copies of all the *Occasional Papers* read before Academy. I promised the Editor of *The Transcript* an article about it early in the New Year. He was greatly surprised to know of its existence and spoke encouragingly of it. If there is anything you want to say about the Academy please do not hesitate to do so. I can furnish you a list of names of wealthy Bostonians whom you may be able to interest in the work of the Academy if you desire it. Some of them may subscribe for the *Occasional Papers.*

Glad my other articles served the purposes of your student friend and hope he paralyzed the natives therewith.

I found in an old bookstore in Cornhill a book which the Academy ought to have for its library entitled *An Historical Account of the Black Empire Comprehending a View of the Principal Transactions in the Revolution of San Domingo with the Ancient and Modern State,* by Marcus Rawsford late Chaplain 3rd W. I. Reg. Published by James Cundee, Ivy Lane Paternoster Row, London 1805. Price $10.00. I would have brought it myself but I could not just then spare the money. The book is finely bound and printed and profusely illustrated with old fashioned wood cuts. The Bookseller informed me that there wasn't another of its kind in this country. I bought Lewis' book printed in 1840 by a committee of Colored gentlemen of Boston for $2.50 and George Livermore's historical paper read before the Mass Historical Society in 1862 entitled "An Historical Research Respecting the Opinions of the Founders of the Republic on Negroes as Slaves, as Citizens, Soldiers and Sailors." This book contains a *facsimile* of the advertisement offering a reward of L10 for Crispus Attucks and is now out of print. I paid $3.50 for it and wouldn't part with it for $20.00. That $10 book is a gem containing valuable historical and statistical data about St. Domingo and hence useful as a book of reference—it is for sale by *Littlefield,* the old bookseller Cornhill, Boston, Mass. Maybe you can triangulate a scheme to get it for the Academy. If you don't I will go for it myself. I'm buying every book I can afford to written by Negroes and get all that have been published recently from the publishers to review so that now I have a pretty fair collection. Lewis' book is called *Light* and *Truth*[35] and bears the stamp of scholarship. It treats of the Negro as a soldier, author statesman, poet etc. from the earliest period of the world's history down to 1840. Lewis was of Indian and Negro blood and a classical scholar, a fact attested by a committee of white men in Boston who examined the manuscript of his book before it was published.

I have just received Washington's "The Future of the Negro etc." and Chesnutt's last book on Douglass.[36] I have dumped Washington, and sent my remarks

35. Robert Benjamin Lewis, *Light and Truth: Collected from the Bible and Ancient and Modern History* (Boston: Benjamin F. Roberts, 1844). Roberts was a well-known figure in Boston and was the plaintiff in the famous separate school case in Boston (*Sara R. Roberts v. City of Boston,* December 4, 1849).

36. *The Future of the American Negro* (Boston: Small, Maynard, 1899). Charles Waddell Chesnutt (1858–1932) was born in Cleveland, Ohio. He was a teacher, a lawyer, and the author of three novels,

about his *rot* to the *American.* It is possible they will be published this week. The burden of Washington's song is that Negroes waste time studying the languages and the classics. I regard his book as the most dangerous yet published by a black man in that it caters to the white man's well-known prejudices on the subject of higher education for Negroes. Washington's cowardly sentiments will put money in Tuskegee's Treasury and in his pocket. But he cannot last the pace he is going. He is a shrewd sick diplomatic darky and his white friends greatly admire him.

I am going to try to get down to Washington this week though I have been away from home so long I have doubts about it still if it be at all possible I will come and shall hope to spend a few moments in social chat with you.

Very cordially yours
Bruce

December 1902–December 1911

Throughout his life, Bruce was impressed by the importance of the people he knows. Two people, in particular, stand out: his employer, Charles S. Clarkson, also referred to as the Surveyor or the General, whom Bruce called "his lifelong and truest white friend," and Charles Anderson, one of the most important black political figures of this period in the North. Bruce frequently invited Cromwell to join his circle and to be a part of his network.

Confidential   258 New Main Street
                                                Yonkers 12/1/02

My dear Mr. Cromwell,

I receive this am and read with a good deal of interest *The Record.* I read every editorial and Lincoln's meaningful article reproduced from *The Transcript.* There is more truth than poetry in some of the things he says and he says them in a way that I like. Washington is the habitat of more different kinds of foul niggers than any other city in the country. I recognized some of the "darks" alluded to notably Sol Morrison, and his brother who are the reputed sons of ex attorney gen'l Garland of Arkansas, Perrenial office holders and professional Negroes. There used to be a "yaller nigger" around Washington when I lived there who claimed to be a cousin of John Sherman. He was a clerk in the Treasury and very uppish. I have

---

two short story collections, and *The Life of Frederick Douglass,* a commissioned biography. He was also awarded a Spingarn Medal in 1928.

forgotten his name, tho' I remember quite distinctly that he was a fool. I have among my effects in Albany a list of all these white darkies. There is a colony of them in Albany. The Schuylers there cut quite a figure socially and old Adam Blakes family has been completely metamorphosed. Blake was a Virginian and a good fellow. The head of the Schuyler family is a Banker and they will not employ a Negro servant within the family under any circumstances. Never mattered for you.

Brother Booker's prounciamento, published simultaneously with Teddys "Solar Plexus" argument is the yawp of a cowardly leader afraid of his shadow, and white southern opinion. For six months past he has been the busiest black politician in America. When I read his letter I am reminded what Madame De Stael is reputed to have said about "Dawgs" and Lincoln's epigram about fooling some of the people, etc.

All letters sent to Roosevelt since General Clarkson has been surveyor and his confidential adviser in southern affairs are forwarded to him at New York and I don't mind telling you *sub rosa* that I have seen every letter written to the Prest. by Booker within the past two or three months. Letters are sent to him by the Prest. from men wanting appointments or their friends, for his opinion of their merit and value to the party. These he endorses and returns and they are in turn sent to the General and when I go to see him about once a week, he says "there Bruce look over these letters, know any of these people, etc. etc." There is one other man that he permits to read this stuff and that man is my friend Charley Anderson[37] alluded to in Roosevelt's letter as the appointee who gets three times the salary paid the Collector of the Port of Charleston. And by the way I want you to know Charley better. I have been telling him about you. He says he met you once or twice in Washington. He is a solid fellow and can do you lots of good. We three together can succeed in landing in a good place if things go well. Charley's friends are my friends and vice versa. Whenever he comes to Washington again I want you to hunt him up and get acquainted with him right. You'll find him one of the squarest, brightest and most sensible young Negroes you ever met and a scholar who *knows* what he knows.

If you will get *The Tribune* for today Dec. 1st you'll find a letter from a white man on Booker's outgivings that will make you say Amen: Kind o' loud like—I

---

37. Charles William Anderson (1866–1938) was born in Oxford, Ohio. After coming to New York in 1886, he became a successful politician and an active Republican. His rise to power was facilitated by his association with Booker T. Washington whose ally he remained until Washington's death. Bruce was a great admirer of Anderson and in many letters sought to have Grandfather meet him.

think *Moses* (B.T.W.) is thoroughly frightened at the notoriety he is getting as the "friend and adviser" of the President. I don't believe his explanation is going to be accepted by the southern press. I understand that it is going to hammer him for his pernicious activity in meddling with appointments for that section. He had no business mixing politics with industrial education and in trying to set himself right before the south. He forgets the French maxim "He who excuses accuses." Booker is an overworked statesman. He needs rest and he is fast approaching the jumping off place. John Durham was appointed solely on his recommendation. I know all about that appt., a good deal more than I am permitted to tell. Yet Quay [?] and Penrose I see by *The Age* of this week are credited with it. Washington visited Durham in Philadelphia two weeks before the appointment was made and discussed the matter with him, later he arranged an interview with the President for Durham and Durham called at the White House and had a chat with the President of an hour's duration. He wanted to be a judge in the Philippines. The President couldn't see his way clear to make such an appointment of a colored man and then he privately had misgivings as to the legal equipment of the applicant who while a good lawyer might not have the experience and training and other necessary qualifications which a judge should possess. Then the political effect of such an appointment was gone over carefully and the matter was compromised by the tender of an assistant attorneyship in the Spanish Claims which was duly considered and gladly accepted. Jack is a sugar expert and in Cuba there are great opportunities for a man who understands the business. He may strike something rich down there and resign. He writes me that he can't make any money on the small salary paid him by the government, etc., etc.

Yours truly
Bruce

Bruce seized the opportunity to know and to assist visiting Africans, thus broadening his knowledge of Africa.

Yonkers, NY
Nov. 11, 1903

My dear Mr. Cromwell,

My friend Dr. Agbebi contemplates leaving here for Washington on Monday next. I shall be obliged to you if you will be good enough to show him such courtesies as one of his station and abilities deserves.

. . . If you will find him a remarkable man, a walking encyclopedia and intensely a Negro, I could wish that you would take him into your own home if that be at all possible.

I have been telling him a good deal about you and your work as educator and journalist, and he has expressed himself as desiring to see much of you. . . . I am going to take the risk of sending him in your care and trust you will be on the lookout for him on Monday evening. His reputation is made. He is now looking on the land of the white man, taking notes and getting ready to say a few things when he gets back to Africa.

Yours very faithfully,

J. E. Bruce

Bruce was proud of his promotion and wished to share his pleasure with Cromwell, indicating also the prominence of the people who recommended him. His African contacts were typical of the kind he made without the opportunity of a face-to-face meeting.

Yonkers, N.Y., November 20, 1903

Dear Mr. Cromwell, I got a surprise from the General the day before yesterday in the shape of a promotion, to the regular service with the rank of Rounds-man, an office much sought after by white men, in the service because it affords so much leisure to the occupant, I am told that I am the only Negro holding such a place in this Department, I have the entire charge of two of the largest Sugar Refineries in this state, employing between 800 and 1000 men of all whom except one whom I had appointed, are white. The General's determination to break down the color line in the public service in these parts is his most distinguished characteristic. My appointment was urged and endorsed by Senator Platt, and Chairman Dunn and my good friend Charley Anderson.

I am enjoying the pleasure of reading the book written by Dr. Africanus Horton "Western Africa" published in 1869, London and the "History of the Gold Coast" by Rev. Carl Christian Reindorf, a native Pastor of the Basel Mission at Christianborg G.C. These works by scholarly Negroes in far off Africa are a revelation to me and an inspiration as well. The Dr has brought with him a great number of books written by Africans—scholars which show that Africa is not as dark as it looks. Those Negroes on the WEST COAST are doing what Negroes in America have not yet begun to do properly—they are writing histories of the African race and doing it mighty well. I am surprised at the great number of Blacks on the other side of the creek who have committed authorship of a high grade and are being quoted by white writers in Europe who write of Africa, as authorities. I think if you would write the Baptist Tract & Book Society for 'WEST AFRICA AND CHRISTIANITY" by Rev Mark C. Hayford, for review they would send you a copy. He is the "Writingest" black man I have ever read after and he makes the white folks look like thirteen copper cents. His book is a veritable literary treasure trove, by all means send for it, and when you get it don't loan it. Ask the Doctor about Hayford he is one of his boys and he ordained him for the ministry. Well what do you think of my Typewriting? My Man

Faithfully yours

J. E. Bruce

This was the period of the ascendancy of Booker T. Washington and the rise of challengers such as W. E. B. Du Bois, about whom Bruce rarely wrote without some negative reference to Washington.

Yonkers, N.Y., Jan 26th, 1904

My Dear Mr. Cromwell:—You are late catching on to Bookers curves, *The Age,* was fixed months ago soon after the famous conference. It was then that I decided to drop out of *The Age* although I had been told that I would not regret my connection with it. I was even asked what depended on the good will of The Sacred Ox (B.T.W). I knew different and took the pains to assure myself as to where and how I stood. And I found the exact spot. I saw very recently a letter from Fortune to Cooper which if it could be quoted would throw some light on the question of "Graft" alluded to by DuBois. Booker is a "very foxy member," but he is very like an Ostrich, he cant find sand enough to cover his whole body. He is buying all the papers that are willing to sell, either for cash or the promise of a job for the editor. All this dirt is going to come out some day and then Booker wont be Ace high except with white people whose tool he is. I have no sort of respect for a leader of his caliber. He is nearing the end of his rope, and he doubtless discovers that his was a big contract.

Yours truly J. E. Bruce

During this period, perhaps because of his growing contact with Africans and his reading, Bruce became increasing interested in the relation of Africans to African Americans and Whites to Africa.

July 27, 1904

My dear Mr. Cromwell,

I note what you say re the African papers and the white folks. *The News of Melbourne, Australia* has a sensational editorial on the Ethiopian Movement.[38] The *crux* of its objection is that Negroes or Blacks have no right to Africanize Africa. How laughable! The white man in some things is several kinds of a fool. . . . The white folks of Europe and America have no idea of the extent of this Ethiopian Movement *so* called—and there is certainly trouble brewing for the white men who are trying to steal *Africa*. That the man who talks to white men about the movement loses the power of speech soon thereafter.

Brother Dancy is a nice man but he has very funny ways and mighty little moral courage. *The Guardian* recently diagnosed his case and did it well. Dancy

38. The Ethiopian Church started in the 1870s in South Africa in reaction to the segregationist practices in the white churches (especially Wesleyan), the desire for personal advancement among a growing group of educated Africans, and a vague feeling of nationalism among the Africans whose traditional institutions were being undermined. The church became more visible among the Wesleyans and, with the establishment of a tribal church in 1884, reached its first peak in 1892 with the founding of the Ethiopian Church. Known as the South African Ethiopian Church, it soon sought affiliation with the African Methodist Episcopal Church in the United States, which

> was achieved in 1896 when James M. Dwane, an ex-Wesleyan, visited the States; and was consummated in 1893 when A.M.E Bishop H. M. Turner made a five weeks' triumphal tour through South Africa. . . .
> Negro Wesleyans and Baptists brought the prestige, finances and organizing experience of their parent bodies in America—though, as many of them were to learn, they were as much foreigners to Africa as were the white missionaries . . . It was this which made them not always as welcome to many Africans as both sides had hoped.

They were often accused "of setting back the indigenous Africans' own movements by the use of alien tactics and methods." By preaching, even before Garvey, "Africa for the Africans" or the anticipation of a "Manifest Destiny," these Afro-American preachers and missionaries fomented discontent and created expectations not welcome by the Whites. "Native discontent was being accentuated in South and Central Africa by the fact that some Africans were beginning to show dissatisfaction with the European native colleges," which the missionaries had started and which compared unfavorably with black colleges in America. There were uprisings and revolts. Yet, it is probably accurate to say that the "American Negro can influence accentuated tendencies already present in the African church separatist movements, with all their political consequences, in the first stage of Ethiopianism from 1892 to 1921 . . . The American Negro entered Africa missionary and uplifter. He added some of the confusion of his own political and social life to an already confused African political scene; this counterbalanced some of the advantages which his capital and organizing experience enabled him to bring to the Africans." (George Shepperson, "Ethiopianism and African Nationalism," *Phylon* 14 [1953]: 9–18).

has been a professional Negro officer holder for years and his spell binding this year aint going to help him to hang on to the boat.

Very truly yours

J. E. Bruce

Bruce never missed an opportunity to promote Cromwell as his friend but also in his capacity as secretary of the American Negro Academy.

Yonkers, N.Y.

August 27, 1904

My dear Mr. Cromwell,

I was quite agreeably surprised to hear from you and greatly enjoyed your all too brief recital of your trip into West Virginia, the home of the octogenarian candidate for Vice-President[39] and was quite amused to learn that you had been his guest in his magnificent private car. After all he isn't so much against social inequality as he would have prejudiced white folks believe.

Your stay on the Graceland was a case of "he who is robbed, not knowing he is robbed is not robbed at all." We colored folks enjoy bits of white folks comforts. And we know from experience that there is absolutely nothing in their objections to the Negro except the pure "*cussedness*" of which they seem to have a monopoly—if their prejudice has any foundation in reason or logic. If it was an innate social characteristic, the white man of Europe would hate and despise us as the white man in certain parts of American does.

. . . I have received a letter from Count de Cardi who is now in London which I have answered. I have asked him to post the name of Mr. John W. Cromwell Journalist and Secy of the American Negro Academy at Washington, D.C. for membership and ok'd it. Your name will therefore come before the Council of the Society at its next meeting. Sir H. H. Johnston KCB U G is chairman of the Council. You will be elected at that meeting and duly notified. M. Count de Cardi will forward the application blank to you for your signature, in a week or ten days and you will have complied with the rule of the Society. Your certificate

---

39. During this period, Cromwell was working for *Pioneer Press* in Martinsburg, West Virginia, which was edited by John R. Clifford, and was probably seeking some scoop on the forthcoming election in which Henry G. Davis of West Virginia was a vice-presidential candidate.

of membership will follow and your name published in the Society Journal. This Society has among its membership the leading Negroes of the world.

Yours truly,

J. E. Bruce.

Bruce was beginning to monitor the international scene, anticipating much that has come to pass.

Yonkers, N.Y. Sept. 8, 1904

Dear Mr. Cromwell:-

My only criticism of the "Jim Crow Negro" received today is that it is too all fired short. I know the . . . [illegible] well, met scores of him in Nashville in '97, and meet him almost daily in New York and Yonkers.

You do the race an incalculable service in this contribution to our literature. We both are able to see alike in these circumstances, and whither we are drifting, it is the "Jim Crow Nigger" in the north as in the south who is making Jordan a mighty rocky road for the self respecting Negro to travel. It is time he should be jumped on and stomped flat. He is very ubiquitous, ignorant, greasy and offensive.

Japan knows that most Malays are Mohammedans. This is the common tie which binds the race together and a stronger tie than a religious one cannot be conceived. Now if Japan starts the fireworks under the protest of a religious or "holy war" the fanaticism displayed by the Crusaders of Western Europe will be insignificant compared to that which will be shown by the Malay Mohammedans. Once this force is aroused Europe herself will not be safe from invasion and domination. My dear brother "It do seem" as that little rascal Bonaparte said that the world is to be either "Cossack or Moslem." His military insight enabled him to look ahead and see the handwriting on the wall. England must abandon India, the U.S. will be ordered out of the Philippines, Russia will be driven out of Siberia, the Dutch will be forced to leave Java and their other possessions acquired by benevolent assimilation—the word for "stealing"—at home. When all this comes to pass—and it is inevitable—Africa will take advantage of the opportunity to free herself from invading Europeans. In this she will be assisted by the Mongols who are willing to do anything against a white man. When Africa revolts Europe will be between two fires and I believe that then is the time that the white race is destined to throw itself into decline by . . . [illegible] itself madly against the invincible front which will be put up by the dark races. The Hausa's in Africa I am told are making more fine dark arms than the Europeans and know how to use them.

Just imagine if you can what kind of a fight these black and brown peoples will put up with when they think of the centuries of wrong they have suffered at the hands of a robber race. The war between Japan and Russia marks the beginning of the end of white domination and the birth of a new "Monroe doctrine" on the other side of the world.

Yours truly
J. E. Bruce

Missionaries were often the source of information for African Americans about Africa; many of the important black religious leaders of this time served in Africa. Bruce had his own opinion of their value.

Yonkers, N.Y. September 22, 1904

My dear Mr. Cromwell:-

I am quite in agreement with your view that while Africa is ready for the American Negro, the American Negro is not exactly ready for Africa. When our men cross the Ocean for Africa they take their chains with them in the shape of uncongenial and incompatible religious and social institutions which are as un-African as our "Afro-Americans" are un-American. And they cannot rid themselves of them but hug them with complacency thinking them ornaments. The trouble in South Africa today results largely from the efforts of American Negro Missionaries to plant the banner of African Methodism in that part of the Fatherland. Methodism is all right in America for the Blacks, but it is wrong in Africa for the Africans who know its history and origin. They know Wesleyanism and what it stands for, but Methodism as brought to them by American Blacks they regard as Wesleyanism doctored by white men and hence a religion of caste. In Africa all Wesleyans worship together, white and black, and these Blacks cannot understand the necessity for a distinctively Negro Church in a country which boasts of the equality of its citizens before God and before the Law. They reason and correctly that there must be something wrong in our social system and they are not inclined to look favorably upon this—to them—new religious cult. The Ethiopian Movement in South Africa, is directly traceable to the pernicious activity of their intentions. With their big talk and swaggering manners they have succeeded admirably in giving a black eye to the A.M.E. and all other branches of the Methodist Church in Africa and have set the English Government to spying and looking with suspicion upon all Clergy men who have the hallmark of the Methodist Church upon them. Then again the Negroes who have gone to win Africa to 'enlighten' the 'heathen' over there have not possessed overmuch of the Force that wins, they have made the mistake too of underestimating the mental and moral capacity of the African on his native heath and have suffered by comparison. There are some wonderfully bright men and women in Africa and God only knows how many.

With all good wishes believe me faithfully yours,

John E. Bruce

The elections of 1904 were imminent with Theodore Roosevelt as Republican presidential candidate and an assured nominee. His opponent was Judge Alton B. Parker (1852–1926). Henry G. Davis of West Virginia was Parker's nominee for vice president and at eighty-one years of age was the oldest major party candidate ever nominated for national office. Earlier, on August 27, 1904, Bruce noted that Cromwell had "a visit to West Virginia, home of the octogenarian candidate for Vice-President."

Bruce always had an interest in the arts, so he knew of Samuel Coleridge-Taylor, the distinguished composer. Coleridge-Taylor was born in England. He was the son of an African physician, Daniel Peter Hughes Taylor from Sierra Leone, and an English mother, Jessie Walmsley, the daughter of a British colonel. From the age of fifteen until his early death from tuberculosis at the age of thirty-seven on September 1, 1912, Coleridge-Taylor was recognized as a musical genius. Hearing the Fisk Jubilee Singers and meeting their leader, Frederick J. Loudin, led Coleridge-Taylor frequently to use African American themes in his works, first in his "African Suite" and then in "Bamboula." Paul Lawrence Dunbar also became an important influence. The two collaborated on a series of African romances, notably, "A Candle Lighting Time" and "Danse Negre." Coleridge-Taylor's works were performed at the Albert Hall, the Crystal Palace, and other famous London concert halls. From 1900 to 1906, he was closely associated with Sir Beerbohm Tree, perhaps the greatest of England's theatrical producers at His Majesty's Theatre in London. At the height of his fame, in spite of discouragement from Dunbar, he made two trips—in 1904 and in 1907—to the United States. His first concert was in Washington, D.C., on November 16, 1904, with a chorus of two hundred African American voices. Coleridge-Taylor was the first black man to give a concert in New York's Mendelssohn Hall and in the New

England Conservatory of Music in Boston. His success in the United States was phenomenal: he gave concerts in major cultural areas of the country—Baltimore, Chicago, Philadelphia, New York, and Boston—and also met with President Theodore Roosevelt. His father returned to Africa, to Gambia, to practice medicine, but neither Coleridge-Taylor nor his mother ever visited Africa.

Yonkers, N.Y. Oct. 14, 1904

My dear Mr. Cromwell:-

The Democratic machine in this country has absolutely refused to nominate candidates to run against Republicans, they are in a state of blue funk, and are as thoroughly demoralized as Lee's troops were at Appomattox. On the other hand the Republicans are all smiles and working like the devil taking no chances and covering every possible point in the game. As to West Virginia, my hope is that we will win out there, though it is exceedingly problematical. Davis has a large barrel and a gorgeous private car as you can testify, it would be an exceedingly sad blow to him to lose out on his own state, as Parker will. Parker's overcaution has done the trick for him. Davis has not been so reserved. He seems to have views on the tariff and the "everlasting nigger question." Bryan has certainly demonstrated his abilities as a Party disorganizer and history will accord to him the palm as the chief nemesis of modern democracy. I am at one with you in the sentiment that the defeat of Parker presages the breaking up of the Democratic Party as a national organization. The attempt of Bryan to reorganize it will make "confusion worse confounded" and many knives and blackjacks will be aimed at his carcass. I know personally Governor LaFollette of Wis. Like Bryan, he wanted to be a tragedian but his diminutive stature was against him, and he took to the study of the law. He is a vindictive little cuss, and might handy with his tongue in a jaw match. He is also an eloquent speaker and as you say rings true on the Negro question. He is as full of ambition as a dog is of fleas, and is a fighter from wayback. I should greatly like to hear and see Mr. S. Coleridge-Taylor when he comes to this country. I had some correspondence with him when his trilogy of "Hiawatha" was first produced in England, and I reproduced in the *Albany Sunday Argus* the press comments from the English papers and wrote a story about him which resulted in the Albany Philharmonic Society taking up "Hiawatha" and producing it some nine months afterwards in the Opera House. I furnished their committee with a photo of Mr. Taylor which he had sent me and which they used in the book which was sold as a souvenir of the occasion. The joke of the matter was that hundreds of people who went to hear "Hiawatha", did not know until the night it was given that its author was a man of color.

Even some of the Albany papers that raved over the trilogy did not know it until their representatives saw the Scorebook. I am sending you herewith an editorial from the *Boston Herald* re Taylor which you perhaps find some use for in the P.P. [Pioneer Press].

Sand Man and good by, Yours truly,
J E Bruce

Oct 29, 1904

My dear Mr. Cromwell,

I sincerely trust that the recital will be not only an artistic, but a financial success. I am glad way down in my heart that the leader and trainer of the chorus that is to sing "Hiawatha" under the direction of its composer, is without *the Caucasian reinforcement*. Mr. Layton is a great musical genius and his fame I hope will go out to the ends of the earth after the 17th. Let me suggest to you the advisability of extending an invitation to General Clarkson to hear "Hiawatha", he has a musical ear and his wife is also quite musical. Send him a circular. I think he would be pleased to see and to meet Mr. Taylor. When I see the General next week I will urge him to go to Washington to this great musical festival.

I congratulate you on your election to membership in the African Society.

Yours Fraternally
J. E. Bruce

Bruce in his complete letter analyzed the final election results and gave much more detail than is included here.

Yonkers, N.Y. Nov. 14, 1904

Dear Mr. Cromwell:

Yours of 12th instant just at hand, contents noted from its tone it is plain that the scandalous conduct of the Republicans throughout the country on the 8th instant, meets your approval. The victory is the biggest ever achieved by the Republican Party in all the years of its existence. The jig is up with the "rebeldevils." I think old *Tillman* will pine away and die now. He ought to have been dead fifty years ago. . . . I agree with you in thinking that there is *danger in reducing southern presentation in Congress.*[40] I am not in favor of it because

---

40. One of the many endeavors to disfranchise African Americans. Between 1890 and 1907, the southern states, with the exception of Kentucky, Maryland, and Tennessee, disfranchised the African Americans.

I see where the Negro will ultimately get the worst of it in the end. The Foxy white southerner will readily accommodate himself to changed conditions join the Republican Party get the offices and still be a Democrat at heart. Under this reduction scheme a small minority of southern Whites would walk away with the offices and the patronage attaching to them would be dispensed always to their advantage. No, *the old way is the best and safest.* Under Grant the Negroes right of franchise was fully protected, his citizenship rights were safe and secure. Roosevelt can do quite as much for us by insisting that existing laws be enforced rather than that new laws be enacted which will minimize our political influence where it should be most potent.

Yours very truly,
John E. Bruce

Bruce covers quite a bit of ground in this letter: an overview of what can be expected of this president, who will and who will not receive a patronage position, and what Cromwell himself should receive and how he should go about getting it. The reference to W. Hayes Ward (1835–1916) is most instructive. Clearly, Bruce thought this was just a matter of making the contact.

Several years earlier, Dr. Ward had asked Bruce and Bishop Walters to undertake a series of articles on Reconstruction. Both men demurred, but then Bruce recommended Cromwell as the most qualified to undertake the task. Dr. Ward felt that if he supplied Bruce with the appropriate books, Bruce could do the work. Bruce urged Cromwell to write Walters and Dr. Ward himself.

On July 31, 1901, Walters wrote Cromwell that he had spoken with Dr. Ward who said if Cromwell "prepared them and they have merit, he will publish and pay you for them." On December 13, 1904, Cromwell received a letter from Hamilton Holt, the managing editor of the *Independent:* "Your article sent to Dr. Ward has been handed to me. Indeed it is an excellent article, but I am sorry we cannot use it. We have had too much on the negro question of late."

There is more to the story than can be related here. Black intellectuals were beginning to assert themselves and to write their own versions of American history. Ward's interest in the subject is hard to understand. In his earlier life, he had been an Orientalist and poet and had not been associated with abolition or abolitionist causes. Having graduated from Amherst College in 1856, from Yale Divinity, and from Andover Theological School in 1859, he became editor of the *Independent.* He was described as a liberal in theology, irenic in temperament, and having a passion for righteousness in civic and national life. He was known for being sympathetic toward but not uncritical of Booker T. Washington. In the controversy over the control of the black press, Ward was protective of it.

Perhaps Cromwell delayed too long in preparing his article; the atmosphere of 1902 was different from that of 1904. Bruce did not seem to understand the situation.

Yonkers, N.Y., Dec. 19, 1904

Dear Mr. Cromwell:-

I have had an eclipse of faith as to the *man* in the White House. What you write me tallies with some other things brought out in a talk with the Surveyor, who is at this writing in Washington . . . He says Roosevelt is all right, and that the adulation which the South is now bestowing on him will be turned into cuss words, when it discovers his drift—He says the President has not forgotten all the pretty (?) things the South has been saying about him and he is a good bater. I am glad that he sees with clear vision the game which the South is trying to play and that he will have the courage to block it. Your informants appear to have the inside track, there's a wonderful sameness about their statements and the Surveyor's. I hope it's all true, but I am prepared for disappointments. I know Roosevelt is not stuck on Southerners. I have heard him express himself strongly on the breed, at Albany when he was governor. If he can overcome the flattery and gush of the Thos Nelson Page *et. al* well and good. I think however that he will be gourd to the occasion. When the us de . . . [illegible] hope for the best. The *Recordship* tussle will be very strenuous. Cummings of Maryland need hardly worry about his political future. I hear that he is handsomely provided for. Brer Powell is serving his last term and New York will get his place. Our old friend Barnett is also to be placed I understand. He did good work in the West. I know of no reason why you should not have a consulate. Malaya, Spain is not bad and I think you could get it with a little quiet work. John Quarles held it down under Grant, and no Negro has been there since.

It's too bad that the *400 of Washington Colored Society* cannot overcome the tendency to split up in factions. I have been reading about the forthcoming inaugural balls. I suppose the question of precedence will be raised and stoutly defended by each side. We sho is gittin mo' like white folks every day. This social nonsense doesn't worry me a bit. I have no patience with these 24 hour Mr. and Mrs. Hoft's. Their antics make me laugh some whatly.

I am glad you have connected with Dr. W. Hayes Ward. He is a mighty fine old man. His paper has plenty of money and it pays good prices for special articles, perhaps you can induce me to commission you to prepare that series of special articles on *Reconstruction* of which I wrote him some time ago, naming you as the one Negro best qualified to attempt and successfully complete such a work. Coming at this time I think these articles would be of particular interest to the American people. Think this over and let me know what your mind is on the subject.

Yours truly,
J. E. Bruce

In one of his more opinionated letters, Bruce discusses the Pan-African Conference held in London in 1900, Booker T. Washington, Du Bois, and his friend, Charles Anderson, who is gradually becoming closer to Washington and therefore is a man to watch. As a young man, Bruce wrote an unpublished treatise, *Washington's Colored Society,* and the frivolous behavior of the "Cullud citizens" of Washington never ceased to interest him.

Yonkers, N.Y. Dec 20/04.

My dear Mr. Cromwell:-

The Pan-African Conference in London to which you allude was a farce to begin with, its promoters were mere adventurers and notoriety seekers. I told Bishop Walters[41] when he was going over there that it would not amount to anything that I had information from a friend of mine in Scotland who had investigated the scheme and saw its finish before it began. It was conceived by a few African and West Indian residents in London, who were thoroughly irresponsible and who had no standing at home. My friend told me that these worked all the philanthropic Englishmen they could reach for funds to carry on this conference and that the greater part of this fund was applied to their personal use. Mr. [Henry Sylvester] Williams, its chief promoter who came to this country with Bishop Walters and whom I met at his house in Jersey City is now in South Africa, practicing law, and incubating a scheme to break into Parliament. He has no more chance of landing than a bob tail bull in fly time. Williams is a West Indian and has all the characteristics of the tribe which is mostly Ego. The Booker

---

41. Bishop Alexander Walters (1858–1917), not unlike many of his contemporaries, shifted his allegiances, leaning first toward Washington and then the Niagara Movement. Later, he joined Du Bois and Trotter in voting for Democrat Woodrow Wilson in the 1912 election. Walters was recognized widely in this country, in England, and in Africa. In July 1900, he attended the Pan-African Conference in London.

Washington panacea is leading the race up to this condition—"gentlemen in the palace, serfs in the field and an impassable gulf between the Negroes in Africa" seem to see with clearer vision than some of us the logical result of this cowardly conservatism and opportunism of the *Modern Moses*. If he is a statesman he hasn't given any proofs of it as yet, cunning and crafty conservatism and cowardice are not characteristics of sure enough statesmen. Booker has been playing both ends against the middle for a long time, and the knee-benders and sycophants have by their fulsome adulation of skill as a phrasemaker made him believe that he is IT. I cannot see him in any other light than that of an experimentalist who has said and done some good things and many foolish ones. *DuBois is my style of Man*, and he is a whole man too, and the coming man. The Banquet for Anderson was a fine affair, the "yallers" predominated and flocked very much together. Charley is a jolly good fellow, and his influence counts in this state, it was sickening to listen to the tommyrot of the sycophants who buzzed around him that night. I think indeed I know that he is on to their curves. Mr. Washington's man Scott[42] gave him a clean bill of health and called him the leader par excellence. Anderson has heretofore been wise enough to keep his own counsel and to do no boasting about the sources of his strength—political, so that whenever he starts out to accomplish anything he generally succeeds. Mr. Washington's friends have found this out and they are most cordial—but it was not always thus. The enlightened Cullud citizens of Washington appear to be contributing their quota to the gaiety of nations by their squabbles over the Inaugural balls, may the best man win.

Charley Crummel, God rest his soul—is dead, Sydney is also dead. I was not acquainted with his sister and cannot say whether she be living or dead.

I wish you and all your family the compliments of the season and God's choicest blessings for the year which like 'Jocund day stands tiptoe on the misty mountain top waiting for 1904, to vacate.

Very truly yours,

J. E. Bruce

---

42. Emmett Jay Scott (1873–1957) was an editor, Republican politician, author, and university administrator. He was born in Texas, and from 1887 to 1890, he attended Wiley College in Marshall, Texas, but did not graduate (for relations between Scott and John W. Cromwell Jr., see pp. 160–61). After leaving Wiley, Scott became a journalist. He worked for three years as a reporter for a white daily newspaper, the *Houston Post*, and then later founded his own weekly paper, the *Houston Freeman*. Scott was an admirer of Washington and wrote favorable editorials on him in his paper. He was especially favorable toward Washington's Atlanta Compromise address in 1895. Scott served as Booker T. Washington's private secretary from 1897 until Washington's death in 1915.

Yonkers, N.Y., Jan 19 1905

Dear Mr. Cromwell:-

I am still very much of a pessimist, and don't expect to see the "Square deal policy" of Roosevelt put into practical operation. I read your bright and breezy political letter in the *PP* and discovered that your right hand has not lost its cunning and that your think thing is in good working order. Hayes devotion to the race I fear will keep him outside, the great works politicians here regard him as a sort of second edition of Nat Turner. He hasn't been as discreet as he might have been. I remember A. W. Harris. He is a bright man but full of political tricks. It will be just like Roosevelt to return J. C. Dancy to his place as I hear he will be. The more fuss and shouting at him by the fellows who want his job the more difficult it will be to get it. Dancy did some pretty good work for Roosevelt up this way and has some assurances which he cannot mention, and will be foolish if he does. The remedy is not in the reduction of Representatives in Congress from the South, but in the honest enforcement of the three amendments. Has the President, has the Congress the courage to enforce them. We'll see. If they cannot enforce them how can they enforce the new legislation on this subject?

Faithfully yours
JE Bruce

As his letter substantiates, Bruce had no use for William H. Ellis, but the story was newsworthy and requires some background to appreciate.

According to the January 1, 1904, issue of the *New York Times,* Ellis, bearing many gifts, was the first American to visit King Menelik of Abyssinia at his court. Ellis gave a glowing account of the great wealth potential in Abyssinia. On this trip, Ellis had preceded Consul Skinner, the American consul general at Marseilles, who was on a government mission to meet the king. Ellis reported that he had paved the way for the success of Skinner's mission by reassuring the king of its positive purpose.

Ellis further explained that he had been interested in the "development of the Negro" and that he had had in fact a cotton farm in Mexico. When this farm venture failed, Ellis decided to reach King Manelik and to start programs there to help the Negro and to help himself. He began by studying the language and the culture. After he met the crown prince, Ellis was invited by the king to visit the country and to assist him in these development projects. Ellis described the meeting in great detail. He gave the king a picture of President Roosevelt at San

Juan Hill and another picture of black troops at the battle of Santiago. King Menelik gave Ellis a personal letter to be delivered to President Roosevelt.

Apparently, a commercial treaty between Abyssinia and the United States had been worked out by Consul Skinner and King Menelik. Ellis asserted that he had paved the way for the development of this treaty because he had preceded Skinner to the king's court and had convinced the king of such an alliance. The actual presentation of the treaty had been entrusted to F. K. Loomis, the brother of Assistant Secretary of State Francis B. Loomis. Mr. Loomis, on leaving the United States, was accompanied by Mr. Ellis, who was now apparently journeying to Abyssinia on private business. On June 20, F. Kent Loomis disappeared suddenly from the steamer *Kaiser Wilhelm II* as the ship was nearing Plymouth. When questioned, neither Ellis nor crew members said that they had noticed any difference in Loomis's appearance or behavior.

Loomis's body was found in the water on July 17; he had an abrasion under his right ear. Then Ellis was designated to continue his journey and to carry the treaty to the king. In August, Ellis met well-known author and traveler Hughes Leroux and boasted that he was the bearer of the signed commercial treaty between America and Abyssinia and that he himself was responsible for the success of the negotiations between the United States and the king, based largely on the earlier contacts he had made.

In November, Ellis was questioned by the State Department on the details of Loomis's death. His responses were satisfactory and "no blame was attached to him in connection with the tragic episode which occurred on his trip from New York to France on June last." To lay the matter to rest, Ellis, accompanied by Gen. Charles S. Clarkson,[43] gave his full account to President Roosevelt. Ellis explained to the president that the duty of carrying the treaty to King Melenik had originally been entrusted to F. Kent Loomis and that he was delegated the mission undertaken by Loomis after Loomis lost his life off the English coast.

Yonkers, N.Y., Nov. 20th 1905

My dear Mr. Cromwell,

Ellis is one of those fool yellow Negroes with an English wife, and supreme contempt for his black mammy's race. He is overdoing the Menelik act all right.

---

43. The *New York Times* (November 23, 1904) reported it was Gen. *James* S. Clarkson who accompanied Ellis, but in his account, Bruce said that it was the "Surveyor."

King Menelik has got the impression that Ellis represents the intelligent Negroes of this country and that he is loyal to his race. The fact is he represents the white capitalists and they are using him to work King Menelik. The man he has sent over here is a sort of special detective with instructions to use his eyes and ears and report what he sees and hears. You would be surprised to know that Ellis is an illiterate man, but has a natural genius for money making and driving bargains. He is a fine looking fellow, a good dresser, wears rings on both hands with a heavy gold chain with an immense diamond charm pendant, makes a big splurge among white men, and retains their friendship by giving handsome presents to them and their wives of jewelry and valuable cuno's. He has no fellowship with Blacks. Wilford Smith, Booker Washington's cross roads lawyer is his bossom friend both being Texans and brokers. I went after Ellis in the *Guardian* last week and I mean to do him up in Sections. I have written *Benito Sylvian* aide de camp to Menelik telling him how much of a black man this yaller man is and what contempt he holds for the black race. The Surveyor got him out of the Loomis scrape. Then he was very much of a Negro and a badly frightened one at that. The Surveyor convinced the Press that he had been greatly misrepresented, that he had no hand in the death of Loomis. Before this interview at Washington it looked bad for Ellis and there is still more suspicion that he knows more about that affair than he cares to have the public know.

The Sun[44] has been after Odell, for three years it has got him and I am not sorry. He is an arrogant, haughty, domineering, pestiferous cuss and doesn't like "niggers" particularly well, and he's a rafter from way back. The situation political is somewhat complicated and it is not safe to guess what all the funny things mean that are happening in politics just now.

Yours truly

JE Bruce

This is a frank discussion on how Bruce handles authority and the responsibilities of his position, and a brief comment on the colored schools in Washington.

44. The *New York Sun*, in several articles from November 15 to November 19, 1905, denounced former governor Benjamin B. Odell Jr. for his flawed leadership as the chairman of the Republican Party in New York. The situation had become so critical that President Roosevelt had designated Senator Thomas C. Platt as the responsible Republican leader in New York through whom any appointments would be made. Odell's behavior had apparently been so flagrant as to be called "Odellian."

Yonkers, N.Y. Nov 9/06

Dear Friend Cromwell,

I was very glad to get your last good favor, and I tried to answer it on the day of its receipt, but could not on account of pressure of business at the Refineries. My leisure moments are all in the past. Since my promotion here to be an assistant US weigher I have had the Devil's own time fighting prejudice to color. I am the first Negro ever appointed a weigher in this Port, and my presence on the docks excites a good deal of unfavorable comment from the poor trash who can do no other. A great many ships unload at night and the weighers are paid $6 per night for this work which last generally from 1 1/2 to 2 hours. These Whites in the service do not like the idea of a Negro receiving such good pay and kick not a little. The Surveyor is determined that I shall remain here and has told the head weigher that he will transfer all the white men here if he hears any more of this talk about "Nigger with a white man's job." Today I went to New York on call and had one of them who got too high transferred to an out of the way post where there are no "nigger weighers." He will receive his transfer notice from the Deputy Surveyor. I have six laborers under me. One of who is a colored man who with nine others I have appointed during the year. Three of the six are Jews and two are Irishmen, and they work well in the traces. The man assigned to take care of my scale house, is an Irishman and he keeps me posted with all that doin and sayin about the "Nigger." Five of my colored men are employed at the Federal Refinery where I am stationed and five are at the National at the other end of the same street. They receive a week's wages of $15 and have been steadily employed since their appointment barring a few days. I don't get a chance to do much writing now, and haven't touched the paper you asked me to write for the Academy in December, and I am very much afraid I shall not be able to do so though I shall not despair until the last moment of grace. I have felt since my appointment to this position that my whole race is on trial and I am devoting every moment of my time to study and to mastering the details of the office. I have cut out a good many social pleasures and my wife and I devote ourselves nights when I am home with tasks of disappointing white critics who would like to see me fail. I am not going to fail. I had the pleasure today of hearing the Deputy Surveyor make a verbal report on my work for the quarter ending Oct. 28, in which he said that it was entirely creditable to me and satisfactory to the Department, and the Surveyor told me that the reason he appointed me was that he knew I would make good and that he wanted him to see to it that I got a white man's chance and to report to him the name of any employee in the service who showed me discourtesies or who tried to embarrass me in any way. I shall have clear sailing now, and will keep both my eyes and ears open.

The Washington Schools (Colored) like some of the Southern American Republics are constantly hatching revolutions and breeding an office-holding aristocracy. By and by Congress will take a hand in your fights and some things will drop tho-

With all good wishes
Faithfully yours
BMG

Cromwell had probably kept Bruce informed about the difficulties he was having with the school department, especially with Roscoe Conkling Bruce. Indeed, Bruce may have been Cromwell's only confidant on these problems.

Yonkers NY, Nov 4/09

Dear Friend Cromwell:

We've just had an election on this end and some of the candidates are not sure whether a mule kicked em, or that they were tossed into outer darkness by dynamite. I sho do feel sorry for Bishop Walters who has been playing into the Tigers hands for several years. The Bishop is developing into a rather shiny politician and grafter. There are some ugly stories about his grafting methods which I don't want to believe but they are so circumstantial one can do no other. The Bishop ought to have more political sense than he gives evidence of possessing and it is pitiful to see him constantly making an ass of himself, playing hot house politics and expelling hot air. The white leaders in both parties here are discussing his political ethics and this is a bad sign for the good Bishop for they'll very likely compare notes only to find that he has been playing both sides against the middle and forgot to cover his tracks. Cobb—forget it—He is simply an echo of B.T.W. Young Bruce appears to be as smooth as his illustrious dad in turning details, they tell me he has a wonderful vocabulary and discount Uriah Heep in the Humility act. He cannot last long however. Somebody will sooner or later trip him up. It pays to be square. I am afraid the Negro school question is going to get into Congress—probably the coming session and that the whole system will be overhauled and revolutionized to the prejudice of colored principals and teachers. This continual crimination and recrimination among colored educators in the district isnt going to help, it is going to hurt somebody and hurt bad in the last analysis, watch it. Did you see the article in last Sunday's Sun on Negroes

who are successfully passing for White and using their black relatives—mothers
etc etc as servants. It is rich.

Yours sincerely

John E. Bruce

Having had several months to observe how President Roosevelt was going to
treat African Americans, Bruce was ready to make certain predictions, most of
which were incorrect. The prominence of William H. Lewis was hard for many
leaders to accept. Although born in Virginia, Lewis, educated at Amherst College
and Harvard Law School, was a product of New England. An early follower of
Trotter and Du Bois, Lewis changed more or less abruptly and became, some say
for the power it would give him, as an active member of the Booker T. Washington camp.

Bruce underestimated Du Bois.

Sunnyslope Farm

Yonkers N.Y.

Nov 16/10

Dear Friend Cromwell:

Lewis has no more chance of being made assistant Attorney General *in fact*
than a bob tail bull in fly time or than C.H.J. Taylor had of becoming the minister to Bogata or the late Bok Bruce as a member of the cabinet for which he
was once named. That job was put up right here in New York, about five weeks
before election. Charley Anderson, Emmet Scott and J. A. Cobb went to Beverly,
the two former by special invitation the latter as interloper and invited by Scott
and Anderson to lend a little dignity to the delegation. They found the president
in a state of mind over the defection in the ranks of the black brethren in New
York, and Mass. and in search of a remedy to check the stampede they told him
a few things which added to the few he knew or had heard, moved him to say
to them for publication that this administration is going to put all previous Republican administrations in the shade in respect of the appointment of Negroes
to office, that, it is going to appoint *some* not a few *but s-o-m-e* Negroes to places
never before held by members of the colored race. I got the story right off the
griddle and sent it out. A few days after its appearance the world was startled
by the announcement that a "Yaller Nigger" named Lewis is going to be made
Asst Attorney General of the B.S. Colored statesmen began to shake their heads
and wooden head Negroes actually shouted for joy, their chests expanded their

mouths began to leak and are still leaking about the great honor that has come of the race. Well it hasnt arrived yet. When it does please send me a spachograph, as you are near the seat of political activity. Mr. Taft will certainly reverse himself in the matter of Brownsville soldiers. If he insists on making it the South will get on its hind legs and howl like . . . [illegible] well and that will settle Mr. Taft so fur as "ouch people" are concerned. But in either event he will be damned if he does and damned if he aint. As usual the brother has made too much noise with his mouth about the contemplated designation of a member of the race. He is a cold blooded Yankee and a white man with a pitying contempt for the black man and an elaborate assortment of dictionary words which he knows how to place to make sound.

If we can make our plans for the Negro Monthly go (and it looks that way) I will certainly be pleased to have your friendly assistance towards making it the success we hope to make it. I dont think much of the *Crisis* nor of the combination with which Prof DuBois is tangled up. I notice, and have heard that the Prof is quite friendly with BT. Washington's chief lieutenant here, my friend C.W.H. and is often out to dinner with him and other Washington worshippers, this looks bad for DuBois future in NY. He may be strong enough to resist the blandishments of the enemy but I "have me doots." Booker generally gets what he goes after and if DuBois does not watch out he'll be a *goner* "shure Put." Now I've written myself to a frazzle and havent said much. Good night, it is nearly two A.M. I am going to "grease my innards" and sleep the sleep of the just. When are you coming this way?

Yours sincerely
John E Bruce

Kelly Miller was a compromiser and an enigma—always in the right circle but never unduly partisan. His position at Howard University, as faculty and administrator, gave him security and prominence, ensuring a continuing presence among the black intellectuals.

Yonkers, N.Y.
Dec 19/10

My dear Mr. Cromwell:

I saw Kelly Miller here a few weeks ago. You know friend Cromwell that among our so called broadminded intellectual men, there is a great deal of jealousy a great deal of hypocracy and deceit. I am not surprised at what you write re

Mr. Kelly Miller. I have heard it before. Washington and DuBois are badly con-
taminated. DuBois exclusiveness and pride of learning unfits him for leadership.
His proper place is an editorial chair. He doesnt attract the masses as Washington can, and does. He has more brains than Booker. But Booker has more
tact is shrewder more resourceful more diplomatic more active. He DuBois has
the best side of the argument but he is woefully lacking in ability to popularize
it. He is too stiff and too exclusive. If he doesnt watch out Booker is going to
clean up for him in New York City. The English in Africa especially South Africa
hate American Negroes and any who go there are constantly watched tho well
treated. The American Negro knows too much English in Africa and they fear
their Blacks will learn a few things from them. Will the American Negro ever
learn to see the white man in all his hideosity. He's a viper whether he live in
Europe or America.

Yours sincerely

John E Bruce

These last two letters from the middle period before the war and before Bruce
had become a follower of Marcus Garvey reveal the quality of the friendship between Bruce and Cromwell and their concern for the race and its leaders. Even
when discussing their concerns, they never lose their humor and mutual affection. Alain Locke has probably never been more perceptively understood than
he was by Bruce on that visit.

this should be read after meal   Yonkers, New York
and before bedtime   12/11/11
Dear Mr. Cromwell:

Well Locke came over and gave us a splendid talk. We kept him over all of
Saturday night and all day Sunday and part of Sunday night and I parted with
him with some reluctance. He is a worthy son of a worthy sire. I remember his
father. Everybody here who met the son is pleased with him. My! but "he have
a mighty intellect and talking ways." I liked him very much and I felt that I had
always known him. Mrs. Bruce was "carried away with him but she has returned."
She fed him on the best of our larder, brought out special jars of preserves and
jam, jam such that I am not even allowed a smell. I did not begrudge Mr. Locke a
bit for the best I had is none too good for any friend of yours, especially when he
is built on the Locke plan. I tried to give him a decent press notice in the papers
here. You know the tendency of the white newspaper, to minimize the best in us

and magnify the worst in us. I succeeded in getting a front page setting in the leading daily here (copy of which I am asking Mrs. Bruce to send you) and a fair resume of his paper which was a thoughtful and scholarly effort. As I sat and looked at the boy seated at my desk in my den I could not help thinking what a Jonah Booker Washington is to the race, and what a mistake his propaganda is. Alain LeRoy Locke was born to scholarship. He'd never make either a good gardener or a good shoemaker and there are thousands of our boys scattered over the country who like him only want freedom for the wings. Ultimately they'll get it. God grant that they'll get it soon. That boy Locke made me feel prouder than ever that I am a Negro. He is a sign of a promise of the coming of better and brighter and let us hope a happier day. God bless him. Our society is proud of the honour in which his coming has conferred upon it. And in a small way expressed his gratitude to him. It encourages young men to know that they are appreciated by the race. This we have tried to make him feel is the attitude of the "Negro Historical" and he can have anything we've got in the grub or cash whenever he comes this way again. Great boy that, and I don't blame his mammy for being proud of him. We have been talking about him ever since he left.

In re to Booker T. I am at one with you in the opinion expressed as to the ultimate effect which the unfortunate scrape into which he has gotten himself will have on his future.[45] There are ugly stories told here and in New York City by seamstresses and cabmen about Booker's fondness for . . . [illegible] and he has some holiday friends with flint lock brains and hair trigger mouths which are beginning to leak. He would display wisdom of the Solomonic brand if he arranged his affairs so as to gracefully to unconscious . . . [illegible] desuetude long about the early part of 1912 for his name now is Ichabod as in Gaelic "Dinmis." *The Guardian Current* publishes a significant review of an Atlanta paper of "My Larger Education" which discovers the trend of the white southern mind toward Booker.

I dont know Mr. Kelly Miller well enough to express an opinion as to his capacity for leadership. But from what I have seen of him and read of him he has not struck me forcibly as being a man of the stamp of which leaders are made. He has seemed to me to be an opportunist, a nonresistant, a compromiser. Self sacrifice does not appear to be in his code of ethics. I thought he made a mistake in tying to the Wizard of Tuskegee. Worshipping the rising son especially a resourceful son like the Wizard is dangerous business for men of resourceful

45. This is in reference to an incident in New York City in March 1911 in which Washington was beaten by a white man who accused him of looking through the keyhole of an apartment occupied by a white woman. The assailant was acquitted, and public attention was diverted by a horrible fire in March 25, which killed scores of men, women, and children.

caliber like Mr. Miller. They can only be satellites when if they had more confidence in themselves and faith in the people they could be fixed stars. Mr. Miller as you well say lost his opportunity—he will be remembered as a great mathematician and as author of "A, to the Leopard Spots" as a brilliant literary effort but a tactless defense of the race which had brought no change to white public sentiment or in the public attitude of our friend the enemy towards us. We have not yet produced a Negro leader who has put into practice the injunction "be as wise as a serpent and as harmless as a dove" showing the white man how smart we are, to put him on his guard and take another tact to defeat the aims we would attain. The white man doesnt care a rah about Negro opinion on any question and he doesnt quote it except in political times to influence Negro votes. He knows there are many superior Negroes and he realizes that they are thorns in his side. He is a diplomat and a liar when he professes to be in full sympathy to Negro aspirations. It is not natural or reasonable to believe that he is no one that is in the ascendant and no individual that resides in a brown stone flat on Easy St. with $10,000 is going out of his way to help another race secure relative position with it or another individual of an alien race to possess the house next to him and a job similar to the one he has. All this Tommyrot expelled by our white friends about equality ad-nauseum looks nice in print. But as Bert Williams says, "all talk."

Sincerely yours,
Bruce

12/29/11

Dear Mr. Cromwell:

Your brief note at hand contents absorbed. What was the character of the juice that palsied yo brain and stopped the flow of thought? The drain on my wallet this Xmas has been heavy and I cannot see the Academy for some weeks yet. I am sending you the African yam I promised you. I got some nice presents this year from West Africa and Panama. Got two Panama hats made especially for Mrs. Bruce and myself and some preserved fruit from home yonder, and a few vegetables. This yam is to be peeled and cooked like potato is cooked.

Happy New Year to you and yours

Sincerely yours
Bruce

P. S. Are you guilty of sending me 1/2 gal of Old Gray Whiskey? There is ½ gal here evidently purchased at Xavier's. Try and find out who did it if you can.

January 1920–August 1923

Jan 7/20

Sub rosa

Dear Friend Cromwell,

Your letter found me at home, recovering from a street car accident, last night. I was thrown to the street from a moving car, in Brooklyn, on my way home from office, and was fortunately saved from instant death by my agility in getting out of the way of a passing heavily ladened motor truck.

My only injury was a cut in the left hand—and the shaking up of my inards. Roland Johnson, son of the Bishop, is the attending physician.

The Company sent its agent to see me this a.m. and as the fault was partly mine, I shall not be able to get full damages, but I will get something for getting mussed up, and for doctor's fees. I am feeling all right after a good rest last night and a hearty breakfast this morning thank you.

I read your letter with much interest and am glad you and madame are pleased with the result of the work of the Academy. It was *your due* and we were *determined* to put over the plan we had worked out in New York or *bust*. We didn't bust, but we did bust up a family ring—which has dominated the Academy for years, and believes its usefulness is now at an end because nepotism is dead.[46] The Rev Frank Jr. told Ferris[47] that he could not understand your tactics that you and he had always been friends the best of friends and he thought that if you had a grievance you should have come to him or his brother and settle it man fashion. Ferris says he seemed much hurt by the suddenness of the shock that killed brother and was somewhat incoherent and incensed, The Academy will go on just the same as though the Grimkés had been dead a thousand years.

---

46. This reference is to Francis Grimké's and Archibald Grimké's reaction to Cromwell's being elected president of the American Negro Academy.

47. William Henry Ferris (1847–1941), author and lecturer, was born in Connecticut. He graduated from Yale in 1899 and earned his master's degree from Harvard Divinity School in 1900. He initially supported Trotter and other "radicals" but soon sought the help of Booker T. Washington. He then shifted his support to Du Bois and the Niagara Movement and ended his life as literary editor of the *Negro World,* Garvey's newspaper. His career reflected the instability and perhaps the characteristics of some of the "Talented Tenth," who found it difficult to follow a consistent and rewarding career. Opportunities soon became obstacles. He was younger than some of his associates and better educated than most. His lasting contribution was his two-volume work *The African Abroad or His Evolution in Western Civilization, Tracing His Development under the Caucasian Milieu,* which was published in 1913. He was a friend of Cromwell from the earliest days of the American Negro Academy.

We together if life lasts will present a program and a series of papers worth *while*. You may rely *wholeheartedly on our support*. We must get a *big* man as a drawing card for the next meeting with minor *satellite* to match. The job won't be a hard one. What did you really think of Randolph's paper?[48] Honest injun. Personally I thought it fine as a rhetorical effort. It was well delivered and ably defended after the attacks upon it were finished. But it wasn't *convincing* Socialism is not the Panacea for the Negroes wrongs because Socialists are not agreed among themselves as to what is the proper solution of the problem. A certain group are attempting to solve with their mouths and on paper. Here in New York they are "fighting like devils for (conciliation) and hating each other for the love of God." Hubert Harrison[49] who used to be as radical as Randolph quit the Socialist party

48. A. Philip Randolph (1889–1979) and Chandler Owen (1889–1967) can be meaningfully understood together because their early adult lives were so intermingled. Both were born in the South: Randolph in Crescent City, just outside of Jacksonville, Florida, and Owen, in Warrenton, North Carolina. Randolph attended the Cookman Institute in Jacksonville, a Methodist missionary school, from which he graduated in 1907, and then moved to New York. Owen graduated from Virginia Union University in 1913 and moved to New York to do graduate work at the New York School of Philanthropy and Columbia University.

Together Randolph and Owen founded an employment agency in Harlem called the Brotherhood of Labor and made their first effort to unionize black workers. In 1917, they cofounded the *Messenger,* a Marxist-oriented monthly. Owen ran unsuccessfully for New York assemblyman in 1920. Owen and Randolph were jailed briefly for allegedly violating the Espionage Act, and the Post Office Department and other government agencies considered them so subversive that their second-class mailing permit was lifted. Their offices were ransacked more than once during the Red Scare hysteria. Owen played a major role in the *Messenger*'s crusade in the 1920s to get Marcus Garvey deported, but by 1923 he had grown disillusioned with Socialist radicalism and had moved to Chicago. He remained a journalist and active in Republican politics.

Randolph was chosen by the black Pullman porters—because he was not an employee of the company, and therefore not susceptible to firing or to harassment—to assist in their fight against the powerful Pullman Company. He successfully negotiated the first contract in 1937, thereby moving Blacks into the labor movement. The *Messenger* was renamed the *Black Worker.* Randolph will also be remembered for two other actions. First, he called off the threat to march on Washington in 1941 after Roosevelt promised and did pass Executive Order 8802 to end racial and religious discrimination in the war industries, government training programs, and government industries. Second, he organized with Bayard Rustin the 1963 March on Washington before the Lincoln Memorial. He remained a Republican committed to integration, pacifism, and nonviolence (Rayford W. Logan and Michael R. Winston, eds., *Dictionary of American Negro Biography* [New York: W. W. Norton, 1982], 476).

49. Hubert Henry Harrison (1883–1927), labor leader, editor, teacher, and author, was born in the Virgin Islands. At seventeen, he moved to New York, where he became a Socialist and a contributor to several racial magazines. In 1917, he left the Socialist Party and founded the Liberty League of Afro-Americans, establishing the *Voice* as its organ. He joined A. Philip Randolph and Chandler Owen in denouncing W. E. B. Du Bois and was chief editor of Garvey's paper, the *Negro World.* He was professor of comparative religion at the Modern School, which was later moved to Stelton, New Jersey. Harrison was one of the more prominent radical leaders of the first quarter

because of *color discrimination* as he told me and he never fails to score it on occasion. Randolph and Owen are on the pay roll of the Rand School as teachers at $85.00 per month and all the extras and it is fair to assume that they are socialist for revenue just as some members of the Right Wing in the old parties are or were. We are all very human and very altruistic when the bung hole is wide open and the pickings are good. Randolph's dream is just a dream, and he may revise it before the Dept. of Justice completes its work of rounding up the Radicals. My compliments to good Mrs. Cromwell and to you. I hope you'll decide to join the "Societié Des Beau Artistes." It will be a killer for some of your critics who are so popular and well known, don't you know. I can work you in to the green taste because the Secretary for whom I rendered a service sometime ago is my *friend* and will put over anything in reason I ask of him as he has assured me confidentially. It takes some pull to pass muster in this body.

> Sincerely yours,
> John E. Bruce

> Treasury Department
> United States Customs Service
> Port of New York

Office of the Surveyor

> March 16/21

Dear Friend Cromwell,

   I am to thank you for your kind interest in my friend Plaatje,[50] and I hope we can get him into Washington, to tell his story. He is a forceful and effective speaker and can make a hit with any audience. He is very much in demand here as his story interests all classes who hear it and evokes indignation at the treatment of the natives which he so faithfully and accurately describes and sympathy for

---

of the twentieth century. He supported Garvey conditionally—emphasizing cultural interest in Africa and a limited return of skilled scientists and technologists who could contribute to African development—and eventually urged his deportation (Ibid., 292–93).

50. Solomon Tshekisho Plaatje (1876–1932) was born in the Orange Free State of Tswana-speaking Barolong people. He was a well-known political leader and spokesman and a prolific writer and pioneer in the little-known history of the African press. He was one of the founders of the South African National Congress (later the National African Congress), and in 1912 he became the organization's first general secretary. He twice traveled overseas to represent the interests of his people. Plaatje was the author of *Native Life in South Africa before and since the European War* and *The Boer Rebellion*. He emulated W. E. B. Du Bois, Robert Morton, and J. W. Cromwell and was a guest in Cromwell's home.

them which always takes a substantial form at the close of his talks. He says we Negroes in America are living in Paradise compared with the lot of the natives of South Africa and that our Jim Crow cars as they have been described to him are palace cars compared with those the natives have to ride in, in South Africa. He is simply amazed at condition of the blacks here and says if his people had our opportunities they'd own all South Africa, in the next 50 years. I have given him Dr. Tanner's[51] address which you sent and he will write him. I am trying to interest the General Education Board here in his cause as, young Rockefeller professes to have deep sympathy for Africans. He is to have an interview in a few days with a representative of Mr. Rockefeller—who is now out of town when he has made arrangements with Dr. Tanner to speak to his Congregation, at Washington, why cannot you write a good story about him for one of the Washington Papers daily or weekly. So that the public can get a line on what he is here for and who he is, etc. You know what to say and do and how to do it. He wants to meet Pres. Harding when he comes to Washington to pay his respects and between you and Dr. Tanner I hope this can be arranged. *It* will have its effect in South Africa. He remembers Dr. Tanner of whom he speaks in high terms and he is eager to get down to Washington to tell our people and the public generally what fine people the Dutch Boers are and how much they love (?) the Square deal for the blacks whose lands they have confiscated and whose natural and civil rights they have denied them, because they now have the power. Read in the current *Negro World* Dr. Gordon's article, on the "Great Steal" in Africa. Did you receive Macauleys open letter to the British Government which I sent you recently. If you have and have read it, I would like to have your opinion of the document. I don't hear anything alarming particularly except that W. H. Lewis is slated(?) for a circuit judgeship and Emmett Scott for Minister to Bolivia a job once sought by C. H. J. Taylor. I haven't heard who is named for the U. S. Consul to Calais France. Then

---

51. Benjamin Tucker Tanner (1835–1923) was an editor and a bishop in the African Methodist Episcopal Church. Following his ordination in 1860, he served as minister of a Presbyterian church in Washington, D.C. In 1862, having retained his affiliation with the A.M.E. Church, he became head of the Alexander Mission in Washington. Tanner was also pastor of churches in Georgetown and Baltimore. From 1868 to 1884, he was editor of the *Christian Recorder*. In 1888, he started the *A.M.E. Church Review,* a quarterly that quickly became a leading black magazine of high literary quality. Tanner advocated racial solidarity and encouraged Blacks to support businesses owned by other Blacks and the black press. Tanner never adopted the form of Black Nationalism advocated by Bishop Henry McNeal Turner but was more a follower of Bishop Daniel A. Payne. One of his seven children, Carlton, became an A.M.E. minister and missionary to South Africa. Another son, Henry Ossawa Tanner, was a distinguished painter.

too there are rumors that the Poro Hair Straightener man of St. Louis is to be Collector of Internal Revenue at this post. I seem to see him confirmed, and installed in office. I said "*seem*" I haven't heard from Scott in nearly two years, and the other day I got from him a fulsome letter praising me in extravagant terms for a letter of mine which appeared in *The Herald* some months ago, about which I had forgotten. I wonder what Scott wants of me? We are going to give Plaatje and the Poet McKay recently arrived from England and now on the Editorial Staff of the *Liberater* a Socialist paper here a stag before Plaatje leaves New York. There must be quite a herd of receptive and faithful candidates around Washington right about now and Congress adjourned to April. It's Awful Mabel!!

Yours sincerely

Bruce Grit

Aaron Eugene Malone, former teacher and traveling Bible salesman, in 1914 became the second husband of Annie Minerva Turbo Malone (1869–1957), the very successful entrepreneur and philanthropist. Annie Malone acquired her fortune manufacturing and selling her "Wonderful Hair Grower." In 1906, she copyrighted the trade name of "Poro" for her business, which was based on a system of franchised agent operators. In 1902, she moved her business from Brooklyn, Illinois, to St. Louis where it was reputed that Sarah Breedlove, later known as the famous Madame C. J. Walker, was one of her agents. She was extremely successful, employing 175 persons in St. Louis and more than seventy-five thousand through franchise schools and supply stations in North and South America, Africa, and the Philippines. She gave liberally to charities, the local YWCA, and Howard University Medical School.

In 1927, Aaron Malone filed for a divorce, demanding half her business, and forced her school, Poro College, into a court-ordered receivership. Malone had become prominent in local and state Republican politics, so the black community in St. Louis was divided over the controversy. But the black press, Poro workers, and leaders, such as Mary McLeod Bethune, rallied to Annie Malone's side. On May 29, 1927, an out-of-court settlement was reached that affirmed her the sole owner of Poro College, and the divorce was granted. In 1930, she moved her business to Chicago's South Parkway where she purchased an entire block. Mr. Malone was apparently still trying to prosper in St. Louis.

107 W 130 St., N.Y.C.
March 17/21

J. W. Cromwell Esq.
Dear Frater,

Your last good letter with the Scoop *re* Flipper, is at hand, and the item will be used with the proper headlines in the *Negro World's* current issue, I know Mr. Flipper by much correspondence which I carried on with him during his fight, from Boston years ago. I helped to get up a mass meeting for him in old Father Grimes[52] Baptist Church on Phillips Street. I am glad to learn of his appointment—though long delayed. He is an able and worthy man, and the race is honored by his appointment. It comes at the psychological moment, when he is no longer a young man and needs the means and leisure which such an office gives. Have you heard that Matthew of Mass is to be an Asst. Atty General, and Welt Lewis is booked for a circuit judgeship? Hope you are well. Kind remembrances to Madam.

Hastily yours
Bruce Grit

Henry Ossian Flipper (1856–1940), the first African American graduate of West Point, was an author and an engineer. He was born a slave in Thomasville, Georgia. He attended American Missionary Association schools, including Atlanta University. In 1873, he was appointed to the United States Military Acad-

52. Rev. Leonard Grimes (1815–1948) was pastor of the Twelfth Baptist Church in Boston. He was born in Leesburg, Virginia, to free parents. He worked at many occupations in various parts of the South and in Washington, D.C. He was sentenced to two years in prison for helping a free man and his wife and seven children escape to Canada. After leaving prison, Grimes returned to Washington and married. In late 1840, Grimes, his wife, and their two children moved to New Bedford. After the death of Rev. George Black, Grimes was called to Boston to be the minister of the Twelfth Baptist Church, which he built from a congregation of only twenty-three to 250 and constructed a new building. Grimes became one of Boston's best-known abolitionists and his church became a center for social protest and an important station on the Underground Railroad, becoming so active in assisting fugitives that it was called "the fugitive slave church." Grimes played an important part in the unsuccessful attempt to rescue Thomas Sims, a fugitive held in jail in Boston. Grimes, Coffin Pitts, and other members of Twelfth Baptist collected funds to buy Anthony Burns from his master, Charles F. Sutter of Virginia. Grimes attended the Rochester National Negro Convention in the summer of 1853 where, without attacking integration as a common goal, the program leaned heavily toward separate, independent actions on the part of African Americans. Grimes, however, joined other Boston leaders such as Charles Remond, John Rock, and William Nell who were in violent opposition to colonization as a solution to the plight of African Americans.

emy, from which he graduated fiftieth out of a class of seventy-six in 1877. He was assigned to the all-Negro Tenth Cavalry Regiment. On November 4, 1881, at a general court-martial, he was accused by his commanding officer, Colonel William R. Shafter, of "embezzling funds and conduct unbecoming an officer and gentleman" because of his alleged failure to turn in nearly four thousand dollars in commissary funds. He was found not guilty of the first charge but guilty of a second, and he was discharged from the army on June 30, 1882. Flipper remained in the West and for the next fifty years engaged in engineering, mining, and surveying work. Between 1892 and 1903, he was a special agent of the Department of Justice in the Court of Private Land Claims. In 1892, he published a book on Spanish laws, thus helping to bring about the return of large tracts of land to their rightful owners. Flipper tried to enter the service in the Spanish-American War, but he was unable to do so. In 1919, he came to Washington as subcommittee translator and interpreter. His sponsor, Albert B. Fall, was found guilty in the Teapot Dome scandal, but Flipper was not implicated, so he left government and went to work for an oil company in Venezuela from 1923 to 1930. He then moved to Atlanta and lived with a brother. Until his death of a heart attack, Flipper insisted that he was wrongly dismissed from the army because of the prejudice of Whites who were particularly angered over his taking horseback rides with one of the few white women in the area of Fort Dix. As late as the 1920s, Flipper continued making official attempts to have his name cleared.

107 W 130 St., N.Y.C.
April 11/21

Dear Friend Cromwell,

Plaatje is in Boston filling an engagement in Tremont Temple, left here Saturday mid-night and will probably be away two weeks. He has asked me to inform you that he has written Dr. Tanner, and that he has gotten no replies to his letters. Will you find out the cause and let me know what's what? Will the "protests" of white women weaken Harding and bring about a compromise. Dare he yield to the insolent demand made upon him? What is your public opinion privately expressed of H. Lincoln Johnson? Is he a white man's "nigger." Is it true that Mary Church Terrell is after the Recordship at the ANP? Say she is and I have given her a boost in the *Negro World*. Things look bad in Europe particularly in England and Lloyd George seems to have his back against the wall. But he is a resourceful old diplomatic liar and may be able to patch up a truce with the miners. England's day is about over however and if she emerges from this trouble she will not be what she once was. I'm praying that the working people will keep up the fight for their rights. India and West Africa are seething volcanoes which may break out at any time. If these peoples had arms of *precision* England would be wiped off the map. And they may do it without them. The world is in travail, and the unexpected may happen at any moment. I met a black Mohamedan a week ago yesterday who told me that when he left Africa the people there were greatly exercized over the hypocrisy of the English and that there was strong talk of an uprising—a holy war—that was two months ago. The men who went to fight for the Allies realize that the English have bumboed them and there is dis-content all over West Africa. Let us hope that something good will result from this discontent. With Ireland, India, Africa and the coal miners in revolt, and Garvey in Jamaica raising the devil among the blacks there England has a few problems on her hands that need immediate attention. I saw the leading Jamaica paper last night, *The Gleaner,* it contained a full page portrait of Garvey, and five columns of a report of his meeting and his speeches. He has set Kingston on fire—The ship for direct trade with Africa will sail from this port May first or thereabouts. It is now on its way here from the Indian Ocean—It is a French vessel and will be rechristened the "Phillis Wheatley."

Yours Sincerely,
Bruce Grit.

Regards to Mrs. Cromwell. God bless her. I cant forget the dinner I et at her table.

260 W. 136 St.
New York City
July 15/21

Personal

Dear Friend Cromwell,

Yours of recent date to hand and I note with pleasure that you will attempt and succeed in writing the introduction.[53] I am deeply grateful to you for your kind interest and willingness to help and will later give you a more *substantial* proof of my gratitude and appreciation. I am forwarding today the printed copy of the *Blyden* paper, and Hookes Mss, pre registered mail. You are to use your

---

53. John Edward Bruce, *The Awakening of Hezekiah Jones: A Story Dealing with Some of the Problems Affecting the Political Rewards Due the Negro* (Hopkinsville, Ky.: Phil H. Brown, 1916).

own discretion as to the length of the introduction. Whether it is short or long I know it will be *good* and *quotable*.

Glad you received and enjoyed the Marcus Garvey Cigar. I've gotten away with two boxes of them in the past two weeks. Garvey has at last reached the United States and is to be in New York Saturday or Monday at the latest. Big preparations are being made to receive him in Liberty Hall. Have you met Pres. King? If so, what is your impression of him? My own opinion of him is that he lacks strength of character and the power of initiative. When he was last here I saw a great deal of him, and I was not favorably impressed with his ability as a Statesman. He leaned too heavily on the white US Fiscal agent who accompanied the delegation and he did not seem to have an original idea or if he had, the courage to advance it. I know of few men of small stature who were really strong characters Samuel J. Tilden, Stephen A. Douglas, Isaiah Wears and Martin R. Delany are notable exceptions. King reminded me of a bell hop who has suddenly been elevated to a position several degrees above him mentally. The first time I heard him speak here I decided that he was a *misfit*. His predecessor in office and who is now acting President of Liberia—Barclay—is as superior to him in mentality and Executive ability, dignity of character and self-confidence as Hypenin to a Saty or the Washington Monument to a fire plug. I fancy that if Barclay were at the head of the Commission we would now have more definite information as to the status of the proposed Liberian loan of $5,000,000. I hear however that there are forces at work in England and Liberia to prevent the granting of the loan. If it should however be granted Liberia will have to install in the Presidential Chair a stronger man than King to keep the United States from stealing the country. King is a real joke . . . i.e. between us. But he takes himself as seriously as though he is what he seemed on his first visit here a year or so ago. The United States cooped him up in the Hotel Astor where he and his wife and Secretary had to eat their meals in their bedrooms. His Keeper the U. S. Fiscal Agent stood guard at the door of his apartment and vised the cards of his visitors and *sat in* at all Conferences. The head of a *Prest Negro state* should not have permitted a white man to dominate and control in these matters. But King seemed to *court it*.

> Yours Sincerely,
> John E. Bruce

260 West 136 Street
New York City, NY
March 13, 1922

Dear Friend Cromwell,

Let me thank you for your last good favour received some days ago, answer to which has been delayed because of duties here which couldn't be "ducked." Yes, we think that we have the situation pretty well in hand, as you intimate, and that there is no *immediate danger*. We are keeping tabs on the grafters who, like buzzards at sight of a dead horse are buzzing around and throwing out hints and making mountains out of ant hills hoping thus to get big fees for doing what can very well be done without their powerful (?) legal aid.

Mr. Garvey has just arrived from the middle West where he had a most successful trip scoring heavily for the U.N.I.A.

Our Sunday night meeting here was a revelation to the natives. Over 6000 Negroes packed Liberty Hall, and cheered him to the echo, when he came to the Platform, the audience rising as one man yelled like mad men, "Garvey, we are with you and we are going to stand by you no matter what happens." and "You're right and we know it, no matter how wrong White man says you are."

The Postal Authorities do not seem to be getting much information from our stockholders, as hundreds of them are sending us the questionnaire sent them by P.O.D. and growling about White men meddling with the affairs of a Negro Corporation. We have been very careful in our replies to these stockholders, telling them that they must use their own judgment as to their replies to the four questions, viz:

(1) How much stock do you own?
(2) From whom did you purchase it?
(3) When did you purchase it?
(4) Are you satisfied?

We intimate to them that if they are *satisfied* with their investment and the management of the Corporation, "Yes" written in Capitals on the Fourth line of the paper ought to satisfy the Postal Authorities that there is nothing to investigate.

I got a tip that the administration at Washington is going to spring some surprises on the black brethren in the way of appointments in the near distance and that the type of appointees will be different; that it is disgusted with the antics of the Henry Lincoln Johnson type who have been talking too loud and too much.

Have you heard a similar report? The appointment of Freeman said to be the beginning of the new deal. Well, we shall see what we shall see. Arrangements are being made to give Charles W. Anderson a big job here, commensurate with his ability and party services. He is one of the few who have kept their own counsel and sawed wood, and he will and "bime by."

Nothing new. Very busy helping to arrange for next *Convention* which will be a hummer.

Duse Mohamed is on the job, and is interesting his West African friends in the movement also Dr. Suliman of Cairo Egypt, blacker than Delany, who speaks Arabic and English with equal facility. We up this way—don't feel no ways discouraged nor cast down. The fight is on and we are going to win.

Yours Sincerely,
John E. Bruce

P.S. My regards to Madame and to you.

B. G. [Bruce Grit]

JEB/BG

5/21/22

Please note new address

258 W 139 St.

NYC

Dear Friend Cromwell:

I received your recent letter a few days ago, and have put off acknowledging it from day to day from sheer laziness. I suppose you know the feeling and how it takes hold of a colored Afro-American Negro when the sun heats the atmosphere in May. After I eat my dinner (i.e.) about 2 hours-after I have performed that important duty, I pound a feather pillow until about 11:30 or 12 then I get up and read, or write until about 2 or 3 and then go to bed regular and sleep until six or seven a.m. I am much better situated now that I have been since I left the farm at Yonkers for going into session with Morpheus and I fear that I am going to get Ferris' habit of taking a hot bath and a beauty nap in broad day and then my correspondents—some of the less important ones will be on the waiting list. I join with you in the sentiments you so beautifully express concerning young Locke and his dear Mother who has passed beyond in the door of Sanctity—to the gloryland. She was a rare good Mother—a noble example of the seldom sort of whom alas our race has too few. A million mothers like her with a million sons of the mental girth of Alain Leroy Locke would be one of the greatest blessings that could be bestowed on our race in this crisis she and her brilliant son are types of what the future holds in store for the Negro who is not yet ready for the opportunities—advantages that await him. I have faith and believe that we shall come into our own after we will have been scourged a little more and that the desire to make the Bible and the spelling book the scriptures . . . or racial and national power will take a firmer grip upon us and help us to find our place in the Sun. Just now we Negroes are too much given to *Seeming* to be, what the acid test proves us not to be. We are the only race group in America that does not seem to be in *earnest* or possess any originality of thought or initiative in race development too many of us are black and brown white men, mere chameleons the victims of our environment the counterfeit presentments of the unconquered and unconquerable white man. Some day let us hope we shall be strong enough—to throw off the spell and brave enough *to be* rather than *seem real* Negroes proud of every clear trickle of our blood and the traditions hoary with age that give to the old grey haired Mother of civilization the Primacy among the cultures races of the world. There is nothing to be ashamed of but everything to be proud of when the Name Africa is spoken. I am delighted to learn that you got the cigars and sorry to be told that because of a throat infection you are having them smoked by Berst. If smoked in your presence you will only be able to enjoy their aroma. Too sorry you won't be able to visit New York during the Convention. I realize that neither of us are as young and spry as we once were and that it would be a tax on your strength to do all the stunts you'd be called upon to perform if you could come. It would indeed be a great pleasure to Mrs. B. and myself—if you could see your way to spend a week here—or longer and take things slowly—sleep all you want to eat when you get ready and browse around the city at your pleasure. It would do you good and put some bones on your meat. I told Woodson the Moneyhawk when he was here a month or so ago that your article was the best in the *Journal of Negro History* that is how his clerk got hold of it as I supposed he must have repeated what I told him so emphatically—well Greener has left the circle. Year by year the ranks grown thinner and our little world seems a more lonesome place to live in. Those of us who are left must be very good or very useful that we are not taken. I'm getting to be a little pessimistic over the activities of the KKK in the North and West and the cryptic silence of the clergy and the best people who treat this group of law breakers in the matter of fact way. I see danger ahead for the Negro and a possible race conflict. I don't like the tactics of the KKK. Its propaganda foreshadows a racial mix-up as sure as you are reading these lines. Within the past two months 8 Negroes have been lynched. If the Dyer Bill[54] passes there will be a . . . [illegible] of lynching in the South just to show the Yankees this is a matter that cannot be regulated by law. Watch it. DuBois is calling a convention in Newark in June to protest lynching and to urge passage of Dyer bill *Cui Bono*? A million Dyer Bills won't change the murderous instincts of the white South which believes in lynching. A few boxes of matches and kerosene cans are the only correctives for the evil. If the Negroes in any town where a lynching takes place had the courage to lay it in the ashes—it would make lynching more expensive and uncertain. Some day the worm is going to turn and white men of the South will be willing to eat out of the Negroes hand when he burns their houses and crops. The KKK is driving the Negro to desperate acts by their subtle methods to secure and make certain white supremacy—we are near the parting of the ways. The Philistines are upon us we have got to fight or die. I've resolved to fight it if I must and to die fighting. Kind regards to Madam and to you.

                                         Yours faithfully,
                                         John E. Bruce

                                         258 W 139th St.
                                         NY City Oct. 14/22
My dear Friend Cromwell:—

   I was just on the eve of dropping you a card when your letter reached me, to ask you "what I have did" to deserve such a snubbing as you have given me for the last month or six weeks. I have generously concluded that you like myself in these latter days find that writing personal letter is more of a discipline than a pleasure because of the physical exertion they intail upon youngsters like you and I—I can write yards of newspaper copy without feeling it, but I seem to balk

54. There was a growing protest against the treatment of African Americans—especially the number of lynchings that occurred each year—so James Weldon Johnson, secretary of the NAACP in 1921, succeeded in getting Missouri representative L. C. Dyer to introduce a bill "to assure to persons within the jurisdiction of every state the equal protection of the law, and to punish the crime of lynching." In spite of southern opposition, the bill passed in the House with a vote of 230–119. The NAACP then mounted the herculean task of securing its passage in the Senate. Twenty-four governors, thirty-nine mayors, twenty-nine college presidents and professors, and a large number of editors, jurists, and lawyers signed a memorial that was sent to the Senate urging the passage of the bill. Full-page advertisements were placed by NAACP in key newspapers, but when the bill reached the Senate floor, southern senators led by Underwood of Alabama and Harrison of Mississippi succeeded in organizing a filibuster that ultimately prevented a vote on the measure.

like a one eyed mule when I am called on to write personal letters and yet I like to receive them and I enjoy reading them when they are as interesting as yours always are. I have been thinking along the lines of your recent, and heed the call. The Academy does not prosper under its present management and it should not be permitted to snuff out its existence by its inaction, lack of interest and pride in the object which called it into being twenty-seven years ago. Our half breed brethren have dual minds and they are not to be expected to think black as did Alexander Crummell. The head of the Academy should be a *seasoned* well equipped mentally black scholar soaked from his toes to the outer surface of his caput in the idea and ideals which Dr. Crummell held when he involved the thought out of which he grew *The American Negro Academy.* If I can in any way bear a hand in helping to bring about this result—health permitting—I shall be only too glad to render what service I can. I was completely disgusted with the Shilly Shally manner with which those responsible treated the Weiner paper,[55] the publication of which would have added a certain prestige to the Academy and to those charged with the duty of preparing it for publication . . . [page missing] Africa by and by will stretch out her hands—unto God and when she does the white man there will have to move and Egypt now as ever the land of mystery will become *in fact* the land of the Blacks what London and Paris are to the Saxons and Gauls, Cairo and Luxor will be to the Blacks. The white people who are now engaged in the laborious work of putting them in order will not remain to enjoy the fruits of that labor. All this wealth belongs to "*We.*"

I trust you are feeling quite well these days, and living within the circle— i.e . . . that you are not overdoing things, but taking life quietly, sleeping plenti-fully and working when you feel the urge and stopping before you get tired. This

---

55. In November 1921, Leo Wiener, professor of Slavic language and literature at Harvard University, accepted an invitation from the executive committee of the American Negro Academy to present a paper on his research in African archaeology and philology. The idea came from Arthur A. Schomburg who had urged Bruce to write an article on Wiener's work for the *Negro World.* Cromwell supported the idea of inviting Wiener to speak at the twenty-fifth annual meeting of the academy. Wiener had already published a three-volume work, *Africa and the Discovery of America,* in which he argued that Christopher Columbus was correct in his judgment that the original inhabitants of America had traded with Africans and that there was a clear and unmistakable African influence that had preceded the period of European encounter. His address, "The Problems of African Civilization," was a discussion of the main ideas in his study. It was anticipated that this paper would be published in the academy's *Occasional Papers.* The executive committee approved its publication in early 1922, but for reasons that were never made clear, Robert A. Phelham, the corresponding secretary, refused to implement the decision, though urged to do so by Cromwell, Schomburg, Bruce, and John R. Clifford. There was some feeling that other members of the academy did not want to publish a paper by a white scholar.

is my programe for a long life and a happy one. Kindest regards to Madame and to you from the both of us.

Sincerely yours

John E. Bruce

258 West 139 Street

New York City,

January 19, 1923.

Dear Mr. Cromwell,

I am very glad of the opportunity you give me to tell you something about the Douglass Cast, a replica in Plaster Paris of the medallion which was carved on one of the Pillars of the Grand Stairway of the State Capitol at Albany New York and which it gave me great pleasure to present to the Bethel Literary Society many years ago, through your good offices.

When the Artist, Mr. Brines had completed the Medallion on the pillar, I told him that I would like very much to have the plaster model for a gift to a Negro Historical Society at Washington of which Mr. Douglass in his lifetime had been a member and of which I myself was a member. He replied that he had no objection personally to giving it to me and would do so if he had authority to dispose of it in that way; that it would be taken up to his studio in the year and after a few days be broken up.

He advised me to go to the superintendent of Buildings, Mr. Perry and make application for it, stating why I wanted it. This I did, finding Mr. Perry who was usually somewhat irascible but was on this day in a particularly good humor. I told him my story in few words. He said: "I remember Frederick Douglass well. He was a great orator, and I heard him speak in New York when he called down Captain Rynders.[56] I was a boy then of sixteen or seventeen years. So you want

---

56. Isaiah Rynders (1804–1885), New York City gang leader and Tammany Hall boss of the Sixth Ward, was a powerful figure during the late antebellum period. He was the leader of the infamous "Empire Club," a band of street toughs first recruited to disrupt Whig political rallies during the 1844 election. For his activities, Rynders was given a series of local federal offices. When not intimidating political opponents, Rynders and his followers participated in a number of rowdy civil disturbances. A staunch defender of slavery, Rynders became the nemesis of New York abolitionists during the 1840s and 1850s. The reference in Bruce's letter is to a speech Frederick Douglass was making in New York on May 7, 1850 when Rynders began to heckle him. Douglass referred to himself as a black man, and Rynders responded, "You are not a black man, you are only half a nigger." Douglass's response elicited roars of laughter: "He is correct, I am, indeed, only half a Negro, a half-brother to Mr. Rynders." This exchange became legendary in antislavery circles and was recounted as late as 1883 at a meeting commemorating the fiftieth anniversary of the New York City Anti-Slavery Society. Later that same year, Rynders acknowledged, in a published interview,

that cast, eh?" I said, "Yes sir, I would like very much to have it to present to my society at Washington." He directed his secretary to write a short note to the chairman of the Committee of Public Buildings stating in brief what I had told him and that he favored disposing of the cast in that way. I then saw this Official, got his consent and he sent me to the Lieutenant Governor with his card stating what I wanted.

The Lieutenant Governor, being an ex-officio member of the all important Committees at the time connected with the completion of the Capitol building, readily assented and gave me a written order to the Sculptor, my friend, Mr. Brines who made the medallion of myself of which I think I sent you a copy. This gentleman kindly had the cast boxed and marked to its destination at Washington.

The following day I paid the cartage to the freight office, 52.50 and freightage bill and this is all I remember of the incident, except the story in the *Washington Star* telling of its arrival and of your presentation of the gift in my name to Bethel Literary Association. If the cast is still recognizable a good treatment with shellac will help to preserve it for many years.

The Douglass home is the place where it ought now to be and photographs should be made of it and sold to visitors. I had several hundred photos of it made and sold them for Twenty-Five cents each. One was sold to the Mayor of Albany and he had it framed and hung in his office.

Yours truly,
John E. Bruce.

258 W 139 St
New York City
Aug. 15/23

Dear Friend Cromwell:

Yours of 8/10/23 found me packing my duds for a trip to North Cambridge Mass where I will spend three weeks resting and loafing after 10 weeks stay in Hospital where I have been under the knife three times and am still alive and kicking. I have been home just one week and have been too weak or lazy or indisposed to be your choice to do more work mental or physical than I have actually been compelled to do. Your letters aroused me somewhat as I had just

---

that Frederick Douglass "did give me a shot, and it was as good a shot as I ever had in my life, when he said to me, 'Oh then, I am only your half-brother.'" (*New York Times,* January 14, 1885; John W. Blassingame, ed., *The Frederick Douglass Papers: Volume 2, 1847–1854,* 1st ser., Speeches, Debates and Interviews [New Haven: Oxford University Press, 1982], 239).

jotted down some notes about this Coolidge man which harmonize with your view of his appearance on the stage at this time. When the Lord's finger touches a Harding and he sleeps it means that he has finished the work that he was sent to do. The job Harding had was a bit too big for him anyhow and was beginning to wear on his intellectuals. His departure from this world was a relief to the men who were looking into the future and saw coming the crash which Warren G. Hardy went to Alaska to temporarily avoid. The great dailies were beginning to criticize his policies or lack of them, regarding domestic and European problems and he felt it keenly. Death was as welcome to him as it was to the men who supported him but had little faith in his program.

Coolidge is going to be a surprise to the Warwicks and other master workmen in the game of politics. His stand as Mayor of Boston or was it Gov.? in the matter of the Police is a *straw* and his letter (recent) to a member of the K. C. commending that organization for its love of law and order is another straw which indicates where he is at. I am waiting to see what he is going to do or say in the Tuskegee Hospital matter. It is a far cry from Franklin Pierce to Calvin Coolidge and it is to be presumed now that Mass. occupies the center of the stage that the performance will be fully up to standard.

My best bet is that Coolidge will be elected our next President unless the State of Mass. ceases to produce Baked beans and the sacred Cod. I think and agree with you that the future is big with promise for those of us who up to ten days ago despaired and were ready to give up the ghost because of the Chio idea like a deadly miasma held the nation in its grip, and the Negro under its iron heels as a thing apart. Coolidge is at least a ray of hope, and may ultimately bring this hope to a full realization of what we all want to be.

Hastily yours
John E. Bruce

My Cambridge Address 35 Prentiss St. Regards to Madame

In 1921, the Veterans Bureau decided to open, at some suitable point in the South, a hospital for the treatment of African American veterans of World War I. Despite vigorous protests from African Americans in all parts of the country, among them the National Board of Directors of the NAACP, the hospital was relocated on the land adjacent to Tuskegee Institute. Other communities had rejected the hospital, but Tuskegee's white citizens had been promised the control of the facility and a major portion of its sixty-five thousand-dollar payroll. Robert Moton, Booker T. Washington's successor as president of Tuskegee, was asked to be patient because eventually African Americans would staff the hospital under a northern white director. When the hospital opened its doors, however, without notification to Dr. Moton, its director was Colonel Robert H. Stanley from Alabama. Colonel Stanley was accompanied by a staff of white medical officers—including white nurses, each of whom would command a black "housemaid" to avoid contamination from the patients and to comply with state law governing racial separation. Moton, described by Du Bois as a "much simpler and more straight-forward type" of Black than Washington, was in a quandary over the situation. He sought help from the NAACP and wrote President Harding that if black physicians and nurses were debarred from service without at least being given a chance to qualify under the civil service rules, it would bring justifiable criticism upon him and upon the Harding administration. Dr. Moton wrote Colonel Stanley asking him to delay the opening of the hospital, but Stanley replied that "there would be no mixture of the races on the staff." Pressure was put on Dr. Moton to acquiesce to the segregated policy. The feeling was so divisive that some several hundred Klansmen paraded through the town of Tuskegee and across the hospital grounds the night before the Fourth of July in an attempt to intimidate the local community. The town's white merchants refused to sell to black customers. The expulsion of the only black physician and the summary dismissal of the black "nurse maids" did not force the federal government to act. Following the parade, about twenty Klansmen went into the hospital and were saluted and permitted to pass. The next day the NAACP wired the president noting the seriousness of the march and requesting the removal of Colonel Stanley and the assignment of a complete colored staff of qualified physicians and nurses, from the commanding officer down. They also requested that, if it was necessary, U.S. troops in Alabama be sent to the hospital to ensure that these physicians and nurses were allowed to do the work to which they had been assigned. President Harding called Dr. Moton into a conference after which the president issued an executive order calling for a special examination for African American applicants for places on the hospital staff. The Civil Service Commission, reported by Du Bois in the *Crisis* of 1923, delayed unnecessarily in arranging for these exams. Harding died suddenly, and the matter was settled by President Calvin Coolidge. Black people were given the right to run their own federally segregated hospital in Alabama's Black Belt, a result anticipated by Bruce.

It is difficult to evaluate the overall significance of this correspondence. There is the obvious inequity because Grandfather was almost a silent partner, whose voice we hear only as Bruce reacts. As Bruce's life was so hectic, complicated, and at times controversial, however, the letters cut through the larger, more muddled picture and become still slides to Bruce's movie reel. There is the ever-changing cast of characters: some old friends, some old enemies, and others that we hardly know.

There was not only a strong bond between Cromwell and Bruce but also an honesty and respect expressed on all subjects with, nevertheless for Bruce, a hope for understanding and approval by Cromwell.

Needing and seeking largesse from those in power, Bruce, from his youngest years, survived on patronage and consequently was almost obsessed with the information on the patronage of others. He himself always had one or more patrons and seemingly evaluated most people on the power they had to help or to hurt him. While most of his patrons were white and Republican, his changing relation to Booker T. Washington and his perpetual affection for Charles "Charley" Anderson also reveal this characteristic.

Throughout his life, Bruce held a number of minor political appointments to supplement his earnings from journalism and newspaper reporting. But he never stopped being a journalist.

Charles S. Clarkson, one of his major patrons, was chairman of the Republican National Committee and in 1889 was appointed assistant postmaster general. Although he served for only one year, he used the title "General" for the rest of his life. In 1892, Charles Clarkson helped Bruce secure a clerk's position in the patent office in the Department of the Interior. But Bruce lost this position when Cleveland began his second term in 1893. In 1897, Bruce was assisted by James S. Clarkson in getting a position as head porter of the New York State Capitol, "In recognition for his sterling work for the Republican organization of the 13th Ward."

In 1902, Gen. Charles S. Clarkson was appointed surveyor of the New York customs office and liaison for black federal appointments and black political strategy by President Roosevelt. General Clarkson appointed Bruce to a position in his department where Bruce remained for more than twenty years until poor health forced his retirement in 1921.

Although both Charles S. Clarkson and James S. Clarkson were important patrons and friends of Bruce, and in spite of the early assistance Bruce received from James S. Clarkson, it was Gen. Charles S. Clarkson whom Bruce always called the "Surveyor" and whom he considered his "life long and truest white friend."[57] Of course, Bruce also judged Clarkson to be his most important patron. As life turns in peculiar ways, however, it seems to me that at the end of his life, Bruce's most important patron, if not friend, was Marcus Garvey.

57. Crowder, *John Edward Bruce,* 69.

Chapter 9

THE TWO HISTORIANS

THE FRIENDSHIP BETWEEN THEOPHILUS GOULD STEWARD AND JOHN WESLEY CROMWELL SR.

~~⊛ ⊛~~

Like John Edward Bruce, Theophilus Gould Steward (1845–1924) has been omitted from the narrative of African American history. Within the powerful circle of the African Methodist Episcopal Church, Steward was a well-known and controversial figure. That he was not included in William J. Simmons's encyclopedic volume *Men of Mark*[1] seems indefensible.

Within the last decade, however, two authors have rescued Steward from oblivion. In *Voices of Dissent: Theophilus Gould Steward (1843–1924) and Black America*,[2] William Seraile has integrated in great detail the life and career of Steward into the fabric of the world in which he lived, enumerating his accomplishments and his failures as a person. More important, Albert G. Miller, in *Elevating the Race: Theophilus G. Steward, Black Theology, and the Making of an African American Civil Society, 1865–1924*,[3] introduced the reader to Steward the theologian. Both authors had much material on which to draw because in addition to his many books, Steward was a regular contributor to the *Christian Recorder* and numerous other magazines.

---

1. William J. Simmons, *Men of Mark, Eminent Progressive and Rising* (Chicago: Johnson Publishing Company, 1970).

2. William Seraile, *Voice of Dissent: Theophilus Gould Steward (1843–1924) and Black America* (Brooklyn: Carlson Publishing, 1991).

3. Albert G. Miller, *Elevating the Race: Theophilus G. Steward, Black Theology, and the Making of an African American Civil Society, 1865–1924* (Knoxville: University of Tennessee Press, 2003).

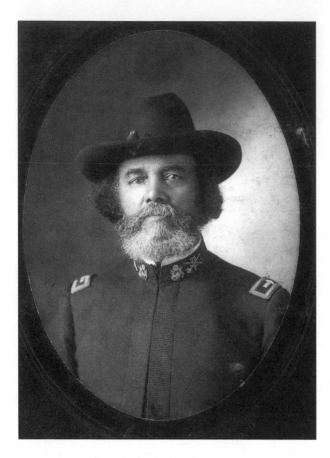

Theophilus Gould Steward, 1843–1924. (Courtesy of the Schomburg Center for Research in Black Culture.)

Both Seraile and Miller underscore the fact that Steward was controversial. He was often argumentative, which earned him a reputation for seeking controversy, and throughout his ministerial career, he was accused of being uncooperative and "a quitter" who always wanted to be right.

The eighteen letters from Steward to Grandfather differ considerably in tone and content from the Bruce letters. Both cover roughly the same span of years, from the 1890s to the middle of the first decade of the twentieth century. Bruce's letters reflect the versatility of his major role—that of an informed and curious journalist—but are never lacking in satire or humor. Steward's correspondence, on the other hand, reveal him to be a man of many parts—a teacher, minister, author, and soldier—who is always serious.

Theophilus Gould Steward was born in Gouldtown, an old community of free mulattoes in Cumberland County, New Jersey, with roots that go back to the seventeenth century. His father, James Steward, a mechanic, came to Gouldtown as a nine-year-old indentured servant. His mother, Rebecca Gould Steward, was a direct descendant of John Fenwick, a seventeenth-century proprietor in West Jersey and one of the founders of the community. Steward had five siblings: two brothers and three sisters. He received his early education at the Gouldtown School, where he had basic instruction in reading, writing, and mathematics. He supplemented his education by attending lectures on literature, politics, and philosophy at the Gouldtown Literary and Moral Improvement Society. He had no further formal education until 1878 when he attended the Philadelphia Protestant Episcopal Church Divinity School, from which he graduated with great acclaim in 1880. At about the same time, Steward took an evening course at the National School of Elocution and Oratory.

In December 1860, at the age of sixteen, Steward joined the A.M.E. Church. In 1862, he was licensed to exhort, and the following year, he received his preaching license. On June 4, 1864, after having been examined at the Philadelphia Annual Conference on doctrine, discipline, and general information, he became a probationary A.M.E. minister.

Steward's ministry began when he was selected by Bishop Daniel Payne to be a missionary to newly freed slaves in Hilton Head, South Carolina. Three days after he arrived in South Carolina, he was assigned to the Beaufort River Circuit, which became the first of his fourteen assignments over the next twenty-seven years.

For his first five assignments, Steward was in Georgia and South Carolina. Among other accomplishments, he organized the first black school in Marion, Georgia, helped write the Georgia Republican platform in 1868, and led a successful protest by Americus, Georgia, freedmen against compulsory labor contracts. He also worked as cashier of the Freedmen's Bank in Macon, Georgia.

Next, at not quite thirty years of age, Steward was sent to Bethel Church in Wilmington, Delaware, a community socially and politically alien to those he had worked for in the South. The congregation of Bethel was composed of working-class families not seeking to alter the social order of the community as were the recently freed former slaves in his southern congregations. Steward did, however, attempt to improve the deplorable education system for Blacks in Delaware and emerged as the leading spokesman for his race in the state.

During this ministry, Steward began to study French and to criticize the A.M.E. Church bureaucracy, initially focusing on church ritual. This was the beginning of an ongoing battle between Steward and church administrators. He also sought to have an A.M.E. missionary established in Haiti and was appointed to undertake this work, arriving in Haiti on June 13, 1873. This was a big mistake. Steward did not understand, and often did not approve of, Haitian culture, and his ability to converse in French was limited. Only the presence of James Theodore Holly, a Presbyterian minister from New Haven and a Black Nationalist, made the experience tolerable.[4] A month after starting a church, which he felt was not being properly funded, Steward, in poor health, returned to the United States.

Steward did not return to Haiti nor was he ever again assigned to a church in the South. He served in Brooklyn, Philadelphia, and Frankfort, Pennsylvania. In 1886, he was transferred to his most formidable challenge, the Metropolitan A.M.E. Church in Washington, D.C., where he remained until 1888. The church building, while new, was poorly funded, but Steward attracted a wide group of outstanding worshippers. It seemed many came to hear Steward preach but maintained their memberships in other congregations.

Wherever Steward served, the picture was always the same: he was known as a builder and an eloquent speaker, who was always needing funds and always involved in some controversy either with the community or with the church hierarchy. Steward was a perceptive observer of the socioeconomic composition of his congregation. Wherever he was, Steward was interested in the quality of education afforded the black community; and with the exception of Washington, D.C., he always found it inferior. Seraile maintained that Steward's northern free background and his near-white complexion always affected his ministry.[5] Steward did complain of the color line in Washington.

In 1888, Steward was transferred to Bethel A.M.E. Church in Baltimore. After his departure, the members of the Metropolitan Church passed a resolution

4. James Theodore Holly (1829–1911) was born in Washington, D.C. He worked with Lewis Tappan as an abolitionist and championed the American Colonization Society. He was also co-editor of *Voice of the Fugitive*. In 1854, he was a delegate to the first National Emigration Convention in Cleveland, and in 1856, he moved to New Haven and became a minister at St. Luke's, a position he held until 1861, and a teacher in public and private schools. In May 1861, he took 110 members of his church to Haiti. His wife, two children, and thirty-nine members of his congregation died of malaria and yellow fever; the survivors left. By 1862 he was a Haitian citizen, and by 1865 he was supported by the American Church Missionary Society and the Board of Missions of the Protestant Episcopal Church. In 1874, he was consecrated the missionary bishop of Haiti, the first African American bishop in the Episcopal Church. Holly never abandoned the belief that emigration was the only way for American Blacks to better their lot. He worked hard to establish schools in Haiti. He died of old age on March 13, 1911, and was buried at Holy Trinity Church in Port-au-Prince, Haiti.

5. Seraile, *Voice of Dissent*, 22.

praising him for "his urbane manner, exemplary piety, Christian bearing and pulpit oratory."[6]

After making some improvement in the education for Blacks in Baltimore, Steward was transferred back to Washington, D.C., in 1890 to Mt. Pisgah Church, and in 1891, the church sent him once again to Baltimore to Walters Chapel. It would seem that the bishops were not favorably disposed to Steward, who had been publicly critical of their decision making, and that they may have moved him as a punishment.

During this time, Steward continued to have health problems and welcomed an opportunity for a change from the rigors of an "itinerary ministry." He had fought and lost too many battles and his memories were bittersweet ones. According to Seraile, "he was a brilliant pulpit orator who possessed outstanding organizational skills. Despite his tremendous success in organizing, renovating and improving A.M.E. churches from Georgia to Brooklyn, his achievements were flawed by his failure in Haiti, and his argumentative personality cost him the presidency of Wilberforce University and election to the bishopric."[7]

As Steward knew Grandfather best when he was serving as the minister of the Metropolitan A.M.E. Church from 1886 to 1888, these eighteen letters comment on that experience and on his experience in the military and contain some brief observations about his later years in Wilberforce.

It is clear from Steward's letters that he and Grandfather were close friends and that they appreciated each other's frankness. The letters reflect those feelings and their mutual awareness of the considerable conflict and tensions within the Metropolitan Church, which disturbed Cromwell, as a member and as an historian and journalist.

In his journal, Grandfather recorded his reactions to the behavior of the ministers, bishops, and members, but he was understandably cautious about sharing his observations with other people.[8] Such observations are rarely a part of the church archives that are available to the public. Either they were not recorded by the participants or observers or they have been destroyed.

The term of an itinerary was usually three years, but in some cases, it was shorter. If the bishop so willed, it could be continued up to five years. As Steward

6. Ibid., 100.
7. Ibid., 109.
8. Seraile quotes Cromwell, as editor of the *People's Advocate,* classifying Washington's "black preachers as unscrupulous, cardplayers, alcoholics and seducers of women" (ibid., 108).

wrote in his letters to Grandfather, he had been surprisingly candid to the bishops concerning the performances of the ministers following and preceding him.

Cromwell had his own assessment of the ministers at Metropolitan A.M.E., which he probably expressed to Steward.[9] He praised John H. Welch, who had literally worked himself to death trying to compensate for the weaknesses of Oscar J. W. Scott, who "through his morality, undignified manner and plotting and scheming had brought reproach to the church." The Reverend Isaac Ross, who was brought into the church by a surprise move, and although he became a bishop, Ross, in Cromwell's opinion, showed a certain lack of character, however popular he was as a preacher and public figure.

Cromwell's main disdain was reserved for Rev. C. Harold Stepteau, who was appointed in 1914 by Bishop Coppin as Ross's successor "against the protest of many members of standing and eloquence." Shortly after his appointment, Rev. Stepteau was accused by the trustees of financial improprieties on two occasions. These charges were apparently kept from church members, for he was able through his contacts to secure another tour at Metropolitan.

It is in this climate of dishonesty and conflict within the church that the letters from Steward must be read. Cromwell certainly wrote to Steward as a trusted friend, and Steward responded to Cromwell in the same manner.

Grandfather was along in years when Stepteau was the minister of Metropolitan A.M.E. Church and clearly was upset with the actions of the bishop, but to him, then and afterward, Theophilus Gould Steward was a man of a different character whose ministry brought prestige and honor to the church. Others must have been in agreement, for Steward was invited back to a warm and appreciative audience, which Grandfather fondly recalls in his journal:

> The career of Rev. Theophilus G. Steward, D.D., an itinerant preacher is inclosed by his appointment as post chaplain in the 25th U. S. Regiment stationed at Fort Missoula, Montana. Dr. Steward certainly *has no superior* as a pulpit orator in the A.M.E. Church. Of him, the words of Rev. J. C. Embry to me that 'he can say what he wants to say better than any other preacher in the A.M.E. Church' will certainly be endorsed by all who have listened to his ministrations of the Word during his pastorate of

---

9. There were eight ministers of the Metropolitan A.M.E. Church during this period: Theophilus Gould Steward (1886–1888); John J. Mitchell (1888–1889); J. W. Beckett (1890–1893); John Albert Johnson (1896–1901); Oscar J. W. Scott (1903–1904); John H. Welch (1907–1909); Isaac Ross (1904–1914); and C. Harold Stepteau (1914–1917).

the Metropolitan A.M.E. Church. Never seemed a pastor better adapted to the great needs of a people than he. Cultured, genial, pious, eloquent, he continued to attract to the church people who never believed it was possible they could see anything good, anything elevating in the Methodist Church. By his personal example he won many a soul to an open profession in the belief of a risen Saviour. When the relations of the church and himself were severed in 1888, there were many sick hearts. An experience of three years has shown that he is the best man yet developed for the place. Without going any further into much that has no legitimate place here and now, suffice it that 1891 found Dr. Steward in charge of a church at Baltimore with his family here where they were located for the increased educational opportunities afforded. Then it was that he was induced to make a formal application for U.S. Chaplaincy. In this, he had the support of the Hon. B. K. Bruce and Hon. John R. Lynch with that of P. M. G. John Wanamaker who had known him in Philadelphia.

. . . Ten years have elapsed, Dr. Steward is once more here. He is now on leave from his regiment stationed in the Philippine Islands now in the possession of the U.S. as an outcome of the war with Spain. Since he has been appointed Chaplain he has been widowed and is now remarried. This time the occasion of his visit to Washington is an engagement to lecture on 'The Philippines' in the Metropolitan A.M.E. Church Sunday, September 8, 1901 he preached from his old pulpit . . . The congregation was an usually large one. Douglass was not there, neither was Bruce, nor Langston, they have all gone to the silent land. One half a generation has passed since he was appointed there as pastor in 1886, yet there were many brought to the church during his pastorate and who worshipped there regularly to welcome him and his message. It was a service of great spiritual uplift; to those who heard Dr. Steward for the first time it was a revelation of his great oratorical and spiritual power.

Monday night the chaplain was entertained by a dinner at Murray's Café. . . . It was the first time that chaplain Steward had been thus honored and he appreciated the occasion accordingly.

At the lecture on the subsequent night nearly three hundred persons were present. As Chairman of the Committee of arrangements I presided and introduced the lecturer. Bishop Jas. T. Holly being in the audience made the invocation.

Chaplain Steward gave a most interesting and entertaining talk on the manners and customs of the Filipinos—their religion and their intellectual culture. As an army officer, he did not refer at all to their politics or military conditions.

1414 Jefferson St.
Baltimore, Md.
May 19, 1891

Mr. J. W. Cromwell
Washington, D.C.
My dear brother:

In looking over the "Post" report of my address last ev'g I see it makes me dogmatize where I only speculated; and in a word gives my positions too strongly. If any unfair criticism should arise in the matter, I will be greatly obliged to you for any kind word you may say in defense. Especially, I am anxious not to be misrepresented as drawing a line between *mixed bloods* and *blacks*. This I never do in *feeling*, much less in discourse except in pure matters of scientific inquiry, etc.

My *principles* do not allow me to draw a *color line* of any sort and I never do it. White men, black men, and mixed men are all the same to me in all relations. Have been ever since I reached my majority.

Those principles I have maintained on more than one marked occasion. In Charleston I openly defied their social customs and in Philadelphia on an occasion, I remember, when I had com . . . [illegible] tickets to white Literary and Social at the *Academy of Fine Arts* it was my pleasure to take with me a thoroughly *black lady.*

I state these things to you as a matter of . . . [illegible]. So I took Helen Handy to a Ladies meeting in Washington and had her preside at the organ and sing and thus opened the way to get the choir mixed to those great meetings.

I know I have no weakness on points of that sort although I do suppose I can set up as good a claim to *blood* as any Negro in the country. But *Bah*! Good conduct and good manners always beat good *blood.*

Sincerely yours
T. G. Steward

In February 1891, the chaplaincy of the Twenty-fifth U.S. Colored Infantry became available. John R. Lynch, a former Reconstruction congressman from Mississippi, tried unsuccessfully to interest the Reverend Francis T. Grimké, the pastor of the 15th Street Presbyterian Church in Washington, D.C., in the position. Grimké suggested Theophilus Gould Steward, whose candidacy was also supported by former U.S. senator Blanche K. Bruce and by Steward's friend Postmaster General John Wanamaker. On July 25, 1891, Steward became the third African American appointed to the chaplaincy since the end of the Civil War.

While Grandfather and Steward had a mutual interest in historical topics and in the Metropolitan A.M.E. Church, the problems of the black soldier were of greater concern to Steward. He was in the midst of the fray, as it were.

Following the Civil War, even before Steward was recruited as the chaplain for the Twenty-fifth Infantry, there was considerable discussion, particularly among the military but also among the general public, of the role of the black soldier. Some, of course, did not think that Blacks were suited for military service, in spite of their record for bravery in war. Even those who accepted Blacks as soldiers insisted that they be under the command of white officers and strictly limited to service in two infantry and two cavalry units. It was believed that Blacks should be excluded from the more specialized and technical branches of the service because they lacked the intelligence to perform those duties.

On January 20, 1877, weighing in on this debate, Gen. William Tecumseh Sherman, as General of the Army, wrote to Secretary of War George W. McCrary that "the word black should be obliterated from the Statute Books and that whites and blacks be enlisted and distributed alike in the Army as has been the usage in the Navy for a hundred years."[10] However, the policy adopted was to assign black enlisted men exclusively in four units, the Ninth and Tenth cavalries and the Twenty-fourth and Twenty-fifth infantries, and not to allow them to serve in the branches of the artillery, engineers, and ordinance.

But the debate was far from over. In 1889, two years before Steward began writing Grandfather, then Secretary of War Redfield Proctor proposed in his annual report that black soldiers should make up two additional regiments of artillery since their record in the service had been excellent. In December 1889, a proposed bill for seven regiments, authorizing President Grant to enlist Blacks at his discretion, was introduced. It failed, as did a similar bill in the next Congress.

Nevertheless, by the time the Spanish-American War broke out in 1898, the army had begun allowing a few black specialists into regiments other than the specified infantry and cavalry units. Steward's letters address some of the problems faced by black troops and their unrecognized abilities as soldiers. Expressed, too, were the unsatisfactory locations of the units—in the northern plains or southwest desert.

The reader of today, familiar with the integrated military service, the acceptance of Blacks in West Point and Annapolis, and the visible appearance of Colin Powell as a military man close to the seat of power, must be reminded of those

---

10. Bernard C. Nalty and Morris J. MacGregor, eds., *Blacks in the Military: Essential Documents* (Wilmington: Scholarly Resources, 1981), 48–49.

years between the end of the Civil War, when the country was still influenced by a weakening egalitarianism, and the two world wars, when Blacks faced overt segregation in the armed services, and of the fight waged by civil rights groups and others for immediate integration of and equal opportunities for Blacks in the military. Idealism (having fought for democracy abroad), political expediency (the rise of a strong black voice), and military realities (the need for a larger army) all combined to bring about changes in the racial policies of the armed forces. On July 26, 1948, President Harry Truman issued Executive Order 9981, declaring that there should be equality of treatment and opportunity for all persons in the armed services without regard to race, color, religion, and national origin. "The actual integration of military units took place with surprising tranquility and comparative speed, considering the controversy that had surrounded the question of segregation in the armed forces."[11]

Could Steward have anticipated this outcome?

During his career in the military, from 1892 to 1906, Steward was stationed in Montana, Nebraska, and Texas, and it was from these posts that he wrote letters to my grandfather. There are no extant letters from Steward when he was a military recruiter in Ohio or from his overseas assignment in the Philippines, an experience he warmly remembered in other letters and lectures. Steward was anxious to go to Cuba with his troops, but unfortunately by the time he received the necessary permission, the Twenty-fifth had been transferred back to the States. Regrettably, these letters reveal little or nothing about Steward's feelings on racial questions as they affected or would affect black soldiers stationed in either Cuba or the Philippines because of the racial complexion of those two populations.

Fort Missoula, Mont.
Feby. 15th, 1892

My dear Cromwell,

If you can get any information respecting a proposed Alaskan Exploring or Surveying Expedition for next summer, I wish you would let me know at once. The rumor has reached here that a military expedition of some sort is to go up there and some of our men are anxious to offer themselves. Cold and the American Negro is all humbug. No troops in the service can stand cold better than the colored troops. We have not had a case of *climate trouble* this whole winter. One man got his foot frozen while hunting; but this occurred through

---

11. Ibid., 295. See also Bernard C. Nalty, *Strength for the Fight: A History of Black Americans in the Military* (New York: The Free Press, 1986).

carelessness on his part. The Garrison of over 300 has not furnished a *death* in the whole six months I have been here so you can see about what the death rate per 1000 is here so far. 300 x 0 x 4 = 0. Of course death must come to some of us some time (if not indeed to all of us).

We enjoy frontier life very much. I have gained 13 lbs in weight and 100% in strength. Can eat and digest anything. I can walk 6 or 8 miles without fatigue, keeping up military step and cadence nearly all the time.

I am solicited to preach 5 nights in a white church next week in a revival meeting and there are also arrangements going on to have me lecture in Helena, pretty soon.

I want to get about 10 first class men to enlist in these companies with a view of becoming non-Commissioned officers and then studying or striving for Commissions. If you know any good men who want to enlist, tell them to write to me.

One thing more, I think if the colored people would make a little effort they could get one of these colored regiments of infantry transferred to the Dept. of the East. They have never been East and are not complaining but justice requires that they should not spend all their days in the wilds and plains of the frontier. They have a plain case and I believe if asked for it would be done. Of course officers are prohibited from such things and I must not be quoted in official circles in this matter.

T. G. Steward

Fort Missoula, Mont.
June 13, '94

My dear Cromwell:

Yours of the 5th recd. I thank you for words of sympathy. We are all well.

If you will look over files of the *Philadelphia Weekly Press* for 1893, you will find that ice-cream was invented by a Philadelphia colored man by the name of Jackson. This will be important in your caterers' article.

You have heard me speak of the general physical character of the Guilds, I'll send you a clipping from a Bridgeton paper bearing upon that subject.

I am now preparing an article on "A crack Colored rifle shot." I shall send it to *Leslies* when done.

My story "Through Tribulation Deep" has been accepted by a Boston publishing house and is likely to come out about August.

Is Scott in the book business yet? I should like him to put in an order for a few copies. If you care to speak to him on the subject you may advise him to address

James H. Earle
Publisher and Imprinter
178 Washington Street
Boston, Mass.

I think he can make good terms. It is not a color story, but simply a religious American tale—a contribution to journal literature. I submitted it to Col. T. W. Higginson who was so well impressed with it that he introduced it to Lee and Shubbard but it was not "sensational" enough for them.

Fort Missoula, Mont.
July 29, 96

Mr. J. W. Cromwell
Washington, D.C.
Dear Brother:

Your very interesting letter reached me some days ago. I thank you for kind words and wish you may have continued pleasant days.

As to your comments and queries respecting the political situation, I must say that I am too far away from the boiling pot to know much as to the soup being concocted. My opinion is that the Republicans are going to have a very hard time of it. If they win they won't know themselves when they get in power; and this remark can apply with much more force to the Dems in case they win. Judgment day seems to have come to both the great parties. Well, let it come! I trust McKinley will win; but if he should fail it will not end the history of the world. You know my views—I believe war is coming—and the niggers will not be "tail pigs" when the war ends. We have got about ten thousand trained soldiers now; and can muster a million fighting men right on the soil—the very best in the country—perfect . . . [illegible] under competent commanders. The average Negro soldier is 3 lbs heavier than the average white and a good deal stronger. He stands the hardships better, is not sick as much, does not die as fast and does not succumb to whisky and cigarettes as much as white troops. All of this is true and you may quote it; but not in such a way as to make the white soldiers mad *at me* as I often have to meet some of them. You may say that I say so from official reports as well as from my own observations. I can prove if ever required to do so: that for the past twenty years the colored troops have been in the very front ranks of the army.

One company of the 24th has just made the finest record in shooting. I suppose ever made in this country. Reports will be in the War Department confirming what I say.

Now about the Metropolitan: when I was there Bp. Gaines complained because it was not filled and said Jenifer would fill it within a very short time if sent there. I replied to him privately that to fill the M. church was a question of both time and labor; and that we would do exceedingly well if we filled it within ten years. Jenifer has been there and the ten years are up—and my views have been fully sustained by experience.

(I find no fault with the work done by Brothers Mitchell, Becket and Jenifer (the three who succeeded Steward). They all worked hard—*so did I*. They met with some success—so did I; and yet there is much to be done.)

You may think it strange that I do not approve of the selection of laymen for church positions when it can be avoided. I think laymen ought to find their positions in the world of business; and keep the positions in the church for ministers growing old in the service. Time will show that the election of Laymen as Presidents of church schools, Editors of church organs and Secretaries of connectional interests will bring about results very difficult to manage. Politics, politics! More than ever will follow. I am entirely satisfied with *all* the elections personally: but I have my principles.

Have you ever noted how few ex-slaves have ever reached the bishopric in our church?[12] Just look the matter up and you will find it an interesting subject. I have mastered it but of course could not publish it as it would be a fire bomb. But it is the truth of history—*slaves can't "get there"* as a rule. Something heads them off.

Trusting I may hear from you some time I am as ever

Your friend and brother

T. G. Steward

Fort Niobrara, Neb.
August 29, '04

Dear Cromwell:

Yours of 6 came to hand and was answered in part immediately.

I enclose today Book C_____ ck for $5.00 which place to my cr with the Academy.

I am sure it was yourself who was the Dr. in the correspondence.

---

12. I assume Steward, who was born free, meant persons who had matured while in slavery, because Grandfather and Bruce were among the many who were born enslaved but became leaders; of course, they were not bishops.

I am not surprised that you do not find your pastor strong as a pulpit man, altho he should be a good average. He has had all the schooling necessary; but is not specifically poetic in nature. He should be practical and I infer he is from what you say.

I look for Roosevelt to win—I look for war before his term expires. I *believe* the end is nigh. The American Negro's day is close. A few years will see him in arms. Nothing but arms can alter his condition. Asia and Africa are going to break out and down will go the *white* fetish (?). Of course this is not to be published.

Steward

Fort Niobrara, Nebr.
Nov. 7, '04

Mr. John W. Cromwell
Washington, D.C.
Dear Brother:

Your brother-in-law George Conn is here and makes a very fine looking soldier. I have taken him under my care and so far he seems very amenable. I am trying to have him study for a commission. In this respects (thinks they) have not made use of a 20th of their opportunities. Let me illustrate: I have been in this regiment near 14 years and during all this time there has been just one candidate and he was given opportunities above the average. Now within this time there could easily have been 40 if they had wished. But of the three other regiments *almost* the same may be said. The chances under the Proctor Law were exceedingly good, and at one time a telegram came to the headmasters of the 25th asking if we had a candidate and the telegram was referred to me to answer and I had to answer "No." (Confidential)

While in the Philippines the chances were good by circumstances as officers were exceedingly scarce. Those of our sergeants were made lieutenants of volunteers and placed on duty right in their own regiment until their Vol. regiment came. Lieutenant Russell (colored) Commander Company H. 25th Infantry and Hoffman and M. Boyer served with companies, the latter as Commissary officer. Green of the 24th took the exam and is now in our regiment and makes a *good* officer. We *must* have more colored officers.

Your brother
T. G. Steward

Sorry to hear Brother Scott is not *coming.*

Fort Niobrara, Neb.
Dec. 13, '04

Mr. John W. Cromwell
Washington, D.C.
My dear Cromwell:

I wrote you some time ago about your brother-in-law and I have now to say that so far he is doing admirably and is holding a leading part in my fine Christmas Chorus choir. We shall have very fine Christmas music. Expect to have 1st and 2nd violins, base viol, flute and clarinet, besides the organ.

But I write now particularly to say that I have read Mrs. Terrell's article on Coleridge-Taylor in the *Independent;* I have read the account of the concerts in Washington as published in the "Star," clipping the latter; but I derived more satisfaction from your account as published in the *Pioneer Press* in W. V.A. than from any of the others. I have clipped this also. Do you know the colored people scored a great *social* success in securing Taylor on his first visit to this country? We are all indebted to the Choral Society.

I read with great interest Judge Terrell's article in *The Age* in which he justly scores some persons whose names I cannot write. We won't have much longer to wait. No births are painless and we already see some signs of travail for the birth of the new era. Eh?

I have thought the *Bethel Literary* might write "Will" to come before it some time in a paper on Journalism, practical journalism.[13] He has maintained himself adequately by this sort of work for the past 25 years. Has been city editor, managing advertiser, business manager—all kinds of reporter and correspondent—always on dailies so that his experience has been rather larger than common. I do not know that he could give the time to prepare much of a paper. He has had some fine pictures made of himself or rather his friends have made them for him. He might send you one should you write him. One thing he could do if he has not destroyed his Mss.—give you a reading of poems. He *had* published hundreds of them. His aim was to write 1000. He has published many anonymously. Write him if you think well of it.

Yours
T. G. Steward

---

13. William Steward, brother of Theophilus Steward.

Fort Niobrara, Nebraska
May 17, 1906

Mr. J. W. Cromwell
Washington, D.C.
Dear Sir:

Enclosed find blanks signed as requested. I will answer your letter in a few days. Can say now that Conn has been doing very well, and has distinguished himself as a member of my choir. He has improved much in his knowledge of music and his ability to sing, and has been faithful in attendance. I will forward today under separate cover a copy of my *Colored Regulars*. I regret to say that the publishers have failed to advertise the book. I enclosed a program of our Easter service.

Yours sincerely,
T. G. Steward

Fort Niobrara, Nebraska
May 17, 1906

Dear Brother Cromwell,

Replying to your request for advice, I wish to say that I have but one idea for the treatment of such a case as you present; and that is to formulate regular charges and press them home with all possible energy. I believe this to be the duty of God-fearing men, not in any spirit of vindictiveness; but for the love of humanity.

It is thought by some that a transgressor cannot be brought to trial, convicted and expelled; I believe it can be done. And moreover, I believe it ought to be done. In this you have all the advice I can give in the matter. Attack this evil as you would attack any other, and may God grant you success.

Yours sincerely
T. G. Steward

P.S. You may remember the fate of Rev. Elisha Weaver. Is the church unable to purge itself? If so, it remains only how long it will be in dying—for sin is known to be fatal.

T. G. S.

It is difficult to know just what problem Steward is alluding to in this letter of May 17th. In 1906, the problems with the *Record* were probably behind Grandfather and those with Booker T. Washington had not yet materialized. As

Steward refers to the Reverend Elisha Weaver, it must have been a problem at the Metropolitan Church, but he does not identify the source. It could have had something to do with Reverend Ross, a person not particularly admired by Cromwell. Elisha (sometimes spelled Alisha) Weaver apparently was a promising preacher in the A.M.E. Church, described as a "Trail Blazer." According to his journal, Grandfather had heard Weaver preach in March 1863. The rumor was that Weaver, in his preaching, had falsified his origins, claiming to be what he was not. This falsification had been uncovered by a black student at Princeton, who until that time had been Weaver's mentor. This disclosure and whatever furor it caused may have been the situation to which Steward alluded.

> Fort Niobrara, Neb.
> May 24, '06

My dear Brother Cromwell,

Answering yours of May 14th I thank you for the information you give me concerning your children and I wish for them each and all still further success. You perhaps know that I am a believer in cumulative capacity or development by generations would perhaps make it clearer. Your father was a man of massive character having abundance of moral and intellectual material. The lives started by him have not reached its full development, we will say, it may concentrate in some descendant as *genius,* or may show itself in several as persons of good intellectual and moral development.

You are probably the line through which the more spiritual of your father's endowments are transmitted hence your children are flowering out for future fruit.

I am saying this without knowing of the mother of your children, but I should reason *a priori* that she too was the possessor of a moral and intellectual heritage of value.

I must also write to you another thing which I am not in the habit of saying publicly. Persons who are not born with such inheritance or under such impulse can have no sympathy with those who are in the current, have no understanding of their thoughts, feelings—or in a word, of their lives. They are more "hop and homing" livers whose lives are bounded by materialism in the form of grab or f . . . [illegible] and whose delight is either sensuous or sexual. To eat, be stared at, be worshipped or envied, are their highest ideals.

> Your brother
> T. G. Steward

Fort McIntosh, Texas
Sept. 22, 1906

Dear Brother Cromwell:

On my arrival here or soon after, I had an interesting letter from you which it was practically impossible for me to do anything with at the time. I found the thermometer here going up to 106, and hot nights as well. I was worn out by excessive labor in moving, and was incapable of taking up anything seriously. This is the hottest place I have ever seen. The average for August was 97, and this was lower than usual. It rarely goes below 75 any time during the 24 hours, and usually reaches 100 as maximum. It is very much worse than the Philippines. It is entirely a Spanish country. The town of Laredo contains about 1500 white Americans and about 60 black Americans, and about 13,000 Mexicans, mostly of the greater class.

If you will get *Harper's Weekly* for Sept. 22 you will see two of our sergeants who were on the Army Team—Sergeants Fox and Tate, both northern men, one from Indiana and the other from New York—this latter fact is for your consideration. Again, ours is the regiment that got two men on the team, and this is just five times our proportion.

Sergeant Fox won the medal for best slow fire, getting a premium of $20 besides, and Tate tied as best skirmisher. They are both exceptionally fine with the rifle. I have seen Sergeant Fox employed in teaching white soldiers how to shoot.

I saw your review of my book. Is it not strange that it does not meet with faster sales?

The colored people now should be clamoring with all their might for another infantry regiment, and should demand all colored officers for it. Now is the time to shout on this line, and I believe Roosevelt would hear them. It is but just.

Sincerely yours
T. G. Steward

Wilberforce, Ohio
March 8, '07

Professor J. W. Cromwell
Washington, D.C.
Dear Brother:

If you can arrange for me a lecture on the Army with some reminiscences of life in the army, for a date in April, I will be glad to come. I should like to make for myself at least $25 so that would not be out of pocket.

I should like a program and respectable entrance fee. If my lectures take I will have circulars.

The investigation is progressing well and Senator Foraker[14] is covering himself in glory.

Yours sincerely

T. G. Steward

P.S. Received your kind and friendly letter.

Wilberforce, Ohio

July 5, '07

Dear Brother Cromwell,

Your very kind and interesting letter came to hand a few days ago. I congratulate you upon your good work and trust it may have a successful issue. It was unfortunate that you let Prof. Scarborough[15] into your plan, if the matter turned out as you say, altho he may not have intended to forestall you, and I am inclined to think his effusions in the *Southern Workman* would hardly affect your publication. I shall be pleased to write an introduction for your book if you wish it; but I incline to the notion that the book will be better without it.[16] I do not know of a case where an introduction helps a book, but I know several where

14. On August 13, 1906, some black soldiers raided Brownsville, Texas, in retaliation for racial insults made against them. One white man was killed and two were wounded. On November 6, 1906, President Roosevelt ordered the discharge of three companies of the Twenty-fifth Regiment. Senator Joseph Foraker (1846–1917) took up the cudgel in the United States Senate in December 1906 in behalf of the black soldiers. Although Foraker was unsuccessful when he ran for reelection, John Cromwell and others organized a public reception for him in the spring of 1909 at the Metropolitan A.M.E. Church as an expression of gratitude.

15. William Sanders Scarborough (1852–1926) was born in Macon, Georgia. He attended Atlanta University and Oberlin College, from which he received a master's degree in 1878. Although he taught at Payne Seminary for a short time, he spent the majority of his professional career at Wilberforce University as professor, vice president, and president. Scarborough was a maverick in his choice of the classics (Greek and Latin), and in 1886, he published *Birds of Aristophanes*. In 1882, he was the third Black elected by the American Philosophical Association. In 1881, he married Sarah C. Bierce, a white colleague on the Wilberforce faculty. Scarborough was a member of the American Negro Academy, a vigorous leader in the A.M.E. Church, and active in Republican politics of Ohio. He published numerous articles in his field and spoke at numerous meetings concerning educational, religious, and racial problems. Scarborough was a unique African American scholar, who clearly saw himself as a person apart and who apparently behaved quite independently, but it is not clear to me just what Steward meant—there may have been jealousy on Scarborough's part, which Steward stressed.

16. Grandfather took Steward's advice. He himself wrote a brief forward to the book in which he expressed indebtedness to Dr. James R. L. Diggs of Selena University, Chaplain Theophilus G. Steward, T. Thomas Fortune, Lafayette M. Hershaw, William C. Bolivar, Daniel A. Murray and Arthur A. Schomburg. The book did not have an introduction.

the introduction detracts from the merit of the work. I think it much better for you to write your introduction, then I might serve you better by writing a review of it.

Sincerely yours,
T. G. Steward

Wilberforce, Ohio
April 1, 1908

Mr. J. W. Cromwell
Washington, D.C.
Dear Brother:

I realize that I met with a "killing frost" on the occasion of my recent visit to your city and up to the present I am unable to account for it; it was so different when I visited there before.

Also, I was anxious to get an opinion as to my lecture. Judging from that one presentation I should infer that it is not what people want. This was its first delivery as a lecture and conditions were unfavorable; still, I think it will remain packed away.

My history work is going on splendidly and I am putting this Department in accord with the Committee of Seven appointed by the American Historical Association and with the College Entrance Examination Board and New York State Dept. of Education. Prof. Albert Bushnell Hart to whom I submitted my course says it is "both practicable and promising."

I should be glad if you could make a trip out here some time.

Well, the T. R. Taft people are drilling themselves pretty heartily now-a-days. Sambo has troubled their digestion greatly. The chief knew it was loaded but did not think the blamed thing would go off so many times. Like Zekes Steve the "lil stream kept on shoutin" until the day was all downer "cussing his tail." If the Dems had a good man they would win in a whoop, I believe.

Lots of Colored men are growing harder anti-Taft every day.

Sincerely yours,
T. G. Steward

Wilberforce, Ohio
May 18, '14

Dear Cromwell,

I am looking anxiously for your book. I am using my "Haitian Revolution" in my advanced history class, as finishing work to the course, of Med. and Modern.

Sincerely,
T. G. Steward

(I see you have a "surprise" pastor.)[17]

Wilberforce, Ohio
May 26, 1914

Mr. J. W. Cromwell
Washington, D.C.
Dear Sir:

On my motion you were given the degree of Master of Arts for meritorious services by the unanimous vote of Wilberforce University. You should be here to commencement with gown and cape.

Sincerely your friend
T. G. Steward

P.S. I have presented but 2 names since being here—my brother Will and yours.
T. G. S.

Wilberforce, Ohio
Sept. 2, 1915

Mr. J. W. Cromwell
Washington, D.C.
Dear Sir:

I have your recent letter in which you speak of some volumes of "scrap book collection" running from 1883 to 1893.[18] You ask: "Would Wilberforce appreciate them to the extent of defraying the expense of transportation?"

Last night I met the chairman of the library committee and spoke of the

---

17. Rev. C. Harold Stepteau's appointment was not welcomed by all at the Metropolitan African Methodist Episcopal Church because he was outside the conference. But Bishop Coppin choose to ignore that fact.

18. Grandfather's collection of scrapbooks is housed in the Moorland-Spingarn Research Library at Howard University. The rest of his papers are in my possession.

matter; he was enthusiastic over it, and said he had the money at hand and would gladly pay expenses.

We have quite a collection of old books, which we hope to get in form for research work during the winter; many collected and arranged by Bishop Payne, original MSS, etc.

As to my book: I am now going to turn my attention almost exclusively to a white market. The newspapers are treating me handsomely, far beyond the colored papers.

I have sold six copies for cash to a house in Sierra Leone, Africa. I get orders from leading book stores; the State Dept. at Washington bought a copy, but I have not been able to sell a copy so far as I have heard elsewhere in Washington, except thru the stores to white persons I presume. It should be in all your schools, for 8th grade reading or 1st year high school.

I am promised its introduction in the schools of Kentucky.

Colored people do not go to the book-stores and buy books—school teachers do not buy books, doctors do not, white doctors bought *Gouldtown,* colored doctors so far as I know have not bought a single copy.

Trust you are doing well.

Yours as ever,
T. G. Steward

Wilberforce, Ohio
Febr. 7, 1916

Professor John W. Cromwell, LLD
Dear Sir:

Yours at hand, I will mail Ms with the $7.50 you suggest requiring for myself only about a dozen copies. I would suggest that the whole issue aside from the number needed for free disposition be sold at rates sufficient to cover expenses.

But after all there might not be so many for sale after supplying the press of the country with free copies. I suggest that you write up the history of the Academy, give a statement of its work and purposes, a succinct account of the several meetings, etc., as an introduction to the publication of the present yearly report. I found the academy much more interesting than I expected.

Did you see the article: "Slave Crime (?) in Virginia?" There appears to be a growing interest in Colored men with respect to South America and I fancy several of our people will be going there before long. We are surely going to quit being "niggers"; that spirit of fight is rapidly supplementing the idea of

"Resolved" and "Protest." I see it brewing everywhere, and I *know* the young American Negro is destined to force recognition by a determined physical resistance.

Sincerely yours,
T. G. Steward.

Madame sends compliments and regards.
T. G. S.

Steward was married twice. With his first wife, Elizabeth Gadsen, he had eight children, several of whom had successful careers. Charles, a graduate of Harvard College and the Tufts University School of Dentistry, married Maude Trotter, the sister of Monroe Trotter. Frank, also a Harvard graduate, served as captain of the Forty-ninth Infantry during the Philippine Insurrection and later practiced law in Pittsburgh. He was also the author of several magazine articles. Theophilus B. taught English in the colored high school in Kansas City, Missouri, and Gustavus taught in the Philippines and at Tuskegee Institute before becoming a cashier for the Supreme Life and Casualty Company of Columbus, Ohio.

Steward's second wife, Susan Maria (Smith McKinney), was the widow of Rev. William J. McKinney, an Episcopal minister in Charleston, and the first African American female physician in New York. There were no children of this marriage. Mrs. Steward died on March 17, 1918.

After serving in several western posts and in the Philippines, Steward retired from the army in 1907 at age sixty-four. He returned to Wilberforce University where he was vice president, chaplain, and professor of history, French, and logic, and where his wife was also employed.

In late July 1911, the Stewards went to England to attend the First Universal Races Congress in London. Steward was a delegate from the A.M.E. Church and his wife delivered a paper. Afterward, they toured England and the continent.

Steward remained a patriotic citizen but was not afraid to criticize the policies of the government with respect to black soldiers or foreign adversaries. He was not a nationalist who identified with African culture, but he was proud of his ancestry and enthusiastically endorsed the scholarship of Carter G. Woodson. Depending on the issue, he was either a supporter or a detractor of Booker T. Washington. Within the A.M.E. Church, he was frequently in disagreement with Bishop Daniel Payne, his earlier mentor, and with Henry McNeal Turner and Richard H. Cain, two prominent and influential bishops in the church. He was also a member of the NAACP.

Steward's position on women was curious. He disapproved of their eligibility for membership in the American Negro Academy and of their elevation in the A.M.E. Church; yet his second wife was a professional woman.

Throughout his life, Steward was a prolific writer and was always anxious to publish his opinion on a variety of issues, usually in the *Christian Recorder.* He wrote three books: *Memoirs of Mrs. Rebecca Steward* (1877); *Genesis Re-Read: Placing the Evolutionary Process within the Context of the Divine Plan* (1885); and *The Colored Regulars in the United States Army* (1899). He was also the author of two pamphlets, "Active Service, or Religious Work among the U.S. Soldiers" (1897) and "How the Black St. Domingo Legion Saved the Patriot Army in the Siege of Savannah, 1779" (1899); a textbook, *Haitian Revolution, 1791 to 1804, or Sidelights on the French Revolution* (1914); and a personal memoir, *Fifty Years in the Gospel Ministry from 1864 to 1914* (1920). With his brother, William, he penned a family history, *Gouldtown, A Very Remarkable Settlement of Ancient Date* (1913); a novel, *Charleston Love Story* (1899); and a poem, "The Aged Patriot's Lament" (1901), which was published in the *Manila Times.*

Steward apparently enjoyed his later years at Wilberforce University, for despite frequent bouts of illness, he continued teaching, reading, writing, and confronting issues. In 1923, he criticized A. Lawrence Lowell, the president of Harvard University,[19] for denying black students dormitory accommodations, and Harvard professor William McDougall[20] for the assertion in his book, *Is America Safe for Democracy?* that only Afro-Americans of mixed blood have shown any marked capacity of any kind. As his correspondence to Cromwell revealed, Steward was frequently concerned about race mixture. At the end of his life, Steward offered his views on what was to continue to be a controversial issue: the racial composition of the staff of the newly opened veterans hospital in Tuskegee, Alabama.

Theophilus Gould Steward died on the afternoon of January 11, 1924, after having earlier in the day taught his regular classes at Payne Theological Seminary.

His military career, at the end, probably shaped his values more than his career in the ministry because he viewed the army as an opportunity for the strengthening of black men as soldiers who could, in turn, teach and drill black students: "soft men cannot carry a hard fight" was his motto.

19. The *Crisis* 25 (March 1923): 199, 218, 230–32.
20. Steward to William McDougall, February 23, 1923, T. G. Steward Papers. According to William Seraile, many of Steward's papers were destroyed in a house fire, and the rest are in the possession of Anna Steward Bishop, his granddaughter. See also William McDougall, *Is America Safe for Democracy?* (New York: Charles Scribner's Sons, 1921), 7.

Epilogue

By the end of the mid 1920s, John W. Cromwell Sr. and most of his circle of friends—certainly Bruce and Steward—had died. With them went the last personal memories of slavery and the hopes engendered by Reconstruction. They saw not only the rise and strengthening of racial segregation but also the emergence of protest in the Niagara Movement, the NAACP, the Urban League, the Garvey Movement, and the national prominence of their leaders: W. E. B. Du Bois, Booker T. Washington, and Marcus Garvey. World War I and the rise of Pan-Africanism broadened their vision, lifting the veil somewhat to reveal these new challenges.

The lives and careers of John W. Cromwell Sr.'s children Otelia, Mary, and John Jr. exemplify the greater opportunities for black intellectuals of the next generation; but at the same time, they faced the restrictions and frustrations of living in a segregated society.

Families under slavery were exposed to many kinds of personal relationships, which were always oppressive for the slave. Freedom, if promised, was often denied. Once free, it became clear that an education was critical in defining and sustaining leadership. For the Cromwell family, the Institute for Colored Youth, started in 1852 by the Quakers in Philadelphia, performed that role. More critical perhaps, because of its persistence under segregation into the twentieth century, was an environment shaped not only by the "double consciousness," of which Du Bois wrote so famously in *The Souls of Black Folk*, but also by a particular double jeopardy. Those Blacks devoted to principles that would hold the leaders of black institutions to the highest standards of competence and integrity found themselves in conflict not only with powerful Whites motivated by racist expectations but also with other Blacks desperately seeking to cling to the artificial rungs of power, not withstanding their own lack of ability or character.

319

I was born into the milieu chronicled in this book: the vanished worlds of black Washington, black Philadelphia, and other outposts of the African American intelligentsia during the century following the Civil War. I have drawn upon my firsthand knowledge of the personalities, events, and environments depicted in my family's archive to bear witness to experience with an intimacy more characteristic of a memoir than a scholarly effort of one whose authority would perforce rely on documentary evidence alone.

Unveiled Voices, Unvarnished Memories is much more than an archive of the Cromwell family's history. It is also a living document, strengthened, I hope, by my editing that makes meaningful what otherwise would be an increasingly remote and fragmented legacy for the world of today.

Appendix

Notes on People Mentioned

❧❧

CHAPTER 1: **Charles Cooper** established a flourishing business in Liberia and was succeeded by his son Henry as a shipbuilder-merchant.

CHAPTER 3: **Mrs. Augustine,** probably wife of Peter Augustine, successful Philadelphia caterer. **George W. Bain,** intermediary in the purchase of Nancy Carney. **Hugh M. Browne,** member of the Hampton-Tuskegee circle, later principal of Cheyney Institute (successor to Institute for Colored Youth), and secretary of the Committee of Twelve. **Joseph Carter,** owner of Nancy Carney. **Alexander Crummell** (1819–1898), teacher, missionary to Africa, and minister of St. Luke's Episcopal Church in Washington, D.C. **Phillip C. Garrett** (1834–1905), graduate of Haverford College, Quaker businessman, reformer, and son of Thomas Garrett, one of the most prominent supporters of the Underground Railroad. **Mrs. Gould,** wife of Rev. Gould, who may be Theodore A. Gould, a poet in Rochester, New York, in 1849. **Richard T. Greener** (1844–1922), born in Philadelphia, educator, lawyer, and consular officer. In 1870, he was the first black graduate of Harvard College. Early in his career he was principal of the Institute for Colored Youth and later principal of the Preparatory School for Colored Youth in the District of Columbia. **Shippen Lewis,** white attorney in Philadelphia who managed Levi Cromwell's business. **William E. Mathews** (1845–1893), born in Baltimore, graduate of Howard University Law School, first African American to work in the U.S. Post Office Department. He was a real estate broker and financier. **Thomas Brackett Reed,** Republican congressman from Portland, Maine, and Speaker of the Fifty-first, Fifty-fourth, and Fifty-fifth Congresses. He was re-elected to the Fifty-sixth Congress and was a prominent candidate for president in 1896.

Dr. Charles Shadd, physician in Philadelphia, graduate of Howard University, Civil War veteran, son of Hanna Shadd, Philadelphia caterer. **Mrs. Andrew Stephens,** whose husband was a prominent caterer and social leader of the black elite in Philadelphia from the late 1870s. In 1894, Andrew Stephens was the sixth black man to win a seat on Philadelphia's Common Council. He served until his death in 1898.

CHAPTER 5: **Frederick G. Barbadoes,** soldier, writer, abolitionist, and son of James G. Barbadoes, who was a signer of Declaration of Principles of the Anti-Slavery Society in Philadelphia in 1833. **Ebenezer Don Carlos Bassett** (1853–1908), born in Connecticut, graduated from the State Normal School, principal of Institute for Colored Youth. In 1869, he was appointed by President Grant as U.S. minister to Haiti and the Dominican Republic. He was the first African American diplomat. **Lewis Harvie Blair,** responding to *Occasional Paper,* no. 11, "Negro and Elective Franchise," did not criticize the paper but wrote his own view that the franchise could only hinder the progress of the Negro in the South. **John Mifflin Brown** (1817–1883) was born in Delaware and studied at Oberlin College. He was an educator, missionary, and author. In 1864, he was editor of the *Christian Recorder* in 1864, and in 1868, he was elected A.M.E. bishop. **James E. Hanley,** contributor to the *Dictionary of American Negro Biography.* **Lafayette McKeen Hershaw,** an employee of the U.S. Department of the Interior, member of District of Columbia Bar, and the American Negro Academy. **Frank Manley,** part owner of the *Record.* **Whitefield McKinlay** was a black businessman, Republican politician, and close friend and staunch supporter of Booker T. Washington. He was an employee of the Government Printing Office, entered real estate and loan business, and received two presidential appointments.

CHAPTER 6: **Dr. Oliver M. Atwood** served on the Board of Education for one year and on two committees relating to school affairs in the District of Columbia. **Parker Bailey** was the first black graduate of the Boston Latin School (1877) and was also a graduate of Harvard College. He was forced to come to Washington to secure a teaching position. **Frederick Lee Barnett** (1852–1936), graduate of Northwestern University, lawyer, and founder of first African American newspaper in Illinois, the *Chicago Conservator.* He was a key anti-Bookerite, the first black assistant state attorney in Cook County, and husband of Ida Wells Barnett, fighter for civil rights and against lynching. **Mary P. Burrill** was a Washington native. She attended Emerson College in Boston and taught dramatics at Dunbar High School. Her sister, Clara, was the wife of Roscoe Conkling Bruce. **Julia Caverno,** professor of Greek at Smith College with whom Otelia Cromwell boarded when she was a student, as black students were not permitted in the dormitories at that time. **William Bruce Evans** graduated from Howard University Medical School. He was the first principal of Armstrong Manual Training School and the father of Lillian Evanti Evans, a well-known singer. **Harry N. Gardner** (1855–1927), professor of philosophy at Smith College (1884–1927). **Majette Gregory,** member of John Munroe Gregory family. Mr. Gregory was principal and tutor at the Howard University Preparatory School. **Grace Hubbard,** associate professor of English at Smith College (1892–1905). **Mary Jordan** (1855–1941), professor of English at Smith College (1884–1921). **Henry L. Moore,** professor of economics at Smith College (1897–1902).

CHAPTER 7: *Aegis,* Dartmouth College yearbook. The *Age,* paper edited by T. Thomas Fortune but controlled by Booker T. Washington. **John G. Baugh,** friend of John Cromwell Sr. from the Virginia days and agent for the *People's Advocate* in Virginia. **Richard Birnie,** 1907 graduate of Harvard and 1911 graduate of Harvard Medical School. **Edwin Jackson Chesnutt,** 1905 graduate of Harvard College. He was the son of Charles Waddell Chesnutt. **Bessie Trotter Craft,** sister of the militant black journalist, William Monroe Trotter, and wife of Henry Craft, grandson of William and Ellen Craft, famous fugitive slaves. **Charley Crummell, Sydney Crummell,** children of Alexander Crummell. **Charles F. Emerson,** dean of Dartmouth College. **George King** did not graduate from Dartmouth. **George Morton Lightfoot** (1868–1947), professor of Latin at Howard University. **Alain Locke** (1885–1954) graduated from Harvard College in 1907 and was the first black Rhodes Scholar (Litt B. Oxford). He was an author and professor of philosophy at Howard University. Locke was a key figure in Harlem Renaissance. **Knocka Lee,** graduate of Sargent College and daughter of Joseph Lee, successful restaurateur in Massachusetts whose clientele was exclusively white. She taught physical education at Dunbar High School. **Wilder P. Montgomery** (Dartmouth 1906) was the son of Winfield S. Montgomery (Dartmouth 1878) and an assistant superintendent of schools in Washington, D.C. *Prince Hall Masons,* an important black fraternal order (see chapter 2). **Emma Goodell Newman,** wife of Charles Newman and daughter of Mrs. Edna Goodell, an important civic leader in the Boston black community at the turn of the century. Emma continued in her mother's footsteps. **Frederick Douglass "Fritz" Pollard,** graduate of Brown University, who was both a college and professional football player. In 1919, he was hired as player-coach of the Akron (Ohio) Indians, making him the first Black to play and to coach in professional football. **Edward French Tyson** was a 1907 graduate of Harvard College and a 1911 graduate of

Howard University Medical School. **Owen M. Waller,** second rector of St. Luke's Episcopal Church. The parish hall was built during his tenure as a memorial to Dr. Crummell. **George H. Walls** operated a bathhouse on the boardwalk below South Texas Avenue in Atlantic City. **Louis T. Wright** (1891–1952), graduate of Clark University (BA) and Harvard Medical School, practiced medicine in New York City and was a hospital administrator. He was an important civil rights leader.

CHAPTER 8: **The African Society** (since 1935, called the Royal African Society) was founded in 1900. Members were amateurs, whose interest in Africa came from their careers as soldiers, statesmen, administrators, merchants, and missionaries, not as professionals or academic students of Africa. A survey of members in 1906 listed twelve Africans but no African Americans. **The Afro-American Council** was an outgrowth of the Afro-American League, which was started in 1889 by T. Thomas Fortune and Bishop Alexander Walters. The organization only lasted until 1890. The strong negative reaction to Washington's famous 1895 Atlanta speech energized Walters and Fortune to call a meeting of key leaders to protest and to form an organization. At the meeting of the council in December 1898, Walters, then president of the council, gave an address of militance and compromise, calling for black voting rights and for property and literacy qualifications to be applied equally to both Blacks and Whites. He contended that these changes would take time and stressed the value of education, including industrial education, hard work, and morality. As members of the council were both conservative and radical, there was much conflict over its goals. Soon Washington anonymously sought to gain control over the council, which he had achieved by 1903. The publication by Trotter in 1901 of a strongly anti-Washington newspaper, the *Boston Guardian,* the publication of *The Souls of Black Folk* by Du Bois denouncing Washington, the "Boston Riot," and the so-called secret meeting held in 1904 by Washington and financed by Andrew Carnegie all foretold the weakness of Washington's leadership and led to the formation of the Niagara Movement in 1905, which was specifically aimed at combatting Washington's policies. Walters was viewed as leaning toward Washington and did not initially join the Niagara Movement, but he was a member by 1908. Walters, Du Bois, and Trotter saw the need for African Americans to split their vote in order to gain the necessary recognition. All three supported Woodrow Wilson, the Democratic candidate in the 1912 election. **Dr. Mojola Agbebi,** president of African Baptist Union for West Africa. **Dr. John Washburn Bartol** graduated from Harvard College in 1887 and Harvard Medical School in 1891. From 1912 to 1915, he was a lecturer at Harvard Medical School. **Edward Wilmot Blyden** (1832–1912), born in the West Indies, made his career in Liberia and Sierra Leone. He was a scholar, diplomat, journalist, and an educator. His most important work, *Christianity, Islam and the Negro Race (1887)*, demonstrated the appeal of Islam to colored people. **George Wallace Briggs** (1875–1959) was born in England. He was one of the founders of the Hymn Society of Great Britain and Ireland and wrote many hymns. **Edward Everett Brown** (1858–1923), born in New Hampshire, studied law in the office of the Honorable John H. White, judge of the Probate Court of New Hampshire, and the Honorable William A. Gaston of Boston. He was admitted to the Massachusetts Bar in 1884 and became deputy health commissioner in 1907. Later, he was a deputy tax collector. "**Buckras**," white people. **Ole Bull (Sarah)** (1850–1910) was a famous Norwegian violinist, who was interested in spiritualism and alternative religions, particularly Hinduism. She was the wife of Ole Bull, a Harvard professor. **Richard Harvey Cain** (1825–1887) was a clergyman, who represented South Carolina in the Forty-third, Forty-fourth, and Forty-fifth Congresses. He was the fourteenth bishop of the A.M.E. Church. **Senator Caldor** (1869–1945) served a decade in the House of Representatives and in the Senate for one term in 1916. **Thomas Junius Calloway** (1866–1930) was born in Tennessee. He was a graduate of Fisk University and Howard University Law School. He was an educator and editor, and he practiced law in Washington, D.C. Calloway was U.S. special commissioner to Paris Exposition (1899–1901) and a leader of Bookerite faction in Washington. **William E. Chandler,** secretary of the navy and future senator from New Hampshire. During the Arthur administration, he directed the southern strategy crafting a policy that gave lip service to protecting the rights of Blacks, while supporting an assortment of lily-white movements. He admired Bruce's commitment to the Republican Party, and Bruce viewed him as an important resource who could influence legislation of relevance to the black community. **Chews,** one of the most outstanding families in Philadelphia (see Roger Lane, *William Dorsey's Philadelphia and Ours: On the Past and Future of the Black City in America* (New York: Oxford University Press, 1991). **James A. Cobb** (1876–1958) was born in Louisiana and was a graduate of Howard University Law School. He was admitted to the District of Columbia Bar in 1900 and was a member of faculty of Howard University Law School (1916–1929) and vice dean (1923–1929). From 1916 to 1935, he was judge of the Municipal Court. He practiced law in the District of Columbia as senior partner in the most prestigious African American law firm, Cobb, Howard, and Hayes. **Dr. Samuel Courtney** (1855–1941) was born in West Virginia, attended Hampton Institute with

Booker T. Washington, and graduated from Harvard Medical School in 1894. He practiced medicine in Boston and was house physician in Boston Lying-In Hospital. Courtney was an alternate delegate-at-large to Republican National Convention in St. Louis in 1896 and in Philadelphia in 1900. He served two terms on the Boston School Committee. **Harry S. Cummings,** Baltimore lawyer. He seconded Theodore Roosevelt's second nomination in 1904. **John C. Dancy** (1857–1920) studied at Howard University Preparatory Department and was the editor of the *North Carolina Sentinel, Star of Zion,* and *A.M.E. Quarterly Review.* He was a staunch Republican and served as a collector of customs at Wilmington, North Carolina, and a recorder of deeds in Washington, D.C. (1901–1911). In 1907, he was invited to dine at the White House by President Theodore Roosevelt. **Martin R. Delany** (1812–1885), editor, author, physician, abolitionist, and nationalist. He was coeditor with Frederick Douglass of the *North Star.* Although he was admitted to Harvard Medical School in 1850, he was forced to leave because of his race. His most well-known publication was *The Condition, Elevation, Emigration and Destiny of the Colored People in the United States, Politically Considered* (1852). **Dr. Depew,** an employee of the treasurer's office of the state of New York. **Dr. Melvil Dewey** (1851–1931) was a librarian who devised the Dewey Decimal system of classifying books. He was the most influential librarian in the development of the profession, and he started the first professional library school in the United States. In 1888, he moved to Albany to become the director of the New York State Library. Dewey founded the American Library Association. **William H. Dorsey** (1837–1923), Philadelphia's first black historian (see Lane, *William Dorsey's Philadelphia and Ours*). **Stephen Arnold Douglas** (1813–1861), U.S. senator from Illinois and vice-presidential candidate. He was famous for his debates with Abraham Lincoln. **John Durham** was from Philadelphia. He was an economist and spent many years as an official of the U.S. Spanish Claims Commission. He also managed a Cuban sugar plantation. His wife was white. **Henry Highland Garnet** (1815–1882), clergyman, abolitionist, editor, temperance leader, and diplomat. He was a delegate to the World Peace Conference in Germany. He served as minister of 15th Street Presbyterian Church in Washington and was appointed minister to Liberia, where he died and is buried. **J. D. Gordon,** once assistant president general of the UNIA. He broke with Garvey and joined African Blood Brotherhood but later returned to UNIA. **Bishop Abraham Grant** (1848–1911) was a conservative and anticolonizationalist. He held nonpolitical jobs in Florida and Texas and was close to Booker T. Washington. **Alfred W. Harris** (1854–1920) was born free in Virginia. He studied law privately with a black lawyer and graduated from Howard University Law School in 1881. Harris practiced law in Petersburg, Virginia, and was elected from Dinwiddie County to the Virginia House of Delegates (1881–1888). **Lewis Hayden** (1811–1889), fugitive slave and leading abolitionist, was a conductor for the Underground Railroad and a member of the Boston Vigilance Committee. He was also an active member of Prince Hall Masons and a state legislator. *Howard's Magazine*: John Bruce was associate editor (see John E. Bruce's letter to John Wesley Cromwell Sr., December 25, 1899, pp. 248–50). **Joseph Ephraim Casely Hayford** (1866–1930), barrister, author, nationalist, head of the Aborigines' Rights Protection Society, and a member of the Gold Coast Legislative Council. He cofounded the National Congress of British West Africa, a major West African political movement in the first quarter of the twentieth century. **Rev. Mark Casely Hayford** (1864–1935), brother of Joseph Ephraim Casely Hayford. **Henry Lincoln Johnson** (1870–1825) was a political opportunist, who was originally on fringe of Washington's circle. In 1919, he secured the post of recorder of deeds at the expense of J. C. Dancy and demanded a position from Taft administration as reward for his role in depriving Judson W. Lyons (1858–1924) of his place on the Republican National Committee in 1908. **Charles Dunbar Burgess King,** president of Liberia (1920–1930). **John Turner Layton** (1841–1916) was born in New Jersey. He studied at Round Lake Conservatory on Martha's Vineyard, Northwestern University, and the New England Conservatory of Music after serving in the U.S. Army in the Civil War. Layton settled in Washington, D.C., in 1883, and he taught music in public schools, served as choir director for Metropolitan A.M.E. Church for forty years, and compiled and edited eleventh edition of the A.M.E. Hymnal in 1897. He received honorary degree from Wilberforce University in 1906. **Helen Longfellow,** probably Miss Ellen Longfellow, niece of the poet. **Dr. J. Robert Love,** clergyman and editor of the *Jamaican Advocate,* was an early Garvey mentor and an acquaintance of Bishop Henry McNeal Turner and Bishop James Theodore Holly. He was a member of the American Negro Academy. **Claude McKay** (1889–1948) was born in Jamaica. He was in England between 1919 and 1921, writing for the *Workers Dreadnaught,* a Communist weekly, and returned to U.S. in 1934. He converted to Catholicism and was the author of "If We Must Die," a famous poem. **President William McKinley** (1842–1901), Republican elected in 1896 and re-elected in 1900. He appointed several African Americans to positions in government and was assassinated on September 24, 1901. Grandfather stood in the rain from 10:30 a.m. to 5:00 p.m. to view the president's remains. **James Matthews** (1846–1894), a lawyer, was appointed recorder of deeds by President Cleveland. He did not win reappointment (see John E. Bruce's letter to John Wesley Cromwell Sr., November 10, 1899, pp. 237–39). **Congressman**

Murray: There were two brothers from New York who served in the U.S. House of Representatives—William Murray (1803–1875) and Ambrose Spencer Murray (1807–1885). Bruce was probably referring to Ambrose Spencer Murray. **Negro Society for Historical Research** founded in 1911 by Bruce, Schomburg, David Bryant Fuller, Wesley Weeks, and William Ernest Braxton, who were in competition with Carter G. Woodson. They published *Occasional Papers* and established a library and sponsored several activities to promote the preservation of and to encourage interest in African American history. **John Knowles Paine** (1839–1906), member of Harvard University faculty (1863–1905), taught vocal music, the history of music, harmony's counterpoint, and instrumental music. He was the author of *Librettos for Opera, History Music to the Death of Schubert,* and *Shall We Have Opera?* **Clifford H. Plummer,** the Boston attorney whom Trotter hired when Washington sued him over the "Boston Riot" incident. But Plummer was secretly in touch with Washington and acted as his underground agent in Trotter's New England Suffrage League. **William Frost Powell** (1848–1920) was an educator and diplomat. In 1897, he was the first American appointed to new title of "Envoy Extraordinary and Minister Plenipotentiary to Haiti" and was involved in many diplomatic issues. **"Recordship tussle,"** the position of recorder of deeds for the District of Columbia was frequently awarded to an African American, as a plum; Frederick Douglass was perhaps the most important of those awardees. **C. H. J. Taylor,** lawyer, editor of *Kansas City World.* He briefly served minister resident in Liberia (1887) and later as recorder of deeds for the District of Columbia. He was highly critical of Radical Reconstruction and believed that all racial troubles originated in politics and political emancipation would result if Blacks ceased being prejudiced toward Whites. He also argued that African Americans hated themselves and their culture but later altered his views. **Robert Thomas Teamoh** (1864–1912), member of Massachusetts House of Representatives (1894–1895), representing Ward 9. He was employed by the *Boston Globe* for twenty years, covering educational news, rarely dealing with black subjects. **Mary Church Terrell** (1863–1954), born in Memphis, Tennessee, was a teacher, author, and civil rights leader. She received both her BA and MA from Oberlin College. Terrell taught early education at Model School of Antioch College, and she taught at Wilberforce University, then in public schools of Washington, D.C. She was the first female president of the Bethel Literary and Historical Association (1892–1893), a member of D.C.'s Board of Education (1895–1901), and founder and first president of the Colored Women's League, which merged with other clubs to form the National Association of Colored Women in 1896. She was married to Robert Henderson Terrell, judge of Municipal Court of the District of Columbia. **Samuel J. Tilden** (1814–1886) was a graduate of Yale Law School and governor of New York. In 1841, he was a presidential candidate. Tilden was a behind-the-scenes tactician and organizer of the Democratic Party. **Nat Turner** (1800–1831), insurrectionary leader, who in August 1831 led a bloody, unsuccessful revolt in Southampton County, Virginia. He was captured, tried, found guilty, and sentenced to death by hanging. **Judge Walker** (1831(?)-1901), possibly Edwin Garrison Walker, son of David Walker, member of 1867 Massachusetts legislature representing Charlestown. He was a member of the Massachusetts Bar. **Isaiah Wears** (1820–1900), born in Baltimore, religious worker for A.M.E. Church, lecturer, scientist, reformer, political figure, and businessman. **George Peabody Wetmore** (1846–1921) practiced law in New York and Rhode Island. He was governor of Rhode Island (1885–1887) and elected to U.S. Senate in 1908. He served as a senator until 1913. **Phillis Wheatley** (c.1753–1784) was captured and enslaved in West Africa and sold in Boston to John Wheatley. She became a celebrated poet first in England and then in the United States. **Egbert Austin "Bert" Williams** (1873–1922), born in Nassau, Bahamas. He was an outstanding entertainer, and after signing with Florenz Ziegfeld to appear in the Ziegfeld Follies, he was transformed into a theater legend. He often appeared in blackface. **James G. Wolff** (1847–1913) was born in New Hampshire. His early education was at Kimball Union College and New Hampshire State College, and he studied law in office of Hon. D. W. Gooch and at Harvard Law School. In 1875, he was admitted to Massachusetts Bar, and in 1907, he served as clerk for district attorney. **Carter Godwin Woodson** (1875–1950), born in Virginia, was self-educated until seventeen years old. He attended Douglass High School in West Virginia and earned his BA from University of Chicago in 1908 and Ph.D. from Harvard University in 1912. He taught in District of Columbia public schools and at Miner Normal School, and he was a founder of the Association for the Study of Negro Life and History in 1912. Woodson established the *Journal of Negro History* in 1916, and in 1921, he organized the Associated Publishers. In 1926, he inaugurated Negro History Week, and in 1926, he started the *Negro History Bulletin*.

CHAPTER 9: **George Conn,** brother of Annie E. Conn, John Cromwell's second wife. **Albert Bushnell Hart** (1854–1943), historian, professor at Harvard University, and son of ardent abolitionist Albert Gaillard Hart. He believed that all history should be based on scientific, sound, and analytical judgment, and he was responsible for expanding history education in schools and colleges throughout the country. **Col. Thomas Wentworth Higginson** (1823–1874), graduate of

Harvard College and Harvard Divinity School. He had strong abolitionist views and knew John Brown, and was a captain of Fifty-fifth Massachusetts Volunteers (all black soldiers) during the Civil War. **John Wanamaker** (1838–1922), well-known Philadelphia merchant, Republican, post master general, and lay minister in his youth, founded the Bethany Sunday School and was the first full-time paid secretary of the YMCA.

Relatives Not on the Genealogical Chart

CHAPTER 3: **Henry Cromwell and his wife, Hester,** listed in 1870 as being from Norfolk, probably a cousin; and **Henry** in Philadelphia is probably a son of Henry and Hester.

CHAPTER 4: **Uncle Charles,** Charles McGuinn, brother of Lucy McGuinn.

CHAPTER 5: **Clara,** wife of William H. Carney Jr.

Index

Page numbers in italics refer to photographs.

JWC Sr. in index refers to J. W. Cromwell Sr. JWC Jr. in index refers to J. W. Cromwell Jr.